GLOBALISING SOCIOLINGUISTICS

This book challenges the predominance of mainstream sociolinguistic theories by focusing on lesser-known sociolinguistic systems, from regions of Africa, Asia, the Caribbean, South America, the European Mediterranean and Slavic regions as well as specific speech communities such as those speaking Nivkh, Jamaican Creole, North Saami and Central Yup'ik.

In 19 chapters, the specialist authors look at key sociolinguistic aspects of each region or speech community, such as gender, politeness strategies, speech patterns and the effects of social hierarchy on language, concentrating on the differences from mainstream models. The volume, introduced by Miriam Meyerhoff, draws together connections across regions/communities and considers how mainstream sociolinguistics is incomplete or lacking. It reveals how lesser-known cultures can play an important role in the building of theory in sociolinguistics.

Globalising Sociolinguistics: Challenging and Expanding Theory is essential reading for any researcher in sociolinguistics and language variation, and will be a key reference for advanced sociolinguistics courses.

Dick Smakman is Assistant Professor in the Leiden University Centre for Linguistics, the Netherlands.

Patrick Heinrich is Associate Professor in the Department of Asian and Mediterranean African Studies at Ca'Foscari University in Venice, Italy.

GLOBALISING SOCIOLINGUISTICS

Challenging and Expanding Theory

Edited by
Dick Smakman and Patrick Heinrich

LONDON AND NEW YORK

First published 2015
by Routledge
2 Park Square, Milton Park, Abingdon, Oxon OX14 4RN

and by Routledge
711 Third Avenue, New York, NY 10017

Routledge is an imprint of the Taylor & Francis Group, an informa business

© 2015 Dick Smakman and Patrick Heinrich for selection and editorial matter; individual contributions, the contributors.

The right of Dick Smakman and Patrick Heinrich to be identified as the authors of the editorial material, and of the authors for their individual chapters, has been asserted in accordance with sections 77 and 78 of the Copyright, Designs and Patents Act 1988.

All rights reserved. No part of this book may be reprinted or reproduced or utilised in any form or by any electronic, mechanical, or other means, now known or hereafter invented, including photocopying and recording, or in any information storage or retrieval system, without permission in writing from the publishers.

Trademark notice: Product or corporate names may be trademarks or registered trademarks, and are used only for identification and explanation without intent to infringe.

British Library Cataloguing in Publication Data
A catalogue record for this book is available from the British Library

Library of Congress Cataloging in Publication Data
Smakman, Dick, 1970- author.
Globalising sociolinguistics / by Dick Smakman and Patrick Heinrich.
pages cm
1. Sociolinguistics–Globalization. 2. Language and languages–Study and teaching–Social aspects. 3. Globalization–Social aspects. 4. Language and languages–Variation–Social aspects. I. Heinrich, Patrick, author. II. Title.
P53.8.S623 2015
306.44–dc23
2014048208

ISBN: 978-0-415-72559-0 (hbk)
ISBN: 978-0-415-72560-6 (pbk)
ISBN: 978-1-3156978-2-6 (ebk)

Typeset in Bembo
by Taylor & Francis Books

Printed and bound by Ashford Colour Press Ltd.

CONTENTS

List of figures viii
List of tables ix
Notes on contributors x
Preface xvi
Acknowledgements xix
Map of places discussed xx

1 "Tings change, all tings change": the changing face of
   sociolinguistics with a global perspective 1
   Miriam Meyerhoff and James N. Stanford

2 The Westernising mechanisms in sociolinguistics 16
   Dick Smakman

PART I
Developing countries 37

Introduction to Part I 37

3 *Ala! Kumbe?* "Oh my! Is it so?": Multilingualism controversies
   in East Africa 39
   Sandra Nekesa Barasa

4 A sociolinguistic mosaic of West Africa: challenges and prospects 54
   Jemima Asabea Anderson and Gladys Nyarko Ansah

5 Southeastern Asia: diglossia and politeness in a
multilingual context 66
Aone van Engelenhoven and Maaike van Naerssen

6 Towards a distributed sociolinguistics of postcolonial
multilingual societies: the case of Southern Africa 80
Rajend Mesthrie

PART II
Less developed countries 93

Introduction to Part II 93

7 Speech community and linguistic urbanization: sociolinguistic
theories developed in China 95
Daming Xu

8 Language variation and change: the Indian experience 107
Shobha Satyanath

9 Gender in a North African setting: a sociolinguistic overview 123
Reem Bassiouney

10 The Creole-speaking Caribbean: the architecture of
language variation 137
Hubert Devonish

PART III
Developed countries 151

Introduction to Part III 151

11 Class in the social labyrinth of South America 153
Elisa Battisti and João Ignacio Pires Lucas

12 The Slavic area: trajectories, borders, centres and peripheries
in the Second World 164
Marc L. Greenberg

13 The study of politeness and women's language in Japan 178
Patrick Heinrich

14 Positive politeness in the European Mediterranean: sociolinguistic notions 194
Irene Cenni

PART IV
Unstable multilingual communities 207

Introduction to Part IV 207

15 Nivkh writing practices: literacy and vitality in an endangered language 209
Hidetoshi Shiraishi and Bert Botma

16 The Jamaican language situation: a process, not a type 223
Hubert Devonish and Kadian Walters

17 *Nutemllaq Yugtun Qaneryararput*: our very own way of speaking Yugtun in Alaska 233
Theresa Arevgaq John

18 Variation in North Saami 243
Ante Aikio, Laura Arola and Niina Kunnas

19 Gaelic Scotland and Ireland: issues of class and diglossia in an evolving social landscape 256
Cassie Smith-Christmas and Tadhg Ó hIfearnáin

Concluding remarks 270
Dick Smakman and Patrick Heinrich

Index 272

FIGURES

2.1 Author's university (N = 493) categorised according to level of English in the country where it is based   24
2.2 Percentage of articles (N = 521) from countries based on HDI position   27
2.3 Percentage of articles (N = 1,547) from three groups of language settings over four decades in two journals   28
2.4 Percentage of articles (N = 339) from three groups of language settings over four separate years in six journals   29
10.1 Use and effects of load-bearing variants   146

TABLES

2.1	Background of well-known sociolinguists	21
2.2	Background of editors of six journals	22
2.3	Regions where university of authors are based	26
2.4	Population size of regions and relative article contribution	26
2.5	Division of published articles across regions	30
2.6	Number of living languages in various regions	30
15.1	Number of publications by Nivkh speakers in Nivkh	215
18.1	A two-dimensional classification of modern North Saami dialects	247

NOTES ON CONTRIBUTORS

Ante Aikio is a Professor of Saami language at the University of Oulu and currently works as a visiting professor of Saami language at the Saami University College in Guovdageaidnu (Kautokeino). His research interests include the description, history and revitalization of Saami languages and comparative Uralic linguistics.

Jemima Asabea Anderson is a Senior Lecturer in the Department of English, University of Ghana, Legon. She teaches foundation courses in English, Phonetics and Phonology of English, Varieties and Functions of English, Discourse Analysis, Pragmatics and Sociolinguistics. Her areas of research interest are cross-cultural pragmatics, speech acts and the codification of English in Ghana. Some of her research articles have appeared in local and international peer-reviewed journals.

Gladys Nyarko Ansah is a Senior Lecturer in the Department of English, University of Ghana, Legon. She holds a PhD in Applied Linguistics from Lancaster University, a Master of Research in Cognitive Linguistics from Brighton University, a Master of Philosophy in Linguistics and a BA in English and Linguistics, both from the University of Ghana. Her current research interests include language and cognition, language and culture, bilingualism/multilingualism, second-language acquisition, and language and politics. She has published several research articles on both local and international platforms.

Laura Arola is a PhD student of Finnish language at the University of Oulu and works as director of education at the municipality of Utsjoki (Ohcejohka) in the Saami native region of Finland. Her research interests include the sociolinguistic situation, vitality and revitalization of Northern European minority languages, especially Saami and Meänkieli. She is currently finalizing her PhD thesis on the sociolinguistic situation of Meänkieli among young people in Northern Sweden.

Sandra Nekesa Barasa is an Assistant Professor in the Department of Communication & Information Studies at the Radboud University of Nijmegen; she is a researcher in the Centre for Language Studies in the Non-nativeness and Communication research group. She holds a PhD from Leiden University. Her research interests include language and communication in social media, computer-mediated communication, youth language and slang, language contact, multilingualism and code-switching, especially in relation to the East Africa region.

Reem Bassiouney (DPhil, Oxon.) is Associate Professor of Linguistics at The American University of Cairo. Her academic books include *Functions of Code-Switching in Egypt* (Brill, 2006), *Arabic Sociolinguistics* (Edinburgh University Press, 2008), *Arabic and the Media* (Brill, 2010), *Arabic Language and Linguistics* (co-edited with Graham Katz; Georgetown University Press, 2012), and recently *Language and Identity in Modern Egypt* (Edinburgh University Press, 2014). Her research and publications focus on topics in Arabic sociolinguistics, including code-switching, language and gender, levelling, register, language policy and discourse analysis. She is also an award-winning novelist.

Elisa Battisti is an Associate Professor in the Department of Linguistics, Philology and Literary Theory at Rio Grande do Sul Federal University. Before joining that university, she taught at Caxias do Sul University. She has taught courses in Linguistics (Sociolinguistics, Phonology) and her research is also in this field. She recently edited a book on language variation in Brazilian Portuguese (with Leda Bisol; EDIPUCRS, 2014), *O português falado no Rio Grande do Sul*, and has contributed to books and journals on sociolinguistics and phonology published in Brazil and abroad.

Bert Botma is a Lecturer of English language and linguistics at the Leiden University Centre for Linguistics. His main research interest is in phonology. Part of his research is in collaboration with Hidetoshi Shiraishi and examines segmental and prosodic aspects of Nivkh phonology.

Irene Cenni is a Lecturer at Ghent University. She is currently teaching at the Department of Translation, Interpreting and Communication. She has taught language acquisition courses and courses in Linguistics and Applied Linguistics at universities in Belgium and in the Netherlands. Her present research interests focus on Italian sociolinguistics and the didactics of Italian as a second language.

Hubert Devonish is Professor of Linguistics in the Department of Language, Linguistics and Philosophy at the University of the West Indies. He is also Coordinator of the Jamaican Language Unit, a Research Unit focusing on issues related to the status and corpus planning of the Jamaican language (Jamaican Creole). His research areas include sociolinguistics, language planning, creole linguistics, phonology and language description. His published books span the range from *Language in Liberation: Creole Language Politics in the Caribbean* (Arawak Press, 2008) through *Talking*

Rhythm, Stressing Tone: The Role of Prominence in Anglo-West African Creole Languages (Arawak Press, 2002) to *A Concise Grammar of Guyanese Creole* (with Dahlia Thompson; Lincom, 2008).

Marc L. Greenberg is Professor of Slavic Languages and Literatures at the University of Kansas and Director of the School of Languages, Literatures and Cultures. He researches primarily Slavic diachrony, dialectology, and language contact, and he has taught sociolinguistics courses focusing on East-Central Europe, the Balkans and ex-USSR. In addition to co-founding and co-editing two Slavic linguistics journals, *Slovenski jezik/Slovene Linguistic Studies* and *Slavia Centralis*, he edited an issue of the *International Journal of the Sociology of Language* (1997) and contributed to Fishman and Garcia's *Handbook of Language and Ethnic Identity*, vol. 2 (Oxford University Press, 2011).

Patrick Heinrich is Associate Professor in the Department of Asian and Mediterranean African Studies at Ca' Foscari University in Venice. Before joining Ca' Foscari he taught at universities in Germany, France and Japan. His present research interests focus on language shift dynamics, language policy and language ideology. His recently edited books include *Handbook of the Ryukyuan Languages* (with Shinsho Miyara and Michinori Shimoji; Mouton de Gruyter, 2015), *Language Crisis in the Ryukyus* (with Mark Anderson; Cambridge Scholars Publishing, 2014), and *Language Life in Japan* (with Christian Galan; Routledge, 2011). His latest monograph is *The Making of Monolingual Japan* (Multilingual Matters, 2012).

Theresa Arevgaq John is an Associate Professor in the Center for Cross Cultural Studies, Indigenous Studies Systems, at the University of Alaska Fairbanks, where she received her PhD in May 2010, entitled *Yuraryararput Kangiit-llu: Our Ways of Dance and Their Meanings*. President Obama selected Theresa to serve on the National Advisory Council on Indian Education in 2011. She recently co-authored a book entitled *Yupiit Yuraryarait: Yup'ik Ways of Dancing* (with James H. Barker and Ann Fienup-Riordan; University of Alaska Press, 2011), which received the prestigious 2011 Book of the Year award from the Alaska State Library Association. She collaborates on a linguistic project, *Improving Alaska Native Education through Computer Assisted Language Learning*. Theresa has published multiple articles in various academic agencies as well as local newspapers. Her professional interest areas include Alaska Native Studies, Indigenous epistemology, ontology, ecology, cosmology and worldview.

Niina Kunnas is Adjunct Professor and University Lecturer of Finnish language at the University of Oulu. She has taught courses in sociolinguistics and minority languages. Her research is also in these fields. She has 42 publications on current situation, variation and change as well as language attitudes of Finno-Ugric minority languages.

Rajend Mesthrie is Professor of Linguistics at the University of Cape Town where he teaches Sociolinguistics, including language contact and variation. He was head of the Linguistics Section (1998–2009), and currently holds an NRF research chair in migration, language and social change. He is a past President of the Linguistics Society of Southern Africa (2002–2009) and a past co-editor of *English Today* (2008–2012). Amongst his book publications are *Introducing Sociolinguistics* (with Swann, Deumert and Leap; Edinburgh University Press, 2009), *Language in South Africa* (ed.; Cambridge University Press, 2002), *A Dictionary of South African Indian English* (University of Cape Town Press, 2010) and *The Cambridge Handbook of Sociolinguistics* (ed.; Cambridge University Press, 2011).

Miriam Meyerhoff is Professor of Linguistics at Victoria University of Wellington. Her research is in language variation (especially in situations of language contact) and language and gender. She is the author of *Bequia Talk* (with James A. Walker; Battlebridge, 2013) and *Introducing Sociolinguistics* (Routledge, 2010), and is co-editor of *The Handbook of Language, Gender, and Sexuality* (with Susan Ehrlich and Janet Holmes; Wiley-Blackwell, 2014). She is a partner investigator in the Dynamics of Language Centre of Excellence (Australian Research Council). She is currently studying variation in a language of northern Vanuatu.

Tadhg Ó hIfearnáin is Head of Irish Language and Literature, an Irish-medium unit within the School of Culture and Communication at the University of Limerick. His main research interests are language policy, ideology and practice, particularly in the context of the modern sociolinguistics of Irish and the other Gaelic languages. His current projects include work on standardization and revitalization and the sociolinguistics of contemporary Manx Gaelic. He edited *An tSochtheangeolaíocht: Feidhm agus Tuairisc* (with Máire Ní Neachtain; Cois Life, 2012), a research-orientated reader in sociolinguistics seen through an Irish-medium lens.

João Ignacio Pires Lucas is an Assistant Professor in the Center of Human Sciences at Caxias do Sul University. He has taught courses in Sociology (sociology of law, political science) and Research Methodology. His research interests are interdisciplinary and focus on themes such as democracy, political parties, language variation, political theory, cultural politics, ideology and university management. He has contributed to books and journals on these themes published in Brazil.

Shobha Satyanath is an Associate Professor in the Department of Linguistics at the University of Delhi, India. She has taught courses on Phonetics, Sociolinguistics, Multilingualism, Language Contact and Historical Linguistics. Her research has focused on (variational) sociolinguistics of Guyana and of diverse Indian settings, language contact varieties in the North Eastern parts of India, dialect geography of Eastern India and on mapping of linguistic diversity of the North Eastern India and the Himalayan regions. Shobha Satyanath is the Editor of *Asia-Pacific Language Variation* (APLV).

Hidetoshi Shiraishi is Associate Professor at Sapporo Gakuin University. His research focuses on the phonology of Nivkh, a language spoken on the island of

Sakhalin and the Lower Amur region in the Russian Far East. His latest publication includes *Nivkh Palatalisation: Articulatory Causes and Perceptual Effects* (with Bert Botma; *Phonology*, 2014).

Dick Smakman is Assistant Professor at Leiden University. He has taught courses in Linguistics (sociolinguistics, phonetics), Applied Linguistics (second-language acquisition, language teaching didactics) as well as language acquisition courses (English and Dutch) at universities in the Netherlands, England, Poland and Japan. His interests include intra- and inter-speaker pronunciation variation, the effects of attitudes on language choices and the sociolinguistics of second-language acquisition. He is currently writing *Discovering Sociolinguistics* for Macmillan (expected in 2016) and in 2015 the second edition of *Accent Building: A British English Pronunciation Course for Speakers of Dutch* was published by Leiden University Press.

Cassie Smith-Christmas is a Research Fellow for Soillse, the inter-university Gaelic language research network. She is based at the University of the Highlands and Islands and also currently holds a fellowship at the Institute for Advanced Studies in the Humanities at the University of Edinburgh. Her research focuses primarily on the intergenerational transmission of Scottish Gaelic, which was the subject of her PhD thesis at the University of Glasgow. Previous publications include articles in *Current Issues in Language Planning*, *Journal of Multilingual and Multicultural Development* and *International Journal of the Sociology of Language*, as well as chapters in the books *Sociolinguistics in Scotland* (Palgrave, 2014) and *Language Variation – European Perspectives IV* (Benjamins, 2013).

James N. Stanford is Associate Professor of Linguistics and Cognitive Science at Dartmouth College in Hanover, New Hampshire. His research focuses on language variation and change in less commonly studied indigenous minority communities, including languages of East/Southeast Asia (Sui, Hmong, Zhuang) and Native American communities. He also studies Eastern New England English features in New Hampshire and Massachusetts. He co-edited *Variation in Indigenous Minority Languages* (with Dennis Preston; Benjamins Publishing, 2009), and he publishes articles in *Journal of Sociolinguistics*, *Language Variation and Change*, *Language in Society*, *Asia Pacific Language Variation*, *American Speech* and other journals.

Aone van Engelenhoven is a Lecturer of Southeast Asian Linguistics (specifically Austronesian languages) at the Department of South and Southeast Asian Studies of Leiden University. His research focuses on linguistic and anthropological issues in Indonesia and East Timor and among Moluccan migrants in the Netherlands. He researches historical linguistics, descriptive linguistics, oral traditions, and language and cognition. He has worked on Austronesian and non-Austronesian languages in Southwest Maluku, minority languages in Indonesia and East Timor, and on Malay.

Maaike van Naerssen is a Lecturer at Leiden University. She is involved in courses in the departments of Linguistics and International Studies focusing on pragmatics, intercultural communication and language and globalization. Her research interests include cross- and intercultural pragmatics and politeness, especially in everyday, mundane, talk-in-interaction. She is currently working on a dissertation about politeness in Dutch and Indonesian informal conversations.

Kadian Walters is a Lecturer of Linguistics and Communication at the University of the West Indies, Department of Language, Linguistics and Philosophy. Her research focuses on linguistic discrimination in Jamaica's public agencies. Her interests include language rights, language ideology, language attitudes and discourse analysis.

Daming Xu is Professor in the Department of Chinese Language and Literature at the University of Macau. Before moving to Macau he taught at universities in Singapore, the US and Mainland China. He was founder-director of the China Center for Linguistic and Strategic Studies at Nanjing University. His English books include *Industrialization and the Restructuring of Speech Communities in China and Europe* (co-edited with Marinus van den Berg; Cambridge Scholars Publishing, 2010) and *A Survey of Language Use and Language Attitudes in the Singapore Chinese Community* (co-authored with Chew Chin Hai and Chen Songcen; Nanjing University Press, 2005).

PREFACE

The motivation for this volume was the editors' awareness of a Western dominance in sociolinguistic theory-making. The incompatibility of several dominant sociolinguistic theories with those outside their Western domain is obvious and undisputed, and this dominance is often expressed by researchers in the field. However, despite this awareness, and despite the fact that non-Western language settings are described extensively in a multitude of publications, these settings somehow seem to contribute less to mainstream theory.

Rather than gathering a set of detailed investigations from various corners of the world, an effort has been made to take the aforementioned incompatibility as the point of departure. Authors were asked to choose one or more well-known theories or models that ill fit in the culture they are studying and to illustrate the incompatibility by referring to existing research. The resultant introductions to the sociolinguistics of various cultures in this volume thus go from case studies to theory, rather than the other way around.

In total, 27 authors from 20 universities across the globe have contributed. Together, they describe 12 larger regions and five smaller communities. Each chapter has its own approach to the issue of theoretical mismatches, and a wide variety of insights and approaches has emerged. Some chapters, for instance Marc Greenberg's chapter on the Slavic area, pay much attention to explaining the coming into existence of a situation in a region from a historical and political perspective. Other chapters, for instance Daming Xu's chapter on China, apply mismatches from a Labovian perspective and try to generate theories that apply specifically to the idiosyncrasies of the local situation and that might work universally as well. Other chapters, like the chapter on Northern Africa, straightforwardly take a certain theory and explain how the theory does not apply to a region or community. There are also chapters containing less predictable approaches, like the chapter on Yup'ik, which discusses the role of dance in social interaction

Preface **xvii**

within a community. In their totality, the chapters draw a lively picture of types of theoretical issues that exist.

Structuring the volume on the basis of region was considered unsatisfactory, since "region" lumps together very different polities, languages and types of communities. Subdivisions on the basis of colonization history or writing traditions were other options, but these approaches were thought to lead to a Western categorization. We therefore took a leap of faith and decided to categorize the chapters on the basis of social and economic development, a factor that is key in shaping distinct types of society and which thus directly affects the sociolinguistic situation. We arranged the chapters according to their respective classification on the Human Development Index (http://countryeconomy.com/hdi). The chapters move from those furthest removed from the Western state of socio-economic development to areas and communities more resemblant of the West in this respect.

Africa and Asia are most strongly represented, together covering about half the chapters, as mismatches seem most pertinent in these regions and because of the relatively high number of living languages in these regions. The Slavic area, covering more than one continent, is described in two chapters, and Central and South America are represented in three. The West is in itself not a coherent unity and there is diversity within the West itself. This book includes chapters that cover parts of the region but do not fit Western paradigms: the North Saami, Yup'ik and Gaelic communities and the European Mediterranean region.

This volume opens with a chapter by Miriam Meyerhoff and James Stanford, who present their take on the issue at hand and who give their first observations on tendencies visible in the subsequent chapters. Chapter 2 tries to draw a factual picture of the nature and extent of the presumed Anglo-Western bias of the field of sociolinguistics by looking at the influence exerted by authors from certain regions as well as the choice of languages discussed in journal articles and books. Chapters 3 to 14 cover the major regions of the globe: each discusses a specific region, while in most cases focusing specifically on a country within that region. Each of these chapters illustrates how one, two or more well-known mainstream sociolinguistic frameworks fail to be easily applicable to the region in question. Chapters 15 to 19 describe the same types of mismatches but focus on smaller communities rather than larger areas.

Compiling this book took about two and a half years, and well over 1,000 e-mails now sit in the inboxes of the editors, suggesting that the Internet deserves the biggest thank you. Without this loyal and efficient friend, this volume would have been impossible or taken ten years. However, we prefer to thank the people behind all the e-mails. We owe much gratitude to the authors for their expertise, and the readiness and enthusiasm with which they shared it with us, in many cases without knowing the editors personally. The many colleagues and other intermediaries who helped find the authors also deserve a big thank you. We are also grateful to everyone at Routledge for helping us realize this volume, in particular Louisa Semlyen, Sophie Jaques, Rosemary Baron and Laura Sandford. Closer to home, we are indebted to Albertine Bosselaar and Max van Arnhem, who proofread the chapters with much enthusiasm and precision. Tradition dictates us to state that any remaining shortcomings and errors are ours.

In discussing, developing and editing the individual chapters we were unashamedly egoistical and tried to produce a book we would ourselves enjoy reading most. Very minor issues aside, we instantly agreed on which direction to take and so we hope that readers will share our interest in the content of these chapters, and develop ideas on how to deal with the issues at hand in the future. Since the readers we imagine will read this book include our own students, we would like to dedicate it to those from whom we ourselves have learned so much. We dedicate this volume to Florian Coulmas and other such inspired teachers.

Dick Smakman and Patrick Heinrich
Nijmegen and Venice

ACKNOWLEDGEMENTS

Every effort has been made to contact copyright holders. If any have been inadvertently overlooked the publishers will be pleased to make the necessary arrangements at the first opportunity.

Map of places discussed adapted from *Introducing Sociolinguistics* by Miriam Meyerhoff, published 2011 by Routledge. Copyright Miriam Meyerhoff. Used with kind permission.

MAP OF PLACES DISCUSSED

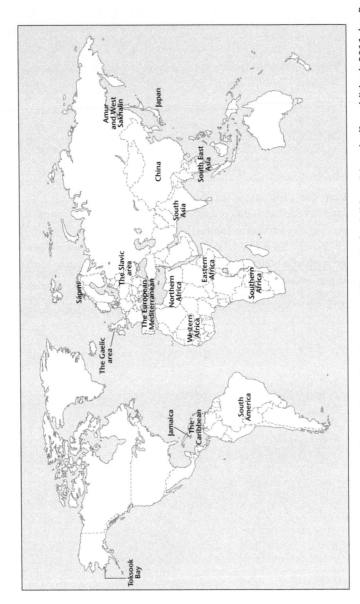

Map of places discussed, adapted from *Introducing Sociolinguistics* by Miriam Meyerhoff, published 2011 by Routledge. Copyright Miriam Meyerhoff. Used with kind permission

1

"TINGS CHANGE, ALL TINGS CHANGE"

The changing face of sociolinguistics with a global perspective

Miriam Meyerhoff and James N. Stanford

1.1 Introduction

In an interview with a teenager from her community, an older woman on Bequia (an island in the Eastern Caribbean) summed up the varied nature of her life experiences: "Tings change, all tings change" ("Things change, everything changes"). Her love for Bequia and her community was in no way diminished by the changes she had experienced, but she was also a realist about the challenges that change presents – not only for her, but for the interviewer, her grandchildren and the community as a whole.

As we consider the face of sociolinguistics in the first decades of the twenty-first century, we are reminded of the philosophical musing of our Bequia speaker. Certainly, much has changed in sociolinguistics since the inception of the field. Some linguists have been concerned with the dynamics of language in society as long as there have been scholarly treatises on language, but as a well-defined discipline of the field of linguistics, sociolinguistics traces its origins to the middle of the twentieth century. Growing out of both the traditions of historical linguistics (Weinreich et al. 1968) and anthropology (Gumperz 1962, 1964), sociolinguistics has since its inception been a field of study that has challenged and changed individual researchers, the academy and the communities of speakers where its work has been undertaken. Periodically, sociolinguistics as a field has taken stock of its ability to challenge and change, and reframed its goals and methodologies in ways that will foreground or refresh our outlook on language attitudes, the documentation of different ways of talking and how these both interact with ways of being (Labov 1969a; Cameron et al.1992; Eckert and McConnell-Ginet 1992; Rickford 1996).

This book represents the ongoing efforts within sociolinguistics to refresh and rechallenge the field. Recent decades have seen a quiet but nonetheless notable shift in the practice of sociolinguistics. In the early years of the field, major studies tended to be focused on urban or monolingual speech communities. But much has changed since then. Social changes have reshaped the demographics and linguistic profile of the traditional, urban locus of speech community studies. Our beliefs about the necessity or, indeed, the feasibility of isolating monolingual speakers in any speech community have changed. Disciplinary boundaries of the academy have softened and increasingly there is space for sociolinguists to define themselves in multiple ways (Sinologist, media studies, discourse analyst, dialectologist, to give one example of a colleague in Australia). We have seen increased engagement with reinvigorated sister fields in linguistics, such as endangered language documentation, where under major initiatives such as the Volkswagen Foundation's Documentation of Endangered Languages programme, salvage work values the details of variation and the details of the social context as essential components of the ecology of any language. Finally, as linguistics itself has matured as a field and gained more prominence as a subject for advanced study, we are seeing an increasing number of sociolinguists who can draw on their previous personal or professional experience with smaller or more isolated communities come into the field.

Not all of these changes are independent. But what all of these changes have done is challenge how we understand sociolinguistics and what we understand the purpose of sociolinguistic research to be. Some of them challenge previous assumptions subtly – simply by participating as an active member of the academy, a speaker of a Chinese minority language may remind us that s/he represents tens of thousands of people whose language has been ignored by sociolinguistic studies up until now (Stanford and Pan 2013), a speaker of Ewe analysing variation in their language steps forward to represent millions of speakers who have previously been invisible (Noglo 2009). Some challenges have been more direct and on record. For example, when there was a general retreat from the logical positivism of the early twentieth century to the post-modernism of the late twentieth century, sociolinguists were among those blowing the trumpets that brought down the walls of what has now come to be known as "first wave" or "second wave" sociolinguistics (Eckert and McConnell-Ginet 1992), or calling earlier sociolinguistics research on its paternalistic stance, and advocating for more genuinely co-operative models of research (Cameron et al. 1992).

Interestingly, a challenge that sociolinguists initially failed to recognise was the challenge to forge new partnerships across sub-disciplines. When the Volkswagen Foundation announced it would spend millions of euros on endangered language documentation at the turn of the century, it did so on the understanding that the documentation of verb paradigms must be accompanied by a broader social perspective that encompassed the role of a language in society, as a vehicle of different styles and a repository of cultural knowledge. This presented a very immediate and material challenge to sociolinguistics and yet few of the funded teams turned to sociolinguists for their expertise, generally instead seeking the advice of other social scientists.

Why might this have been? Why did sociolinguistics fail to seize the moment and become part of the VW schemes? The reasons are complex (and beyond the scope of this chapter to tease out), but one reason that we must entertain is that in responding to the intellectual and social challenges of the late twentieth century, the field of sociolinguistics failed to grasp the increasingly global nature of research. This book, with its global scope and its broad perspective, stands both as a reproach to the field, and as one of the latest challenges to it.

Our purpose in this chapter is to articulate some of the major issues that the challenge of globalising sociolinguistics presents to us as a field. Globalising sociolinguistics is a major enterprise – it involves getting away from the WEIRD subjects that dominate social science research and have had a disproportionately strong influence on sociolinguistics as well. WEIRD, meaning Western, Educated, Industrialised, Rich and Democratic (Henrich et al. 2010), may not apply in entirety to sociolinguistics, but it is a reasonable generalisation about the cultural frame that has dominated sociolinguistics research for much of its history. We highlight some of the valuable new insights that a less WEIRD research perspective can provide, drawing from work in this volume as well as prior work. A wide-ranging volume like this raises many more issues than can be covered in one chapter, so we have chosen to focus on five themes that we believe are especially pertinent. Some of these we have already intimated, and none of them are entirely independent of the others. They are:

(1) the multilingual reality of most people's experience;
(2) the notion of standard languages, and how these interact with local vernaculars;
(3) the native speaker;
(4) the application of third wave approaches to sociolinguistics with a global perspective; and
(5) cross-cultural collaboration.

1.2 The multilingual reality

Hard statistics are impossible to find, but general wisdom seems to hold that more people in the world are bilingual or multilingual than are monolingual. This presents challenges for sociolinguists, both those working in more exotic and thoroughly multilingual speech communities and those working on urban dialectology in countries where there is one normative language (e.g. English in New York, French in Paris). We see the main challenges here as being to do with (1) sampling and access to the people whose language practices we may be concerned with, and (2) how we theorise our speech community and analyse our results. Here, we deal first with challenges of access and sampling.

An increasing number of sociolinguistic studies are engaged with documenting the variation and patterns of language use in multiethnic and multilingual communities. Studies in European and North American cities have led the way here (Boyd et al. 2015; Cheshire, Gardner-Chloros and Gadet 2011; Cheshire, Kerswill, Fox and Torgersen 2011; Cornips 2014; Nagy 2014), and they have shown that, by and large, the methods of urban dialectology can be adapted for a focus on multilingual communities and ethnic minorities in modern cities. Issues of course do arise with making contacts and recording successfully in ethnic enclaves. Most professional sociolinguists are themselves exemplars of pretty WEIRD upbringings, and success on these projects has depended on using a team-based approach, which combines the expertise of the professional sociolinguists with insider fieldworkers or other social scientists working with the target communities. Ideally, the process involves training community insiders and moving towards the participatory research model advocated by Cameron et al. (1992).

The challenge of gaining access to parts of the speech community that the researcher is an outsider to is by no means new. Labov (1972a) showed that a research team that includes local fieldworkers can be effective in gaining the trust and co-operation of speakers of urban minorities, and anthropology has a long tradition of dealing with the problem through participant observation and lengthy fieldwork. We'll come back to this point in Sections 1.5 and 1.6.

The sociolinguistic analysis of these communities has followed established routines – data on attitudes, linguistic security, domains of language use and the details of variation have all been analysed in the manner of the classic sociolinguistic field studies (Shuy, Wolfram and Riley 1967; Labov 1972b; Trudgill 1974; Cheshire 1987; Milroy 1987). But in addition to the challenges of sampling and access in such diverse communities, these projects have also raised questions about which language(s) it is appropriate to record people speaking, since many such communities are characterised by intense multilingualism, code-mixing and blended varieties (cf. Mesthrie 2008).

The rewards associated with engaging with these challenges are potentially substantial. Cheshire et al.'s (2011) work in London has shown us that findings from the multilingual and multicultural inner city may turn sociolinguistic truisms on their heads. Their work has found younger boys from migrant families (not teenagers, and not young women) leading changes that are spreading through the rest of the community.

Other research has highlighted the intense creativity of liminal speakers within an ethnically diverse city community. For example, Hmong American communities in some of the large cities they have migrated to in the US classify themselves into several subgroups, such as White Hmong and Green Hmong. In cases of intermarriage, wives are traditionally expected to learn the dialect of the husband's family. Stanford's (2010) research found, however, that some wives are agentively challenging this traditional sociolinguistic expectation, along with other gendered traditions. Using dialect choices as a proxy, these women are negotiating new social positions for themselves and their daughters within Hmong American urban society, taking advantage of a liminal period of immigration and acute cross-cultural contact in large US cities. In this way, investigations of culturally diverse minority communities can lead to new perspectives on sociolinguistic behaviour. There is an obvious challenge for sociolinguists if we want to try and capture this diversity of experience and to broaden our sense of what sociolinguistic knowledge can and should be.

Most of the essays in this volume deal with multiethnic and multilingual communities or else monolingual communities undergoing acute contact with other languages, so the volume provides a valuable opportunity to consider sociolinguistic research in these settings. As a starting point on this topic, we direct readers to fascinating discussions of complex multilingualism in South Asia (Satyanath), Eastern Africa (Barasa), Southern Africa (Mesthrie), West Africa (Anderson and Ansah), the Mediterranean (Cenni) and the Slavic world (Greenberg), among others in the volume.

1.3 Standards, norms and local vernaculars

The contact and relationship between regional and national standard languages and the common language of the home is an important consideration for sociolinguists. Ferguson's (1959) distinction between the High and Low languages of diglossic speech communities drew a sharp line between standard languages and local vernaculars and initially characterised the tension between, say, classical and local varieties of Arabic as a relatively stable phenomenon. Subsequent research has found many analogues of a functional dynamic between a High and a Low language in communities around the world, but they have also shown that they vary in their temporal stability. A somewhat looser notion of functional diglossia (that is, a relatively stable alternation between varieties or codes on the basis of function or domain at the level of society and the individual), remains well suited for describing the sociolinguistic ecology of many communities across the globe. Several chapters in this volume grapple with the challenge of analysing diglossia in diverse sociolinguistic research settings, including Southeast Asia (Van Engelenhoven and Van Naerssen), East Africa (Barasa), West Africa (Anderson and Ansah), the Caribbean (Devonish; Devonish and Walters) and Scotland/Ireland (Smith-Christmas and Ó hIfearnáin).

Questions about what serves as a standard, and whether there is an identifiable standard within a speech community and who validates the standard are ones that sociolinguistics take seriously, and indeed there is a long tradition in sociolinguistics of combining social activism with descriptive work (e.g. Wolfram 1993; Rickford 1997; Wolfram et al. 1999), even of very subtle patterns of variation (Labov 1969b; Wolfram et al. 1997). As we try to reframe the sociolinguistic enterprise in more global terms, the role of language as a tool for power, prestige, status and gatekeeping becomes even more central. Many of the chapters in this volume highlight why language standards cannot be ignored; community ideologies about standards remain powerful means of oppressing or privileging sectors of society in many parts of the world. For example, Aikio, Arola and Kunnas (this volume) find very little dialect levelling in North Saami, and they attribute this lack of levelling to the lack of a single prestige variety. North Saami speakers value a notion of dialect "purity", expressed in terms of "keeping to one's own dialect". In this way, each community maintains its traditional regional dialect.

One of the spectres that raises its head when we start to consider language standards is the role of language in education. This has been and remains a major issue in multilingual countries worldwide, because the choice of languages for education plays a crucial role in defining someone's life opportunities, particularly the opportunities of those who are not lucky enough to speak the standard language of education at home or in their everyday life.[1]

It is worth bearing in mind that the study of variation depends fundamentally on establishing some kind of "standard", so the notion is not purely of significance for applied sociolinguists. This is because what any analysis of variation typically does is that it defines a baseline against which variation is measured. A researcher can define the baseline or norm as the form or structure that is associated with the educational or metropolitan standard of any particular language, but they can also define it as being the most frequently used form in the community. We can see how this operates by looking at work on Bequia English, which uses both approaches to define the baseline.

Walker and Meyerhoff (2006) analysed use of the copula in Bequia, and they explored different ways of modelling its presence or absence. One way to model the absence of the copula in Bequia English is to take Standard English norms as the baseline. Because Standard English requires an overt copula in most syntactic frames, we can take every place where Standard English would use a copula as the baseline, and treat any Bequia English utterance without an overt copula as reflecting the application of some rule for deletion. The problem with this kind of set-up for an analysis of variation is that it models Bequia English as a derived form of English. This may be historically correct, but one could ask why not treat it as a grammar in its own right now, instead of perpetuating vaguely colonial attitudes towards it as a deviant form of English? Such criticisms are valid ones and they apply quite broadly. Researchers should consider them when they undertake analyses of sociolinguistic variation in the growing range of global speech communities gaining attention today.

On the other hand, Walker and Meyerhoff (2006) also have language-internal reasons for modelling the presence/absence of the copula in Bequia English as a case of deletion. The vast majority of sentences in Bequia English that correspond to copula sentences in Standard English do have an overt copula in Bequian. So if we are to take the most frequent form of a variant as the baseline in modelling variation, this fact would also favour the idea that there is a copula in Bequia English that speakers delete with variable frequency. (In fact, Walker and Meyerhoff work through possible models in more detail even than this.) In the case of the Bequia English copula, the researchers could look to both the form associated with the metropolitan standard and to the form found most frequently in the community to support their decision to take the standard against which variation is measured as presence of a copula.

A second example will serve to illustrate how token frequency can push a researcher to treat one form as the baseline over another, especially when the sociolinguistic work has moved into the domain of less well-described languages. Meyerhoff's work on Nkep in Vanuatu (Meyerhoff 2012, 2015) considers the distribution of different forms of subject prefix in finite clauses. Since there is no local standard of Nkep that one could refer to, it would not have been meaningful to define the norm socially, and since the historical source of some of the prefixes is also unclear, it was not reasonable to suppose one set was older and a precursor to the other. So in this case, the distribution of different forms was used to guide the analysis of variation, and the least frequent prefixes were treated as the application of the variable rule.

A third and final example, based on Stanford's work on the use of tone in Sui, will show how social factors sometimes trump all others in defining the norm. Sui society is organised around loyalties to clans. In rural Sui villages, speakers maintain the clan dialect features of their home villages throughout the lifespan, regardless of mobility and contact (Stanford 2009). This pattern is best observed in the context of marriage and in-migration. Following customs of clan exogamy, women in rural Sui regions are expected to marry a man from another clan. At the time of marriage, the wife moves to the husband's village, but she does not acquire the husband's dialect. Instead, she is expected to maintain her original clan dialect − a strict social norm that overrides her physical location. In other words, the norm is not defined in an extra-local manner, such as the large-scale norm found in Standard French ideology, nor is it defined in terms of mathematical majority in a given local community. For Sui, the norm for a particular individual is socially defined according to personal heritage: You are expected to speak like your home clan speaks, regardless of your current place of residence or social networks. This cultural pattern is then passed on to the children, who learn the father's (local village) dialect, not the mother's dialect, even though the mother is typically the primary caregiver for young children (Stanford 2008).

In sum, there is both a mathematical sense of a norm that researchers can orient their analysis to, and a social sense of norm that the analysis can be oriented to. Either way, the quantitative approach requires the researcher to take some kind of stand on what might be considered standard or normative for a group of speakers, regardless of whether their language variety enjoys any formal recognition or even whether it enjoys any orthographic standardisation.

Well-established and well-described languages allow us to look to the internal language history and previous descriptions, and also to the orthographic norms for explicit cues about what might be treated as normative or standard within the community. However, as we globalise sociolinguistics, we need to recognise that this may not be an option, especially for smaller, less well-described languages. In these cases, the researcher's own selection preferences may play a role in deciding which features or structures to elevate to the status of standard. Hence, the challenge for us, as analysts, is to state our decisions clearly and to make the rationale behind them completely transparent. This is essential for a global sociolinguistics because if we choose to treat one form as the standard or norm and another form as the application of some variable process, this can snowball and have implications for the rest of our analysis (and even subsequent work on the language situation).

Moreover, while notions of socioeconomic class and style-shifting can sometimes help researchers define a locally relevant "standard" (e.g. Labov 1972b), such tools can be problematic in other communities. Chapters in this volume that touch on these issues include Smith-Christmas and Ó hIfearnáin (Gaelic), Xu (China), Battisti (South America) and Bassiouney (Northern Africa).

Imagine, for instance, that you have completed the analysis of subject prefixes and you discover that the modality of the clause seems to play a very strong role in constraining where certain prefixes are found in your data. There is now a strong temptation for you, as an analyst, to group anything else that might be influenced by the modality of the clause into some kind of sociolinguistic natural class. However, the effect of modality on the other features might be much more attenuated than it was on the subject prefixes. If that is the case, using modality as the basis for creating some kind of natural class may be giving it undue prominence in the grammar of the language.

For example, Mendes (2010) analyses Brazilian Portuguese variation between EG, *estar+gerúndio* ("be + Gerund"), and TP, *ter+particípio* ("have + Past Participle"). Mendes must carefully consider how to frame the research question (2010: 44): Should the alternation between EG and TP be viewed as the dependent variable conditioned by aspect or should aspect be treated as the dependent variable instead? Mendes uses diachronic evidence to justify his decision to treat EG and TP as "interchangeable" variants to be analysed in relation to aspect. Mendes (2010: 33) notes, "Without taking into account these diachronic facts of the semantics of TP, it would probably be reasonable to deny the possibility of variation in the uses of EG and TP." Because Portuguese is a world language, such diachronic information is easily available to a variationist researcher. Of course, when dealing with many smaller languages, researchers would not have this resource. Fundamental research issues like this are all the more challenging in small, understudied language communities that may have little or no written literature, historical records, or prior linguistic work. Clearly a global sociolinguistics will have to take this into consideration.

1.4 "Native speakers" and inclusion/exclusion

As a more global sociolinguistics embraces more heterogeneous speech communities than it traditionally has in the past, researchers must confront another question that was largely taken for granted in foundational studies of the speech community. *Who* exactly are we studying? Many of the first social dialect studies that were undertaken focused expressly on only those people who had grown up in the community, people who one might consider native speakers of the local variety. The term is seldom deployed in sociolinguistic research, but it is important to recognise that sociolinguistics in the latter half of the twentieth century was arguably as much obsessed with the idea of capturing native speaker knowledge as formal linguistic studies were.

The notion of native speaker has received a good deal of scrutiny in recent years. Davies (2003, 2013) provides an extended discussion of how the notion of the native speaker has both helped and limited research and research methodologies in second-language acquisition studies. Davies acknowledges that the notion of the native speaker (and, equally, the notion of a "standard language") is very useful when researchers are developing theory and trying to apply the theories they have developed, but he also makes a case for understanding the native speaker as an object of enquiry. For Davies, being a native speaker of a language is not an immanent state of being; instead it is inextricably linked to an ongoing set of achievements, and these achievements may be driven by individuals' emotions and affect. The status of native speaker is, according to Davies, something that individuals can gain or lose across a lifespan – in this respect his work can usefully be read in conjunction with sociolinguistic research on variation across the lifespan (Guy and Boyd 1990; Sankoff and Blondeau 2007; Wagner and Sankoff 2011). Although Davies grounds his discussion in specific case studies, it is primarily a reflective and theoretical approach to the ongoing processes that underpin a person's claim to be a native speaker (it is not a post-modern deconstruction of the term, in the manner of Jørgensen et al. 2011).

Hackert (2012) presents a rather wide-ranging historical sociolinguistic consideration of the notion of the native speaker. Although her focus is primarily on the emergence of the English native speaker as a category in the latter half of the nineteenth century, her discussion and sources are decidedly global. She positions the English native speaker in relation to European scholarly traditions and also in relation to the language politics, racial politics and nationalism that were all central to the consolidation of the British Empire in the nineteenth century. Not coincidentally, it was at precisely the same time that English was becoming more and more a global communication medium that some scholars began the navel-gazing and jingoism that almost *required* the invention of something like the native speaker as a means of demarcating who is "in" and who is "out". Corder's (1973) characterisation of the speech community foreshadows Hackert's sociopolitical perspective on the category of the native speaker, since for Corder membership in a speech community is defined on the basis of others' perceptions of whether one is a member.

Perceptions of authenticity (who is "in" and who is "out" when we study a speech community, e.g. Eckert 2003) are particularly in focus when the speech communities we are dealing with have multiple codes, not all of which are used and shared equally by all members. Should we accede to lay notions that older speakers are "better" speakers of a language, or exclude people who do not use the language we are primarily interested in as the main medium of communication at home?

To give one example, many speakers in Hog Harbour (a village in northern Vanuatu) consider their Nkep good enough to participate actively or passively in community meetings, to hold conversations with friends and to make arrangements for daily activities in the family. However, they may not consider their Nkep good enough to tell traditional (*kastom*) stories and they may want to defer to older members of the community, or refuse to have their versions of these stories recorded. A sociolinguistic description of Hog Harbour means trying to understand what people consider to be "good enough" Nkep and why this varies in different domains and with different tasks/audiences. This creates an "inclusion paradox" – in order to understand who the community considers to be good speakers and why, you have to include everyone in the community in your study, including the people who are not considered good speakers. Struggling with the inclusion paradox is likely to be a pervasive feature of global sociolinguistics; ideologies and beliefs about whether someone is "good enough" in a language or not provide us with vital information about how people orient to ongoing linguistic and social change – exactly the kinds of problems that sociolinguistics holds dear to its heart. Nagy (2009) suggests a set of documentation methods that researchers can use to systematically describe such complexities in a lesser-studied language community.

In the present volume, John grapples with the challenge of defining "speaker" in the context of Central Yup'ik in Alaska. She notes that formal assessments of fluency may not always be available as a measure in some communities. Instead, she stresses the importance of a social or community definition. For Yup'ik, she finds that the local definition of "speaker" hinges on whether or not the person can communicate with an elder; it is not simply a matter of passing a fluency examination.

1.5 The waves of sociolinguistics

As we consider the future of a globalised sociolinguistics, we believe it is important to remember that some analytical trends and theoretical developments have only been made possible because they have been enabled by the rich descriptive knowledge about certain languages and speech communities that have accrued over decades. One such development that we think is worth unpacking in this way is "third wave" sociolinguistics (Eckert 2012). Third wave approaches to sociolinguistics are focused on documenting how social meaning is ascribed to language variants through social interaction. In this regard, it is seen as a departure from first and second wave approaches to variation that tended to focus on describing correlational relationships between variants and social or demographic categories, which might have been established by the researcher on the basis of very superficial knowledge of the community.

The challenge of responding to a third wave approach to language variation has greatly energised the field of sociolinguistics over the last 20 years and it has had the very valuable effect of encouraging researchers to give careful consideration to apparently anomalous or unpredicted uses of language that might occur in their data. Personally, we enjoy reading this work enormously but we also think it is worth noting that unless you have a fully-fledged description of a language, it can be very hard to aspire to third wave analysis – no matter how much you would like to undertake it.

The reason for this is rather simple: focusing on the social meaning of variation can only be fruitfully done once you have worked out what aspects of variation are socially meaningful. A lot of variation is "noise", and competent members of the speech community simply filter noise out. For example, the intra-speaker variation associated with whether or not I have a cold or whether parts of my tongue are numb because I have just been to the dentist doesn't get ascribed social meaning. And this is not because it's idiosyncratic. They are just as iterable across individuals and just as potentially performative as the variation associated with using a high rising intonation contour on a declarative statement. The reason that nasal speech produced when you have a cold gets ignored and high rising declaratives don't is because we don't ascribe social meaning to the typical producers of nasal speech (people who have a virus), but we do ascribe social meaning to the typical producers of some intonation patterns (people who are young, people who are (a particular kind of) female). Basic correlational, second wave work on the sociolinguistics of less well-known or less well-described speech communities is a highly effective way of determining which kind of variation we might be dealing with.

Eckert (2000) acknowledged that the important work she did which laid the foundations for a third wave approach depended on the solid descriptive work that had already been done on the Northern Cities Shift. It is not a coincidence that third wave analyses tend to be associated with minutely scrutinised varieties (such as North American English) or otherwise well-described languages and social settings (such as modern Beijing and Hong Kong Chinese, Zhang 2005). But not everyone working to globalise sociolinguistics has the luxury of a solid description of the fundamentals of the language variety/ies they are working on. An analyst can't ask what categories "mean" to speakers until they have a firm hold on what the categories are. We believe that as researchers, and as a field, it is important that people working on smaller and less well-described languages should not feel apologetic about using first or second wave approaches in their study of variation. It is, if you like, a strategic essentialism – a necessary first step if the language is going to be available at some stage for the more socially situated analysis of a third wave approach. For less commonly studied communities, then, sociolinguistic research may need to start from a basic Lévi-Straussian structural foundation and then later explore how the meanings of linguistic forms relate to Bourdieuian notions of what we do with those forms, right through to hexis and social capital.

1.6 Cross-cultural collaboration

Lastly, we would like to highlight the importance of collaboration as a tool in globalising sociolinguistics. Many sociolinguists working in communities around the world have a commitment to long-term and collaborative relationships with their communities, but we believe that there are particular analytic challenges for researchers studying smaller or less well-known languages since they are usually working in isolation or near isolation.

As a profession, we often take for granted the comfort we enjoy in the company of others. Researchers (and we are not exempt from this) sometimes pick the features they decide to focus on because they know they will have a ready-made community of colleagues that are also concerned with the same issues. There is nothing wrong with this and some of the best sociolinguistic work (that is, the work that has had the furthest reach and the most lasting impact) has come from people working in detail on the same or similar problems, sometimes over decades (Guy 1991; Labov et al. 2006; Otheguy et al. 2007; Guy and Cutler 2011). When we consider sociolinguistics as a whole, we would hazard to suggest that the majority of past research projects have been conducted in researchers' own "home" communities or ones that are linguistically and culturally closely related.

There is a danger with this: "the rich" may simply keep getting richer. "The rich" in this case are the languages – the already well described and well known get even more attention, while the descriptions and results arising from the study of languages that are less well known are marginalised. Consciously or unconsciously, they can be considered inherently less significant.

If we can challenge ourselves to move beyond the limits of parochialism, we will be able to engage with a far wider range of sociolinguistic questions. After all, many subfields of linguistics – including what some people believe is core linguistics, such as phonetics, phonology, morphology, syntax – have greatly benefited from the fresh perspectives that data from lesser-studied languages can offer. We are convinced that sociolinguistics will benefit as well. Two new scholarly initiatives are taking positive steps in this direction: the conference series New Ways of Analysing Variation – Asia/Pacific and the new peer-reviewed journal *Asia-Pacific Language Variation*.

One certain way to increase the amount of research being conducted in lesser-studied language communities is to develop collaborative work models with local "cultural insiders". For an outside researcher entering a new community, it typically takes months or even years to learn enough about the language and culture to be able to conduct a sensible sociolinguistic study and interpret the results. Long-term cultural experience is crucial for operationalising research activities and determining locally meaningful sociolinguistic questions (and this is also directly relevant to the discussion of third wave sociolinguistics above). But mobilising an "army of Westerners" who would spend years learning each of these languages and cultures would be inefficient and probably undesirable – it is perilously close to academic colonialism. Moreover, Western researchers would be wise to learn from the many other sociolinguistic traditions around the world, some of which predate Western research on this topic. In this volume, for example, Heinrich describes Japan's *gengo seikatsu* "language life" research tradition (Sibata 1999; Chambers 2012).

How, then, can we quickly and realistically encourage new sociolinguistic research projects in diverse communities around the world? One answer lies in healthy collaborations between "outsider" researchers and local community members. A truly globalised sociolinguistics will need collaborative partnerships where local community members can combine their insights with outside research perspectives and methods, that is, a balance of emic and etic perspectives. Moreover, collaborative research relationships are mutually beneficial; in cases where no trained researchers are available in a given community, the local researcher can be trained and started on a lifetime of research through fieldwork experience, conference talks, publications and integration with the international scholarly community.

Many of the essays in this volume present a positive and definitive role model in this regard. An impressive number are written by authors with intimate insider knowledge of the communities studied, and the range of topics covered are commensurately rich.

1.7 Conclusion

The intriguing studies in this volume all strive towards the shared goal of globalising sociolinguistics. While some classic theories and models of sociolinguistics may need to be adjusted when they are applied to diverse societies around the world, we can always learn from prior work and build upon it. Rather than "starting from scratch" theoretically, we believe it is best to take knowledge from prior theories as a starting point and build upon those ideas with the many new perspectives gained from a more global approach (Nagy and Meyerhoff 2008; Stanford and Preston 2009). As this volume shows, it is productive and rewarding to work on global languages using methods that have come out of Western sociolinguistics traditions. A global sociolinguistics challenges us conceptually and methodologically. The fact that we may need to jettison some aspects of practice or theory should not deter us from addressing the interesting and rewarding issues raised in trying to meet these challenges.

In this chapter, we have focused on five particularly pressing issues: the ubiquity of multilingualism, standards and local vernaculars, the challenge of defining "native speaker", the "waves" of sociolinguistics and the role of collaboration. We look forward to the continuing efforts of sociolinguists around the world in tackling these and many other challenges, as we work together to build a truly globalised sociolinguistics.

Note

1 There are a number of excellent texts and monographs available that cover the ground raised by the educational implications of a more globalised perspective on sociolinguistics (e.g. Hornberger and McKay 2010; Makoni 2011; Omoniyi 2004).

References

Boyd, Sally, Michol Hoffman and James Walker (2015) Sociolinguistic Practice among Multilingual Youth in Sweden and Canada. In: *Language, Youth and Identity in the 21st Century*. Jacomine Nortier and Bente A. Svendsen (eds). Cambridge: Cambridge University Press.

Cameron, Deborah, Elizabeth Frazer, Penelope Harvey, M.B.H. Rampton and Kay Richardson (1992) *Researching Language: Issues of Power and Method*. London: Routledge.

Chambers, Jack K. (2012) Professor Sibata's *haha* and other Sociolinguistic Insights. New Ways of Analyzing Variation: Asia-Pacific 2. Tokyo, Japan, 2 August.

Cheshire, Jenny (1987) Syntactic Variation, the Linguistic Variable and Sociolinguistic Theory. *Linguistics* 25(2): 257–82.

Cheshire, Jenny L., Penelope Gardner-Chloros and Françoise Gadet (2011) Multicultural London English/Multicultural Paris French. In: *Franco-British Academic Partnerships: The Next Chapter*. Maurice Fraser and Philip Lane (eds), 134–44. Liverpool: Liverpool University Press.

Cheshire, Jenny, Paul Kerswill, Sue Fox and Eivind Torgersen (2011) Contact, the Feature Pool and the Speech Community: The Emergence of Multicultural London English. *Journal of Sociolinguistics* 15: 151–96.

Corder, S. Pit (1973) *Introducing Applied Linguistics*. Harmondsworth: Penguin.

Cornips, Leonie (2014) Language Contact, Linguistic Variability and the Construction of Local Identities. In: *The Sociolinguistics of Grammar*. Tor A. Åfarlí and Brit Maehlum (eds), 67–90. Amsterdam: John Benjamins.

Davies, Alan (2003) *The Native Speaker: Myth and Reality* (second edition). Clevedon: Multilingual Matters.

——(2013) *Native Speakers and Native Users. Loss and Gain*. Cambridge: Cambridge University Press.
Eckert, Penelope (2000) *Linguistic Variation as Social Practice: The Linguistic Construction of Belten High*. Malden: Blackwell.
——(2003) Elephants in the Room. *Journal of Sociolinguistics* 7(3): 392–431.
——(2012) Three Waves of Variation Study: The Emergence of Meaning in the Study of Sociolinguistic Variation. *Annual Review of Anthropology* 41: 87–100.
Eckert, Penelope and Sally McConnell-Ginet (1992) Think Practically and Look Locally: Language and Gender as Community-based Practice. *Annual Review of Anthropology* 21: 461–90.
Ferguson, Charles (1959) Diglossia. *Word* 15: 325–40.
Gumperz, John (1962) Types of Linguistic Communities. *Anthropological Linguistics* 4: 28–40.
——(1964) Linguistic and Social Interaction in Two Communities. *American Anthropologist* 66(6.2): 137–53.
Guy, Gregory R. (1991) Explanation in Variable Phonology: An Exponential Model of Morphological Constraints. *Language Variation and Change* 3: 1–22.
Guy, Gregory R. and Sally Boyd (1990) The Development of a Morphological Class. *Language Variation and Change* 2(1): 1–18.
Guy, Gregory R. and Cecelia Cutler (2011) Speech Style and Authenticity: Quantitative Evidence for the Performance of Identity. *Language Variation and Change* 23: 139–62.
Hackert, Stephanie (2012) *The Emergence of the English Native Speaker: A Chapter in Nineteenth Century Linguistics Thought*. Berlin: Mouton de Gruyter.
Henrich, Joseph, Stephen J. Heine and Ara Norenzayan (2010) The Weirdest People in the World? *Behavioral and Brain Sciences* 33: 61–135.
Hornberger, Nancy H. and Sandra Lee McKay (eds) (2010) *Sociolinguistics and Language Education*. Bristol: Multilingual Matters.
Jørgensen, J. Normann, Martha Karrebæk, Lian Malai Madsen and Janus Spindler Møller (2011) Polylanguaging in Superdiversity. *Diversities* 13(2): 23–38.
Labov, William (1969a) The Logic of Nonstandard English. In: *Georgetown Monograph on Languages and Linguistics* (Vol. 22). James Alatis (ed.), 1–44. Washington, DC: Georgetown University Press.
——(1969b) Contraction, Deletion, and Inherent Variability of the English Copula. *Language* 45(4): 715–62.
——(1972a) *Language in the Inner City*. Philadelphia: University of Pennsylvania Press.
——(1972b). *Sociolinguistic Patterns*. Philadelphia: University of Pennsylvania Press.
Labov, William, Sharon Ash and Charles Boberg (2006) *The Atlas of North American English*. Berlin: Mouton.
Makoni, Sinfri (2011) A Critical Analysis of the Historical and Contemporary Status of Minority Languages in Zimbabwe. *Current Issues in Language Planning* 12: 437–55.
Mendes, Ronald (2010) Aspectual Periphrases and Syntactic Variation in Brazilian Portuguese. In: *Aspect in Grammatical Variation*. James Walker (ed.), 27–48. Amsterdam: John Benjamins.
Mesthrie, Rajend (2008) "I've Been Speaking Tsotsitaal all my Life without Knowing It": Towards a Unified Account of Tsotsitaals in South Africa. In: *Social Lives in Language – Sociolinguistics and Multilingual Speech Communities: Celebrating the Work of Gillian Sankoff*. Miriam Meyerhoff and Naomi Nagy (eds), 95–109. Amsterdam: John Benjamins.
Meyerhoff, Miriam (2012) Indefinite Verb Agreement in N'kep. New Ways of Analyzing Variation: Asia/Pacific 2. Tokyo, Japan, 2 August.
——(2015) Turning Variation on its Head: Analysing Subject Prefixes in Nkep (Vanuatu) for Language Documentation. *Asia-Pacific Language Variation* 1(1): 79–109.
Milroy, Lesley (1987) *Language and Social Networks* (second edition). Oxford: Blackwell.
Nagy, Naomi (2009) The Challenges of Less-commonly Studied Languages: Writing a Sociogrammar of Faetar. In: *Variation in Indigenous Minority Languages*. James Stanford and Dennis Preston (eds), 397–418. Amsterdam: John Benjamins.

——(2014) A Sociolinguistic View of Null Subjects and VOT in Toronto Heritage Languages. *Lingua*. http://dx.doi.org/10.1016/j.lingua.2014.04.012.
Nagy, Naomi and Miriam Meyerhoff (2008) The Social Lives of Language. In: *Social Lives in Language – Sociolinguistics and Multilingual Speech Communities: Celebrating the Work of Gillian Sankoff*. Miriam Meyerhoff and Naomi Nagy (eds), 1–17. Amsterdam: John Benjamins.
Noglo, Kossi (2009) Sociophonetic Variation in Urban Ewe. In: *Variation in Indigenous Minority Languages*. James N. Stanford and Dennis R. Preston (eds), 229–44. Amsterdam: John Benjamins.
Omoniyi, Tope (2004) *The Sociolinguistics of Borderlands: Two Nations, One Community*. Trenton: Africa World Press.
Otheguy, Ricardo, Ana Celia Zentella and David Livert (2007) Language and Dialect Contact in Spanish in New York: Towards the Formation of a Speech Community. *Language* 83: 770–802.
Rickford, John (1996) Regional and Social Variation. In: *Sociolinguistics and Language Teaching*. Sandra L. McKay (ed.), 151–94. Cambridge: Cambridge University Press.
——(1997) Unequal Partnership: Sociolinguistics and the African American Speech Community. *Language in Society* 26: 161–98.
Sankoff, Gillian and Hélène Blondeau (2007) Language Change across the Lifespan: /r/ in Montreal French. *Language* 83(3): 560–88.
Shuy, Roger, Walt Wolfram and William Riley (1967) *Linguistic Correlates of Social Stratification in Detroit Speech*. USOE Final Report No. 6–1347.
Sibata, Takesi (1999[1959]) Subjective Consciousness of Dialect Boundaries. In: *Handbook of Perceptual Dialectology* (Vol. 1). Dennis R. Preston (ed.), 39–62. Amsterdam: John Benjamins. (Translated by Daniel Long (1999) Hōgen kyōkai no ishiki, *Gengo kenkyū* 36: 1–30.)
Stanford, James N. (2008) Child Dialect Acquisition: New Perspectives on Parent/Peer Influence. *Journal of Sociolinguistics* 12(5): 567–96.
——(2009) "Eating the Food of our Place" – Sociolinguistic Loyalties in Multidialectal Sui Villages. *Language in Society* 38(3): 287–309.
——(2010) The Role of Marriage in Linguistic Contact and Variation. Two Hmong Dialects in Texas. *Journal of Sociolinguistics* 14(1): 89–115.
Stanford, James N. and Preston, Dennis R. (eds) (2009) *Variation in Indigenous Minority Languages*. Amsterdam: John Benjamins.
Stanford, James N. and Yanhong Pan (2013) The Sociolinguistics of Exogamy: Dialect Acquisition in a Zhuang Village. *Journal of Sociolinguistics* 17(5): 573–607.
Trudgill, Peter (1974) *The Social Differentiation of English in Norwich*. Cambridge: Cambridge University Press.
Wagner, Suzanne and Gillian Sankoff (2011) Age Grading in the Montreal French Inflected Future. *Language Variation and Change* 23: 275–313.
Walker, James and Miriam Meyerhoff (2006) Zero Copula in the Eastern Caribbean: Evidence from Bequia. *American Speech* 81(2): 146–63.
Weinrich, Uriel, William Labov and Marvin Herzog (1968) Empirical Foundations for a Theory of Language Change. In: *Directions for Historical Linguistics*. Winifred Lehmann and Yakov Malkiel (eds), 95–188. Austin: University of Texas Press.
Wolfram, Walt (1993) Ethical Considerations in Language Awareness Programs. *Issues in Applied Linguistics* 4: 225–55.
Wolfram, Walt, Donna Christian and Carolyn Adger (1999) *Dialects in Schools and Communities*. Mahwah: Lawrence Erlbaum.
Wolfram, Walt, Natalie Schilling-Estes, Kirk Hazen and Chris Craig (1997) The Sociolinguistic Complexity of Quasi-isolated Southern Coastal Communities. In: *Language Variety in the South Revisited*. Cynthia Bernstein, Tom Nunnally and Robin Sabino (eds), 173–87. Tuscaloosa: University of Alabama Press.
Zhang, Qing (2005) A Chinese Yuppie in Beijing: Phonological Variation and the Construction of a New Professional Identity. *Language in Society* 34: 431–66.

2

THE WESTERNISING MECHANISMS IN SOCIOLINGUISTICS

Dick Smakman

2.1 Mainstream theory and exceptions

This volume demonstrates the many shapes that sociolinguistic systems can assume. Such breadth of variation cannot easily be captured in a single theoretical framework. Yet, ever since the mid-1960s frameworks have arisen that describe the workings of language variation in speech communities; models illustrating how, for instance, class or gender affect language use or how politeness is reflected in language. Some of these frameworks have remained relatively unchallenged and have, over the preceding decades, been elaborated on and sharpened.

It is well known that some of these theories have been developed under a relatively strong degree of Western influence and may not necessarily encompass cultural patterns that are less commonly known than those of predominantly monolingual societies like the United States, the United Kingdom and many of the European nations. Coulmas (2005: 19–20), amongst others, demonstrated how, despite the universality of language variation, variationist sociolinguistics is predominantly a Western science and that concepts developed within a Western paradigm should be applied with caution to non-Western societies. Introductory books and articles on sociolinguistics have long been taking the approach of presenting the best-known theories and adding information on deviant communities as contrastive material that puts certain generalisations into perspective. As many existing theories have proven to be high quality and durable, there has been reluctance to develop new ones to overrule them and instead they keep serving as default models.

The awareness of this issue is evident and a consensus seems to exist that systematically challenging and extending mainstream theories to cover a broader and more representative set of communities is overdue. The readiness and even eagerness of authors to write a chapter for this book spoke volumes in this respect.

2.2 Chapter overview

This chapter tries to draw a factual picture of the issue by demonstrating the degree and nature of an alleged Western bias in sociolinguistic theory-making. It demonstrates the factors contributing to the persistent Western image of the field. The data for this description are introductions into sociolinguistics as well as international journals focusing on sociolinguistic issues. Journal publications in particular provide us with authorship information and with the choices authors have made to study a certain variety.

To establish the opposition of cultures and language settings (i.e. "Western" versus "non-Western") we are actually dealing with, Section 2.3 discusses the area that is often typified as "the West". In Section 2.4, an overview is given of the available publications in the sociolinguistic field; well-known introductions into sociolinguistics and some examples of publications that focus on sociolinguistic situations in lesser-known areas. That section draws a picture of the material that those wishing to explore the field will have at their disposal. In Section 2.5, important names in the field are looked at; important authors and editors, their home university and their language background. Sections 2.6 to 2.8 discuss the authors: Section 2.6 gives estimates on their language background; Section 2.7 presents the relative contribution by authors from different areas to the total number of publications; and Section 2.8 gives estimates on the human development status of the country where authors are active. In Section 2.9, the languages under investigation are the focus; which languages are mentioned in the titles of journal articles? Section 2.10 summarises the main conclusions, and Section 2.11 tries to elaborate on the workings of the possible cultural bias and make suggestions towards a better balance in theory-making.

Despite an inevitable and unsatisfactory crudeness in ordering data linguistically and geographically, this set of overviews will go a long way in outlining the nature of the challenge researchers face.[1]

2.3 Variation within "the (Anglo-)West"

Terms such as "European", "Anglo-Western" and "Western" are sometimes used to highlight contrasts, although these terms are intrinsically uneasy and not necessarily representative of tangible realities. What these qualifications mean exactly is debatable. Hence, it is also debatable that there is such an entity as the "non-West".

The "West" could refer to different sets of countries, depending on what context and which criteria would be applied: race, culture, geography, history or language. Historically, Europe is the West, and this area was originally mainly contrasted with the civilisations and cultures of the Middle and Far East. Changing views of the cultures of the world and factors such as international immigration and the effects of colonialism have made the West an increasingly problematic entity. The term denotes geographic and cultural oppositions that are no longer realistic or relevant. Moreover, the internal variation within the West and the non-West are too large for any tenable opposition between these two to be applicable.

In a modern interpretation, the West is mostly associated with Europe and countries which due to colonialism have considerable European-descended populations, such as the United States (Thompson and Hickey 2005). Yet even this subdivision of the world is not workable. Not all boundaries of Europe coincide with clear-cut cultural or linguistic boundaries. Within Europe, the cultural differences among countries are considerable, and few Europeans would agree that North-Western, Southern and Eastern Europe are culturally similar. The term "European" is, by some Europeans, associated with the European Union and its economic ramifications, not with some overarching cultural or other commonality.

Sociolinguistically, an important agreement within the European language families is the dialect continuum (see also Lefevre 1976). Europeans share the experience of dialect agreement crossing national boundaries, lively patterns of regional language variation and the strong social connotations that go with this patterning. Dialects are the dominant forms of daily communication in many parts of Europe. Europeans are also used to the concept of a language that has over the decades developed a standard variety. Resemblances in the development of the European nation states have brought about resemblances in the development of such prestige varieties.

A special leading role is sometimes awarded to the United Kingdom. North-West European sociolinguistic models and the one in the United Kingdom are comparable to a high degree. The UK model has been influential in the development of theory, and, for instance, social class is still associated with the system in that country today. However, Swedish research into social variation revealed that although Bernstein's (1971) theory of the Elaborated and Restricted Codes applied to Swedish society as well, the tendencies are far from being as dramatic as those described by Bernstein for British society (see Loman 1976). This is due to the incomparability of British class and class perceptions with those in mainland Europe. In North-West Europe, in particular, egalitarianism and income levelling in the last century have led to the decrease of dominant higher social classes and subservient working classes. Kurth (2003: 6) explained how the differences between the Enlightenment in Britain and mainland Europe caused important divisions within the West, which still have their effects today. The mismatch becomes even more prominent in the area outside North-West Europe. Mioni and Arnuzzo-Lanszweert (1979: 81) indicate that dialects in Italy are structurally different from those in, amongst others, Great Britain. This structural difference affects their sociolinguistic position in society as well. Not all standards and dialects, so Mioni et al. argue, have the same relationships of diglossia and societal bilingualism among one another, as a function of regional differences and social class.

It seems that mainland Europeans feel most strongly culturally connected to surrounding countries, especially those who speak similar languages. Strong ties exist between Swedes and Norwegians and, for instance, between Germans and Dutchmen. Similar sentiments exist in southern and eastern European countries. Neighbouring languages are different and usually not mutually intelligible, but the cultural and linguistic similarities are obvious and genetic relationships close. So, a European theoretical framework spearheaded by the United Kingdom is not realistic.

Discussing the United States and Europe within the same theoretical framework is even more problematic. The dialect continuum and the social patterning of language are what sociolinguistically distinguish Europe from the United States, and even more so from countries like Australia and New Zealand – the reality of noticeably different dialects in villages, towns and cities which might be a mere ten miles apart. Smakman (2012) found that when it comes to the concept of standardness, lay perceptions of the actual existence of such a language in the United States and New Zealand were very different from European perceptions (in this case in England, Poland, The Netherlands and Flanders). The European view even seemed to have more in common with that of Japan, in that in both cases an undisputed standard language exists, which is based in a certain city or area and which has an exceptional social and historical status. There is also the European social situation, with its remnants of class divisions and the linguistic emblems that accompany those; subtle pronunciation differences and lexical choices can have a particularly powerful perceptual impact on interlocutors. So, the European perspective in certain respects resembles that of countries with a language variation situation that has developed over many centuries from a dialectologically plurifom landscape. Europeans will feel less of a sociolinguistic connection with the landscapes as they exist in those countries that do not share this history, even if these countries are Western.

Indeed, the American perception of language and ethnicity in particular is unlike that of mainland Europe. Smith and Lance (1979: 127–40) describe the uniqueness of the sociohistorical forces that have shaped the American language variation situation. European sociolinguistics, however, has nevertheless traditionally leaned relatively strongly on Anglo-American traditions and assumptions. European research readily followed American developments, often without adding their own spin on the theory. Löffler (1994) explained how in (Western) Germany Labov´s criticism of the Deficit Hypothesis was readily adopted, as it was felt that the courage to put forward arguments from the German perspective and research tradition was lacking. Also, in order to catch up with international sociolinguistic progress, sociolinguists in Western Germany felt it necessary to latch on to the American system. In the process, the idea that Germany had its own sociolinguistic patterns was pushed to the background (see also Clyne 1995: 200–201). The awareness of ethnically determined language variation is relatively recent in Europe, with third- and fourth-wave immigrants maintaining an ethnic dialect. The Anglo-American model works to a degree; for instance, sociolinguistic patterns such as those found by Labov in New York were found in the cities of Eskiltuna and Uppsala (see Nordberg 1972, 1975; Widmark 1973), but the agreement is not substantial enough to fit into one shared model.

2.4 Available introductory books and journals

To establish the forces active in the possible Anglo-Western dominance of the field, we will first consider the availability of writings on sociolinguistics to students and researchers. Since the early 1970s, a constant flow of introductions into sociolinguistics has been generated. It is not possible to produce a complete list of introductions that have been popular and influential over the years, and reprints and new editions make any data on what the leading sources may be tentative. Nevertheless, a search in a number of digital university libraries, online bookshops and prescribed books for sociolinguistics courses at several universities across the world leads to a set of about 30 titles that often reoccur, and which can therefore be considered important standard works.

Early examples are Joshua Fishman's *Sociolinguistics: A Brief Introduction* (1970), William Labov's *Sociolinguistic Patterns* (1972) and *Sociolinguistics: Selected Readings* by J.B. Pride and Janet Holmes (1972). The subsequent decade yielded introductions such as Richard Hudson's *Sociolinguistics* (1980), Jack Chambers and Peter Trudgill's *Dialectology* (1980) and Peter Trudgill's (ed.) *Applied Sociolinguistics* (1984). The 1990s brought us, amongst others, Janet Holmes' *An Introduction to Sociolinguistics* (1992) and Suzanne Romaine's *Language in Society: An Introduction to Sociolinguistics* (1994). More recent well-known introductions are Florian Coulmas' *Sociolinguistics: The Study of Speakers' Choices* (2005), Miriam Meyerhoff's *Introducing Sociolinguistics* (2006) and *Introducing Sociolinguistics* by Rajend Mesthrie, Joan Swann, Ana Deumert and William Leap (2010). Most of these publications have had more than one edition over the years. Publications from the United States and the United Kingdom are the most numerous. The authors are generally well known and the majority of them are native speakers of English.

Searching through digital libraries and descriptions of sociolinguistics courses at various universities shows that eight to ten introductions to sociolinguistics keep reoccurring as important reading material, mostly from the past two decades. It is, unfortunately, not possible to systematically investigate which books are used as course books across the various continents. This information is not always available online, and the language used on websites is not always English, which makes it all the more difficult to research even a representative subset of universities. It can be assumed that in many cases general, mainstream introductions are used in combination with descriptions of the local sociolinguistic situation. Books on more local or regional situations are widely available, such as *Arabic Sociolinguistics* by Reem Bassiouney (2009), *The Handbook of Hispanic Sociolinguistics* by Manuel Díaz-Campos (ed.) (2011), *Language and Society in Singapore* by Afendras Evangelos and Eddie Kuo (eds) (1980), *Aspects of Chinese Sociolinguistics: Essays by Yuen Ren Chao* by Anwar S. Dil (ed.) (1976) and *Studies in South African Sociolinguistics* by Rajend Mesthrie (ed.) (1995). Some of these more regionalised introductions are in English, others are not. Examples of non-Anglophone introductions are *Vvedenie v sociolingvistiku* ("Introduction to Sociolinguistics") by Russians Aleksandr Švejcer and Leonid Nikol'skij (1978) and *Sosiolinguistik: Suatu Pengantar* ("Sociolinguistics: An Introduction") by Indonesian Nababan (1993). It is possible that the role of general introductions may be minor in certain areas and that students are simply asked to take notice of these theories whilst focusing on the more regional description.

Journals are available as well, such as *Language in Society, International Journal of the Sociology of Language, Language Variation and Change, Discourse and Society, Journal of Linguistic Anthropology* and *Journal of Sociolinguistics*. These journals are in English. Journals in other languages are available too, such as *Journal of Chinese Sociolinguistics*, which is mostly in Mandarin Chinese. Descriptions of more local situations are also available in articles in these journals, some of which are not in English, for instance Janez Dular's *Ohranjanje maternega jezika pri slovenski manjsini v Porabju* ("Native language maintenance among the Slovene minority in Porabje") (1986).

2.5 Influential names in sociolinguistics

To form an idea of the backgrounds of the people active in sociolinguistics, two lists were compiled. The first list was of 21 well-known sociolinguists that have been active since the start of sociolinguistics as a separate discipline in the 1960s. Second, a list of editors was compiled of six important journals in the field: *Language in Society, International Journal of the Sociology of Language, Language Variation and Change, Discourse and Society, Journal of Linguistic Anthropology* and *Journal of Sociolinguistics*.

The list of influential sociolinguists contained William Labov, of course, and other well-known productive authors in the field from both present and past. These authors have written introductions into sociolinguistics and/or have simply been prolific producers of influential research. Two authors whose names appeared on the list and two who were not on the list were then asked to check whether they agreed with the list, so that a final list could be compiled. Two of these four authors were not from the stereotypical West. They were asked to indicate if they thought names should be added or deleted. In most cases, names were added, making the list longer. A few names were removed from the original list. Table 2.1 shows the country of origin (i.e. the country of birth) of the influential 26 sociolinguists in the resultant list.

These scholars are also usually the authors of the sociolinguistics introductions mentioned in Section 2.4 and most are native speakers of English. The same authors often write reviews of each other's books on the back covers and, by doing so, form a network.

TABLE 2.1 Background of well-known sociolinguists

Country of origin	Number of scholars
United States	8
United Kingdom	7
Canada	4
Germany	3
New Zealand	2
South Africa	2

Then the editorial boards of the six journals were looked at. In total, 190 editors appeared in lists provided online by the publishers. The publishers were Cambridge University Press, De Gruyter, Sage and Wiley. The universities behind the names of the complete editorial teams ("Editor", "Editor in Chief", "Reviews Editor", "Honorary Member", "Editorial Board" and "Associate Editor") are listed in Table 2.2.

TABLE 2.2 Background of editors of six journals

Area where home university is based	Number of editors
United States & Canada	75
United Kingdom & Ireland	38
Mainland Europe	28
Asia	19
Australia & New Zealand	17
Africa	7
Central & South America	6

The editorial impact of the United States, the United Kingdom and Europe is paramount although Asian scholars also have a noticeable say. Numerically, the roles of New Zealand and Australia are surprising, if one takes into consideration their population sizes (see Table 2.4 below). The *Journal of Linguistic Anthropology* and *Language Variation and Change* editors in particular are predominantly from North America. Five of the seven African editors are on the *International Journal of the Sociology of Language* team.

Together with reviewers, the editorial teams influence which articles are published and which are not. No reliable data are available on the background of actual reviewers in the field, and thus no assumptions can be made on those. The editorial teams influence which reviewers are contacted; networks play an important role in the selection as well as information on university websites (if editors search the web for experts in the field). No reliable long-term rejection data are available for any of the six journals.

2.6 The language background of authors

Another relevant factor is the cultural and language background of authors who manage to get through the selection. Non-native speakers are confronted with Erling's (2004: 84) "publish in English or rather perish" principle – journals usually rely on submissions written in English. Publications by non-native speakers are indeed often in English, and statistics presented by Ball and Tunger (2005) even show that, in for instance Poland, in 1975 approximately 65 per cent of articles were published in Polish, compared with only 10 per cent in 2000. This demonstrates the appeal of being recognised in "the supranational community" (Duszak and Lewkowicz 2008: 109) of the academic world. It is safe to assume that more and more publications will be in English in the future.

For authors whose native tongue is not English, a minor or major barrier exists. Authors who work at a university in a country with English as the dominant native tongue are more likely to write English well than authors from countries where this is not the case. A safe assumption is also that if English is the dominant surrounding native tongue a large percentage of these authors are in fact native speakers. For those authors from countries where English has successfully become a foreign or second language (Scandinavian countries, for instance), producing idiomatic written English is also relatively problem-free.

Finding out the native countries and native tongues of authors is not realistic, amongst other reasons because many authors work for foreign universities or because people move to other countries during their lifetime. A safer way to describe the background of the researchers is to look at the university where they are stationed at the moment when their article was published. The underlying assumption is that the traditions and research approaches from that university play a dominant role in the researcher's theoretical analyses, and that they are relatively often natives from that same country.

For all six journals under investigation, it was possible to go as far back as 1993 and check how things have developed over the years. Publishers increasingly provide an author's home university. Before 1993, an author's university information was not consistently available for all six journals. Three years were selected as the source of information, with a ten-year interval between them: 1993, 2003 and 2013. These three years might reveal some tendencies in the backgrounds of the authors. The number of articles written in each of the three decades is 110 (in 1993), 185 (in 2003) and 226 (in 2013). In total, 521 articles were encountered, and the home universities of these authors were noted down. If author names occurred multiple times then they were counted as such.

To estimate the general level of English of the authors, the English Proficiency Index was used (www.ef.nl/epi/). The EPI is published yearly by Education First, an education company that specialises in language training. The organisation draws its data from a large corpus of online English tests. Some countries are not listed in this index; in 28 of the 521 cases the level of English in the country where an author's university was based was unknown. Figure 2.1 shows the general level of English of the countries where article authors were based if known. The bars represent percentages, so as to reveal relative contributions of authors with certain backgrounds.

No strong tendencies across time are visible. The dominance of universities in Anglophone countries is clear. Of the authors, across the three years studied, 62.3 per cent are from a university based in such a country. There seems to be a positive relationship between working at an Anglophone university and the chances of being accepted as an author. Authors who are at universities where English proficiency is "high" and "very high" constitute 22.1 per cent of the total. Of the authors, 15.6 per cent work at a university in a country where English has not successfully gained ground – "moderate", and "(very) low".

The aspect of the written style of an article usually comes down to a command of academic English from a linguistic and stylistic point of view. Traditionally,

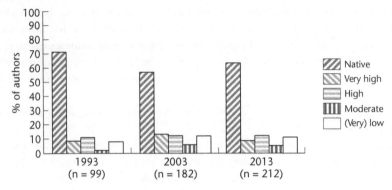

FIGURE 2.1 Author's university (N = 493) categorised according to level of English in the country where it is based

native speakers of English determine the norm regarding what constitutes correct English (Jenkins 2000: 30), and non-native speakers simply need to learn these rules if they want to use the language and be accepted. A command of the grammar and the lexicon is not the only feature of an academic writing style. When writing, non-native speakers inevitably apply an argumentative style which incorporates their own cultural habits. Variation exists in the presence of textual components, the steps towards contextualising the research, the way knowledge is shared with readers, degree and manner of argumentation and elaboration, and the status and handling of previous research. Half a century ago, Kaplan (1966) already demonstrated that authors may apply their own culture's writing style when writing in English. Kaplan (1966: 12) argued that logic in rhetoric is a result of cultural conventions. As a result, L2 writers transfer their L1 rhetorical and stylistic habits as well as their writing abilities into the target language, which may cause the text to be perceived as less attractive (Duszak 1994: 291). Even editing by native speakers may not solve this issue, as such editing involves correcting grammatical and other errors that are mainly at the sentence level (Smakman and Duda-Osiewacz 2014). In other words, an author's rhetorical style may play a role in the acceptance or rejection of articles, and a deviant style may be perceived as a quality issue and may hinder acceptance.

Non-native authors could also write in their own language. An author may decide to do so for practical or principled reasons. There are advantages to writing in one's native tongue about languages one is personally familiar with. This choice makes the resultant texts all the more meaningful and expressive. This leads to a dilemma if one's native tongue is not English, because the chances of international publication and of others reading these texts outside one's country or speech community are smaller if one writes in anything but English. Some of Ulrich Ammon's publications, for instance, are in German; like his 1979 article "Regionaldialekte und Einheitssprache" ("Regional Dialects and Community Language"). An example of a sociolinguistics-related publication on the Slovenian language situation is Dular (1986), mentioned in Section 2.4, which is accessible only to readers with a Slovenian background. In the Netherlands, Jo Daan (1910–2006) and Toon Weijnen (1909–2008) spent much of their professional careers researching and discussing Dutch dialects in a sociolinguistic context. Weijnen contributed to the understanding of laymen's perceptions of regional language variation through his *Pijltjesmethode* ("Arrows Method"), in which perceived (according to dialect speakers) dialect agreement with regard to neighbouring villages and towns was measured. This method (Weijnen 1966) constitutes a very efficient and innovative attempt to inventory lay perceptions regarding language variation as a function of geographical, linguistic and attitudinal factors. Publications hereon were in Dutch, so while this method from the mid-1960s was an insightful folklinguistic approach to measuring social aspects of dialects, the Arrows Method remains largely unknown outside Flanders and the Netherlands.

It is convenient for authors to use sources written in languages they understand. It is often the case that sources on a specific community are only available in the language spoken in the country this community belongs to, and this is not always English. In Ammon's 1979 article, for instance, 22 of the 28 articles he uses to support his points are in German. In a 1997 article, entitled "Slovene Language Issues in the Slovene-Hungarian Borderland" by Necak-Lük, 40 of the 49 references are not in English and thus not accessible to most readers. In his 1979 article entitled "Quelques problèmes de l'hégémonie culturelle en France: Langue nationale et langues regionals" ("Some Issues Regarding the Cultural Hegemony in France: National Language and Regional Languages"), Jean Baptiste Marcellesi refers to 52 articles, all of which are in French. It is more of a rule than an exception that English publications only refer to Anglophone articles and do not quote from articles written in German, Slovenian, French or, say, Mandarin. Due to this, Anglophone articles tend to draw from a different set of sources.

2.7 Relative contribution of authors from different regions

Let's see how the production of articles by authors from universities from various regions compares. The same six journals are used. Table 2.3 shows a ranking order on the basis of regional origin of authors' universities, added up for all three years under investigation (1993, 2003 and 2013).

The role of United States universities is striking; a third of all articles are from a university in the US. The table shows that European universities are also reasonably well represented. A normal distribution of universities would be one where a high population number of the country in question would be matched by a high number of publications coming from that area. Table 2.4 shows to what degree there is a numerical balance in this sense. It contains the relative number of inhabitants in a region (percentage of the world's population), according to a rough estimate (http://en.wikipedia.org/wiki/World_population), and the relative number of authors from universities in the area in question according to the above calculations.

26 Dick Smakman

TABLE 2.3 Regions where university of authors are based

Region	Articles (N = 521)	
	number	percentage
US	174	33.4
UK	63	12.1
Canada	28	5.4
Australia	26	5.0
France	22	4.2
Germany	20	3.8
Denmark	17	3.3
Malaysia	15	2.9
Spain	12	2.3
Belgium	11	2.1
Brazil	11	2.1
China	11	2.1
Finland	11	2.1
Netherlands	10	1.9
South Africa	10	1.9
Other (< 10)	80	15.4

TABLE 2.4 Population size of regions and relative article contribution

Region	% inhabitants (N = 7.2 billion)	% articles (N = 521)
Asia	59.8	10.4
Africa	15.5 } 81.0	3.1 } 17.7
Central & South America	5.7	4.2
Europe	10.4	37.6
North America	7.9 } 18.8	38.8 } 82.3
Australia & New Zealand	0.5	6.0

The numerical imbalance in this table is evident; Asia and Africa have the highest under-representation of authors, and Europe, North America, Australia and New Zealand (i.e. the prototypical Anglo-West) have the highest over-representation. Authors at Western universities produce well over four-fifths of all publications while representing less than one-fifth of the world population.

2.8 The economic background of authors

Another insightful method of categorising the universities where authors worked is on the basis of economic development, because an underlying issue in the discussion regarding the Western nature of the field is that the more economically developed countries seem to be dominant. The Human Development Index as developed by

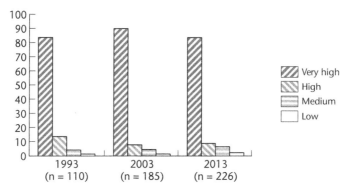

FIGURE 2.2 Percentage of articles (N = 521) from countries based on HDI position

the United Nations Development Programme (www.undp.org/content/undp/en/home.html) can be used to this end. The chapters in the current volume are categorised on the basis of this index. Figure 2.2 contains information on the position on the Human Development Index of the country where the university of the authors is situated. Again, the total number of home universities of authors is set at 100 per cent in each year under investigation.

Authors from universities in countries that are high on the HDI have been dominating the field. This graph suggests that at least in the last two decades there has been a dominance of articles from more affluent regions, which in fact form 85.2 per cent of the total. One should bear in mind that the total number of articles is increasing; in fact, it has more than doubled. This amplifies the effects seen in the graph.

2.9 The languages investigated

To discover the relative interest in languages from inside and outside the Western realm, let us look at the choice of languages that were studied in journal publications. To develop an idea of these choices over the decades, the two oldest of the six journals studied were looked at first, namely *International Journal of the Sociology of Language* and *Language in Society*. Both journals were established in the first part of the 1970s, enabling a four-decade overview of the development of choices made by experts in the field.

All articles published over the 40 years in question were taken into consideration. Delving into the articles themselves led to the realisation that establishing which languages were dealt with in the text was not realistic, as a language-independent approach was often applied, and more than one language was used as supporting material. For this reason, the explicit mentioning of a language variety, speech community or country in the article title was adhered to. The assumption was that in these cases this language, community or country was the main focus of attention. In roughly half the articles a speech community, country or language variety was mentioned. If no language was mentioned or if it was not categorisable then the article title was not counted. On the basis of this subset of titles, the following division could be made:

(1) Inner Circle English areas (the United Kingdom, the United States, Australia, New Zealand, Ireland, Canada; see Kachru 1992);
(2) Europe;
(3) Other.

The first two categories coincide to a large degree with what is popularly called "the West". Languages of immigrants who had moved to or from the "Other" area were put in the "Other" category. Immigrants within one of the three areas were allocated to the area in question. So, African immigrants in France were part of the "Other" category, Malaysians in China were part of the "Other" category, and Czechs in Slovakia ended up in the "Europe" category. The few instances of immigrants from Europe to the Inner Circle area or vice versa were also placed in the "Other" category. Native populations (Native Americans, for instance) in Inner Circle or European areas were also put in the "Other" category. Figure 2.3 shows the relative representation of each area over four decades.

The results suggest that there is a considerable interest in what can roughly be qualified as non-Western languages and cultures and that this interest is not decreasing – more and more articles on these languages are appearing. It is worth noting that the *Journal of the Sociology of Language* has regular special issues, in which a specific area is discussed. The proactive inclusion of lesser known sociolinguistic systems in this journal in particular has affected the results.

The above result, including the difference between the two journals, was an incentive to review all journals in a similar way and gain a broader view of the contemporary situation and of the subdivisions in the "Other" category. *Journal of Sociolinguistics* started in 1997, and this year was taken as a convenient point of

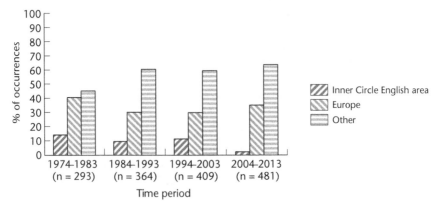

FIGURE 2.3 Percentage of articles (N = 1,547) from three groups of language settings over four decades in two journals

departure. All titles from all six journals from the years 1998, 2003, 2008 and 2013 were taken into consideration. Any recent tendencies would become clear that way, and the totality of titles could represent the state of affairs in recent decades. Figure 2.4 shows the relevant data regarding the journals and language settings. Only articles that contained a reference to a language or community were taken into consideration (43.2 per cent of the articles).

Some caution is necessary in interpreting the results in Figures 2.3 and 2.4. The data are based on the titles that bore the name of a language or community, but a quick look at the abstracts of those that did not contain such information reveals that in a high number of cases English is used as the language to demonstrate a sociolinguistic point. In other words, English has, in many cases, the status of the default language of investigation. European and non-Western languages, on the other hand, were usually explicitly mentioned in the title.

Nagy and Meyerhoff (2008: 9–10) did study the actual languages studied in articles (not just the titles), namely in two journals: *Journal of Sociolinguistics* and *Language Variation and Change*. They found that linguistic situations in the United States received relatively more attention while fewer articles reported from regions with more of a multilingual base, such as Africa. Nagy and Meyerhoff (2008: 10) indicated that "[t]hese trends provide a further motivation for linguists to increase our efforts to make our research findings accessible to the public". One such effort is Stanford and Preston's (2009) volume on under-represented minority communities, which book focuses on descriptions of specific aspects of lesser-known sociolinguistic systems. Furthermore, the individual chapters in Bolton and Kwok (1992) describe a linguistic phenomenon in a specific country or community. *The Routledge Handbook of Sociolinguistics around the World* (Ball 2010) does deal with larger areas and can thus be considered a good source of background information on sociolinguistic systems across the globe because it focuses on "notable features" (Ball 2010: xviii) of the regional and smaller-scale sociolinguistic settings.

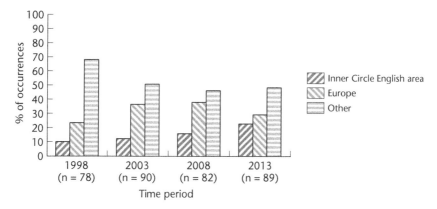

FIGURE 2.4 Percentage of articles (N = 339) from three groups of language settings over four separate years in six journals

Our results suggest that the attention paid to non-Western languages as a group is considerable. However, whether the attention paid to various language settings is balanced depends on population size and number of languages spoken within areas. Tables 2.5 and 2.6 below provide information on these issues. Table 2.5 shows the subcategories within the "Other" category alongside the "Europe" and "Inner Circle" categories (added up across all four years under discussion).

The relative interest in European language variation is strong. The most striking imbalance between population size and number of articles lies in the lack of attention for Asian language settings. Another striking result is the attention paid to Native American languages; no fewer than 17 articles concerned this group of languages (this is not visible in the table).

The richness of language variation in the various regions and sets of communities is difficult to measure, but the number of living languages per region gives some impression in this respect. Presumably a high number of living languages is indicative of much language variation. Table 2.6 shows data given by Ethnologue (Lewis et al. 2014) on the number of living and institutional languages spoken in various areas. The table confirms that Asia and Africa deserve most attention, as do the smaller islands in the Pacific Ocean. The Anglo-West scores relatively low.

TABLE 2.5 Division of published articles about various regions

Investigated region	% articles (N = 339)
Asia	19.5
Africa	12.4
Europe	31.9
South and Central America	9.7
Inner Circle	13.6
Non-Western communities in Western regions	9.4
European in Inner Circle or vice versa	2.1
Western communities in non-Western regions	1.8

TABLE 2.6 Number of living languages in various regions

Region	Living languages	Institutional languages
Asia	2303	203
Africa	2146	174
Melanesia, Micronesia, Polynesia	1100	66
South and Central America	783	32
North America	254	5
Australia, New Zealand	212	5
Europe	120	72
Russian Federation	105	19

2.10 Summary

This chapter tried to find support for the view that there is a strong Western bias in sociolinguistics. Most of all, it tried to ask the question what the nature of such a bias is, if it exists, and what the mechanisms are that keep the bias intact.

The chapter started by emphasising that within the area called "the West" too much internal variation exists for it to be considered a source of contrast with the "non-West". A contrastive study of the two areas is thus problematic.

The availability of introductory books and journals to researchers and students – both general and more specific to a region – does not seem to be an issue. Those wishing to familiarise themselves with the field have many sources at their disposal, both Western and non-Western. However, the international popularity of influential introductions is problematic in the sense that they are generally written by Western authors. Journals are readily available; the most influential are in English. The important names within the field, who oftentimes write such introductions, often have an Anglo-Western background. Editors, and possibly also reviewers, from the United States and the United Kingdom are dominant in editing teams of journals, followed by European and Asian editors. Authors of the journals that these editors are in charge of are often also mainly from universities in Anglophone countries, and the Inner Circle countries, led by the United States, are highly dominant in producing sociolinguistic output. Asian universities and those in Africa suffer the most from this imbalance. The over-representation of universities in countries high on the Human Development Index is even more obvious than the dominance of Anglophone universities.

When it comes to the focus on languages in journals, it turns out that there is a strong interest in non-Western languages. European language variation nevertheless receives the most attention despite a relatively low number of languages within this continent. English is not always mentioned explicitly in titles but nevertheless sometimes emerges as a source of theory-making. Despite the strong interest in non-Western language, the non-West is not equally represented when taking into consideration population size and language diversity.

2.11 Discussion

The interest in non-Western languages and cultures is considerable, especially when bearing in mind the publications about non-Western areas that are not written in English (which this chapter has not touched upon). Nevertheless, varieties of English, and the English language in general, have been receiving considerable attention and are probably an important source of theory-making along with European varieties. English deserves relatively much attention, one might argue, because of its wide and varied usage across the world. Indeed, it seems to be an important default means through which theories are tested.

With the over-representation of researchers from the West, a logical conclusion is that the non-West is oftentimes researched by those not from the area itself.

Studying a language that is not the researcher's native language and which is not within the researcher's cultural realm has many advantages; such as a high degree of objectivity of the researcher. The disadvantage, however, is that authors automatically apply their own cultural norms when researching a language that is not their own, and they may suffer from a certain degree of deafness when it comes to recognising certain features. It takes native speakers to recognise such intricacies, and languages being studied by both native speakers and outsiders may lead to the best results. At the moment it seems that researchers affiliated with US universities are particularly active in studying non-Western languages, and that will inevitably lead to a theorisation style based on paradigms from the United States.

The actual existence of sources describing speech communities all over the world is not really an issue. The availability of these works to an international audience, however, is sometimes hindered by the fact that they are written in the local language. Translating articles may be the answer here; having authors write articles in their preferred language, using the sources they prefer to use, and having the complete articles be translated into English. Ammon's 1979 German article mentioned above, for instance, contains an English summary, which may be considered a first step. The advantages of translation are obvious, but disadvantages also exist. My own PhD dissertation was a phonetic and sociolinguistic description of Dutch in the Netherlands, and reactions from the field included criticism of the fact that it was written in English and not Dutch. A simple truth is that for Dutchmen it is comfortable to read about Dutch in Dutch, and English causes an uncomfortable distance between the reader and the topic. This is true in other countries as well. But all in all, the advantages of translating or of writing/summarising in English seem to outweigh the drawbacks.

Critical deviations from mainstream theories exist and have reached a large reader audience and new generations of sociolinguistics, but the many critical exceptions have not always led to adjustments in mainstream theory. This is possibly due to the lack of a systematic stocktaking of the deviations. Inventorying all sociolinguistic idiosyncrasies and crystallising them out into more general theories, or developing parallel theories to existing ones, seems to be an important challenge. Regional frameworks might be a good idea. Brown and Levinson's Politeness Theory (1987) and Bernstein's (1971) codes would then constitute the Anglo-Western framework.

There are a number of interrelated mechanisms at play. One issue is the online availability of journals. Not only is there a fierce article reviewing system, so as to keep the standard high, the high subscription rates of journals also contribute to their exclusiveness. The status of online free-access publications is still relatively low. There is an unequal distribution of Internet connections around the globe and some African and Asian countries in particular have relatively little or slow access to the World Wide Web. Such access affects networking options and the opportunities of searching the web for researchers to collaborate with or ask to be reviewers. The language used on Internet pages is also a factor in determining readership. Large groups are automatically excluded from the common networks of researchers on such language grounds. The importance of publications for career development is another issue. If a government's or university's policy is to evaluate researchers on the basis of article output, then this leads to more output. Such a policy is not always the case. Then there are the funding opportunities; the strong connection between university output and a country's position on the Human Development Index is likely due to an imbalance in the opportunities of project funding, travel and conference financing.

A practical solution is for researchers from well-budgeted universities to try and find joint funding for collaboration with researchers from other universities and to combine forces. Universities would need to allow for some of the budget to go to another university's researcher. The added advantage is that the language of a lesser-known region could be studied by someone not from the region in collaboration with someone from that region. Establishing free-access journals that invite authors, based on cultural origin, and aim at collaboration within and across regions is a possible solution. A focus on general theory rather than the description of a specific region or community seems advisable, so that active efforts are made to combine findings from different areas into a common theory. Rather than focusing on a region, they could focus on a theme, which is then approached from several regional angles.

Note

1 Determining the population figures of the various regions of the globe is tricky. There are countries that belong to two continents; Russia and Turkey are both partly European and partly Asian. Moreover, there are areas that are disputed in this sense. For practical reasons and for intuitive reasons regarding cultural agreement, certain choices were made. First of all, Turkey and Russia are both considered to be part of Asia in this chapter. For Russia in particular this is not satisfactory, because while most of Russia lies in Asia, most Russians live in the European part of the country. The results were not affected in any serious way by this subdivision, because relatively few articles were about Turkish and Russian varieties. Furthermore, the United Kingdom and Ireland were not automatically considered to be European; this is indicated where relevant. The Caribbean was counted as part of Central America, South Africa was not included in the Inner Circle countries and was instead treated as part of Africa. The whole of Canada was considered part of the Inner Circle. The two poles were not counted and North America included Greenland (but no publications from Greenland are in the data).

References

Ammon, Ulrich (1979) Regionaldialekte und Einheitssprache in der Bundesrepublik Deutschland (BRD). *International Journal of the Sociology of Language* 21: 25–40.
Ball, Martin J. (2010) *The Routledge Handbook of Sociolinguistics around the World*. London: Routledge.
Ball, Rafael and Dirk Tunger (2005) *Bibliometrische Analysen. Daten, Fakten und Methoden. Grundwissen Bibliometrie für Wissenschaftler, Wissenschaftsmanager, Forschungseinrichtungen und Hochschulen*. Jülich: Forschungszentrum Jülich GmbH.
Baptiste Marcellesi, Jean (1979) Quelques problèmes de l'hégémonie culturelle en France. Langue nationale et langues régionales [Some Issues Regarding the Cultural Hegemony in France: National Language and Regional Languages]. *International Journal of the Sociology of Language* 21: 63–80
Bassiouney, Reem (2009) *Arabic Sociolinguistics*. Edinburgh: Edinburgh University Press.

Bernstein, Basil (1971) *Class, Codes and Control: Theoretical Studies Towards a Sociology of Language* (volume 1). London: Routledge & Kegan Paul.
Bolton, Kingsley and Helen Kwok (1992) *Sociolinguistics Today: International Perspectives*. London/New York: Routledge.
Brown, Penelope and Stephen C. Levinson (1987) *Politeness: Some Universals in Language Usage*. Cambridge: Cambridge University Press.
Chambers, Jack and Peter Trudgill (1980) *Dialectology*. Cambridge: Cambridge University Press.
Clyne, Michael (1995) *The German Language in a Changing Europe*. Cambridge: Cambridge University Press.
Coulmas, Florian (2005) *Sociolinguistics: The Study of Speakers' Choices*. Cambridge: Cambridge University Press.
Díaz-Campos, Manuel (ed.) (2011) *The Handbook of Hispanic Sociolinguistics*. Malden: Wiley-Blackwell.
Dil, Anwar S. (ed.) (1976) *Aspects of Chinese Sociolinguistics*. Stanford: Stanford University Press.
Dular, Janez (1986) Ohranjanje maternega jezika pri slovenski manjšini v Porabju [Native language maintenance among the Slovene minority in Porabje]. *Slavistična Revija* [The Slavonics Journal] 34: 121–34.
Duszak, A. (1994) Academic Discourse and Intellectual Styles. *Journal of Pragmatics* 21: 291–313.
Duszak, Anna and Jo Lewkowicz (2008) Publishing Academic Texts in English: A Polish Perspective. *Journal of English for Academic Purposes* 7: 108–20.
Education First LTD (2014) English Proficiency Index. Online available at: www.ef.nl/epi/ (accessed 17 August 2014).
Erling, Elizabeth J. (2004) English as the Language of the European Academic Community: Questions from the Freie Universität Berlin. In: *Speaking from the Margin: Global English from a European Perspective*. Anna Duszak and Urzuka Okulska (eds), 77–90. Frankfurt am Main: Peter Lang GmbH.
Evangelos, Afendras and Eddie Kuo (eds) (1980) *Language and Society in Singapore*. Singapore: Singapore University Press.
Fishman, Joshua (1970) *Sociolinguistics: A Brief Introduction*. Rowley: Newbury House.
Holmes, Janet (1992) *An Introduction to Sociolinguistics*. London: Longman.
Hudson, Richard (1980) *Sociolinguistics*. Cambridge: Cambridge University Press.
Jaakkola, Magdalena (1976) Diglossia and Bilingualism Among Two Minorities in Sweden. *International Journal of the Sociology of Language* 10: 67–84.
Jenkins, Jennifer (2000) *The Phonology of English as an International Language*. Oxford: Oxford University Press.
Kachru, Braj B. (1992) *The Other Tongue: English Across Cultures* (second edition). Champaign: University of Illinois Press.
Kaplan, Robert B. (1966) Cultural Thought Patterns in Inter-cultural Education. *Language Learning* 16: 1–20.
Kurth, James (2003) Western Civilization, Our Tradition. *The Intercollegiate Review* (Fall/Spring): 10–18. Online available at: www.mmisi.org/ir/39_01_2/kurth.pdf (accessed 20 May 2014).
Labov, William (1972) *Sociolinguistic Patterns*. Philadelphia: University of Pennsylvania Press.
Lefevre, Paul (1976) *Le libéralisme à Bruges 1893–1940*. Bruxelles: Université Libre de Bruxelles.
Lewis, M. Paul, Gary F. Simons, and Charles D. Fennig (eds) (2014) *Ethnologue: Languages of the World* (seventeenth edition). Dallas: SIL International. Online available at: www.ethnologue.com.
Löffler, Heinrich (1994) *Germanistische Soziolinguistik* [Germanistic Sociolinguistics] (second edition). Berlin: Erich Schmidt.
Loman, Bengt (1976) Linguistic Performance and Social Evaluation: A Sociolinguistic Attitude Test. *International Journal of the Sociology of Language* 10: 85–102

Mesthrie, Rajend (ed.) (1995) *Language and Social History: Studies in South African Sociolinguistics.* Cape Town: David Philip.
Mesthrie, Rajend, Joan Swann, Ana Deumert and William Leap (2010) *Introducing Sociolinguistics.* Edinburgh: Edinburgh University Press.
Meyerhoff, Miriam (2006) *Introducing Sociolinguistics.* Abingdon: Routledge.
Mioni, Alberto M. and Anna Maria Arnuzzo-Lanszweert (1979) Sociolinguistics in Italy. *International Journal of the Sociology of Language* 21: 81–108.
Nababan, P.W.J. (1993) *Sosiolinguistik: Suatu Pengantar.* Jakarta: Gramedia.
Nagy, Naomi and Miriam Meyerhoff (2008) Introduction. In: *Social Lives in Language: The Sociolinguistics of Multilingual Speech Communities, Celebrating the Work of Gillian Sankoff.* Miriam Meyerhoff and Naomi Nagy (eds), 1–16. Amsterdam/Philadelphia: John Benjamins.
Necak-Lük, Albina (1997) Slovene Language Issues in the Slovene-Hungarian Borderland. *International Journal of the Sociology of Language* 124: 99–128.
Nordberg, Bengt (1972) Morfologiska variationsmonster i ett centralsvensk stadsprak [Morphological Variation in a Central Swedish City]. In: *Sprak och samhalle: Spraksociologiska problem* [Language and Society: Language-sociological Issues]. Bengt Loman (ed.), 14–44. Lund: CWK Gleerup Bokforlag.
——(1975) Contemporary Social Variation as a Stage in a Long-term Phonological Change. In: *The Nordic Languages and Modern Linguistics 2. Proceedings of the Second International Conference of Nordic and General Linguistics, University of Umeå, June 14–19.* Karl-Hampus Dahlstedt (ed.), 587–602. Stockholm: Stockholm University.
Pride, John B. and Janet Holmes (eds) (1972) *Sociolinguistics. Selected Readings.* Harmondsworth: Penguin.
Romaine, Suzanne (1994) *Language in Society: An Introduction to Sociolinguistics.* Oxford: Oxford University Press.
Smakman, Dick (2006) *Standard Dutch in the Netherlands: A Sociolinguistic and Phonetic Description.* Utrecht: Landelijke Onderzoeksschool Taalwetenschap (LOT).
——(2012) The Definition of the Standard Language: A Survey in Seven Countries. *International Journal of the Sociology of Language* 218: 25–58
Smakman, Dick and Agnieszka Duda-Osiewacz (2014) A Contrastive Rhetoric Analysis of Scholarly Publications by Polish and Anglophone Authors. *Journal of Language Teaching and Learning* 4(2): 29–47.
Smith, Riley and Donald Lance (1979) Standard and Disparate Varieties of English in the United States. Educational and Sociopolitical Implications. *International Journal of the Sociology of Language* 21: 127–40.
Stanford, James and Dennis Preston (2009) *Variation in Indigenous Minority Languages.* Amsterdam: John Benjamins Publishing Company.
Švejcer, Aleksandr Davidovič and Leonid Borisovič Nikol'skij (1978) *Vvedenie v sociolingvistiku* [Introduction to sociolinguistics]. Moskva: Vysšaja škola.
Thompson, William and Joseph Hickey (2005) *Society in Focus.* Boston: Pearson.
Trudgill, Peter (ed.) (1984) *Applied Sociolinguistics.* London: Academic Press.
United Nations Devlopement Progamme (2014) Empowered Lives. Resilent Nations. Online available at: www.undp.org/content/undp/en/home.html (accessed 17 August 2014).
Weijnen, Antonius Angelus (1966) *Nederlandse dialectkunde* [Dutch Dialectology]. Assen: Van Gorcum.
Widmark, Gun (1973) Språkförändring och socialgruppsbyte [Language Change and Social Group Replacement]. In: *Förhandlingar vid sjunde sammankomsten för svenskans beskrivning.* Christer Hummelstedt (ed.), 10–23. Åbo: Åbo akademi.
Wikipedia (2014) World Population. Online available at: http://en.wikipedia.org/wiki/World_population (accessed 17 August 2014).

PART I
Developing countries

Introduction to Part I

The countries in Chapter 3 to 6 share a low to intermediate position on the Human Development Index; this index is a composite measurement of life expectancy, education and income. From the perspective of this composite statistic Southeast Asia and the three African areas, which will be discussed in the four chapters to come, are all furthest removed from the prototypical West. These factual differences inevitably affect the sociolinguistic situation in these regions.

Taken together, the three African parts discussed roughly constitute Sub-Saharan Africa. This area notably includes the large Bantu area. Multilingualism in this area is particularly alive, and the culture of speaking more than one language daily and using heavy code-switching evokes many questions regarding the systematicity in the parallel use of two or more languages in informal discourse. The countries in the Sub-Sahara region share a history of nineteenth-century colonisation and of a relatively recently acquired independence in the second part of the twentieth century. The same is true for Indonesia, which acquired its independence during the aftermath of the Second World War and which is the main subject of the Southeast Asia chapter. Like the three African regions, this region can be typified by a highly complex sociolinguistic setting, due not only to the language left behind by colonists but also the diverse tribal and linguistic settings. How indigenous and imported traditions interact and influence each other is an important field of sociolinguistic research. Studying it requires more than a knowledge of mainstream sociolinguistic approaches and the respective languages spoken in these polities. Lack of a knowledge of indigenous approaches has resulted in either having these approaches be ignored or in having sociolinguists uncritically reproduce ideologically loaded research findings.

An additional relevant aspect of Indonesia, which by population and area is one of the largest countries in Southeast Asia, is the geographical setting of its speakers. The archipelago contains many thousands of islands (estimates vary), almost a thousand of which are claimed to be permanently inhabited. Yet, a shared linguistic identity exists, embodied in one standard language. This is the official lingua franca for peoples living as far as 3,000 miles apart, whose native dialects are highly different from each other and not always mutually intelligible.

All countries discussed in this section have been colonised and this experience has unsettled the local language ecologies. Nation building and social modernisation further impacted on the sociolinguistic situation of the societies and communities discussed here. Today, we encounter in these regions legacies of the pre-colonial and colonial period, as well as the effects of modernisation attempts that paid little attention to these distinctions but sought a solution for perceived language issues based on Western experiences. For these and other reasons, the sociolinguistic differences and ensuing inapplicability of mainstream sociolinguistic theoretical frameworks as described in the following chapters should be especially pressing for these particular regions.

3

ALA! KUMBE? "OH MY! IS IT SO?"

Multilingualism controversies in East Africa

Sandra Nekesa Barasa

3.1 Introduction

The East Africa region is sometimes referred to as Eastern Africa. As expected for every large region in the world, many sources do not seem to agree on the countries that belong to the East Africa region. Some sources, for example Wikipedia, claim that this region not only consists of Kenya, Uganda and Tanzania but also includes countries from the horn of Africa, like Eritrea, Ethiopia, Djibouti, Somalia, South Sudan, and the Indian Ocean's islands, like the Seychelles, Madagascar, Mozambique, Réunion, Mayotte and Comoros. Other sources claim that the East Africa region includes the aforementioned countries plus Rwanda, Burundi, the democratic republic of Congo, Malawi, Zambia and Zimbabwe. The discussion in this chapter narrows the region down to Kenya, Uganda and Tanzania as three countries within the East Africa community (EAC). The EAC is an intergovernmental regional cooperation comprising Kenya, Uganda, Tanzania, Burundi, Rwanda and South Sudan. According to the World Factbook CIA maps, the total population of Kenya, Uganda and Tanzania is around 127 million people (in July 2013).

This chapter presents a selection of sociolinguistic issues in East Africa that have not yet been adequately captured by existing theoretical frameworks. All the issues deliberated upon converge under the umbrella of multilingualism, which is a second nature to linguistic discussions involving the African continent. It should be understood from the onset that the multilingualism phenomenon in East Africa is not comparable to that of Western countries (Auer 1999; Ogechi 2002), and therefore Western sociolinguistic models might not capture it satisfactorily.

3.2 The sociolinguistics of East Africa

A major sociolinguistic feature that is observable in the East Africa region is that all the countries have a relatively similar sociolinguistic situation with the common denominator being that they are all multilingual. Each of the countries hosts over 40 indigenous languages in addition to the national and official languages such as Swahili, Luganda and English. These countries are not only characterised by a complex pattern of indigenous African languages and lingua francas but they also share a common Anglophone colonial background (Simango 2006). It is also notable that each of these countries possesses English and Kiswahili in its linguistic repertoire. An average literate citizen of this region is expected to possess an indigenous language, a national lingua franca – for example Kiswahili or Luganda (for Uganda) – and English, the official language.

Early work on East African languages was initiated by German missionaries such as Ludwig Krapf and Johannes Rebmann in the mid-eighteenth century. Their efforts involved Bible translation into indigenous languages, developing dictionaries and recording language demographics. Bamgbose (1995: 2) explains that scientific linguistic research by scholars in Africa formally started in the early 1960s. By the mid-1960s, it was clear that research in the West Africa region mainly dealt with the syntactical and phonological description and documentation of language data, while research in the East Africa region concentrated on themes such as language policy, planning and implementation, language use and proficiency, and literature.

Schmied (2006) offers an elaborate background to sociolinguistic research in East Africa. He explains that in the period between the late 1960s and early 1970s, the Ford Foundation funded a major sociolinguistic survey in East Africa. This resulted in a number of descriptive publications. They included Ladefoged et al. (1972) for Uganda, Whiteley (1974) for Kenya, and Polomé and Hill (1980) for Tanzania. Note that all the researchers who took part were from the West; that is, they were all British – except Polomé, who was Belgian. However, the 1980s and 1990s witnessed an upsurge of studies by East African native scholars, including Wa Thiong'o (1986), Abdulaziz (1988), Bokamba (1993), Mazrui and Mazrui (1993), Mbaabu (1996) and Chimerah (1998). All these scholars were concerned with English and Swahili in East Africa. Other publications that are trendsetters in the region include Myers-Scotton (1993b, 1993c) on code-switching between English, Swahili and vernacular languages in Kenya, Webb and Kembo-Sure (2000), and King'ei (1999, 2000) on general linguistics as it pertains to African languages. Other significant studies focused on the exceptional Kenyan youth slang "Sheng". These include Abdulaziz and Osinde (1997), Githiora (2002), Shitemi (2002), Kießling and Mous (2004), Bosire (2006), Rudd (2008) and Githinji (2009).

3.2.1 Accessibility of existing literature and language demographics

Generally, most previous studies used conventional and standard methods of data collection and analysis, with the ethnographic approach being the favourite. Data collection methods include recorded conversations, interviews, personal observation of conversations and questionnaires. Respondents are usually natives from the region. They fall in a wide range, including children, students from university and high school, young urban professionals, residents of rural areas, cities, slums and members of "hoods". For data analysis, both qualitative and quantitative methods are used and often complement each other. It is worth mentioning that, in some cases, the quality of research is not up to date because of various factors such as lack of expertise, materials and funding.

One main problem faced by researchers in East Africa is that many of the indigenous languages are understudied and thus there is very little literature available to go by. This is linked to the fact that there is a major shortage of linguists in the region. One of the causes of this shortage is the difficulty in attracting students for linguistic training because other disciplines offer much better job opportunities. As a matter of fact, most of the students who study languages like English and Swahili do so as an area of specialisation for a Bachelor of Education degree in order to gain employment as a language teacher in high schools. Specialisation in linguistics and especially in indigenous languages would restrict one's job opportunities, given that vernacular languages are not taught in schools though Luganda as a national language is an exception.

Another problem experienced during research in East Africa is related to reviewing of existing literature. Although some linguistic research has been carried out by graduate students and other researchers in East African universities, it is often difficult to obtain copies of their dissertations and publications. These documents are stored in the archives of the local university libraries but are not easily available to "outsiders" due to "official restrictions and the long bureaucratic procedures involved" (Githinji 2009: 52).

In discussing problematic issues that researchers face in conducting sociolinguistic research in East Africa, a basic but controversial issue arises: how many languages does each of the countries in the region have? Despite linguistic research accruing to slightly over 50 years, there is no clear answer to this. The number of all the indigenous languages per country in the region is estimated like a back-of-the-envelope calculation. Ogechi (2003), Djité (2008) and Githinji (2009: 23) point out that the Constitution of Kenya Review Commission (CKRC) (2000: 95) states that Kenya has 70 languages. Lewis et al. (2013) put the number at 68. Whiteley (1974) claims that there are 34 languages in Kenya, while Webb and Kembo-Sure (2000) indicate that the country's languages amount to 42. Most linguistic researchers, like Myers-Scotton (1993a) and Ogechi (2003), use the figure of 42 languages. In an attempt to circumvent this, a new trend has emerged where researchers indicate the number of languages in Kenya as being "over 42" (Barasa 2010). Kamusella (2009) explains that part of this uncertainty is caused by the constant discovery of new languages (vital and extinct) in many underdeveloped countries.

It is very likely that the problem of ambiguity of demographics in the East African region has persisted partly due to the ambiguity in the definition and the differentiation of the terms "(standard) language", "dialect", "code" and "variety" (Myers-Scotton 1993c; Simango 2006). Ogechi (2009: 1) poses the question: "How distinct is the term 'language' from 'dialect' […]? How are these terms used either distinctively or interchangeably in Kenya?"

The questions above are discussed in this chapter together with other theoretical approaches that do not adequately explain some of the concepts exhibited by the sociolinguistic situation in East Africa. These include: the divergence between language policy and actual practice, issues in code-switching generalisations and the challenges faced in defining a standard language in a highly multilingual context.

3.3 Walk the talk: language policy versus societal practice

Stewart (1968) asserted that for a language to be considered as standard, it should have vitality as one of its features. This declaration was supported by Giles et al. (1977), who built on it to come up with one of the earliest ethnolinguistic frameworks known as "ethnolinguistic vitality". According to this model, the vitality of a language is determined by its status, the demographics of speakers and institutional support. The observation of the situation in the East African region shows that only part of the ethnolinguistic vitality framework holds, and that more factors need to be included for it to apply.

Similar to other regions, language policies in East Africa are mostly reinforced in formal institutions such as education, legislature, the judiciary and mass media (Giles et al. 1977; Michieka 2005; Muaka 2011). The policies are also tacitly promoted through the economy, religion and culture. According to the ethnolinguistic vitality model, it should naturally follow that, given this promotion, a language gains "high vitality", which means that it ends up being spoken and used widely, and that it is assured of continuity through generations. Conversely, speakers of a language with "low vitality" are likely to abandon it and adopt another language (Giles et al. 1977; Meyerhoff 2011: 113). However, a concern that should be raised here is that this may not always be the case. It is possible for a language to score low in terms of the three main components of the model – that is, status, demographics and institutional support – but still maintain a high vitality position.

One of the main gaps in the vitality model is its downplay of the issue of language contact. Low vitality and language endangerment are always the outcome of contact between a weaker community and a stronger one. There is no endangerment without contact. Another weakness in this model is pointed out by Yagmur and Ehala (2011: 104) who explain that in spite of a language's generally low vitality rating, the speakers may propel and maintain it at a higher vitality position if they uphold a strong community identity (Johnson et al. 1983; Saint-Blancat 1985). Such a situation may then convince the government to recognise the language and give it a status in the national language policy. A case in point is the sociolinguistic situation in Uganda.

Katende (2009) explains the situation in Uganda by pointing out that the problem of the Ugandan national language policy is a longstanding one, with no easy solution in sight. Uganda's official language is English; however, the choice of a national language has been contentious with some opting for Luganda while others prefer Swahili. Luganda is an indigenous Ugandan language and is used by the greater majority of Ugandans. It has a high vitality rating due to its well-established high status, demographics and institutional support. This high vitality automatically nominates Luganda as a standard language based on Stewart's (1968) and Bradley's (2012) argument that vitality is a major feature for a language to be considered standard. Swahili, on the other hand, has had a low score in all the three major components of the ethnolinguistic vitality model (status, demographics and institutional support). Despite Luganda meeting all the high vitality criteria, it is not popular among some Ugandans, especially those who have a different first language. They argue that Luganda is not suitable as a national language because it is closely related to the Buganda subnational kingdom, and that making it a national language would elevate the Baganda people, which is unfair to the other communities. They advocate Swahili because it is neutral and does not favour any particular community. In addition, it is widely spoken throughout the East African region. Those against Swahili argue that the language is closely associated with soldiers who propagated the 1966 war, and the unpopular rule of Idi Amin. In an attempt to appease both groups, in 2005 the government voted for Swahili as a national language alongside Luganda. This goes a long way in proving that it is possible for a language (in this case Swahili in Uganda) to maintain a "self-induced high vitality" status even though it scores low on the checklist of the ethnolinguistic vitality model.

Despite the promotion of Swahili to the status of a national language in Uganda's constitution, it is observable that a majority of Uganda's general population has snubbed it. This, however, has not deterred the progress of the language; in fact, it has motivated its speakers to value it more. This is reminiscent of Patten's (2001: 703) explanation that, in such a case, the speakers of language X (Luganda, in this case) will complain about why a new language (Swahili) should be introduced in the policy, yet its (Swahili) speakers can also speak X (Luganda) anyway. The puzzling outcome is that "the more some linguistic group is able to speak another language, the stronger its case to have its own language recognized".

It is conspicuous that Uganda's language policy is merely rhetorical, since so far not much has been done to develop Swahili as a national language in terms of institutional support or campaigns to endear it to the people (prestige planning), and give it a generally high vitality status as a national language driven by the majority. This scenario in Uganda is not exclusive. A similar though perhaps less glaring scenario regarding Swahili and English can be observed in Tanzania, where, although English is supposedly the official language according to the language policy, it still lacks one of the ethnolinguistic language vitality components, that is demographics (Simango 2006). Nonetheless, it is still popular, especially among the educated professionals. The Ugandan and Tanzanian governments in this case are caught between both international and national pressure, leading to the prescription of national and official languages without adequately considering relevant measures for a successful implementation.

3.4 A storm in a teacup: seemingly random code-switching as the norm

The issue of code-switching has been complicated right from the earliest interpretations. Weinreich (1953: 73), in one of the earliest studies, claimed that "the ideal bilingual switches from one language to the other according to appropriate changes in the speech situation [...] but not in an unchanged speech situation and certainly not within a single sentence" (as cited in Boztepe 2005: 2). Currently, this claim has been surpassed by many code-switching studies worldwide. Code-switching instances incorporating Swahili and English have been recorded, where switches occur without any change in the speech situation. Additionally, there are cases where the switch is either intra-sentential or even in a single word distinguishing the morpheme and content word (Barasa 2010), thus indicating no change in the speech context.

In his "contextualization cues" approach, Gumperz (1982: 98) states that "[c]ode switching signals contextual information equivalent to what in monolingual settings is conveyed through prosody or other syntactic or lexical processes. It generates the presuppositions in terms of which the content of what is said is decoded." As an elaboration to this, Gumperz proposed an inventory of six common functions of conversational code-switching that should accommodate all code-switching situations. These are: quotation marking, addressee specification, interjection, reiteration, message qualification and personalization versus objectivization. This view is contradicted by Myers-Scotton (1993c), Gafaranga (2000) and Barasa (2010) based on evidence from code-switching in East Africa (including Rwanda). To begin with, while it is true that code-switching may perform these functions in some contexts, it is important to note that code-switching does not necessarily signal contextual information. Furthermore, it can simply occur as what Myers-Scotton refers to as the "unmarked choice" (Myers-Scotton 1993c: 114). In other words, code-switching has no identifiable motivation in many instances (Myers-Scotton 1993c; Barasa 2010).

In addition to the inapplicability of some functions of code-switching in East Africa, it is useful to point out that there exists a number of reasons for code-switching that have hardly been covered in mainstream literature. These include: insignificant cultural value of the languages involved, complete or identical proficiency in two or more languages, identity through informality and creativity (especially in intra-word code-switching).

Designs in code-switching often have an underlying assumption that the languages involved are culturally charged. However, it is possible for speakers to randomly switch between languages, which for them have little or no significant cultural value. Most such speakers have an identical proficiency in the languages incorporated (Auer 1999: 312). This mostly manifests itself through languages other than the mother tongue, which is assumedly culturally loaded. These "culturally neutral" languages include English and Swahili in situations where they are considered as non-native languages.

Code-switching has been tagged by Myers-Scotton (1993c) as an informal way of speaking. In this way, speakers want to create an identity through informal speech. An example of this is when Kenyan politicians address crowds. The tendency is to use code-switching to create a sense of informality, in order to connect with the public. In this way, the people are likely to be convinced by the "down to earth" identity of the politician. For this effect to occur, politicians must of course be highly proficient in the dominating language as well but refrain from using it in such a context.

Intra-word code-switching can purely be a result of creativity (Barasa 2010). This manifests itself in code-switching using a matrix language, where a single word is made up of two or more languages. Such words are fluid and not conventionalised in speech. An indiscriminate example of intra-word code-switching between Swahili and English is in the word *walini*buy*ia* ("they bought for me"). In this instance, *wa-li-ni* is used as a prefix marking class, tense and person in Swahili, "buy" is a verb in English and *-ia* is a prepositional suffix in Swahili. In most cases of this kind of intra-word code-switching, the affixes of the word are in Swahili or other agglutinative Bantu languages, while the root is in English. This, however, does not rule out possibilities where the affixes are in English and the root is in Swahili or an indigenous language such as the word *un*bwogo*able* in the Kenyan context, where *un-* is an English prefix and *-able* is a suffix. These two affixes have been sandwiched by the Luo word *bwogo*, which means "scare" in the Luo language. The whole word translates to "undefeatable". This word was coined and popularised by the song "Who can bwogo me?", also known as "Unbwogable", from the Kenyan musical group Gidi Gid Maji Maji. Such random instances prove that code-switching can stem out of creativity.

3.4.1 Trilingual code-switching: an oversight?

Ogechi (2002) and Barasa (2010) assert that an unexpected observation in mainstream literature on code-switching is that trilingual code-switching and triglossia face a general oversight. The majority of code-switching studies only focus on bilingual code-switching, thus totally ignoring any form of code-switching encompassing more than two donor languages/codes, yet this kind of code-switching is evident in East Africa. Ogechi (2002: 5) notes that for a long time the possession of more than one language/code has been subsumed under bilingualism or multilingualism. As a matter of fact, most of the research involving the possession of more than two languages is generally done within bilingualism or second-language acquisition studies (Hoffmann 2001b: 13). Yet, for fairness sake, the manifestation of trilingual code-switching should be dealt with independently. Scholars like Abdulaziz (1972), Enninger (1979), Krier (1992), Clyne (1997), Clyne and Cain (2001), Hoffmann (2001a, 2001b) and Ogechi (2002) have recognised this gap and conducted studies on trilingualism. Hoffmann (2001b: 14) defines trilingualism as "the presence of three languages in one speaker". Trilingual code-switching is largely an unexplored field, although it is a well-known fact that a majority of multilingual Africans are "trilinguals"; however, the code-switching studies using data from Africa have either been silent on trilingual code-switching – for example Myers-Scotton (1993b) and Kamwangamalu (2000) – or explicitly denied observing any trilingual code-switching in their data, for example Haust (1995). Perhaps this has been brought about by the assumption that in a setting of three languages, the trilingual speakers cannot adequately master and be completely proficient in all the three languages. Abdulaziz (1972: 211) controverted this notion after studying code-switching in a trilingual context in Tanzania. His study was based on code-switching between English, Swahili and vernacular (Kinyakyusa/Kipare).

These concerns acknowledge that there are difficulties in accounting for code-switching in East Africa by applying mainstream sociolinguistic frameworks based on Western languages.

3.5 Back to the drawing board: defining the standard language

The controversial issue of the number of languages present in East Africa is persistent. It appears that the earliest distinction of indigenous languages, dialects and variations in the region was mainly based on geographical proximity, socio-historical factors and political influences; thus, in many cases regardless of the linguistic structure (Barasa 2010). Currently, it is not uncommon to witness discrepancies in language demographics based on political interests and idiosyncrasies by various governments in the region. The appropriate approach to solve this would be to determine the actual number of languages based on sociolinguistic investigation.

For East Africa, such an investigation would entail questions such as what is a standard language? How is it determined? What is the relationship between standard languages and dialects? Is there a link between national lingua franca(s)/national languages and the standard language? At a first glance, these questions may seem fairly straightforward, especially from a non-African point of view. However, it may not be quite clear in the multilingual African setting. Indeed, Smakman (2012: 30) was aware of this fact in his remark that the presence of more than one national language in a country with a "complex sociolinguistic scenario" is bound to affect the definition of a standard language in such a country. The next section intends to use Finegan's (2007) definition of a standard language, Bourdieu's (1977, 1993) cultural capital theory, and some of Smakman's (2012) findings on the characteristics of a standard language, to argue that there is more complexity in East Africa for their perspectives to be fully applicable.

3.5.1 What is a standard language?

Finegan (2007: 14) defines a standard language as a language variety used by a group of people as a lingua franca in their public discourse. In many cases, such a language has undergone the process of standardisation. This definition seems limited, and it would encounter some shortcomings in the East African multilingual environment.

First and foremost, the high linguistic diversity and impressive multilingual repertoires pose a challenge in identifying the so-called standard language. This diversity in repertoires is partly the outcome of a complementary allocation of language functions across domains of usage; people choose different languages depending on the domains of communication such as school, neighbourhood, religion, trade and government. This is made even more complex by language variation and individual networks. For example, a person may choose which language variety to use in order to index social class, gender and context (Milroy and Milroy 1992: 12). An example of these diversities in Kenya is when English is used at school, Swahili in the neighbourhood and a vernacular language at home. However, the variety of Swahili used at the local market in the neighbourhood would be different from the one used by the same speaker in a market in another location such as Mombasa or Dar es Salaam, or even when speaking with a Kenyan of Indian or Somali origin. Similarly, the English used away from official settings is likely to be the Kenyan variety of English also referred to as Kenyan English. According to Finegan's definition, both English and Swahili, and their different varieties, would qualify as standard languages. An additional scenario worth mentioning is the use of the Sheng slang as a lingua franca for inter-ethnic communication in urban areas. In such a case, should Sheng be regarded as the standard language even though it is slang?

Another theory that can be contested in the East African context is Bourdieu's (1977, 1993) cultural capital theory, which claims that social mobility, power and status can be propelled by factors such as education, intellect, language and physical appearance, among others. In the language trajectory, Bourdieu proposed the concept of linguistic capital in linguistic markets whereby language is equated to financial capital. This means that if invested or used appropriately as a resource, language can yield a high profit of power and status in the linguistic market. According to Bourdieu, each linguistic market has a dominant or legitimate language or variety that is recognised as a source of power. Such a language can be either inherited or acquired over time and perfected by its speakers who use it to their advantage. The Kenyan multilingual situation is reminiscent of what Bourdieu (1977, 1993) described as "a single dominant linguistic market where the rule of the legitimate language [or variety] is merely suspended, its domination temporarily absent, when the vernacular [another language or variety] is used" (as cited in Milroy and Milroy 1992: 4). The main setback in Bourdieu's theory in a highly multilingual context such as East Africa is the fact that the issue of the "legitimate language" is not clear given that many language varieties, abstand languages and even dialects exist, which could all be viewed as legitimate. Such contexts call for reconsideration of what a standard language is.

The second issue in identifying a standard language is related to political and social implications. In as much as a (indigenous) language/dialect is a public lingua franca, it is still a major challenge to officially invest it as "the standard language". Several scholars, including Hudson (1980), Wardhaugh (1986), Appel and Muysken (1987) and Milroy and Milroy (1992), explain that standardising a language involves a number of stages, with the most important being selection, acceptance, diffusion, maintenance, elaboration of function, prescription and codification. Smakman (2012: 29–30) avers that "[t]he tribal background of many speakers in the African countries makes it hard to construct or impose a national standard language in these countries". Such a move would fuel disgruntlement in "left out" communities. The most acceptable way to establish an indigenous language as a standard national lingua franca would be either to reward the country's ethnolinguistic diversity by elevating all the languages in question to a standard language status (for example

Luganda and Swahili in Uganda), or to settle for languages that do not have ardent local tribal ties (such as Swahili and English in Kenya). The latter option has its drawbacks, but it may be more appealing to countries with many independent ethnolinguistic groups with an underlying need to ensure a standard national lingua franca. It should be pointed out that this recourse is not solely based on communicative requirements of a standard language, but on the elaborated function of language as a means of fostering and reproducing nationalism and social cohesion.

3.5.2 A code-switched language as a standard language?

As already discussed, the frequent use of a particular language as a lingua franca in public discourse does not always qualify it as a standard language. Some additional characteristics that may serve to augment its status include media usage, acceptability, and informality (King'ei 2000; Lafon and Webb 2007). Based on these features, the question that arises is: can code-switching as a variety be regarded as standard language? If the aforementioned features are considered in the Kenyan situation, then the popular code-switched hybrid variety between Swahili and English (which are both standard languages) might qualify as a standard language. The use of code-switching in Kenya is common in the media, especially radio and television programmes, and social media. It is also used in formal public discourse such as political rallies and debates. It is the norm in informal private discourse, such as in offices, shops, at home, among friends and acquaintances. It is accepted by most people who understand both languages. As a matter of fact, Smakman (2012: 50) would perhaps classify such a code-switched hybrid variety as an "inclusive standard language", that is "socially cohesive". Therefore, in theory, such a code-switched hybrid variety would make a good candidate were it a stable language, but the main restraint in actual practice is the fact that it is not conventionalised, and it is not stable (yet) to be used in formally written communication and documentation. Hence, the main point here is that some definitions and features tagged on languages/varieties in Western society are too general, and are likely to create confusion if taken literally in the African setting. In essence, a definition of standard language which is based on South Africa but is suitable for the East African situation is by Lafon and Webb (2007: 12–13), who propose that a "fully-fledged standard language" should

- be accepted by the community for use in high-function formal contexts such as teaching, government communication and legislation – in other words, it should be the language of power;
- be taught in schools and therefore be known by the literate people;
- have a strong link with written language such as in dictionaries, grammars and newspapers.

In the East African context, this checklist only applies to English, Swahili and Luganda. It does not fully cover the code-switched variety, vernacular languages or slang.

3.6 What is the relationship between standard languages and dialects?

Smakman (2012: 26) states that "dialects and standard languages are opposites" from a sociolinguistic point of view. By and large, most Western investigations, including Smakman's (2012), consider standard languages as being the standardised version of dialects. In other words, standard languages emerge from one or more dialects. Whereas this view easily holds for monolingual societies, it does not fully concur with the multilingual societies. In East Africa, most indigenous languages, for example Luhyia, Maasai and Kalenjin, have dialects which are equivalent to what Kloss (1967: 29) referred to as "abstand languages". Nonetheless, there is no abstand language that can be elevated or claimed to be the standard since some of them are independent and mutually unintelligible. To make matters more complex, some of these languages only exist arbitrarily for regional classification purposes, and perchance as labels used to refer to the community at large. Examples include the terms "Luhyia" and "Kalenjin", which are considered as languages but are, in fact, umbrella-like labels denoting a cluster of abstand languages, and thus cannot be equated to being the standard language that has emerged from dialects.

3.6.1 Is there a link between national languages and the standard language?

In Western countries, national and standard languages are closely related. Smakman (2012) conducted a study in seven diverse countries, in an attempt to answer the question what is a standard language (according to lay users). The question itself was not cause to debate for the respondents. There was the underlying assumption that the national language is the standard.

Most Western countries have an uncontested lingua franca such as Dutch (Netherlands and Flanders), Polish and Japanese (Poland and Japan), and English (US, UK, New Zealand). These lingua franca languages ascended in the course of modernisation of these countries. Smakman's findings indicate that in each of these countries almost all native inhabitants can be assumed to speak a variety that resembles the standard/national language, and all can be assumed to understand the national/standard language. This renders the language a successful lingua franca in these countries. Consequently, there is no question of a choice of a national language that might exclude communities that do not actually speak it. However, it is possible to disagree on the choice of a national language, let alone the standard variety of the language. A majority of Ugandans speak Luganda. They do not speak Swahili and cannot fathom why it should be flaunted as a national language.

3.7 Conclusion

The main theme of this chapter has been on issues related to multilingualism in East Africa. The discussion demonstrates that multilingualism comes with several complex issues that have not yet been adequately covered by existing studies based on non-African contexts. The concerns raised here are just the tip of the iceberg, and should therefore be an eye-opener and a challenge for researchers to exploit the resources offered by the abundant yet under-utilised data present in the East African region.

Further reading

Mbaabu, Ireri (1996) *Language Policy in East Africa: A Dependency Theory Perspective*. Nairobi: Educational Research and Publications. (This book is worthwhile in providing a clear and detailed background of the politics that surround the formation and implementation of language policies in East Africa.)

Myers-Scotton, Carol (1993c) *Social Motivations for Codeswitching: Evidence from Africa*. Oxford: Clarendon Press. (This book is a must-read in order to understand the phenomenon of code-switching in East Africa. Myers-Scotton uses English, Swahili and vernacular to advance a strong theoretical framework explaining why bilinguals use code-switching in discourse.)

Simango, Silvester (2006) East Africa. In: *Sociolinguistics: An International Handbook of the Science of Language and Society*. Ulrich Ammon, Norbert Dittmar, Klaus Mattheier and Peter Trudgill (eds), 1964–71. Berlin: Mouton de Gruyter. (This is a book chapter that presents a sociolinguistics profile of East Africa in a nutshell. It captures the language situation in Kenya, Uganda, Tanzania, Malawi and Zambia in both the pre-colonial and post-colonial era. It is useful in laying a foundation for sociolinguistic studies in East Africa.)

References

Abdulaziz, Mohamed (1972) Triglossia and Swahili-English Bilingualism in Tanzania. *Language in Society* 1(2): 197–213.
——(1988) A Sociolinguistics Profile of East Africa. In: *Sociolinguistics*. Ulrich Ammon, Norbert Dittmur, and Klaus J. Mattheier (eds), 1347–53. Berlin: De Gruyter.
Abdulaziz, Mohamed and Ken Osinde (1997) Sheng and Engsh. Development of Mixed Codes Among the Urban Youth in Kenya. *International Journal of the Sociology of Language* 125: 43–64.
Appel, René and Pieter Muysken (1987) *Language Contact and Bilingualism*. London: Edward Arnold.
Auer, Peter (1999) From Codeswitching via Language Mixing to Fused Lects: Toward a Dynamic Typology of Bilingual Speech. *International Journal of Bilingualism* 3(4): 309–32.
Bamgbose, Ayo (1995) Three Decades of African Linguistic Research. In: *Theoretical Approaches to African Linguistics: 25th Anniversary of the Annual Conference on African Linguistics at Rutgers University between March 25–27, 1994*. Akinbiyi Akinlabi (ed.), 1–17. Trenton: Africa World Press.
Barasa, Sandra (2010) *Language, Mobile Phones and Internet: A Study of SMS Texting, Email, IM and SNS Chats in Computer Mediated Communication (CMC) in Kenya*. Utrecht: LOT.
Bokamba, Eyamba (1993) Language Variation and Change in Pervasively Multilingual Societies. Bantu Languages. In: *Conference on African Linguistics. Topics in African Linguistics: Papers from the XXI Annual Conference on African Linguistics, University of Georgia, April 1990*. Salikoko S. Mufwene and Lioba J. Moshi (eds), 207–47. Amsterdam: John Benjamins.

Bosire, Mokaya (2006) Hybrid Languages. The Case of Sheng. In: *Selected Proceedings of the 36th Annual Conference on African Linguistics.* Olaoba F. Arasanyin and Michael A. Pemberton (eds), 185–93. Somerville: Cascadilla Proceedings Project. Online available at: www.lingref.com/cpp/acal/36/paper1423.pdf (accessed on 7 January 2014).
Bourdieu, Pierre (1977) *Outline of a Theory of Practice.* Cambridge: Cambridge University Press.
———(1993) *Soziologische Fragen.* Frankfurt: Suhrkamp.
Boztepe, Erman (2005) Issues in Code-Switching. Competing Theories and Models. *Teachers College, Columbia University Working Papers In TESOL & Applied Linguistics* 3(2): 1–27. Online available at: http://journals.tc-library.org/index.php/tesol/article/view/32 (accessed on 3 March 2014).
Bradley, David (2012) Vitality of Minority Languages. In: *Encyclopedia of Chinese Language and Linguistics.* Rint Sybesma (ed.), 1–5. Leiden: Brill. Online available at: www.academia.edu/1555914/Vitality_of_languages_in_China (accessed on 12 February 2014).
Chimerah, Rocha (1998) *Kiswahili. Past, Present, and Future Horizons.* Nairobi: Nairobi University Press.
Clyne, Michael (1997) Some of the Things Trilinguals Do. *The International Journal of Bilingualism* 1(2): 95–116.
Clyne, Michael and Helen Cain (2001) Trilingualism in Related Languages – Dutch-German-English Near and Far. In: *Kulturen-Sprachen-Übergänge.* Gunther Hirschfelder, Dorothea Schell, Adelhei Schrutka-Rechtenstamm (eds), 135–52. Köln: Böhlau.
Constitution of Kenya Review Commission (2000) *The Main Report of the Constitution of Kenya Review Commission, 18th September, 2002.* Online available at: www.constitutionnet.org/files/KERE-423.pdf (accessed on 12 June 2014).
Djité, Paulin (2008) *The Sociolinguistics of Development in Africa.* Clevedon. Multilingual Matters.
Enninger, Werner (1979) Language Convergence in a Stable Triglossia plus Trilingualism Situation. In: *Anglistik, Beiträge zur Fachwissenschaft und Fachdidaktik.* Peter Freese and Karin Feywald (eds), 43–63. Münster: Regensberg.
Finegan, Edward (2007) *Language. Its Structure and Use* (5th edition). Boston: Thomson Wadsworth.
Gafaranga, Joseph (2000) Language Separateness: A Normative Framework in Studies of Language Alternation. *Estudios de Sociolinguistica* 1: 65–84.
Giles, Howard, Richard Bourhis and Donald Taylor (1977) Towards a Theory of Language in Ethnic Group Relations. In: *Language, Ethnicity, and Intergroup Relations.* Howard Giles (ed.), 307–48. London: Academic Press.
Githinji, Peter (2009) *Sheng, Styleshifting and Construction of Multifaceted Identities. Discursive Practices in the Social Negotiation of Meaning.* Saarbrücken: VDM Verlag.
Githiora, Chege (2002) Sheng: Peer Language, Swahili Dialect or Emerging Creole? *Journal of African Cultural Studies* 15(2): 159–81.
Gumperz, John (1982) *Discourse Strategies.* Cambridge: Cambridge University Press.
Haust, Delia (1995) *Codeswitching in Gambia. Eine soziolinguistische Untersuchung von Mandinka, Wolof und Englische in Kontakt.* Köln: Rüdiger Köpper Verlag.
Hoffmann, Charlotte (2001a) Towards a Description of Trilingual Competence. *The International Journal of Bilingualism* 5(1): 1–17.
Hoffmann, Charlotte (2001b) The Status of Trilingualism in Bilingualism Studies. In: *Looking Beyond Second Language Acquisition. Studies in Tri- and Multilingualism.* Jasone Cenoz, Britta Hufeisen and Ulrike Jessner (eds), 13–24. Tübingen: Stauffenburg Verlag.
Hudson, Richard (1980) *Sociolinguistics.* Cambridge: Cambridge University Press.
Johnson, Patricia, Howard Giles and Richard Bourhis (1983) The Viability of Ethnolinguistic Vitality: A Reply. *Journal of Multilingual and Multicultural Development* 4: 255–69.
Kamusella, Tomasz (2009) *The Politics of Language and Nationalism in Modern Central Europe.* Basingstoke: Palgrave Macmillan.

Kamwangamalu, Nkonko (2000) INFL as a Marker of Matrix Language in Codeswitching in a Diglossic Context. In: *The Proceedings from the Main Session of the Chicago Linguistic Society's Thirty-sixth Meeting*. Arika Okrent and John Boyle (eds), 197–207. Chicago: Chicago Linguistic Society.

Katende, Bob Robert (2009) National Language Still Eludes Uganda. *Independent*, 13 October. Online available at: www.independent.co.ug/reports/special-report/1933-national-language-still-eludes-uganda (accessed on 16 September 2013).

Kießling, Roland and Maarten Mous (2004) Urban Youth Languages in Africa. *Anthropological Linguistics* 46(3): 303–41.

King'ei, Kitula (1999) *The Challenge of Expanding the Lexicon of an African Language. The Case of Kiswahili in East Africa*. Cape Town: The Centre for Advanced Studies of African Society.

——(2000) *Classification of Ugandan Languages*. Cape Town: Centre for Advanced Studies of African Society.

Kloss, Heinz (1967) Abstand Languages and Ausbau Languages. *Anthropological Linguistics* 9: 29–41.

Krier, Fernande (1992) L'alternance langagière comme stratégie discursive dans une situation plurilingue. *Bulletin de la Société de Linguistique de Paris* 87: 53–70.

Ladefoged, Peter, Ruth Glick and Clive Criper (1972) *Language in Uganda*. London: Oxford University Press.

Lafon, Michel and Vic Webb (2007) The Standardisation of African Languages: Language Political Realities. *IFAS Working Paper* 11. Online available at: ?www.ifas.org.za/?research/?pdf/?Cahiers-IFAS_11.pdf (accessed on 3 March 2014).

Lewis, M. Paul, Gary F. Simons and Charles D. Fennig (eds) (2013) *Ethnologue. Languages of the World*. Dallas: SIL International. Online available at: www.ethnologue.com/country/KE (accessed on 3 March 2014).

Mazrui, Alamin M. (2004) *English in Africa After the Cold War*. Clevedon: Multilingual Matters.

Mazrui, Alamin M. and Ali Mazrui (1993) Dominant Languages in a Plural Society. English and Kiswahili in Post-colonial East Africa. *International Political Science Review* 14(3): 275–92.

Mbaabu, Ireri (1996) *Language Policy in East Africa: A Dependency Theory Perspective*. Nairobi: Educational Research and Publications.

Meyerhoff, Miriam (2011) *Introducing Sociolinguistics* (2nd edition). London: Routledge.

Michieka, Martha (2005) English in Kenya: A Sociolinguistic Profile. *World Englishes* 24(2): 173–86.

Milroy, Lesley and James Milroy (1992) Social Network and Social Class: Toward an Integrated Sociolinguistic Model. *Language in Society* 21(1): 1–26.

Muaka, Leonard (2011) The Dynamics of Language Use among Rural and Urban Kenyan Youths. In: *Selected Proceedings of the 40th Annual Conference on African Linguistics*. Eyamba Bokamba (ed.), 217–30. Somerville: Cascadilla Proceedings Project.

Myers-Scotton, Carol (1993a) Common and Uncommon Ground. Social and Structural Factors in Codeswitching. *Language in Society* 22(4): 475–503.

——(1993b) *Duelling Languages. Grammatical Structure in Codeswitching*. Oxford: Clarendon Press.

——(1993c) *Social Motivations for Codeswitching: Evidence from Africa*. Oxford: Clarendon Press.

Ogechi, Nathan (2002) A Trilingual Codeswitching in Kenya. Evidence from Ekegusii, Kiswahili, English and Sheng. PhD dissertation, University of Hamburg. Online available at http://ediss.sub.uni-hamburg.de/volltexte/2005/2749/pdf/Binder1.pdf (accessed on 3 March 2014).

——(2003) On Language Rights in Kenya. *Nordic Journal of African Studies* 12(3): 277–95.

——(2009) The Language Situation in Kenya. Paper presented at a symposium conducted as part of the IUPUI Fulbright Hays Group Projects in Eldoret, Kenya.

Patten, Alan (2001) Political Theory and Language Policy. *Political Theory* 29(5): 691–715.

Polomé, Edgar and P. C. Hill (1980) *Language in Tanzania*. Oxford: Oxford University Press.
Rudd, Philip (2008) Sheng: The Mixed Language of Nairobi. PhD dissertation, Ball State University.
Saint-Blancat, Chantal (1985) The Effect of Minority Group Vitality upon its Socio-psychological Behavior and Strategies. *Journal of Multilingual and Multicultural Development* 6(1): 31–45.
Schmied, Josef (2006) East African Englishes. In: *The Handbook of World Englishes*. Braj B. Kachru, Yamuna Kachru and Cecil L. Nelson (eds), 188–202. Malden: Blackwell.
Shitemi, Naomi (2002) Pidginization: Sheng, the Melting-pot of the Kenyan Languages and an Anti-Babel Development. *Kiswahili* 64: 1–15.
Simango, Silvester (2006) East Africa. In: *Sociolinguistics. An International Handbook of the Science of Language and Society*. Ulrich Ammon, Norbert Dittmar, Klaus Mattheier and Peter Trudgill (eds), 1964–71. Berlin: Mouton de Gruyter.
Smakman, Dick (2012) The Definition of the Standard Language: A Survey in Seven Countries. *International Journal of the Sociology of Language* 218: 25–58.
Stewart, William (1968) A Sociolinguistic Typology for Describing National Multi-lingualism. In: *Readings in the Sociology of Language*. Joshua A. Fishman (ed.), 531–45. The Hague: Mouton.
Wardhaugh, Ronald (1986) *An Introduction to Sociolinguistics*. Malden: Blackwell Publishing.
Wa Thiong'o, Ngũgĩ (1986) *Decolonising the Mind: The Politics of Language in African Literature*. London: Heinemann.
Webb, Vic and Edward Kembo-Sure (eds) (2000) *African Voices: An Introduction to the Languages and Linguistics of Africa*. Oxford: Oxford University Press.
Weinreich, Uriel (1953, 1968) *Languages in Contact*. The Hague: Mouton.
Whiteley, W. H. (1974) *Language in Kenya*. Nairobi: Oxford University Press.
World Factbook CIA Maps (2013) *World Factbook CIA Maps*. Online available at: www.cia.gov/library/publications/the-world-factbook/ (accessed on 3 March 2014).
Yagmur, Kutlay and Martin Ehala (2011) Tradition and Innovation in the Ethnolinguistic Vitality Theory. *Journal of Multilingual and Multicultural Development* 32(2): 101–10.

4

A SOCIOLINGUISTIC MOSAIC OF WEST AFRICA

Challenges and prospects

Jemima Asabea Anderson and Gladys Nyarko Ansah

4.1 West Africa: a history of colonialism

West Africa is located in sub-Saharan Africa. The region consists of 15 countries, which form the politico-economic block ECOWAS (Economic Community of West African States): Benin, Burkina Faso, Côte d'Ivoire, the Gambia, Ghana, Guinea, Guinea-Bissau, Liberia, Mali, Mauritania, Niger, Nigeria, Senegal, Sierra Leone and Togo. Major ethnic groups in the region include: Akan, Ewe, Fulani, Hausa, Igbo, Mandinka, Yoruba and Wolof. Major religions in the region include: Christianity, Islam and various forms of Traditional African Religion, e.g. Voodoo.

Countries within the region share common history: the West African coast endured centuries of slave trade which affected all the countries in the region, and, in addition, nearly all countries in the region have a colonial history. The Gambia, Ghana, Nigeria and Sierra Leone are former British colonies; France colonised Benin, Burkina Faso, Côte d'Ivoire, Guinea, Mali, Niger and Senegal; Portugal colonised Guinea-Bissau, while Germany claimed Togoland, but was forced to divide it between France and Britain following the First World War, due to the Treaty of Versailles. Only Liberia retained its independence but at the price of major territorial concessions.

4.1.1 The languages of West Africa

One consequence of the European colonisation of the region was the division and re-organisation of some ethnolinguistically related groups into different nation states. Whereas, for instance, the Ewes are spread across four post-colonial nation states in the region – i.e. Ghana, Togo, Benin and Nigeria – the Wolofs are spread across Senegal, Mauritania and the Gambia. Various dialects of Akan are found in Ghana and

La Côte d'Ivoire, while the Hausas are found in Nigeria, Niger and La Côte d'Ivoire, overlapping with the Akan-speaking regions. Thus, the artificial division of ethnolinguistically related people into different nation states is one of the many colonial legacies in the region.

West Africa is one of the most ethnolinguistically diverse areas in the world. According to Ethnologue (Lewis et al. 2013), there are approximately 889 living languages with a speaker population of approximately 274,899,000. All countries in the region maintain the use of a European language as the national or official language, that is the exclusive medium of governance, education, mass media and international communication (Bokamba 2011). Nevertheless, many citizens across the region either do not speak these European languages at all or they do not have enough competence in them. Lewis et al. (2013) further explain that out of the 889 languages in West Africa, only 74 are institutional, that is have been developed to a point where they are used and sustained by institutions beyond the home and community. Of these languages, 211 are developing, are in vigorous use, have spawned a literature and are being used by some members of the population. However, they are neither widespread nor sustainable. The majority of these languages, 509, are in vigorous use among all generations but unstandardised, while 49 of them are endangered; the intergenerational transmission of these languages has been interrupted even though the child-bearing generation can still use them. This means that revitalisation measures can be put in place to ensure natural intergenerational transmission of these languages. Finally, 46 of the languages across West Africa are believed to be facing extinction; the only fluent speakers (if any) are older than child-bearing age, and it would be too late to put in revitalisation measures to restore a state of natural, intergenerational, transmission.

4.2 Sociolinguistic studies in West Africa

There have been quite a number of studies on several sociolinguistic topics in the region since the post-independence period of the 1960s and 1970s. Earlier studies focused on traditional topics such as language in educational policy in the face of high multilingualism (Ansre 1969; Spencer 1971; Chumbow 1987), language spread in multilingual communities (Bokamba and Tlou 1977), and pidgins and creole studies (Hancock 1971), and so on. These studies had very little, if anything at all, to say about bilingualism or multilingualism, discourse analysis, ethnography of communication and language shift in the region (Bokamba 1990). However, there has recently been an increase in sociolinguistic studies in the region that have focused more on such topics as language shift (Omoniyi 2009; Bodomo et al. 2009; Igboanusi 2009), linguistic diversity (Ansah 2008), and language choice and language use (Anderson 2009). The main focus of this chapter is to give a broad overview of the major sociolinguistic concerns of West Africa and to assess whether they corroborate current sociolinguistic theories. The topics we shall dwell on here are multilingualism, language shift, code-switching, pidgins and creoles, New Englishes and politeness.

4.2.1 Multilingualism

According to Singh (2010) and Connell and Zeitlyn (2010), studies of multilingual situations in West and Central Africa have mainly focused on two areas – urban settings and the interaction between indigenous languages and former colonial languages (Banjo 2000; Chumbow and Bobda 2000). Trudell (2009) has examined some specific aspects of multilingualism in Africa and identifies several sub-categories of multilingualism in sub-Saharan Africa. Multilingualism in West Africa has often been discussed in terms of language policy, a topic that has received a lot of research attention in the region. Given the level of linguistic diversity in the region, perhaps this should not come as a surprise at all.

Language policy may be defined as a legislative or governmental action taken to solve language problems and conflicts within institutions, nation states or supra-national bodies. Language policies across West Africa have typically made former colonial languages the exclusive media of national and international communication, even after independence was achieved. This situation has been bemoaned, lamented, described and explained in many different ways using different sociolinguistic theories. For instance, Ansre (1976) and Bamgbose (1991) have explained the phenomenon in terms of the Rationalisation Hypothesis – that language policy makers in Africa appear to be influenced by these four main arguments: (1) the efficiency of European languages; (2) building national unity (on the basis of a dominant language); (3) national development and progress; and (4) cost effectiveness in choosing former colonial languages as the exclusive official languages. Myers-Scotton (1993) and Bamgbose (2000) have explained the use of former colonial languages in national and international communicative functions at the exclusion of indigenous languages in terms of the Elite Closure hypothesis and "language exclusion" respectively. Bokamba (2011) also describes the language policies of West Africa as neo-colonialist and "Ukolonia", that is, the colonisation of the mind. Thus, the ideas espoused in Anglo-Western-based sociolinguistic theory that language planning and language policy are conscious and sustained efforts or attempt to solve language and communication problems in multilingual communities (e.g. Fishman 1974; Weinstein 1980) are different from the underlying ideologies of language planning and language policy in highly multilingual West Africa. From the discussion above, it is obvious that the apparent underlying ideology for language planning and language policy across West Africa is often creating or widening the gap in the power relations between the minority elite and those who constitute the majority of the population. Current sociolinguistic theories on language planning and language policy in multilingual communities do not always quite capture these realities of language planning and language policy in West Africa.

These studies on language planning and language policy in West Africa provide a lot of insight into aspects of high multilingualism and its challenges in the region. For instance, they explain how indigenous languages are not made, by legislature, a key part in the collective national or regional identity across West Africa. However, they do not describe or explain in detail how the lack of intentional and institutional support to develop indigenous languages has the potential to undermine the current apparent stable multilingualism in the region. This is, perhaps, a confirmation of Singh's (2010) contention that no contemporary sociolinguistic theory can do full justice to the sociolinguistic complexities of a multilingual society.

Wolff (2010) distinguishes three aspects of multilingualism in Africa: territorial multilingualism, institutional multilingualism, and individual and social multilingualism. Whereas territorial multilingualism describes the geographic distribution of languages across national, sub-national or supra-national (regional) territories, institutional multilingualism deals with language policies and institutionalised language practices at any kind of social, educational and political level while individual and social multilingualism deals with language choice and language use by individuals and social groups.

In some regions of Africa where linguistic diversity is high, for example South Africa and East Africa, legal instruments have been deliberately employed to reinforce and sustain individual and social multilingualism. For instance, the post-Apartheid constitution of South Africa recognises nine indigenous languages and two transplanted languages as official languages – all 11 languages have or are given equal status. In other words, the constitution of South Africa proffers language rights to at least some indigenous groups in the country. Similarly, the use of Kiswahili as a national and regional language across East Africa is supported by a legislative instrument.

The situation is different in West Africa. The use of indigenous languages, even including those with a high vitality profile, are relegated to inter- and intra-group communication. Even though various countries may have adopted one form of bilingual language in education policy at some point, such policies have been merely nominal and experimental in rural basic education situations. No country within the region has legislative instruments that recognise any of the indigenous languages as an official language. The lack of any legislature at the moment may not be as worrying as the lack of sensitivity or the lack of political will among political leaders in the region to address this problem.

For instance, none of the four institutions and the eight specialised committees of ECOWAS (which recognise English, French and Portuguese as their working languages) is dedicated to addressing language issues and language needs in the region, even though the African Academy of Languages collaborates with the Committee to monitor the implementation of ECOWAS Regional Culture Development and Integration on some language issues. Thus, a very alarming picture can be painted indeed.

4.3 The consequences of complex multilingualism in West Africa

With the level of multilingualism described above, it is obvious that there are complex language contact situations in West Africa. When speakers of different languages interact, language contact occurs – their languages interact and influence one another. In prolonged language contact situations, a number of language conditions may emerge. For instance, speakers of one language may converge to or even abandon their own language for another language (language shift). More commonly, speakers of the languages in contact tend to become bilingual/multilingual in the languages and alternate between them either by mixing them or switching between them (code-switching/code-mixing). Sometimes, the languages are mixed to the point of fusion to form a hybrid language (pidgins and creoles). In what follows, we discuss some of these language conditions that have emerged in West Africa and point out how current sociolinguistic models are either able or unable to adequately account for them.

4.3.1 Language shift

Language shift is a very common occurrence in West Africa, and the phenomenon is triggered by different factors. De Klerk (2002: 222) suggests that shift occurs "when linguistic minorities find themselves in contact with a language which offers greater practical and economic rewards or carries higher prestige". There are more than 800 languages spoken in West Africa. Interestingly, several speakers of these languages are, for one reason or another, adopting languages other than the language of their communities. While some of these speakers are adopting new languages voluntarily, others are compelled by political, social and economic factors to abandon the languages of their communities for other languages (Nettle and Romaine 2000; Batibo 2005).

In West Africa, there are three major types of language shift patterns. First of all, many indigenous languages are being displaced by ex-colonial languages such as French, English and Portuguese. In Ghana and Nigeria, English is displacing many indigenous languages. There are reports that show that English is quickly gaining the status of a first language in some communities in Ghana (Bodomo et al. 2009). Second, there are reports of shifts from minority languages to major or dominant languages. For instance, Akpanglo-Nartey and Akpanglo-Nartey (2012) describe language shift of this nature in Ghana where speakers of relative minority languages, Efutu, Ga-Adamgbe and the Togo-Mountain languages, are mainly shifting to Akan and also to some degree Ewe. They report that among the Efutu speakers of Winneba, the shift is very significant – there are children of Efutu L1 speakers who speak Akan but no Efutu at all. The third category of language shift is triggered by factors such as urbanisation, migration and industrialisation (Igboanusi 2009). Thus, one main mismatch with Western theory on language shift in West Africa is that the shift is from indigenous West African languages towards other regional African languages rather than national or official languages. Another mismatch is that the linguistic exclusion that language policies in West Africa create may be said to be working favourably for language maintenance. Contrary to the view that linguistic diversity tends to translate into violent conflicts, the phenomenon (high multilingualism) does not translate to violent conflicts in West Africa.

In sociolinguistic models, language shift is often associated with diglossia where domains of linguistic behaviour are boxed into a kind of complementary distribution, and where the domains are hierarchically ranked (Ferguson 1959). In West Africa, this does not happen. What does happen may be closer to Fishman's (1967) extended diglossia where the H roles and L roles may be played not by different varieties of the same language but by different languages, usually the colonial language and an indigenous language, respectively. Even then, this is not applicable to all cases of bi- or multilingualism in West Africa as the majority of the population are multilingual in languages that do not include any colonial language. Igboanusi (2009) presents a collection of studies that bring different perspectives to language shift in West Africa. For instance, Omoniyi (2009) argues that language shift existed long before colonialism and that colonisation should not be seen as the precursor of language shift in West Africa. He bases his argument on the premise that, long before the advent of colonialism, ethnic wars had occurred in West Africa and after these wars some ethnic groups had taken others as vassals, which resulted in many different forms of language contact and language displacement cases. In the same collection, Juffermans and McGlyn (2009) study language shift in the Gambia and observe that there is a lot of language tolerance and accommodation in the Gambia that lead to viable multilingualism and extended code-switching. Consequently, language shift from indigenous minority languages, e.g. Sarer spoken in the Gambia, to major languages, such as Wolof, is restricted to only certain domains of language use. Bodomo et al. (2009) adopt the concept of multilingual language shift to describe the phenomenon in highly multilingual West Africa. They argue that the type of language shift that occurs in highly multilingual contexts is different from that which is obtained in less multilingual environments in some Western countries. Agyekum (2009) also investigates language shift in Ghana and identifies two types of language shift: intranational (where there is a shift from indigenous languages to major indigenous languages) and international (where there is a shift from indigenous languages to ex-colonial languages, such as English and French).

4.3.2 Code-switching

Another major focus of research in the sub-region has been code-switching. In November 2007, a conference was held in Ghana on code-switching in West Africa. This conference gave a boost to research on code-switching in the region. In Nigeria, Essien (1995) studies Ibibio–English code-switching, Amuda (1994) discusses Yoruba–English code-switching, while Akinremi (2011a, 2011b) examines different aspects of English–Ibo code-switching. In studies from other countries in the sub-region, Haust (1995) explores code-switching involving Mandinka, Wolof and English, while Juillard (1995) examines code-switching involving four languages: Wolof, Diola, Mandinka and French. In Ghana, interests in these studies date back to the 1970s and 1980s (Forson 1979, 1988). Forson describes code-switching as a "third tongue" in both formal and informal in-group interactions. Asilevi (1990) describes English–Ewe code-switching in conversational discourse and observes that code-switching is used pervasively especially in in-group interactions. Recent studies have shown that code-switching occurs in different domains including religion

(Albakry and Ofori 2011), classroom contexts (Asilevi 1990; Amekor 2009; Ezuh 2009; Brew-Daniels 2011), and in informal academic discussions (Quarcoo 2012). Code-switching has also been reported to occur in the media (Anderson and Wiredu 2007; Yevudey 2009; Amuzu 2010a, 2010b; Vanderpuije 2011). Most of these studies have drawn on Myers-Scotton's Markedness Model or the Matrix-Language Framework to discuss the grammatical structures or socio-pragmatic aspects of code-switching.

Code-switching is usually regarded as one of the natural consequences of language contact situations. In West Africa, a highly multilingual region where free trade and movement is encouraged (by ECOWAS), the appearance of code-switching is not surprising. In many cases language contact is so intense that even when language shift has not occurred words and phrases from the languages in contact infiltrate each other. In other words, while people whose languages are in contact may not share a common language in the sense of being bilingual they tend to acquire (consciously or unconsciously) words and phrases from other languages which become part of their linguistic repertoire. Typically, the speakers are not even conscious of their code-switching habits. In this regard, code-switching in West Africa, which may be seen as the norm rather than a way to assert one's self, makes a personal or political statement. This contradicts existing sociolinguistic theories. Nevertheless, there are other instances where West African code-switching conforms to prevailing existing theories. For instance, people consciously switch codes or languages for favours, especially those of a socio-economic and political nature. Various forms of code-switching, both situational and metaphorical, occur in many facets of life in West Africa, ranging from everyday conversations among friends and family, through radio and television programmes, to music and movies. In Ghana, for instance, code-switching occurs in many radio programmes and in commercial advertisements on both radio and TV. There are also instances of code-switching in Ghanaian hip hop (hiplife) music that has recently developed. In all these instances, code-switching occurs between English and Akan mainly, but also between English and the other major Ghanaian languages. It is interesting to note that in recent times, Ghanaian English pidgin is beginning to feature a lot in code-switching in Ghana, especially in commercial adverts on radio and television. However, the phenomenon rarely occurs in the print media in Ghana. The situation is not so different in Nigeria. For instance, Babalola and Taiwo (2009) have studied code-switching in Nigerian hip-hop music and found that most code-switching in that context occurs in three languages, namely, English, Nigerian pidgin and Yoruba.

4.3.3 Pidgins and creoles

There are different forms and functions of the varieties of pidgins that are spoken along the West Coast of Africa. Although the pidgins spoken in Nigeria, Sierra Leone, Liberia, Ghana and Cameroon are described as West African pidgins, they play different roles in the communities where they are used. For instance, compared with the varieties of pidgin that are used in Nigeria and Cameroon, Ghanaian pidgin is a highly stigmatised variety of pidgin with very limited functions. There are two main varieties of pidgins spoken in Ghana – the educated pidgin and the uneducated pidgin. Huber (1999, 2004a, 2004b) describes these two varieties as "institutionalized pidgin" and "non-institutionalized pidgin".

The main difference between these two varieties is that, while the educated/institutionalised variety is used mainly in schools or institutions and by people with at least a secondary school level of education, the uneducated or non-institutionalised variety is used by people without any secondary education, typically unskilled labourers, taxi drivers or housemaids. Generally, the educated variety is used predominantly by male students in senior high schools and universities and is used mainly as an in-group language that enables speakers to convey a sense of intimacy and solidarity. There are a few self-reports of females who speak the educated variety of pidgin but the number is not significant. The females who speak the uneducated variety are perceived to be women of low morals. Ghanaian pidgin is highly stigmatised and so it is not used in formal contexts at all. It is thus also generally not used in the media or for religious purposes. However, there are growing numbers of infomercial and commercial adverts which are produced in pidgin. There are also religious songs by predominantly Nigerian artists (and some Ghanaian artists as well) that are sung in pidgin commonly in Ghanaian Pentecostal churches.

The situation in Cameroon and Nigeria is different. In Nigeria, pidgin is used as a medium of wider communication. The same thing applies to Cameroon, where Kamtok or Cameroonian Pidgin is spoken. According to Menang (2004), even in Doula, which is a predominantly French-speaking area, about 87 per cent of persons interviewed in a survey conducted by the Department of English, University of Yaounde, reported that they spoke Kamtok. Unlike the situation in Ghana, Menang reports that Cameroonian Pidgin is used by Christian missionaries for evangelism and liturgical services. There are also Bibles and other Christian literature written in Kamtok. Kamtok is also used for radio broadcasts, newspaper publications, and so on. This situation where a pidgin is also used as a home language, like Kamtok in Cameroon, has not arisen in Ghana. There are also reports that about 97 per cent of children of school-going age acquire Kamtok before they start school. This language is also used as a medium of instruction in nursery schools. Singler (2004a, 2004b) also reports the prevalence of Vernacular Liberian English in Liberia, also known as Liberian Pidgin.

4.3.4 New Englishes

One area that has attracted the attention of sociolinguists in the sub-region is the emergence of new varieties of English or French in this highly multilingual context. The sociolinguistic consequences of the co-existence of English or French and indigenous West African languages has been the focus of many studies. Especially among the Anglophone countries the notion of Nigerian English, Cameroonian English, Ghanaian English and Gambian English and the like have been given a lot of attention. Book-length discussions have been given in Sey's *Ghanaian English* (1973), Simo-Bobda's *Cameroon English Phonology* (1994), Kropp-Dakubu's *English in Ghana* (1997), Bamgbose's *New Englishes: A West African Perspective* (1997), Awonusi and Dadzie's *Nigerian English: Influences and Characteristics* (2004) and Anchimbe's *Cameroon English: Authenticity, Ecology and Evolution* (2006). Journal articles, dissertations and book chapters have also emerged on these topics.

4.3.5 Politeness

Another important research area has been in the field of politeness. Nwoye (1992) points out in his much-cited paper that the kind of activities that are regarded as face-threatening acts or high-imposition acts in Western societies are not regarded as face-threatening acts amongst the Igbos. This finding has been corroborated by Agyekum (2004), Obeng-Gyasi (1996), and Anderson (2009), who have examined the notion of politeness in Akan and English in Ghana. Basically, this research challenges the assumption that the realisation of face-threatening acts is universal. The findings from these studies underscore the point that for these African cultures, which are more collectivist cultures, the notion of face is more of a group property rather than an individual property.

4.4 Conclusion

In this essay, we have re-examined the challenges and prospects of the sociolinguistic situation in West Africa, one of the most linguistically diverse regions in the world. Many studies have tried to fit the West African sociolinguistic mosaic into Western-oriented sociolinguistic theories. In this essay, however, we have presented the West African sociolinguistic situation as unique in many respects from what existing theories propound. For instance, we have pointed out that existing theories in sociolinguistics appear inadequate when accounting for aspects of several sociolinguistic phenomena (e.g. multilingualism, language planning and language policy, language shift and code-switching) in West Africa. In other words, a critical examination of sociolinguistic phenomena in West Africa reveals that the sociolinguistic realities in the region challenge many of the existing theories in the field. This calls for an expansion in such theories to be able to adequately account for sociolinguistic phenomena in linguistically highly diversified communities.

Further reading

Bamgbose, Ayo (1991) *Language and the Nation: The Language Question in Sub-Saharan Africa*. Edinburgh: Edinburgh University Press.
Batibo, Herman (2005) *Language Decline and Death in Africa*. Clevedon: Multilingual Matters.
Connell, Bruce and David Zeitlyn (2010) Sociolinguistic Studies of West and Central Africa. In: *The Routledge Handbook of Sociolinguistics around the World*. Martin J. Ball (ed.), 203–15. London: Routledge

References

Agyekum, Kofi (2004) The Socio-cultural Concept of Face in Akan. *Pragmatics and Cognition* 12(1): 71–92.

——(2009) Language Shift: A Case Study of Ghana. *Sociolinguistic Studies* 3(3): 381–404.

Akinremi, Ihuoma A. (2011a) Patterns, Processes and Mechanisms in Igbo-English Code-switching. Paper presented at the 2011 Annual Conference of the Linguistics Association of Ghana. Kumasi: Kwame Nkrumah University of Science and Technology.

——(2011b) Towards a Grammatical Theory of Code-switching: The Case of Igbo-English Code-switching. Paper presented at the 2011 Summer Conference of the Society for Pidgin and Creole Linguistics. Accra: University of Ghana.

Akpanglo-Nartey, Jonas and Rebecca Akpanglo-Nartey (2012) Some Endangered Languages of Ghana. *American Journal of Linguistics* 1(2): 10–18.

Albakry, Mohammed and Dominic Ofori (2011) Ghanaian English and Code-switching in Catholic Churches. *World Englishes* 30(4): 515–32.

Amekor, Collins K. (2009) Code-switching as Medium of Instruction in Selected Schools in the Volta Region. MA thesis, English Department, University of Ghana.

Amuda, A. Ayonade (1994) Yoruba/English Conversational Code-switching. *African Languages and Cultures* 7: 121–31.

Amuzu, Evershed Kwasi (2010a) Code-switching as Communication of Multiple Identities. Messages from the Ghanaian Context. Paper presented at the 8th Faculty of Arts Colloquium, University of Ghana, 13 April.

——(2010b) *Composite Code-switching in West Africa. The Case of Ewe-English Code-switching*. Saarbrücken: Lambert Academic Publishing.

Anchimbe, Eric A. (2006) *Cameroon English: Authenticity, Ecology and Evolution*. Frankfurt am Main: Peter Lang.

Anderson, Jemima Asabea (2009) Polite Requests in Non-Native Varieties of English. *Linguistic Atlantica* (30): 30–59.

Anderson, Jemima Asabea, Gladys Nyarko Ansah and Patience Afrakoma Mensa (2009) Domains of English in Ghana and its Use for Specific Purposes. In: *English for Academic and Specific Purposes in Developing, Emerging and Least Developed Countries*. M. Krzanowski (ed.), 122–29. Reading: Garnet Education.

Anderson, Jemima Asabea and J. F. Wiredu. (2007) Code-switching as a Linguistic Resource in Ghanaian Advertisements. Paper presented at the International Conference on Code-switching in West Africa: Theory and Implications. University of Ghana.

Ansah, Gladys Nyarko (2008) Linguistic Diversity in the Modern World. Practicalities and Paradoxes. *The International Journal of Language, Society and Culture* 26: 1–8.

Ansre, Gilbert (1969) The Need for a Specific and Comprehensive Policy on the Teaching of Ghanaian Languages. In: *Proceedings of the Conference on the Study of Ghanaian Languages*. J. R. Birnie and Gilbert Ansre (eds), 5–11. Legon: Ghana Publishing.

——(1976) *Four Rationalizations for Maintaining the International Seminar on African Languages in Education*. Kinshasa: Mimeographed.

Asilevi, F. (1990) English-Ewe Code-mixing in Controversial Discourse: A Case of English as a Second Language in Ghana. MA thesis, Department of Linguistics, University of Ghana.

Awonusi, Segun and A. B. K. Dadzie (2004) *Nigerian English. Influences and Characteristics*. Lagos: Concept Publication.

Babalola, E. Taiwo and Rotimi Taiwo (2009) Code-switching in Contemporary Nigerian Hip-Hop Music. *Itupale Online Journal of African Studies* 1: 1–26. Online available at: www.cambridgetoafrica.org/resources/Baba_1.pdf (accessed on 21 June 2014).

Bamgbose, Ayo (1991) *Language and the Nation: The Language Question in Sub-Saharan Africa*. Edinburgh: Edinburgh University Press.

——(1997) *New Englishes. A West African Perspective*. Trenton: Africa World Press.

——(2000) *Language and Exclusion: The Consequences of Language Policies in Africa*. Hamburg: LIT Verlag.

Banjo, Ayo (2000) English in West Africa. *International Journal of the Sociology of Language* 141: 27–38.
Batibo, Herman (2005) *Language Decline and Death in Africa*. Clevedon: Multilingual Matters.
Bodomo, Adams, Jemima Asabea Anderson and Josephine Dzahene-Quarshie (2009) A Kente of Many Colours: Multilingualism as a Complex Ecology of Language Shift in Ghana. In: *Sociolinguistic Studies* 3(3): 357–79.
Bokamba, Eyamba G. (1990) African Languages and Sociolinguistic Theories. *Studies in the Linguistic Sciences* 20: 3–34.
——(2011) Ukulonia in African Language Policies and Practices. In: *Selected Proceedings of the 40th Annual Conference on African Linguistics*. Eyamba G. Bokamba, Ryan K. Shosted and Bezza Tesfaw Ayalew (eds), 146–67. Somerville: Cascadilla Proceedings Project.
Bokamba, Eyamba G. and Joshia S. Tlou (1977) The Consequences of the Language Policies of African States vis-à-vis Education. In: *Language and Linguistic Problems in Africa: Proceedings of the Seventh Conference on African Linguistics*. Paul F. Kotey and Haig Houssikian (eds), 35–53. Columbia: Hornbeam Press.
Brew-Daniels, J. (2011) Two-English Code-switching in the Classroom. A Case Study of Some Selected Colleges of Education in Ashanti Region. Master's thesis, Department of English, University of Ghana.
Chumbow, Berban Sammy (1987) Towards a Language Planning Model for Africa. *Journal of West African Languages* 17(1): 15–22.
Chumbow, Berban Sammy and Augustin Simo Bobda (2000) French in West Africa: A Sociolinguistic Perspective. *International Journal of the Sociology of Language* 141: 39–60.
Connell, Bruce and David Zeitlyn (2010) Sociolinguistic Studies of West and Central Africa. In: *The Routledge Handbook of Sociolinguistics around the World*. Martin J. Ball (ed.), 203–15. London: Routledge
De Klerk, Vivian (2002) Xhosa as a "Home Appliance"? A Case Study of Language Shift in Grahamstown. In: *Opportunities and Challenges of Bilingualism*. Li Wei, Jean-Marc Dewaele and Alex Housen (eds), 221–48. Berlin: Mouton de Gruyter.
Essien, Okon (1995) The English Language and Code-mixing: A Case Study of the Phenomenon in Ibibio. In: *New Englishes: A West African Perspective*. Ayo Banjo, Ayo Bamgbose and Andrew Thomas (eds), 269–83. Ibadan: Mosuro.
Ezuh, Sampson Kobla (2009) Investigating the Effect of Using Code-switching in Instruction on the Performance of Students of Senior High Schools in the Volta and Central Regions. MA thesis. Department of Linguistics, University of Ghana.
Ferguson, Charles (1959) Diglossia. *Word* 15(3): 325–40.
Fishman, Joshua A. (1967) Bilingualism With and Without Diglossia – Diglossia With and Without Bilingualism. *Journal of Social Issues* 23(1): 29–38.
——(ed.) (1974) *Advances in Language Planning*. The Hague: Mouton.
Forson, Barnabas (1979) Code-switching in Akan-English Bilingualism. PhD thesis, University of California.
——(1988) Code-switching, Our Third Tongue? *Universitas* 10: 180–94.
Hancock, Ian (1971) A Survey of Pidgins and Creoles of the World. In: *Pidginization and Creolization of Language*. Dell Hymes (ed.), 509–25. Cambridge: Cambridge University Press.
Haust, Delia (1995) *Code-switching in Gambia: Eine soziolinguistische Untersuchung von Mandinka, Wolof und Englisch in Kontakt*. Köln: Rüdiger Köppe Verlag.
Huber, Magnus (1999) *Ghanaian Pidgin English in its West African Context. A Sociohistorical and Structural Analysis*. Amsterdam: John Benjamins.
——(2004a) Ghanaian Pidgin English. Phonology. In: *A Handbook of Varieties of English. A Multimedia Reference Tool* (volume 1). Bernd Kortmann, Edgar W Schneider, Clive Upton, Rajend Mesthrie and Kate Burridge (eds), 866–73. Berlin: Mouton de Gruyter.
——(2004b) Ghanaian Pidgin English. Morphology and Syntax. In: *A Handbook of Varieties of English. A Multimedia Reference Tool* (volume 2). Bernd Kortmann, Edgar W. Schneider, Clive Upton, Rajend Mesthrie and Kate Burridge (eds), 866–78. Berlin: Mouton de Gruyter.

Igboanusi, Herbert (2009) Language Shift in West Africa: An Introduction. *Sociolinguistic Studies* 3(3): 299–306.
Juffermans, Kaspar and Caroline A. McGlynn (2009) Sociolinguistic Profile of the Gambia. *Sociolinguistic Studies* 3(3): 329–56.
Juillard, Caroline (1995) *Sociolinguistique urbaine: La vie des langues à Ziguinchor (Sénégal)*. Paris: Éditions du CNRS.
Kropp-Dakubu, M. Esther (1997) *English in Ghana*. Accra: Black Masks.
Lewis, Paul M. et al. (eds) (2013) *Ethnologue: Languages of the World* (16th edition). Online available at: www.ethnologue.com (accessed on 14 June 2013).
Menang, Thaddeus (2004) Cameroon Pidgin English. Kamtok Phonology. In: *Varieties of English* (volume 4). Bernd Kortmann, Edgar W Schneider, Clive Upton, Rajend Mesthrie and Kate Burridge (eds), 902–17. Berlin: Mouton de Gruyter.
Myers-Scotton, Carol (1993) Elite Closure as a Powerful Language Strategy: The African Case. *International Journal of the Sociology of Language* 103: 149–63.
Nettle, David, and Suzanne Romaine (2000) *Vanishing Voices. The Extinction of the World's Languages*. Oxford: Oxford University Press.
Nwoye, Onuigbo G. (1992) Linguistic Politeness and Socio-cultural Variations of the Notion of Face. *Journal of Pragmatics* 18: 309–28.
Obeng-Gyasi, Samuel (1996) The Proverb as a Mitigating and Politeness Strategy in Akan Discourse. *Anthropological Linguistics* 38(3): 521–49.
Omoniyi, Tope (2009) The Sociolinguistics of Colonisation: A Perspective of Language Shift. *Sociolinguistic Studies* 3(3): 307–28.
Quarcoo, M. (2012) Bilingualism Among the Youth: The Role of Language Practices and Values among Students in Ghanaian Universities. PhD thesis, Department of English, University of Ghana.
Sey, Kofi Abakah (1973) *Ghanaian English: An Exploratory Survey*. London: Macmillan.
Simo-Bobda, Augustin (1994) *Cameroon English Phonology*. Bern: Peter Lang.
Singh, Rajendra (2010) Multilingualism, Sociolinguistics and Theories of Linguistic Form: Some Unfinished Reflections. *Language Sciences* 32: 624–37
Singler, John Victor (2004a) Liberian Settler English-phonology. In: *A Handbook of Varieties of English* (volume 1). Bernd Kortmann, Edgar W Schneider, Clive Upton, Rajend Mesthrie and Kate Burridge (eds), 65–75. Berlin: Mouton de Gruyter.
——(2004b) The Morphology and Syntax of Liberian Settler English. In: *A Handbook of Varieties of English* (volume 2). Bernd Kortmann, Edgar W Schneider, Clive Upton, Rajend Mesthrie and Kate Burridge (eds), 71–89. Berlin: Mouton de Gruyter.
Spencer, John (1971) Colonial Language Policies and Their Legacies. In: *Current Trends in Linguistics* (volume 7). Thomas Sebeok (ed.), 537–47. The Hague: Mouton de Gruyter.
Trudell, Barbara (2009) Multilingualism in Sub-Saharan Africa: Describing a Phenomenon, Leveraging a Resource. Paper presented at the International Conference on Multilingualism, Bamako, 19–21 January.
Vanderpuije, J. A. (2011) GA-English Code-switching in Television and Radio Advertisements. MA thesis, Department of Linguistics, University of Ghana.
Weinstein, Brian (1980) *Language Planning in Francophone Africa: Language Problems and Language Planning* 4(1): 55–77.
Wolff, H. Ekkehard (2010) Multilingualism and Language Policies in Anglophone and Francophone Africa from a Sociolinguistic Macro-Perspective, with Reference to Language-in-Education Issues. Paper presented at the 5th International Expert Workshop for Alumni of Ghana in Dakar, 26 November–1 December.
Yevudey, Elvis (2009) Ewe-English Code-switching on Radio. BA Long Essay, Linguistics Department, University of Ghana.

5

SOUTHEASTERN ASIA

Diglossia and politeness in a multilingual context

Aone van Engelenhoven and Maaike van Naerssen

5.1 Linguistic profile of Southeastern Asia

This chapter will discuss the sociolinguistic situation of Southeastern Asia. Following general consensus, Southeast Asia is taken to refer to the area south of China and east of India. This area includes the ten countries that form the Association of Southeast Asian Nations (ASEAN) – Brunei Darussalam, Cambodia, Indonesia, Laos, Malaysia, Myanmar, the Philippines, Singapore, Thailand and Vietnam – plus the Democratic Republic of Timor-Leste (commonly known as East Timor).

In the nineteenth century, much of the Southeast Asian territory came under Western colonial rule. Except for Thailand, all other countries experienced some form of colonisation, which markedly affected their course of history. Before Western rule, the political map of Southeast Asia comprised an indefinite number of political centres; these were more or less autonomous provinces. The colonial powers created new political frameworks and imposed modern bureaucratic systems on them, resulting in the bordered states we know today (Steinberg 1987: 173ff.).

Languages from at least four different language families are found in this region. First, there is Austronesian, which includes most languages spoken in Malaysia, the Philippines and Indonesia. Most languages of Vietnam and Cambodia belong to the Austro-Asiatic family. Furthermore, the language families Tai (which includes the official languages of Thailand and Laos) and Sino-Tibetan, which includes Chinese and Myanmar, are found in this region (Comrie 1990). Migration and the colonial language policies have further complicated the language situation.

While the countries of Southeastern Asia are very different in many ways – for instance in size, gross domestic product, religious beliefs and literacy rate – what most of them share is a plurality of languages, cultures and ethnicities existing within their borders. In most of the countries, multilingualism is considered standard. Aside from the national language(s), people often speak one or more indigenous/local languages. According to Lewis et al. (2013), over 700 languages are spoken in Indonesia today, with speaker numbers ranging from tens of millions to just a handful, making it the most plurilingual country in the region by far.

In this chapter we will discuss the issue of politeness, illustrated by a case study on Malay, the diglossic situation found in large parts of Southeastern Asia as represented by a case study on Tetum and the phenomenon of language concealment as exemplified by the Leti and Makuva languages in East Indonesia and Timor-Leste. Malay is a member of the Malayic branch in the West Malayo-Polynesian subgroup of the Austronesian language family (Blust 2013). It is the national language of Indonesia (where it is referred to as Bahasa Indonesia), Malaysia, Brunei and Singapore (where it is called Bahasa Melayu). While Malay is widely used and almost all inhabitants have an active knowledge of the language, first-language speakers are almost exclusively found on the Malay Peninsula (Errington 1998; Sneddon 2003; Simpson 2007a). Tetum is a member of the Timor branch in the putative Central Malayo-Polynesian subgroup of the Austronesian language family, and one of the official languages of East Timor, alongside Portuguese.

Language documentation – being language description and lexicography – spearheading in the former colonial research programmes has been continued as such in most countries in insular Southeast Asia. A more sociolinguistic research tradition developed initially in Malaysia, Singapore, Brunei Darussalam and the Philippines for reasons of language planning, but it has always been subordinate to descriptive linguistics in Indonesia. The rise of language rights awareness within the multilingual context of insular Southeast Asia enables sociolinguistic research on indigenous language development through mother tongue-based education. Only in Brunei Darussalam has the use of local languages in education been proscribed (Skutnabb-Kangas 2000; Rau and Florey 2007; Kosonen and Young 2009).

5.2 Politeness in the Malay-speaking world

A persistent stereotype about Southeastern Asia is that the people are very polite. And indeed, scholars from the area state that ambiguity and evasiveness is prominent in Malay-speaking society (Aziz 2000). The classic approach to politeness is often said to be too Anglocentric, focused on an individualistic society and unable to account for more group-oriented communities (e.g. Eelen 2001).

Every speaker holds cultural values and beliefs about how one should behave and express themselves in certain situations, but what behaviour is considered appropriate is highly dependent on those values and beliefs.[1] Considering the multitude of languages and cultures represented in Southeast Asia, intercultural communication is an everyday matter. Matters of politeness are of course influenced by this multiculturality.[2]

5.2.1 Mainstream approach to politeness

The phenomenon of politeness is difficult to grasp to begin with and can be approached in many ways. To this date the only comprehensive theory is Brown and Levinson's influential politeness theory (1987). It has been successfully applied to several speech communities but has received much comment and criticism as well (for discussion see, e.g., Eelen 2001; Watts 2003; Leech 2007). Even though a lot of progress has been made since, and several more recent theories have emerged, it is still the starting point for a lot of research concerning politeness, and it will be in this brief discussion on Malay politeness phenomena.

Most people seem to think of politeness as ways of speaking that avoid causing conflict or confrontation. Brown and Levinson approach politeness as the strategic orientation to participants' face: the public self-image every speaker wants for himself. This sought-after self-image consists of two related aspects or wants:

negative face – the need to be unimpeded by others; freedom of action and freedom from imposition;
positive face – the need to be approved of and appreciated.

According to Brown and Levinson (1987: 65) some acts – such as requesting – are inherently face-threatening and require softening. When in conversation, speakers choose specific strategies to show their care for their interlocutors' face wants. For example, using a nickname or form of endearment can, in the right circumstances, enable a feeling of appreciation, thus enhancing the hearer's positive face. Brown and Levinson (1987: 74–76) suggest that the decision about what strategies would be best to use is based on the assessment of three factors – the social distance (D) between speaker and hearer, the relative power (P) of the speaker with respect to the hearer and the cost of the imposition (I).

An important point to make here is that Brown and Levinson assume speakers to generally follow Grice's Cooperation Principle (CP) and the associated maxims (Grice 1975). Abiding by the CP ensures that speakers provide information they believe to be true (the maxim of Quality), complete and as informative as required, that is provide enough and not too much information (the maxim of Quantity), relevant (the maxim of Relevance), and unambiguous and clear (the maxim of Manner).

5.2.2 Malay norms of politeness

However, with respect to the approach discussed above Aziz (2003: 178) claims that "[...] in order to be polite to a hearer, an Indonesian speaker seemed to always have to violate one or more maxims", most often the maxims of Quantity and Manner. Consider the following example.

A regular customer has asked the restaurant owner to prepare her a special type of food that is not on the menu. The restaurateur responds as follows:

Malay response
"How about if you substitute it with another type of food? You said you like trying new food. By chance, I'm trying a new recipe now. It will be delicious, Madam. I'll give you a promotional price."[3]

English response
"Well, not today actually. It has been really busy. So how about I'll cook you the special some other time?"

The Malay restaurant owner could have simply said "no", maybe with a short explanation about being too busy. Instead, he asks her if she would not rather try something new, states that he remembers her telling him that she enjoys trying new food, and goes on to tell her he is in fact trying a new recipe right at this moment and adds that he will give her a discount. This response provides more information than the hearer needed, violating the maxim of Quantity and could, arguably, be regarded to violate the maxim of Manner as well, since the answer does not seem to be as clear, orderly and brief as it could have been and thus might lead to misunderstandings. His lengthy reply is considered polite because while the restaurant owner does in fact say "no" to the request, at the same time he recognises he might be causing a disadvantage to the hearer and tries to offer a solution.

Violations of a maxim form a class of politeness strategy in Brown and Levinson's model and are called off-record strategies, which they report to be the "very most pervasive in all the social interactions [they] have studied" (1987 [1978]: 213ff.). By violating a maxim, the speaker indicates to the hearer he has to infer the speaker's intended meaning rather than take his utterance literal. While the abundance of maxim violations in Malay reflects the above mentioned observation, it is unclear how to analyse the individual utterance in terms of off-record strategic language use. Politeness Theory is primarily concerned with what strategies (i.e. forms) are used to lower the threat to one's face; the problem here is that no particular form or strategy can be identified that conveys the implicit message. The response in the discussed example in its entirety implicitly communicates "no", but the utterances in that response carry meaning as well and are difficult to account for from a politeness theory perspective. These individual utterances seem to communicate their literal meaning instead of adding to the implied message; one starts to wonder why.

Aziz (2003) argues that indirectness is part of the social norm when refusing a request and proposes a principle of mutual consideration. This principle incorporates the speaker's and hearer's mutual understanding and consideration of each other's feelings to preserve social harmony. Similar results are reported for Malay speakers using English (Satter et al. 2011). This is in line with the ethos of indirectness generally observed in Indonesian social interaction (Hassall 1999) and the reported orientation towards, and public rhetoric of, solidarity (Wouk 1998, 2001) which implies greater care for positive face. More generally, values of Malay are said to include indirectness, humility, accommodation and politeness, which "are all rooted [in] one common trait of a Malay i.e. conflict-avoidance" (Awang, et al. 2012: 204; see also Asmah 1995). A similar tendency to avoid confrontation is reported for Brunei (McLellan 1996; Othman and McLellan 2000) and the Philippines (Ginting and Kleiner 2000).

Interestingly, however, several more recent studies about the realisation of speech acts in the region seem to contradict this idea of conflict avoidance. Hassall (1999, 2003) reports direct questions to be most often used when asking for information and query preparatory requests to be the most found type of requests in Indonesian, where one might have expected a stronger preference for hints if indirectness would really be the norm.[4] Adrefiza and Jones (2013) show that responses to apologies in Indonesian (said to be a collective society) and in Australian English (a so-called individualistic society) are in fact very much alike; Henry and Ho (2010) and Ho et al. (2012) present similar data on Brunei complaints. Evidenced by the number of recent publications and the divergent results presented in them, the final word has not been said about this matter yet.

Further complicating the description and analysis of politeness in Malay is the fact that the majority of speakers are multilingual. In the next section we will discuss the role of multilingualism and diglossia in South East Asia.

5.3 Language policy, multilingualism and diglossia

The multitude of its languages and the mutual contacts of its speech communities make insular Southeast Asia an excellent research area to study multilingualism, broadly defined here as the use of at least two languages in one speech community (after Edwards 2012). The multilingual character of a country influences its national language policy, as for example in the choice of national and official languages. Singapore is the only country in the region where each ethnic group that is recognised as such by the state has its own official language – Mandarin for the Chinese, Malay for the Malays and Tamil for the Indians – to which English has been added as an official fourth language. English is also an official language in the Philippines beside Filipino, the national language. Although it is a very important language in trade and interethnic communication, English has no official status in Malaysia and Brunei Darussalam as Malay is the only official national language. A similar situation is found in Indonesia, where Malay – redubbed as Indonesian – functions as the national and only official language in interethnic communication as well. The national language status of Malay is rather symbolic in Singapore where English is used for official communication, including interethnic official communication (Asmah 2007; Gonzalez 2007; Simpson 2007a, 2007b).

5.3.1 Mainstream approach to multilingualism and diglossia

The phenomenon of using different speech variants in formal and informal domains is generally referred to in sociolinguistic literature as diglossia. It is traditionally assessed by nine characteristics: (1) Speech variants are functionally different, because of which they are labelled "high variant" (H) and "low variant" (L); (2) H has more prestige than L; (3) the presence or absence of a literary heritage; (4) L is typically learnt at home, whereas H is taught at school; (5) H is the speech variant that is standardised; (6) each variant pertains to its own domains; (7) H is grammatically more complex than L; (8) H and L have exclusive lexicons; and (9) H and L have exclusive phonologies (Hudson 2002).

If the speech variants belong to the same language, for example as dialects, then the system is labelled classic diglossia, whereas extended diglossia refers to a system where the speech variants are different languages (Fishman 1967). This definition implies that, because of their multilingual character, on a macro level most societies in Southeast Asia have extended diglossia, while classic diglossia may only be found in either very remote or isolated areas. On a micro level, however, classic diglossia can be attested within one speech community, as for example the palace language of the Malay-speaking community in Brunei Darussalam, the existence of four different respect vocabularies in the Javanese language in Indonesia and the formulaic speech in Ifugao epics in the Philippines (Fatimah and Saxena 2009; Quinn 2011; Stanyukovich 2010).

5.3.2 Timor-Leste and diglossia

The problem related to multilingualism and diglossia in Southeast Asia is particularly obvious in Timor-Leste, which is the smallest nation in Southeast Asia, after Singapore and Brunei Darussalam. It is located on the eastern half of the island of Timor. The National Institute of Linguistics (INL: Institutu Nasionál Linguística nian in Tetum and Instituto Nacional de Linguistica in Portuguese) identifies 16 indigenous languages, of which the majority belongs to the Austronesian language family and four belong to what has recently been named the Timor-Alor-Pantar language family. Portuguese, Indonesian, English, Hakka and Yue are the foreign languages that are spoken (van Engelenhoven 2006; Schapper et al. 2012; Blust 2013).

Intensive contact between most ethnolinguistic groups, often resulting in intermarriage, and the fact that most languages share the grammatical features of the East Timorese Sprachbund enables individual multilingualism, in which each speaker may use up to four languages, depending on their background and the locale where speech is used (Taylor-Leech 2009).

When Timor-Leste gained independence from Indonesia in 2002, the creolised variant of Tetum in the capital Dili, which was heavily influenced by Portuguese, was identified as the model on which Tetun Ofisiál ("Official Tetum") was to be developed. This choice was based on the creole's historical role as lingua franca in the country and the fact that it was not linked to any of the speech communities in the country. Because it had no literary tradition, it was generally considered unsuitable as an official language; unlike Portuguese, the language used prior to the Indonesian occupation. Consequently, both Tetum and Portuguese are listed as co-official languages in the constitution, whereas the remaining 15 indigenous languages have national language status. Indonesian and English have a working language status (Hajek 2000).

As a member of the Community of Portuguese Language Countries (Comunidade dos Países da Língua Portuguesa, CPLP) Timor-Leste's language policy takes Portuguese as an inextricable part of its national cultural heritage. Notwithstanding its official status, however, Portuguese is spoken only by a small segment in Timorese society (Hull 2002; Corte-Real et al. 2007). Tetum on the other hand is known in most districts, except in the districts of Lautém in the extreme east and the exclave of Oecussi in Indonesian West Timor, respectively. In these monolingual regions, Indonesian (either the standardised form or a local variety) is traditionally used in contact with outsiders.

The main task of the INL is the standardisation and promotion of Official Tetum. It devised the "standard orthography" (*ortografia padronizada*) as a unifying spelling system for all Tetum sociolects and dialects and their different pronunciations. A similar approach was used in the Philippines, where Tagalog was the model for Filipino (*wikang Filipino* "Philippine language"), which is still not embraced as a national language by most Filipinos whose first language is not Tagalog (Gonzalez 1998; Hull and Eccles 2004; Steinhauer 2005).

To counter its unpopularity related to the consistent mismatch between spelling and pronunciation, the *ortografia padronizada* was declared the official orthography for Tetum in 2004 and became the basis for the orthographies of the national languages and all loan words. The unified orthography for Malay and Indonesian devised by the Language Council of Brunei, Indonesia and Malaysia (Majelis Bahasa Brunei-Indonesia-Malaysia, MABBIM) also applies to all loans, albeit without specifically mentioning the local languages. The latest orthographic proposal of the Commission for the Filipino Language (Komisyon sa Wikang Filipino, KWF) applies to all Philippine languages and Spanish loans. All other loans from foreign languages, however, follow their original orthography in Latin script (Asmah 2007; Komisyon Sa Wikang Filipino 2007).

The INL published many Tetum language materials, among others a standard dictionary (Correia et al. 2005) that contains many neologisms based on Portuguese. A monolingual standard grammar has, however, not yet been published. An innovation of Tetum grammar can be seen in the masculine and feminine gender inflections of Portuguese-derived adjectives; this is comparable to Filipino, as Filipino adjectives loaned from Spanish also display gender inflection (Hull and Correia 2005; Jubilado 2008; van Engelenhoven 2006; Alburquerque 2012).

During the first years of independence, education was confined to the reintroduction of Portuguese in society and the introduction of Tetum in the educational system. Inspired by the efforts of the Philippine government to enhance mother-tongue-based multilingual education, a similar educational pilot programme for the national languages of East Timor has been set up (Taylor-Leech 2011).

5.3.3 Other relevant issues: language concealment

Since the 1970s, a new trend in linguistics evolved that focused on language ecology, that is "the interactions between any given language and its environment" (Haugen

2001; see also Mühlhäusler 1995). The specific kind of language ecology that concerns us here is what Steffensen and Fill (2014: 8) call "symbolic ecology" – the co-existence and interaction of several languages in a given geographical area. In other words, in any context where languages meet it may happen that one language comes out as a winner and removes another language from the "languagescape". In the extended diglossia model that contains genetically unrelated languages, the high variety language, as for example Malay in Indonesia, will take over all diglossic functions of the local languages in the country (see Hudson 2002).

Steffensen and Fill (2014) observe that language endangerment or extinction and the related issues of maintenance and revitalisation became main topics in language ecology research. Within descriptive linguistics this interest led to what would become known as documentary linguistics (Himmelmann 1998), which focuses on recording and archiving spoken material of especially highly endangered languages. The archives would enable profound research on languages that are either extinct or endangered as well as the revitalisation of some of them. A related trajectory of research focuses on what became known as "linguistic rights", the right of individuals to speak and to receive education in their own language (Skutnabb-Kangas 2000). A basic assumption in the context of language ecology, which is implied but not always well articulated, is that loss of a language equals loss of cultural knowledge and therefore in itself means a threat to the intellectual legacy of all humanity (Davis 2010).

Ongoing research in Timor-Leste, East Indonesia and the East Indonesian diaspora in the Netherlands, however, revealed a sociolinguistic phenomenon called "language concealment" where the disappearance of a language from society is an attempt of cultural knowledge conservation rather than a loss (Florey and van Engelenhoven 2001). Language concealment occurs when a minority group of speakers decides to hide their own language and exclusively speak the majority language in the community they reside in. Although the reasons to conceal one's language may be different, the initial motive to do so is usually pressure from the surrounding majority culture.

The East Indonesian languages Leti and Serua exemplify this in a migration context. Their numerical insignificance and ethnolinguistic divergence from the Central Moluccan majority among the Moluccan exiles in the Netherlands made Leti parents refrain from using their indigenous language in public. Van Engelenhoven (2002) elaborates how in the Moluccan exile community an ideology evolved in which it eventually would go back to Indonesia to create an independent Republic of the South Moluccas (Republik Maluku Selatan, RMS). The idealised inhabitant for this republic was imagined after the "Alifuru concept", the idea among Central Moluccans that the mountain tribes of Seram Island were least influenced by outside forces and therefore culturally still "pure". Partly induced by the need of their children to meet the requirements of this idealised inhabitant, Leti families managed to fit the "Alifuru concept" by concealing their language.

Although not directly influenced by this RMS ideology, Seruan speakers initially also considered explicit expressions of their language and culture as "inappropriate" and hid them from Dutch society until at least 2000. Halfway through the twentieth century, the Serua community in Indonesia, along with two other language communities, was relocated from its indigenous island to a specially created district in the Central Moluccas. Although already severely threatened by this multilingual context, Serua became acutely endangered during the civil war in 2000 when the district was flooded by fugitives from diverse ethnolinguistic regions in Indonesia. It was this acute endangerment in Indonesia that overruled the concealment of Serua in the Netherlands and encouraged the leaders of the community to look for the help of linguists to document their language (van Engelenhoven 2003).

The sixteenth national language of Timor-Leste, Makuva – alternatively referred to as Lóvaia – displays a case of language concealment in a context where a majority language is introduced in a region. Makuva is the original language of the Tutuala sub-district where everyone now speaks Fataluku as a first language. Just as with Leti and Serua, Makuva is considered as a receptacle of traditional knowledge, because of which it needs to be protected against outsiders and their influences (of which the Fataluku language is an instance). The knowledge of Makuva, therefore, is now confined to a group of chosen specialists that carry out traditional rituals, such as prayers to ancestors. These specialists are expected to eventually transfer their knowledge of Makuva to a qualified candidate in the next generation. Consequently, Makuva is no longer a "living" language that changes through time but rather a language "in coma" and reserved exclusively for ritual use. This explains why in the literature Makuva was considered to be nearly extinct, since it no longer appeared in the public domain. Ongoing research shows that in fact Makuva has become a ritual register in the dominant Fataluku language (Hajek et al. 2003; van Engelenhoven 2010).

Because it has received little attention in the sociolinguistic literature thus far, there does not appear to be an analytical model yet that accurately explains language concealment.

5.4 Conclusion

The multilingual character of Southeast Asia and its complex historical backgrounds make it difficult to present one coherent overview on sociolinguistic research in the region. In this chapter, we have highlighted a few topics of research that prove to be problematic for classic sociolinguistic approaches. First, we have discussed the problem of applying politeness theory to Malay discourse, due to its focus on specific strategies. The lengthy and evasive responses produced in Malay do not fit the Gricean-based model very well. An alternative approach would ideally be able to incorporate the importance of mutual feelings towards the situation and indirectness in interaction, and account for the reported preference for direct questions.

Second, the language situations in East Timor and the Philippines represent an alternative path in language standardisation. In the Philippines and East Timor it was a language without a written tradition – an L variant in both classic and extended diglossia – that was standardised and became official. The main reason for this was the fact that the languages in question, Tagalog and Tetum, functioned as contact languages and did not belong to a single (ethnic) group and were in that sense neutral.

The final topic of interest we discussed is not yet accounted for in any sociolinguistic theory or approach we know of – concealing a language, seemingly, as a strategy of maintenance. The Makuva language, which is not in fact extinct, but rather "in coma", serves as one of the primary examples of language concealment as found in this region.

Whereas the case studies in this chapter focused on insular Southeast Asia, the phenomena discussed are equally relevant to the languages and societies in mainland Southeast Asia.

Notes

1 A distinction can be made between such a commonsense understanding of politeness (first-order politeness) and a technical, scientific conceptualisation (second-order politeness). Separating these two orders of politeness is important to ensure that the analyses that are made in fact talk about the same phenomenon. This point was raised by Watts (2005 [1992]) and has since been applied in numerous politeness studies (see Eelen 2001; Watts 2003).
2 Some research had been done about intercultural communication in the area. However, most studies report on communication in English between speakers from one of the Southeast Asian countries with speakers from outside the area (e.g. David and Dumanig 2011 on Malaysia–Philippine relations; Ismail 2007 on Malaysia–Australia relations; Storz 1999 on Malaysia–China relations) instead of the intercultural contact between people(s) within the borders of one nation, which might bring a whole new aspect of intercultural communication to the table.
3 Original example (taken from Aziz 2003: 179, ex. 3a): "*Ganti aja deh Bu dengan masakan lain. 'kan Ibu katanya suka byoba makanan baru. Kebetulan saya lagi nyoba resep baru. Dijamin enak deh Bu. Saya kasih harga promosi deh.*"
4 That said, Hassall presents data on initiating turns, where Aziz and Wouk mainly focus on responsive turns, which might be responsible for the different outcomes. More research is needed in order to make reliable statements about this.

Further reading

Guan, Lee Hock and Leo Suryadinata (eds) (2007) *Language, Nation and Development in Southeast Asia*. Singapore: Institute of Southeast Asian Studies. (The essays in the volume evaluate the successes and drawbacks of language policies in Southeast Asia.)

Rappa, Antonio L. and Lionel Wee (2006) *Language Policy and Modernity in Southeast Asia. Malaysia, the Philippines, Singapore, and Thailand*. New York: Springer. (This book presents an interdisciplinary approach to language policy in the designated countries.)

Simpson, Andrew (ed.) (2007) *Language and National Identity in Asia*. Oxford: Oxford University Press. (This volume provides an excellent overview of the history and development of the national languages and identities in the region.)

References

Adrefiza and Jeremy F. Jones (2013) Investigating Apology Response Strategies in Australian English and Bahasa Indonesia: Gender and Cultural Perspectives. *Australian Review of Applied Linguistics* 36(1): 71–101.

Alburquerque, Davi Borges de (2012) Para uma política de implantação terminológica em Timor-Leste [Towards a Politics of Terminological Implantation in Timor-Leste]. In: *Congresso internacional de dialetologia e sociolinguística – Anais* [International Congress of Dialectology and Sociolinguistics – Annals]. Abdelhak Razky, Marilúcia Barros de Oliveira, Alcides Fernandes de Lima (eds), 1185–94. São Luis: Editora da Universidade Federal do Maranhão.

Asmah Hj Omar (1995) Indirectness as a Rule of Speaking among the Malays. In: *Verbal Interaction at Play. Rules of Speaking*. Zainab Abdul Majid and Loga M. Baskaran (eds), 47–60. Petaling Jaya: Pelanduk Publications.

——(2007) Malaysia and Brunei. In: *Language and National Identity in Asia*. Andrew Simpson (ed.), 337–59. Oxford: Oxford University Press.

Awang, S., M. Maros and N. Ibrahim (2012) Malay Values in Intercultural Communication. *International Journal of Social Sciences and Humanity* 2(3): 201–5.

Aziz, Aminudin E. (2000) Indonesian Speech Act Realization in Face Threatening Situations. *Monash University Linguistic Papers* 26(2): 53–68.

——(2003) Theorizing Linguistic Politeness in Indonesian Society. *Linguistik Indonesia* 21(2): 167–87.

Blust, Robert (2013) *The Austronesian Languages* (revised edition). Canberra: Asia-Pacific Linguistics.

Brown, Penelope and Stephen Levinson (1987) *Politeness: Some Universals in Language Use*. Cambridge: Cambridge University Press.

Comrie, Bernard (ed.) (1990) *The Major Languages of East and South-East Asia*. London: Routledge.

Correia, Adérito Guterres, George Saunders, Geoffrey Hull, Rosa Tilman and Mario Soares (2005) *Disionáriu nasionál ba Tetun Ofisiál* [National Dictionary for Official Tetum]. Dili: Instituto Nacional de Linguística.

Corte-Real, Benjamim Ajaúro de Brito and Regina H. Pires de Brito (2007) Aspectos da política linguística de Timor-Leste. Desvendando contra-correntes [Aspects of the Linguistic Policy of Timor-Leste. Untangling Counter Currents]. In: *Língua Portuguesa. Reflexões lusófonas*. Neusa Barbosa Basto (ed.), 75–84. São Paulo: Editora da PUC-SP.

David, Maya Khemlani and Francisco Perlas Dumanig (2011) Social Capital and Politeness Strategies in Fostering Ethnic Relations in Malaysia and Philippines. *IARS International Research Journal* 1(1): 1–14.

Davis, Wade (2010) Last of Their Kind. What is Lost when Cultures Die? *Scientific American* 303: 60–67.

Edwards, John (2012) Bilingualism and Multilingualism: Some Central Concepts. In: *The Handbook of Bilingualism and Multilingualism* (second edition). Tej K. Bhatia and William C. Ritchie (eds), 5–25. Chichester: Wiley-Blackwell.

Eelen, Gino (2001) *A Critique of Politeness Theories*. Manchester: St. Jerome.

Errington, J. Joseph (1998) *Shifting Languages: Interaction and Identity in Javanese Indonesia*. Cambridge: Cambridge University Press.

Fatimah Awg Chuchu and Mukul Saxena (2009) Socio-cultural Hierarchy in the Palace Language of Brunei Darussalam. *Southeast Asia. A Multidisciplinary Journal* 9: 42–51.

Fishman, Joshua A. (1967) Bilingualism with and without Diglossia: Diglossia With and Without Bilingualism. *Journal of Social Issues* 23: 29–38.

Florey, Margaret and Aone van Engelenhoven (2001) Language Documentation and Maintenance Programs for Moluccan Languages in the Netherlands. *International Journal of the Sociology of Language* 151: 195–219.

Ginting, Eva and Brian H. Kleiner (2000) Conducting Business Effectively in the Philippines. *Management Research News* 23(7/8): 107–10.

Gonzalez, Andrew, FSC (1998) The Language Planning Situation in the Philippines. *Journal of Multilingual and Multicultural Development* 19(5): 487–525.

——(2007) The Philippines. In: *Language and National Identity in Asia*. Andrew Simpson (ed.), 360–73. Oxford: Oxford University Press.

Grice, H. Paul (1975) Logic and Conversation. In: *Syntax and Semantics* (Volume 3). Peter Cole and Jerry L. Morgan (eds), 41–58. New York: Academic Press.

Hajek, John (2000) Language Planning and the Sociolinguistic Environment in East Timor: Colonial Practice and Changing Language Ecologies. *Current Issues in Language Planning* 1(3): 400–414.

Hajek, John, Nikolaus Himmelmann and John Bowden (2003) Lóvaia, an East Timorese Language on the Verge of Extinction. *International Journal of the Sociology of Language* 160: 155–67.

Hassall, Tim (1999) Request Strategies in Indonesian. *Pragmatics* 9(4): 585–606.

——(2003) Requests by Australian Learners of Indonesian. *Journal of Pragmatics* 35: 1903–28.

Haugen, Einar (2001) The Ecology of Language. In: *The Ecolinguistics Reader. Language, Ecology, and Environment*. Alwin Fill and Peter Mühlhäusler (eds), 57–66. London: Pinter.

Henry, Alex and Debbie G.E. Ho (2010) The Act of Complaining in Brunei – Then and Now. *Journal of Pragmatics* 42(3): 840–55.

Himmelmann, Nikolaus P. (1998) Documentary and Descriptive Linguistics. *Linguistics* 36: 161–95.

Ho, Debbie G.E., Alex Henry, Sharifah N.H. Alkaff (2012) "You Don't Seem to Know How to Work" – Malay and English Spoken Complaints in Brunei. *Pragmatics* 22(3): 391–416.

Hudson, Alan (2002) An Outline of a Theory of Diglossia. *International Journal of the Sociology of Language* 157: 1–48.

Hull, Geoffrey (2002) *Timór Lorosa'e, identidade no política nasionál/ Timor-Leste, identidade e política nacional* [East Timor, Identity and National Politics]. Lisbon: Instituto Camões.

Hull, Geoffrey and Adérito Guterres Correia Correia (2005) *Kursu gramátika Tetun* [Tetum Grammar Course]. Dili: Instituto Nacional de Linguística.

Hull, Geoffrey and Lance Eccles (2004) *Gramática da língua Tetum* [Tetum language grammar]. Lisbon: Lidel.

Ismail, Jumiati (2007) Challenges in International Business Communication: A Study of Language, Culture and Inter-cultural Issues in Malaysian-Australian Business Discourse. PhD dissertation, University of Western Australia.

Jubilado, Rodney (2008) The Filipino Language in the Malaysian Linguistic Space. *Jati* 13: 148–58.

Komisyon Sa Wikang Filipino (2007) *Ang ortograpiya ng wikang pambansa* [The Orthography of the National Language]. Manila: Komisyon Sa Wikang Filipino.

Kosonen, Kimmo and Catherine Young (eds) (2009) *Mother Tongue as Bridge Language in Instruction. Policies and Experiences in Southeast Asia*. Bangkok: The Southeast Asian Ministers of Education Organization.

Leech, Geoffrey N. (2007) Politeness: Is there an East–West Divide? *Journal of Politeness Research* 3: 167–206.

Lewis, M. Paul, Gary F. Simons and Charles D. Fennig (eds) (2013) *Ethnologue: Languages of the World* (17th edition). Dallas, TX: SIL International. Online available at: http://ethnologue.com (accessed 23 March 2014).

McLellan, James (1996) Some Features of Written Discourse in Brunei English. In: *Language Use and Language Change in Brunei Darussalam*. Peter W. Martin, Conrad K. Ożóg and Gloria R. Poedjosoedarmo (eds), 223–35. Athens: Ohio University Centre for International Studies.

Mühlhäusler, Peter (1995) *Linguistic Ecology: Language Change and Linguistic Imperialism in the Pacific Region*. London: Routledge.

Othman, Noor Azam Hj and James McLellan (2000) Brunei Culture, English Language: Textual Reflections of an Asian Culture Located in the English-language Output of Bruneians. *Asian Englishes* 3(1): 5–19.

Quinn, George (2011) Teaching Javanese Respect Usage to Foreign Learners. *Electronic Journal of Foreign Language Teaching* 8: 362–70.

Rau, D. Victoria and Margaret Florey (eds) (2007) *Documenting and Revitalizing Austronesian Languages*. Honolulu: University of Hawai'i Press.

Satter, Hiba Qusay Abdul, Salasiah Che Lah and Raja Rozina Suleiman (2011) Refusal Strategies in English by Malay University Students. *GEMA. Online Journal of Language Studies* 11(3): 69–81.

Schapper, Antoinette, Juliette Huber and Aone van Engelenhoven (2012) The Historical Relationships of the Papuan Languages of Timor and Kisar. *Language and Linguistics in Melanesia* 1: 194–242.

Simpson, Andrew (2007a) Indonesia. In: *Language and Identity in Asia*. Andrew Simpson (ed.), 312–36. Oxford: Oxford University Press.

——(2007b) Singapore. In: *Language and Identity in Asia*. Andrew Simpson (ed.), 374–90. Oxford: Oxford University Press.

Skutnabb-Kangas, Tove (2000) *Linguistic Genocide in Education or Worldwide Diversity and Human Rights?* Mahwah: Erlbaum Associates.

Sneddon, James (2003) *The Indonesian Language: Its History and Role in Modern Society*. Sydney: University of New South Wales Press.

Stanyukovich, Maria V. (2010) Филиппинский эпос и связанные с ним искусственные конструкции // "Калевала" в контексте региональной и мировой культуры. [Philippine Epic and Related Artificial Constructions // "Kalevala" in the context of regional and world culture]. In: Материалы международной научной конференции, посвящённой 160-летию полного издания "Калевалы" [Materials of the International Scientific Conference Devoted to the 160th Anniversary of the Full "Kalevala" Edition]. Karelian Research Centre (ed.), 156–16. Petrozavodsk: Russian Academy of Sciences.

Steffensen, Sune Vork and Alwin Fill (2014) Ecolinguistics: The State of the Art and Future Horizons. *Language Sciences* 41: 6–25.

Steinberg, David Joel (ed.) (1987) *In Search of Southeast Asia. A Modern History* (revised edition). Honolulu: University of Hawai'i Press.

Steinhauer, Hein (2005) Colonial History and Language Policy in Insular Southeast Asia and Madagascar. In: *The Austronesian Languages of Asia and Madagascar*. Alexander Adelaar and Nikolaus Himmelmann (eds), 65–86. London: Routledge.

Storz, Moni Lai (1999) Malay and Chinese Values Underlying the Malaysian Business Culture. *International Journal of Intercultural Relations* 23(1): 117–31.

Taylor-Leech, Kerry (2009) The Language Situation in Timor-Leste. *Current Issues in Language Planning* 10(1): 1–68.

——(2011) Timor-Leste: Sustaining and Maintaining the National Languages in Education. *Current Issues in Language Planning* 12(2): 289–308.

van Engelenhoven, Aone (2002) Concealment, Maintenance and Renaissance: Language and Ethnicity in the Moluccan Community in the Netherlands. In: *Language Maintenance for Endangered Languages. An Active Approach*. David Bradley and Maya Bradley (eds), 272–309. London: Routledge Curzon.

——(2003) Language Endangerment in Indonesia: The Incipient Obsolescence and Acute Death of Teun, Nila and Serua (Central and Southwest Maluku). In: *Language Death and Language Maintenance: Theoretical, Practical and Descriptive Approaches*. Mark Janse and Sijmen Tol (eds), 49–80. Amsterdam: John Benjamins.

——(2006) Ita-nia nasaun oin-ida, ita-nia dalen sira oin-seluk, "Our Nation is One, Our Languages are Different": Language Policy in East Timor. In: *Diversidade cultural na construção da nação e do estado em Timor-Leste* [Cultural Diversity in Nation and State Building in East Timor]. Paulo Castro Seixas and Aone van Engelenhoven (eds), 106–31. Porto: Publicações Universidade Fernando Pessoa.

——2010 The Makuva Enigma: Locating a Hidden Language in East Timor. *Revue Roumaine de Linguistique* 80(2): 161–81.

van Engelenhoven, Aone and John Hajek (2000) East Timor and the Southwest Moluccas: Language, Time and Connections. *Studies in Languages and Cultures of East Timor* 3: 107–24.

Watts, Richard J. (2003) *Politeness*. Cambridge: Cambridge University Press.

——(2005 [1992]) Linguistic Politeness and Politic Verbal Behavior: Reconsidering Claims for Universality. In: *Politeness in Language. Studies in its History, Theory and Practice* (second revised edition). Richard J. Watts, Sachiko Ide and Konrad Ehlich (eds), 43–69. Berlin: Mouton de Gruyter.

Wouk, Fay (1998) Solidarity in Indonesian Conversation: The Discourse Marker *kan*. *Multilingua* 17: 381–408.

——(2001) Solidarity in Indonesian Conversation: The Discourse Marker *ya*. *Journal of Pragmatics* 33: 171–91.

6

TOWARDS A DISTRIBUTED SOCIOLINGUISTICS OF POSTCOLONIAL MULTILINGUAL SOCIETIES

The case of Southern Africa

Rajend Mesthrie

6.1 The languages of Southern Africa

Southern Africa comprises the following independent countries: Angola, Botswana, Lesotho, Malawi, Mozambique, Namibia, South Africa, Swaziland, Zambia and Zimbabwe. A formal alliance of these countries does not exist, though the SADC (Southern African Development Community) is the body that comes closest to this, in its mission to enhance economic development in the region.[1] Historically, Southern Africa was home to hunters and gatherers known as the Khoikhoi and the San – who may well constitute the "oldest genetic material" on the planet from which all of current humanity derive (via "African Eve"). Linguists now concur that there is no linguistic unity between the languages previously labelled Khoesan, and that there appear to be three unrelated families that they designate (for want of a better current label) "non-Bantu click languages". Many of these languages are in decline today, though Nama survives as an important language of Namibia. The Bantu languages are the most numerous in the region, and are historically considered a "Southern Bantu" offshoot (with south-eastern and south-western branches) of Proto-Bantu which must have originated in central-west Africa (in the area around the present-day Western Cameroons). Bantu languages have official status in many of the Southern African countries, often in tandem with a colonial language (e.g. Sotho and English in Lesotho). European explorations in the region largely date back to the fifteenth century and colonisation to the seventeenth century, resulting in the presence of Portuguese, Dutch and English as the main colonial languages in the region.[2] Thus Portuguese is the sole official language of Angola and Mozambique, while English is the sole official language of Namibia. South Africa has 11 official languages, and Zimbabwe looks set to recognise no fewer than 16. This should alert readers to the different socio-political and symbolic dynamics surrounding language in the region (see Mesthrie 2008 on language and nation building in South Africa).

Bantu languages were able to resist the full onslaught of European colonisation in ways that were not possible in Australasia and the Americas, and remain the majority languages of the region. This is not always a demographic majority for any one language, since most countries in the region are multilingual. However, clear majorities are Swati (also known as Swazi) in Swaziland, Tswana in Botswana, Shona in Zimbabwe and Sotho in Lesotho. The region thus continues with policies that are partially endoglossic and partially exoglossic. At state level a colonial language is dominant, though at intermediate levels and "on the ground" indigenous languages proliferate.[3] For several reasons, the Southern African language situations are hard to capture in existing sociolinguistic paradigms. One source of the region's sociolinguistic complexity is that colonial languages are not spoken by the majority, yet they retain a large measure of power and prestige. A second source of complexity is that in many large urban centres multilingualism is common, and the borderlines between languages continue to change and become blurred. Youth language practices of males exploit this fluidity and are sometimes claimed to result in new urban lingua francas (e.g. Town Bemba in Zambia and Tsotsitaal in South Africa). Four notable issues which to a large extent challenge the dominant approaches within sociolinguistics arise from this complexity: (1) issues of standardisation of indigenous languages; (2) issues concerning language prestige; (3) lack of salience of the Western variationist sociolinguistic model for a majority of languages; and (4) the robustness of contact-related variation over social dialect variation. I will illustrate these four related areas mainly from South Africa. It is hoped that this account will stimulate research on these topics within the entire region and eventually contribute to mainstream theory-making.

6.2 Issues pertaining to standardisation

In the Western tradition language standardisation is associated with the cultivation of a public form of a language within a territory for wider regional and functional communication than associated with any of the pre-existing dialects. This often went hand in hand with the rise of nation states in Europe (see Coulmas 1989). A standard language is something of an idealisation – the norms associated with it are more often applicable to formal usage. At the level of informal standard use, language continues to change, even in the written forms in which the standard is best realised. Haugen (1972) outlined four stages in the standardisation process:

- selection of norm (choice of variety on which the standard is based);
- codification of form (in grammar, dictionaries, usage guides);
- implementation (promotion of the norm);
- elaboration (ongoing development of the standard for different functions).

Several things are taken for granted in this model:

(1) that the economic and political system of the territory is relatively autonomous and integrated and has reached a stage where it both needs and can support the standardisation process;
(2) that writing already exists as a widespread tool in the society;
(3) that the education systems and media that will promulgate the standard are in place;
(4) that an ideology supporting the standard has developed or will soon develop;
(5) that the language for which a standard form is being developed is widely known and accepted in the territory;
(6) that this register of the language would achieve prestige and become associated with social mobility, aspirations and power.

These conditions were not always met in the colonial world. In Southern Africa most countries did not meet these conditions, yet standard forms of the languages were developed for use in writing, religion and education. The following discussion is an adaptation of what I wrote earlier (Mesthrie 2002: 16).

The earliest written texts for Southern African languages were translations of the Gospels by Western missionaries with the aid of their African assistants. In many territories the dialect selected by the missionaries for writing came to have prestige, partly because of this association. The rise of African languages thus did not follow from the more familiar bases of standardisation familiar in the West – urbanisation and the prestige accruing from the economic and social status of certain groups of speakers. Rather, it was based on the external force of missionary influence. This has developed into a modern-day paradox. The standard varieties of African languages are associated with the rural areas, where the missions were based and survived, and where the population all spoke the dominant language of the region. These are no longer centres of prestige, given the subsequent absorption of Black people into an industrialised economy based largely on mineral wealth. Mining and industrialisation saw the growth of new cities, in which an urban Black labour force arose, drawing from many areas in Southern Africa. Urban multilingualism became a reality in the late nineteenth century, and the following century saw the large-scale influence of the different languages upon each other, eventually resulting in partially restructured urban forms of African languages (see Calteaux 1996). This went hand in hand with the acquisition of colonial languages like Portuguese and English. The latter had the most prestige as the language of education and the means by which Western culture reached the Black townships of South Africa. Thus today high-status Black people are more likely to be urban-wise, "modern" people, who speak English and non-standard urban varieties of African languages, showing extensive borrowing of vocabulary, code-switching and neologisms. In Mesthrie (2002: 16) I posed the question thus: did the standardisation of African languages via the mission presses, sermons and nineteenth-century dictionaries take place too early to be effective as a norm representing black social and political aspirations and achievements?

The situation for indigenous languages in urban areas thus goes against the model of social and dialect variation evident in Trudgill's (1986: 41) well-known pyramid diagram where the large number of regional varieties are spoken by the lower classes whereas the standard dialect is used by the highest social class. This model would not work for a language like Zulu, where the language of the highest class is more likely to be an urban variety, considered non-standard. By contrast the language of some rural centres might well count as more standard. This standard has high status among traditional leaders, praise poets and orators.

The multilingual collision in colonial and post-colonial South Africa has resulted in a distributed sociolinguistics. It seems to me, based on over 100 interviews with young Black university students in the period 1992 to 2013, that their preferred organisation of speech repertoires is:

- oral proficiency in the language(s) of the home and neighbourhood, either in a traditional rural form or an urban restructured form or both, depending on speakers' individual histories;
- oral proficiency in the street language in urban areas – these are youth "anti-language" registers of the urban varieties, formerly used by males alone, but now attracting some female users;[4]
- oral and written proficiency in English, as promoted in classrooms.

In only the last domain is a standard form prized by young, urban speakers.[5] The dynamics of African language use amongst younger speakers require that it be community-oriented. In urban areas this is decidedly not a standard form.[6] In rural areas the older norms of languages like Xhosa and Zulu still have authority, though the interviews suggest dialect levelling among younger people (within an African language like Xhosa or across closely related languages like Tswana and Sotho). This distributed sociolinguistics is supported by a language ideology among the young. Students frequently complain that their home language as taught in schools is "hard" or too "deep", and that they are unfamiliar with some of its standard and advanced terms. They also report alienation from the prescriptive attitude of some school teachers towards loanwords and neologisms in their speech. These themes are taken up in part below.

6.3 Issues concerning the prestige of dominant languages

Although sociolinguistics as a discipline supports cultural and linguistic diversity, and sociolinguistics textbooks cover material from a range of places on the planet, some territories and languages are perhaps better represented than others. This is partly a reflection of the global research hierarchy. Obviously, some countries have a far bigger pool of researchers, whose work often engages with the variation they are most familiar with. That English is frequently the medium as well as the main exemplar language is a reflection of the initial establishment of sociolinguistics in Anglo-American contexts. (In fairness all textbooks in the discipline that I am familiar with do cover a range of languages and societies.) In this section I wish to scrutinise what might be called the sociolinguistic typology of the prestige language (see Kahane 1986). Characterisations of the prestige accent in England also follow a pyramid model (Trudgill 1986: 42) in which the highest social class uses Received Pronunciation (RP) whereas the lower classes use localised accents.

The dynamics of the prestige language have been contested internationally in the paradigm known as "World Englishes". Following Kachru (e.g. 1986), it is accepted that the dynamics of Anglo-American English, its social nuances, and speakers' judgements about grammaticality, prestige and acceptability do not translate intact in contexts outside of this Inner Circle. Instead, the "Outer Circle" generates its own norms based on an essentially pluricultural and multilingual ethos, with due regard to the realities of postcolonial and global policies and politics. Two early studies within the Kachruvian paradigm were those of Chishimba (1984) and Magura (1984), both scholars based in Southern Africa. It is not necessary to go into the details of this paradigm here, since it deals largely with L2 varieties in contradistinction to the L1 English of the Anglo-American variationist scholarship. (Good overviews occur in Kachru 1986; McArthur 1998; and Mesthrie and Bhatt 2008.) Rather, I wish to focus on the complexities of English in South Africa in which both L1 and L2 varieties have co-existed for some time.

Lanham and Macdonald (1979) charted the history of English in South Africa, suggesting first a levelling out of social and regional variation from British antecedents in different ways in the two early colonies (Natal and the Cape). This was followed by a large degree of regional convergence, class differentiation and gender status as the country moved from pre-industrialised colonies to an industrialised country, following the discovery of diamonds and gold. The two exceptions are:

(1) the influence of a competing and pre-existing colonial language, Afrikaans;
(2) a colonial trichotomy between the existence of a local prestige variety (called the Standard by Lanham and Macdonald), an international prestige variety (oriented to RP) and a local somewhat stigmatised L1 English, showing contact with Afrikaans (and which carries some covert prestige).

At the same time other L2 varieties evolved in South Africa amongst the Black majority, amongst people classified "Coloured", and amongst a fairly large Indian immigrant community (see respectively de Klerk 2006; Wood 1987; Mesthrie 1992).[7] Of particular interest is the relationship between these varieties in post-apartheid South Africa, which abolished racial discrimination, instituted freedom of association and installed a democratically elected, non-racial, predominantly Black government. The country now permits quality education on a non-racial basis (though in practice this is limited to those who can afford it, or who live in proximity to good schools). To some extent the Labovian model (1972) is vindicated by the sociolinguistic patterns of the young new elites generated within the post-apartheid educational system. Mesthrie (2010) investigates the degree to which young South Africans of different backgrounds were adopting key variants in their new networks that had previously been associated with White L1 speakers.

The variant he focused on was GOOSE fronting, that is central and front realisations of the /u:/ vowel, reported by Lass (1995: 99) as "peculiarly 'White'". Mesthrie found that middle-class young Black speakers matched the erstwhile White norm considerably more than their Indian and Coloured counterparts. The latter two were divided between their new access to prestige White models and prestige L1 English norms already developed within their own communities. Young, middle-class Black speakers did not feel this pressure, as their community languages continued to play a role in cultural and community matters, and the L2 English of their older generation did not provide a compelling model for middle-class status.

The above account can be reconciled with the main tenets of Labovian sociolinguistics, and indeed draws its methods and assumptions from it. However, there is another aspect to new developments in South African English that challenge the above model. This comes from the very different linguistic ecology and multilingual ethos of this post-colonial nation. One strand of power and status is globally oriented, with prestige models of English afforded by the UK, White South African English and US English via television. This is what the new young elites are responding to; and given their own high status in the new South African society they are promoting such models even further. On the other hand, a more Africanist strand reflects *its* power and new political prestige via multilingualism that includes a noticeably African variety of English.[8] English is the dominant language in South African parliament, at government meetings, and on radio and television. In a deracialising society a diversity of accents and styles can be heard at even the highest levels of the media pyramid. The majority of announcers, newsreaders, sports journalists in the visual and sound media, and politicians in parliament and government are Black, and themselves show a range of accents and styles. Because it is used by a large number of people in influential positions, traditional Black South African English is experiencing an upsurge in usage and prestige, especially amongst those with an Africanist political bent. One young, female, Black parliamentarian (and member of an opposition party) who has a clearly "crossover" accent has been accused by members of the ruling party of being "un-African" (*Cape Times*, 15 January 2013 reporting on attitudes to MP Lindiwe Mazibuko). While political motives are at work here, this is a clear indication that the prestige of traditional Black South African English is (to the critic) not just covert. Scholars who have carried out surveys among Black teachers suggest that a majority of them accept some features of traditional Black South African English as standard or correct, especially in schools where this is the main variety in use. Constructions like the extension of the progressive to include stative verbs (e.g. *He is having a cold*) were judged to be standard (see Gough 1996; van der Walt and van Rooy 2002). All of this calls into question a mono-pyramid model of the prestige language for the present and near future.

6.4 Issues pertaining to sociolinguistic variation

One of the most successful schools of sociolinguistics in the West is based on the hierarchical model of structured heterogeneity (Labov 1972). This hierarchy is robustly evident from studies of American and British English in the last 50 years. The main early assumptions of the Labovian model are summarised by Mesthrie et al. (2009: 92) as follows:

- Society is hierarchically structured, like a ship or layered cake.
- Social class is basic to this structure; other categories like gender and ethnicity are also significant factors which cut across class stratification.
- Social class can be characterised as a composite of several factors pertaining to education, income and so on.
- Much variation in language correlates with this pre-determined hierarchy.
- Style can be arranged on a single dimension from least to most formal, according to context.
- Style shows a correlation with linguistic variants similar to that of social class.

Pierre Bourdieu (1991) makes strong connections between Labov's work and French socioeconomic hierarchies of prestige. His editor J.B. Thomson (Bourdieu 1991: 18) puts it thus:

> Linguistic utterances or expressions are always produced in particular contexts or markets, and the properties of these markets endow linguistic products with a certain "value". On a given linguistic market, some products are valued more highly than others; and part of the practical competence of speakers is to know how, and to be able, to produce expressions which are highly valued on the markets concerned.

This model of hierarchical prestige is obviously predicated on the dynamics that have evolved in what are essentially late-modern, post-industrialised, capitalist societies. The Labovian model does not seem to apply to more traditional societies, where issues of power, prestige, status and gender might be arranged differently. In Southern Africa there have been no large-scale studies of African languages from a variationist perspective, presumably because the model does not resonate in this context. Studies of variation in African languages have largely focused on three aspects: (1) the effects of contact with European languages, especially in the use of loanwords, in loanword phonology and code switching (which is discussed in greater detail below); (2) gendered use of language, evident in traditional hlonipha ("women's language of respect", Finlayson 1984); and (3) the rise and proliferation of antilinguistic youth language registers (see Mesthrie and Hurst 2013). (I omit here the large body of applied linguistic work on language planning and policy, translation, and taboo and the semantics of health.) Other types of variation reported for African languages appear more lexical and overt: the use of a separate women's register in Xhosa after marriage, that treats as taboo the initial syllable of in-laws' names (Finlayson 1984); a young man's initiation language or register in Xhosa (Finlayson 1998); and a special royal courtly register in languages like Venda that bestows synonyms to everyday terms (van Warmelo 1971). All of these appear to be traditional topics within anthropological linguistics, rather than typical fodder for urban variationists.

Labovian linguistics becomes more relevant when a new hierarchical arrangement comes into play within colonial bilingualism, consisting of an indigenous language and a new superposed language of power and prestige. To a small extent "Labovian effects" then enter the indigenous language. This can be seen in the phonological treatment of loanwords. Treating loanwords in the phonology of the indigenous language as opposed to using a phoneme from the colonial language opens up a degree of hierarchical variation. Thus the traditional form of the English loanword "rice" in Zulu is *i-layisi*; but this form that turns an /r/ into an /l/ is considered old fashioned and rural, with younger speakers using the variant *i-rayisi*, with the newly introduced phoneme /r/. Ngcobo (2013) demonstrates how sociolinguistic factors affect the morphological classification of loanwords in Zulu according to the degree of bilingualism in Zulu and English and the educational standing of the speaker. Zulu's 17 or so noun classes are – in common with other Bantu languages – semantically motivated, though in the course of time this has become a less rigid classificatory system.[9] Thus, for example, class 1 (with prefix *u-*) typically comprises nouns referring to human beings, with their plural equivalents falling into class 2 (with prefix *aba-*). Loanwords from English and Afrikaans are usually assigned to a noun class on semantic or phonological grounds (or both). Thus *isi-Ngisi* "English" is assigned to class 7 with prefix *isi-*, on the basis of its semantics ("language"). And *u-tisha* "teacher" is assigned to sub-class 1a for "human beings". Class 5 (with prefix *i-*) is a common class into which loanwords are placed, since it denotes inanimates: hence *i-shalofu* "shelf". In contrast *um-shini* "machine" is assigned to class 3 on the basis of the initial consonant "m" of the English word, which is given a vowel to bring it in line with Zulu phonological and morphological patterns. The noun is treated as a regular member of class 3 and assigned a plural (in class 4), hence *imi-shini* "machines". Thus the English word has been resegmented with *m* treated as part of the noun class prefix, and *-achine* or *-chine* as part of the stem. Ngcobo (2013: 32) shows how such resegmentation is avoided (or resisted) by younger educated speakers, who prefer to maintain the phonological structure of the English loanword. Thus a common new borrowing like *iselulafoni* "cellphone" is put into class 7 by some speakers, who treat the prefix as *is(i)-*. Younger speakers put this loanword in class 9, with prefix *-i* and keeping *se-* as part of the stem (as in English).[10] The presence and acquisition of a new prestige language thus opens up pathways to social (and ideological) differentiation familiar in variationist sociolinguistics, by offering new variants via loanword choices as well as their phonological form.

6.5 Issues pertaining to multilingual norms and code-switching

Code-switching seems a natural outgrowth of multilingualism in modern urban societies. In important ways the switching of languages parallels the stylistic and interactional changes shown by speakers who are monolingual. Myers-Scotton (1985) demonstrated this in an analysis of an American monolingual English television programme in which the compere strategically switched to a "lower" style to indicate temporary rapport with a game-show participant. Myers-Scotton shows parallels between code-switching and what she calls "lexical colouring" in relation to style and power in language. In fact Myers-Scotton's work on the social motivations of switching, developed on the basis of data from East Africa, is an important piece of multilingual sociolinguistic theorising that deserves to be taken seriously in understanding style shifting in monolingual western societies or sectors of society. I will briefly outline the model here, with examples from South African research that corroborate her findings while adding some minor refinements. Myers-Scotton (1992, 1993) begins with a pragmatic account of communication that involves a model of rights and obligations between speakers in the same society. Speakers have rights (to be listened to, to be taken seriously) but they also have obligations (to speak meaningfully within the context, to get to the point if time is an issue). Speech always involves a negotiation between these rights and obligations between interlocutors. In multilingual societies historical factors lead to certain languages accruing characteristic roles and perceived qualities relating to degrees of power, prestige, status, and solidarity. Myers-Scotton (1992) showed how multilingual speakers in her studies in Kenya switched between languages to challenge and change the balance of rights and obligations existing up to that point in the conversation. A sequence of unmarked code choices may be used to gain co-operation with speakers – for example a Kenyan national speaking Swahili to a security guard as an unmarked choice between strangers, but switching to Luyia to suggest the solidarity of historical ties, once the security guard deduces that they are of the same ethnic background. On the other hand, a switch to a marked choice may be used to go against social expectations, to temporally break conventions for a particular purpose. Myers-Scotton (1992) gives the example of a passenger using English to a bus conductor (rather than Swahili) to exaggerate social distance for particular reasons – in this case because he believes the conductor to be taking advantage of him. Generally South African studies (Finlayson and Slabbert 1997; Herbert 1997) corroborate Myers-Scotton's model. In addition, Herbert found a kind of parallel in speaker turns not mentioned by Myers-Scotton. University students were observed to initiate conversation with fellow students in an African language and then shift to English, the language associated with status and education. Thus the solidarity code always preceded the H (or "High") code. Thereafter, the rights and obligations model determined the degree of switching. Finlayson and Slabbert (1997), however, suggest a major difference in their studies of multilingual adults in the same geographical area (the Witwatersrand), noting that speakers of Zulu are reluctant to switch and accommodate to other speakers of African languages. From a Myers-Scotian perspective this is tantamount to the language accruing an imbalance in which speakers' rights are generally emphasised above their obligations. However, it is not difficult to imagine a scenario where a Zulu speaker seeking an urgent favour did switch to another language. Younger speakers who opt as much as possible for an urban mixed form (Tsotsitaal or Iscamtho) in contexts that allow it are, in fact, defusing some of the power and authority of Zulu associated with their elders.

The African research, with its layers of multilingualism, shows more starkly how power, ideology and youth identities are involved in code-switching than research in societies in which the hegemony of one language is sealed (English in the UK, French in France, etc.), or in which power sharing between high-status languages occurs (French and English in Canada). Proficient speakers often need to be able to balance their languages in the same speech event or context, rather than deploy them chronologically according to discrete domains.

6.6 Conclusion

A multilingual and formerly colonised society like South Africa shows the difficulty of a unified sociolinguistic model predicated on an unambiguously prestigious language. As shown in this chapter aspects of power, prestige and solidarity are distributed across speakers' repertoires. This has implications for many key concepts in linguistics and sociolinguistics, including criteria for conceptualising a native speaker. However, I would not go so far as some analysts who argue that there are no rules underlying combinations of languages, or even that languages themselves do not exist, only multilingual resources. Careful attention to domains of use, needs and intentions of speakers, their degrees of "involvement" (versus alienation) in the society, and the prevailing rights and obligations associated with languages or combinations of languages will demonstrate greater cohesion than apparent to the outside observer.

Notes

1 The SADC includes a few other countries not generally considered "Southern African" – e.g. Tanzania.
2 As is well known, South African Dutch developed into Afrikaans in the course of time.
3 South Africa has the additional complexity of two ex-colonial languages being official – Afrikaans and English.
4 The term "antilanguage" is taken from Halliday's (1978) insightful analysis of secret codes of the underworld, in which phonological and semantic patterns of the mainstream language are symbolically overturned.
5 In many areas, this standard English is not achieved, on account of lack of access to the relevant model (see, e.g., De Klerk 2006). Instead, a discernible Black variety of English has arisen, and is possibly on the rise.
6 An exception might be the form of African languages as used on radio and television, an important topic for language standardisation that awaits the scrutiny of African-language specialists.
7 "Coloured" in South African colonial and apartheid terms denotes a social group of multiple ancestries, distinguished from "Black" and "White".
8 However, the government's use of only English in the most public and official situations has had its critics, most notably the late Neville Alexander (e.g. 2002).
9 The qualification "or so" is necessary to cover slight uncertainty concerning subclasses and of elements that would now be considered adverbials rather than nouns.
10 Ngcobo (2013: 27) calls this class 9a, a sub-class of 9, which involves loanwords without a nasal in the prefix.

Further reading

Herbert, Robert K. (ed.) (1993) *Foundations in Southern African Linguistics*. Johannesburg: Witwatersrand University Press.
Mesthrie, Rajend (ed.) (2002) *Language in South Africa*. Cambridge: Cambridge University Press.
Webb, Victor (2002) *Language in South Africa: The Role of Language in National Transformation, Reconstruction, and Development*. Amsterdam: Benjamins.

References

Alexander, Neville (2002) Linguistic Rights, Language Planning and Democracy in Post-apartheid South Africa. In: *Language Policy. Lessons from Global Models*. Steven J. Baker (ed.), 116–29. Monterey: Monterey Institute of International Studies.
Bourdieu, Pierre (1991) *Language and Symbolic Power*. Cambridge: Polity Press.
Calteaux, Karen (1996) *Standard and Non-standard African Language Varieties in the Urban Areas of South Africa: Main Report for the STANON Research Programme*. Pretoria: HSRC Publishers.
Chishimba, Maurice (1984) African Varieties of English: Text in Context. PhD dissertation, University of Illinois.
Coulmas, Florian (1989) Language Adaptation. In: *Language Adaptation*. Florian Coulmas (ed.), 1–25. Cambridge: Cambridge University Press.
de Klerk, Vivian (2006) *Corpus Linguistics and World Englishes: A Study of Xhosa English*. London: Continuum.
Finlayson, Rosalie (1984) The Changing Nature of Isihlonipho Sabafazi. *African Studies* 43(2): 137–46.
——(1998) The Linguistic Implications of the Xhosa Initiation Schools. *Language Matters* 29: 101–16.
Finlayson, Rosalie and Sarah Slabbert (1997) "We just Mix" – Code-Switching in a South African Township. *International Journal of the Sociology of Language* 125: 65–91.
Gough, David (1996) Black English in South Africa. In: *Focus on South Africa*. Vivian de Klerk (ed.), 53–78. Amsterdam: John Benjamins.
Halliday, Michael A.K. (1978) *Language as Social Semiotic*. London. Edward Arnold.
Haugen, Einar (1972) *The Ecology of Language*. Stanford: Stanford University Press.
Herbert, Robert (1997) The Meaning of Language Choices in South Africa. In: *African Linguistics at the Crossroads*. Robert K. Herbert (ed.), 395–415. Cologne: Rüdiger Köpper Verlag.
Kachru, Braj (1986) *The Alchemy of English: The Spread, Functions and Models of Non-native Englishes*. Oxford: Pergamon.
Kahane, Henry (1986) Typology of the Prestige Language. *Language* 62(3): 495–508.
Labov, William (1972) *Sociolinguistic Patterns*. Philadelphia: University of Pennsylvania Press.
Lanham, Leonard and Carol Macdonald (1979) *The Standard in South African History and its Social History*. Heidelberg: Julius Groos Verlag.
Lass, Roger (1995) South African English. In: *Language and Social History: Studies in South African Sociolinguistics*. Rajend Mesthrie (ed.), 89–106. Cape Town: David Philip.
Magura, Benjamin (1984) Style and Meaning in African English: A Sociolinguistic Analysis of South African and Zimbabwean English. PhD dissertation, University of Illinois.
McArthur, Tom (1998) *The English Languages*. Cambridge: Cambridge University Press.
Mesthrie, Rajend (1992) *English in Language Shift: The History, Structure and Sociolinguistics of South African Indian English*. Cambridge: Cambridge University Press.
Mesthrie, Rajend (ed.) (2002) *Language in South Africa*. Cambridge: Cambridge University Press.
Mesthrie, Rajend (2008) South Africa: The Rocky Road to Nation Building. In: *Language and National Identity in Africa*. Andrew Simpson (ed.), 314–28. Oxford: Oxford University Press.

——(2010) Socio-phonetics and Social Change. Deracialisation of the GOOSE Vowel in South African English. *Journal of Sociolinguistics* 14(1): 3–33.
Mesthrie, Rajend and Rakesh Bhatt (2008) *World Englishes: The Study of New Linguistic Varieties.* Cambridge: Cambridge University Press.
Mesthrie, Rajend and Ellen Hurst (2013) Slang Registers, Code-switching and Restructured Urban Varieties in South Africa: An Analytic Overview of Tsotsitaals with Special Reference to the Cape Town Variety. *Journal of Pidgin and Creole Languages* 28(1): 103–30.
Mesthrie, Rajend, Joan Swann, Ana Deumert and William Leap (2009) *Introducing Sociolinguistics.* Edinburgh: Edinburgh University Press.
Myers-Scotton, Carol (1985) "What the Heck, Sir?" – Style Shifting and Lexical Colouring as Features of Powerful Language. In: *Sequence and Pattern in Communicative Behaviour.* Richard Street Jr. and Joseph Cappella (eds), 103–19. London: Edward Arnold.
——(1992) Codeswitching in Africa: A Model of the Social Functions of Code Selection. In: *Language and Society in Africa: The Theory and Practice of Sociolinguistics.* Robert K. Herbert (ed.), 165–79. Johannesburg: Witwatersrand University Press.
——(1993) *Social Motivations for Code-Switching: Evidence from Africa.* Oxford: Clarendon.
Ngcobo, Mtholeni (2013) Loanword Classification in isiZulu: The Need for a Sociolinguistic Approach. *Language Matters* 44(1): 21–38.
Trudgill, Peter (1986) *Sociolinguistics* (second edition). Harmondsworth: Penguin.
van der Walt, Johan and Bertus van Rooy (2002) Towards a Norm in South African Englishes. *World Englishes* 21(1): 113–28.
van Warmelo, N.J. (1971) Courts and Court Speech in Venda. *African Studies* 30: 355–70.
Wood, Tahir (1987) Perceptions of and Attitudes towards Varieties of English in the Cape Peninsula, with Particular Reference to the "Coloured Community". MA thesis, Rhodes University (Grahamstown, South Africa).

PART II
Less developed countries

Introduction to Part II

The regions and countries discussed in this section of the volume are not only in similar positions on the Human Development Index, that is higher than the previous set of countries/regions, they also have in common that they are sociolinguistically highly transitional. For some of them, most notably China, the position on this index is changing, making their sociolinguistic future hard to predict, and creating an increased necessity towards sociolinguistic description of the current transitional period.

In China the sociolinguistic situation has developed relatively independently from Western colonial powers, making it a particularly interesting setting to compare with other sociolinguistic situations; those that developed without abrupt, intrusive and long-term outside linguistic and cultural interference and dominance, namely the settings in most of the Western European countries. What is true in both China and Western Europe may in fact be universally true for such societies. China deserves special attention because of its swift move up the Human Development Index; changes, including sociolinguistic ones, are taking place at a high rate. Chinese theories regarding the linguistic effects of heavy urbanisation may be of particular interest to Western European sociolinguists; in that and other respects China's sociolinguistic situation is at a more advanced stage and may give the West a glimpse of the future.

The three regions of South Asia, North Africa and the Caribbean are all dealing with the effects of colonisation and its language legacy. In all three regions, a dominant language is present which carries the ambiguous status of language of the uninvited former coloniser on the one hand, and that of language of social opportunity, officiality and overtly high status on the other. Independence, economic growth and the ensuing self-assurance are currently leading to situations where more localised languages, including mixed ones, are challenging the status of the formerly undisputed high-status language.

In India, the case discussed in the South Asia chapter, we find highly distinct language ecologies. When studying shift in style, the picture emerging from sociolinguistic studies in India is also quite different and unexpected. This chapter informs us about the situation in India, while at the same time creating awareness of widespread assumptions underlying sociolinguistic style shift and audience design. One such assumption is that linguistic diversity is the battlefield in which social inequality is practised. Specific ideologies regarding phenomena such as "standard language", "written language", "lingua franca", "dialect" and "minority language" have long been applied in mainstream sociolinguistics, but their definitions and connotations are far from universal. Language does not directly and predictably serve as an index of social inequality.

The chapter on North Africa cautions the reader not to treat gender as referring to fixed categories. Instead, gender is "being done" in specific contexts. It is therefore necessary to de-essentialise concepts of language and society before applying them to specific case studies. In this chapter language variation emerges as a fluid resource to explain expression of social structure. The chapter on the Caribbean also hints at the need to reconsider existing categories and discusses diglossia and the Creole continuum from a fresh perspective. It is argued, in particular, that the experiences of colonisation have been underestimated by diglossia theory. Colonisation results in an uneven distribution of linguistic codes and hence to a different functional loading of these codes in comparison with diglossia in non-colonised societies. In order to study language choices in such contexts, a shift away from "language" or from "continuum" is practised and in its place we find a system where elements of individually distinct "linguistic pools" are mixed in patterned ways.

7
SPEECH COMMUNITY AND LINGUISTIC URBANIZATION

Sociolinguistic theories developed in China

Daming Xu

7.1 Introduction

The most prominent topic of mainstream (Anglo-European) sociolinguistics in the last decade seems to be indexicality. Efforts are being made to define the ranges of sociolinguistic symbolism; that is, what indicates or marks what in what order or field (Silverstein 2003; Eckert 2008, among others). While rejecting macro-social categories (socio-economic class, race, gender, age, etc.) as too vague and overarching, researchers tended to resort to smaller social units for closer connections of language use and social identities (Milroy 1980; Meyerhoff 1997; Eckert 2000; Zhang 2005, among others). In the following, I will introduce a slightly different approach to the question, as characterized in a number of studies in Chinese sociolinguistics. While initially being intrigued by the findings of sociolinguistic stratification (Labov 1966) and sociolinguistic interaction (Gumperz 1982, 2003), Chinese sociolinguists attempted to integrate the two into an interaction-based sociolinguistic system. We proposed the Theory of Speech Community (TSC; see Xu 2004, 2006b, etc.) and the Theory of Linguistic Urbanization (TLU; see Xu 2006a; van den Berg and Xu 2010, etc.) to account for the complexity of sociolinguistic indexicality, the former dealing with the "ranges" issue and the latter with its dynamic aspect. While the two theories mentioned above will be the focus of this chapter, for a more general account of Chinese sociolinguistics, readers are referred to Zhou (2010) and Gao (forthcoming). The theories contrast with the mainstream theories in that they do not only take a static view of sociolinguistic symbolism but also demonstrate how this symbolism has arrived in a process of community formation.

7.2 China's language situation

The relatively independent and rapid development of Chinese sociolinguistics in the twenty-first century is evidently contextualized in the fast-paced and far-reaching changes of contemporary Chinese society. China, the most populous country in the world, is also richly multiethnic and multilingual. The latest census tallied 1,370 million persons in China and they are designated as belonging to 56 different ethnic groups (Population Census Office 2013). Among the groups, "Han" is the majority group taking up 91.51 per cent of the total population while the remaining 8.49 per cent comprises 55 minority groups. The government websites list more than 80 languages, and recent publications in China report more than 130 languages.[1] Through a history of over two millennia, the written standard of the Chinese language has emerged on the basis of a continuous literary tradition. In the early twentieth century, a spoken standard was officially launched after the founding of the Republic of China, but it would not be fully implemented until the 1950s. The unifying powers of the shared writing and literary traditions have always been felt, and the standardization efforts building on it have made obvious results – especially in the last few decades, since the official standard called "Putonghua" was effectively popularized.

Among the changes that have taken place in China recently, the processes of industrialization, urbanization and the transition from a planned to a market economy have been felt particularly and they have directly impacted on language situations in China. A host of new language phenomena emerged, some previously uncommon ones became common, and some previously normal ones became atypical. In other words, languages and dialects are disappearing while new linguistic varieties emerge, and new media of language communication modify old linguistic forms and produce new ones. At the same time, the ways in which people use language have also changed. The examples include, evidently, netspeak, code-mixing, linguistic hybridization, new pragmatic strategies and many other innovative ways of using language (State Language Commission 2006–11).

However, as will become clear below, the most fundamental linguistic changes are the restructuring and reorganization of speech communities due to the unprecedented scale and magnitude of mass migration and social mobility.

7.3 Sociolinguistics in China

Sociolinguistics was introduced in China in the 1980s, but its initial stage of development was limited by a lack of research focus and a lack of organization. At the turn of the twenty-first century, sociolinguistics in China entered a new stage. In 2001, the First International Conference on Chinese Sociolinguistics was held in Beijing. Following that event, the Association of Chinese Sociolinguistics (ACS) was founded and the *Journal of Chinese Sociolinguistics* was launched in 2003. In the same year, the Sociolinguistics Laboratory of Nanjing University (SLNU) was set up. From then on, sociolinguistics in China was conducted in a more organized fashion, and, due to the leading roles played by ACS and SLNU, a few new research focuses were gradually formed. Subsequently, the China Centre for Linguistic and Strategic Studies (CCLASS) was set up at Nanjing University in 2007. Building on the sociolinguistics tradition in Nanjing, CCLASS initialized a new trend of applied research, namely applying sociolinguistics theories to resolve current problems in society. A series of attempts were made to integrate sociolinguistics theories and findings with the evaluation and formulation of language policies (Xu and Wang 2012). For instance, issues and problems arising from the restructuring and reorganization of speech communities were investigated, and the results of this research influenced the formation of public policy.

While mainstream sociolinguistics theories provide us with the general framework for the analysis of speakers' identities and intents (Meyerhoff 2006), the changing realities in China prompt us to adopt the more dynamic perspective of linguistic symbolism and indexicality, which started our theorization attempts. Our focus on theoretical thinking was also due to the pressure involved with dealing with problems of language, communication and identity in the population perspective of the country.

7.4 The Theory of Speech Community

As pointed out by Patrick (2002), the "speech community", although a time-honoured concept, remains controversial and lacks focused treatment (Patrick 2002: 573–74). Consequently, it has become clear that the situation is caused by the lack of a general theory on speech community. A theory is needed in which speech community as a concept takes up a central rather than a peripheral position, while linking up to other important concepts in sociolinguistics. Xu (2004) is an attempt to build the theory. According to the theory, the speech community is a system of speakers that itself deserves focused study as much as other linguistic systems such as phonology or syntax (Xu 2004). With the complement of a system of speakers, the set of linguistic systems becomes more complete. Currently, a grammaticality judgement, that is whether a particular form belongs to a particular system, tends to be an arbitrary decision, which is sometimes seen in the disagreement among "native speakers", the power of decision lies with the speech community, not with individuals. It is through the establishment of a speech community that we may define a language and not the other way round (see Lyons 1970).

Patrick (2002) points out the tautology in defining a speech community with its language and, vice versa, its language with the community. Therefore, the question regarding language and speech community is: which comes first? The Speech Community Theory (Xu 2004) provides a definite answer to this question: the speech community comes first. First, a group of speakers form a speech community through sustained interactions among themselves. Then, a language may be generated in the speech community. There can be a speech community without a recognized language, but there cannot be a language that is not traceable to a particular speech community (Xu 2004: 21).

Patrick (2002) also raises the question whether a speech community is a real entity. In our theory, the answer, again, is yes (Xu 2004: 22). By extending a sociological theory of community (Tönnies 1955; Cohen 1985; Smith 2001; Wagner 2004/2005), we regard the speech community as a social organization, an organization of speakers. As an existing phenomenon, it is discoverable and definable through objective measures of its features and strengths. Through this perspective, the formation process of a new speech community can be revealing, and thus I will introduce a case of speech community formation in the following.

7.4.1 The application of the Theory of Speech Community: the formation of the Kundulun speech community

The study of variation in Mandarin nasal finals in the Kundulun community is focused on the formation process of a new speech community (Xu 2010). Mandarin is the largest dialect of the Chinese language, boasting over 900 million speakers. The so-called "Mandarin nasal variation", referring to the variable realizations of the nasal rhymes (called "nasal finals" in Chinese linguistics) in natural speech, was found in all Mandarin varieties that have been investigated (Barale 1982; Xu 1992, among others). The Kundulun community in Baotou Municipality, Inner Mongolia, originated in the 1950s and it was formed with a sudden influx of industrial migrants who spoke a host of different Mandarin and non-Mandarin dialects. The community was first investigated sociolinguistically in 1987 and re-investigated in 2006 (Xu 1992, 1993; Xu and Wu 2006; Xu 2010, among others). In both investigations, Mandarin was found to be the major linguistic variety of the community.

In the study, three linguistic variables in Mandarin nasal finals – nasalization of the vowel nucleus of the syllable, deletion of the consonantal coda of the syllable and retroflexion of the vowel nucleus of the syllable – were identified. The realizations of the variables in audio-taped speech were examined, that is whether the nasalization, retroflexion or deletion actually occurred in each token of the realization. In the 1987 investigation, 70 speakers were interviewed and in the 2006 investigation 83 speakers were interviewed. The data on the speakers' performances in nasal variation were subjected to a quantitative analysis. In line with standard procedure in variation analysis, the variation of Mandarin nasal finals was analysed for their internal (linguistic) and external (social) constraints. For each of the variables, its internal and external constraints were obtained through an examination of a host of social and linguistic factors using the Variable Rule Program (VARBRUL) (Sankoff 1988; Tagliamonte 2012, among others).

When the first investigation was carried out in Kundulun in 1987, we expected to have results resembling what was found in most of the other investigations at the time (predominantly conducted in highly industrialized societies). However, it turned out that many external constraints found elsewhere were not found here, and the internal constraints also appeared to be fewer. The second investigation of the community was conducted in 2006. Interestingly, the results of the second investigation were remarkably different in that many more external and internal constraints were found.

In the investigations, the variables were examined with ten phonological factors as potential internal constraints. Importantly, all three variables had an increased number of constraints in the later investigation. In the first investigation, out of the ten potential ones, only seven constraints were actually found for nasalization and for deletion, and only five were found for retroflexion. In contrast, in the second investigation, all ten constraints were found for nasalization, nine for deletion and six for retroflexion.

In comparison with the changes in internal constraints, the changes in external factors were more drastic. Seven socio-stylistic factors were included in the analysis as potential external constraints. In the first investigation, out of the seven potentials only three were actually found for nasalization, two for deletion and none for retroflexion. Moreover, certain social constraints which were commonly found in other speech community investigations, such as age, gender and education, were not found for any of the variables in this investigation. By comparison, the 2006 investigation found that all three variables were constrained, whereas the 1987 investigation found that only two of them were constrained. Moreover, all variables had an increased number of constraints. Now nasalization was constrained by all seven factors, deletion by six and retroflexion by five.

The study also noted the expansion of ranges of variation for the variables. The range of variation refers to the difference between the largest factor weight and the smallest factor weight of the factor group in the results of VARBRUL analyses (Xu 2010: 133). There were 19 internal constraints found for the three variables in both investigations. Remarkably, all of them enlarged their ranges of variation in the later investigation with the exception of one, which decreased only slightly (Xu 2010: 134–35).

A set of constraints for a variable makes up a constraint pattern (Tagliamonte 2012). From the above results, we can see that the constraint patterns for nasal variation in Mandarin as spoken in Kundulun were enriched and strengthened during the time between the two investigations. This is shown both by the increased number of constraints and the enlarged ranges of variation.

According to TSC, the nature of a constraint pattern is "the shared evaluation of linguistic variables" and "uniformity of abstract patterns of variation", which are two defining features of a speech community (Labov 1972; Patrick 2002; Xu 2004). Therefore, the richer and stronger patterns of variation represent increased "shared-ness" and "uniformity" in the behaviours and attitudes of community members (Xu 2010: 132).

The Kundulun case shows the maturation process of a speech community with reference to its history as a migrant community. In the initial stage of dialect contact, speakers do not have much in common in their evaluation of the linguistic variables because they have just arrived from different speech communities. Consequently, there is a shortage of constraint patterns when viewed at the level of the speech community. However, with a sustained period of daily interactions, the speakers gradually adjust towards each other in their speech. In time the sociolinguistic patterns of usage and evaluation will form.

The Kundulun study shows that constraint patterns emerge and strengthen over time, and we interpret this as a process of speech community formation. It is known that a new dialect may emerge as a result of long-term speech accommodation in a dialect contact situation (Trudgill 2003: 35). However, as predicted by TSC, a new dialect may or may not emerge, but if it does it emerges in a speech community (Xu 2004). Therefore, linguists have so far ignored a precondition for the emergence of a language, which, first and foremost, has to originate in a speech community. In studies of similar language situations, the Koineization perspective is usually adopted, which differs from the one adopted in the Kundulun study. Although they refer to some social conditions, Koineization studies are more concerned with the linguistic systems of forms. What is missing is the system of speakers that is the basis of the systems of forms.

7.4.2 Other demonstrations of the Theory of Speech Community

There have by now been several dozens of studies on speech communities in China employing the perspective of TSC (see papers in Xu and Gao 2005; van de Berg and Xu 2010, among others). For instance, Fu (2011) made a thorough investigation of the Fu village in Wuwei county, Anhui province. He interviewed every one of the 249 villagers living there. While collecting speech data from them, he also gauged the villagers' language attitudes, migrant histories and other social traits. Among the variables he studied was the address term for a male parent. Three different terms, *Da-da*, *A-ye* and *Ba-ba*, with the same referential meaning, were used in different families of the village in spite of the fact that they all speak the same dialect. Initially, on the basis of sociolinguistic literature, Fu suspected that age, education and migrant history were possible constraints of the variation. Then he brought in the factor of social mobility in his analysis. In adopting TSC, he found that the spread of the new term *Ba-ba* was more aptly explained with the structural change of the speech community, which was in turn motivated by social mobility.

As another example of application of TSC, Xu and Wang (2009) proposed the concept of the Global Chinese Community (GCC) by applying TSC. The component of "identification" of speech communities (Xu 2004) is emphasized in the application. Different from the models of language spread, the GCC is not geographically defined, but the community is based on its members' identification with "Huayu" (the term used in overseas Chinese communities for Standard Chinese) and their use of Huayu. Hence, the internal cohesion of the GCC is much stronger than that of the International English-knowing Speech Community (Kachru 2005) because the former is characteristically a product of its membership's act of identity.

The Chinese studies mentioned above represent an attempt towards a paradigm shift in sociolinguistics and in linguistics. They differ in their perspective from many studies of similar sociolinguistic settings. The studies of new-town or migration effects on language changes have been carried out successfully in many places (Britain and Trudgill 2005; Kerswill and Williams 2000, among others). In most of these studies, social factors including migration and others are brought in to explain linguistic variation and change. The explanations show why a language is the way it is and how a new dialect is formed. However, contrasting to their society-explains-language approach, TSC allows us to go in the opposite language-explains-society direction.

When we show how a speech community is formed we try to explain why the society is the way it is due to its linguistic conditions.

7.4.3 The Theory of Linguistic Urbanization

The accelerated process of urbanization in China started in the last decade of the twentieth century, as a consequence of the impact of the economic reforms taking place at the time. As a result, China's urban population reached 52.6 per cent of the total population in 2012, while it was only 26 per cent in 1990. On the basis of the current trend, it is projected that 70 per cent of China's population will live in urban areas by 2035. The populations of many big cities in China have doubled in a matter of one or two decades, with rural-to-urban migration as the major source of growth.

A number of Chinese sociolinguists responded to this situation of urbanization (Yang 2002; Xu 2010; Fu 2011, among others). When it was set up, the Sociolinguistics Laboratory of Nanjing University adopted the so-called Urban Language Survey (ULS) as its special area of research,[2] on top of the commonly accessed areas of language variation and change and language contact. A small seminar with the theme of ULS took place at the inauguration of the laboratory in 2003. Since then it has grown into a series of conferences with an increasing number of participants. So far, the conferences have been held in many different places in Mainland China, Hong Kong, Japan, Germany and the Netherlands. The studies shown at the conferences addressed issues of social communication in urban settings, identity formation and re-formation induced by language shifts, and formation and restructuring of speech communities, as well as other issues in sociolinguistics. Like a spin-off from its predecessor, ULS inherits all the theories and methods from the general enterprise of sociolinguistics, but it is now gradually relinquishing its "sociolinguistics for language" orientation. It embraces more of a "sociolinguistics for society" orientation. One of the results is TLU (Xu 2012).

The TLU attempts to model the changing linguistic realities in the societal process of urbanization. The dynamic perspective of TLU would have been initially inspired by the sociolinguistic focus on language change, especially change-in-progress, but TLU focuses on changes in the structure of a speech community and changes in the relations among speech communities. It goes from description to explanation, from understanding the changing language situation to an understanding of the nature of language.

7.4.4 The Nanjing language survey

In the Nanjing language survey, which was conducted in Nanjing in 2002, a new method was developed, adapted from Labov's (1966) "rapid and anonymous survey" method. A specific communicative event, "asking the way", was chosen as a window to look into language communication in urban settings. Specifically, language use was observed with fieldworkers posing as individuals walking in the street and seeking directions from passers-by. In order to be representative of the whole city, a sampling method was developed with a city map. The survey locations were selected with a random digit table from a list of serially numbered areas, which were defined in a gridded city map. The focus of observation was on the subjects' language use, that is what language variety or varieties they would use in response to the request for direction. As a sociolinguistic investigation, the speakers' demographic features, such as age and gender, were also systematically noted down. The research question was: Is Nanjing a speech community, and how do we determine the status of a speech community?

According to TSC, a speech community is an effective body of language communication made up of a population (Xu 2004). Therefore, the effectiveness of communication was studied as a variable in the Nanjing survey. Because the speech event of "asking the way" was an encounter between two strangers, there was no guarantee that there would be a successful case of communication. Therefore, the concept of speech community was operationalized into "successful communications" among strangers in the street in the study. Three values were defined for the variable of effective communication: "successful", "partially successful" and "unsuccessful". Other variables of language use being studied were the "insider language" and the "outsider language". The former refers to the language use with a known person (e.g. walking together) while the latter refers to the language use with strangers (e.g. with the direction-seeker). As shown by the results, the insider and the outsider language use was frequent in different varieties (Xu 2006b: 181).

The Nanjing investigation makes explicit what a speech community is. In sociolinguistics, an urban community is usually tacitly accepted as a speech community without evaluation or justification. Although it is not problematic for most cases, it is not an infallible truth. For instance, in some cities where the population includes a large proportion of new residents, whether there is a speech community is cast in doubt. However, it is found that Nanjing remained a speech community in spite of the influxes of migrants as results of urbanization. It is found that most cases of communications were successful (96 per cent), which means that among the unacquainted speakers in Nanjing effective communication was default. To achieve this, the speakers would have to share some language codes and also the norms on how to behave in the specific situation where communication takes place (Xu 2006b: 184).

On the basis of the survey, the researcher concluded that Nanjinghua was the base dialect for the Nanjing speech community (being used over 60 per cent and around 50 per cent as an insider and outsider language, respectively) and Putonghua was the next important code (being used around 10 per cent and over 30 per cent as insider and outsider language). Therefore, Nanjing was a Nanjinghua-Putonghua bi-dialectal speech community. As shown by the results, a speech community is not completely uniform, but is an "ordered heterogeneity" (Weinreich et al. 1968). Members of the community do not use just one linguistic code and different codes are used to different degrees. However, just as Nanjinghua is the symbolic language for the community, the success rates of communication, the sharing rates of the set of language codes and the similar patterns of language choice, and other survey results all show the main trends in the community.

The "ordered heterogeneity" is also shown by the structure of the speech community. As shown by the survey data, the Nanjing speech community can be separated by location into core and marginal areas. Language choice behaviours were found to be more typical of the main trend in core areas than in the marginal areas. The "heterogeneity" issue, first raised by Weinreich et al. (1968), contradicts the assumption of mainstream linguistics that there is uniformity. As shown by the Nanjing results, while language as an idealized formal system can be uniform, the speech community is an ordered heterogeneity.

Apart from addressing theoretical issues, the Nanjing Language Survey (Xu 2006b) contributes to the standardization of Urban Language Survey methods. With similar methods, a large number of surveys have been conducted in Chinese cities. Researchers also adapted the method in studies of address terms used in public places (Ge 2005), and in measuring the spread of Putonghua in proportion to mobile population (Zhang and Xu 2008).[3] For a general survey, readers are referred to van den Berg (forthcoming).

7.5 Conclusion

Contemporary Chinese society has provided special motivations for the development of sociolinguistics. China is the largest country in the world population-wise, and an ancient civilization that is now experiencing an unprecedented scale and magnitude of economic and social changes. It is simultaneously becoming one of the most linguistically complex and dynamic places in the world. The proliferating and aggravating problems of changing linguistic realities call for a solution with the aid of both new and old theories. Consequently, TSC and TLU were developed to meet these needs. The former stems from the variationist tradition of sociolinguistics but moves on to focusing on the structures of the speech community instead of structures of sounds and sentences. The latter was initially motivated by the need for descriptions for practical purposes such as management and planning (Li 2010; Spolsky forthcoming), but, through the combination with the speech community theory, it now provides a new understanding of language.

The theories may have more general appeals than just their applications in China. The TSC explains the juncture between language and society, and it also creates bridges between linguistics and sociology. With the community-primacy principle of TSC, the questions about how language operates and changes are one step closer to being answered. That "language is an adaptive system" (The Five Graces Group 2009) may be the first step in answering the question. It then begs the question, what motivates these adaptations? The question is answered if we apply TSC. A language is not really a living thing nor can it really adapt. It has the illusion of life by being attached to a living entity – the speech community. A speech community, as a social system, is by definition a "living system" (Miller

1978; Bailey 2006). It is an oversimplification to say that language changes in its social context. It omits the important link between language and society – the speech community. What we see as changes in language are artefacts of adaptations of speech community towards changes in society.

Now we may return to the issues on the ranges of indexicality. Where does the sociolinguistic symbolism stop? It stops at the end of a speech community, as shown by the fields of its interpretation (Eckert 2008). Moreover, it is structured inside the speech community. The structures and structuring of the speech community are revealed vividly in its movement, as shown by the cases of speech community formation and linguistic urbanization.

Notes

1 The statuses of many Chinese varieties as an independent language or dialect of another language are in controversy, much as it is elsewhere. However, it is not necessary for us to go into the controversy here.
2 Although ULS is, strictly speaking, a research tool, it is nevertheless seen as an area of research. It refers to a group of studies that focus on the urbanization impacts on languages and speech communities. These studies use a variety of sociolinguistic methods but most often the social survey method.
3 "Mobile population" is a translation of a term in Chinese, *luidong rekou*, sometimes also translated as "floating population". The concept arises in the Chinese context as any resident in PRC is required to make a residential registry. Zhang and Xu (2008) refer to people who live in Nanjing but whose official residential registries are not in Nanjing. In pre-reform years (before the 1980s), it was illegal to live for a long period where your registries are not. Now, the mobile population is officially recognized and individuals can be given "temporary registries" which can last for years.

Further reading

Xu, Daming (2004) *Yanyu shequ lilun* [Speech Community Theory]. *Journal of Chinese Sociolinguistics* 1: 18–28.
Xu, Daming (2006a) Urban Language Survey. *Journal of Chinese Sociolinguistics* 2: 1–15.
Xu, Daming (2010) The Formation of a Speech Community: Mandarin Nasal Finals in Baotou. In: *Industrialization and the Re-structuring of Speech Communities in China and Europe*. Marinus van den Berg and Daming Xu (eds), 120–40. Newcastle: Cambridge Scholars.

References

Bailey, Kenneth D. (2006) Living Systems Theory and Social Entropy Theory. *Systems Research and Behavioral Science* 23(3): 291–300.
Barale, Catherine (1982) A Quantitative Analysis of the Loss of Final Consonants in Beijing Mandarin. PhD dissertation, University of Pennsylvania.
Britain, David and Peter Trudgill (2005) New Dialect Formation and Contact-induced Reallocation. Three Case Studies from the English Fens. *International Journal of English Studies* 5(1): 183–209.
Cohen, Anthony P. (1985) *The Symbolic Construction of Community*. London: Tavistock.
Eckert, Penelope (2000) *Linguistic Variation as Social Practice*. Oxford: Blackwell.
——(2008) Variation and Indexical Field. *Journal of Sociolinguistics* 12(4): 453–76.

Fu, Yirong (2011) *Yanyu shequ he yuyan bianhua yanjiu: Jiyu anhui fucun de shehui yuyanxue diaocha* [Studies of the Speech Community and Language Change: A Sociolinguistic Investigation of the Fu Village in Anhui]. Beijing: Peking University Press.
Gao, Yihong (forthcoming) Chinese Sociolinguistics. In: *Encyclopedia of Chinese Linguistics*. Zev Handel et al. (eds). Leiden: Brill.
Ge, Yanhong (2005) *Nanjingshi Xiaojie chenghuyu de diaocha fenxi* [The Investigation of the Address Term Xiaojie in Nanjing]. *Journal of Chinese Sociolinguistics* 2: 196–206.
Gumperz, John J. (1982) *Discourse Strategies*. Cambridge: Cambridge University Press.
——(2003) On the Development of Interactional Sociolinguistics. *Language Teaching and Linguistic Studies* 1: 1–10.
Kachru, Braj B. (2005) *Asian Englishes beyond the Canon*. New Delhi: Oxford University Press.
Kerswill, Paul and Ann Williams (2000) Creating a New Town Koiné: Children and Language Change in Milton Keynes. *Language in Society* 29: 65–115.
Labov, William (1966) *The Social Stratification of English in New York City*. Washington: Centre for Applied Linguistics.
——(1972) *Sociolinguistic Patterns*. Philadelphia: University of Pennsylvania Press.
Li, Yuming (2010) Language Planning in the People's Republic of China: Language Function Planning. In: *Industrialization and the Re-structuring of Speech Communities in China and Europe*. Marinus van den Berg and Daming Xu (eds), 24–34. Newcastle: Cambridge Scholars.
Lyons, John (1970) *New Horizons in Linguistics*. London: Penguin.
Meyerhoff, Miriam (1997) Engendering Identities: Pronoun Selection as an Indicator of Salient Intergroup Identities. *University of Pennsylvania Working Papers in Linguistics* 4(2): 23–68.
——(2006) *Introducing Sociolinguistics*. London: Routledge.
Miller, James G. (1978) *Living Systems*. New York: McGraw-Hill.
Milroy, Lesley (1980) *Language and Social Networks*. Oxford: Blackwell.
Patrick, Peter (2002) The Speech Community. In: J.K. Chambers, Peter Trudgill and Natalie Schilling-Estes (eds), *The Handbook of Language Variation and Change*. Malden: Blackwell Publishers.
Population Census Office (2013) *Tabulation on the 2010 Population Census of the People's Republic of China*. Beijing: China Statistics Press.
Sankoff, David (1988) Sociolinguistics and Syntactic Variation. In: *Linguistics. The Cambridge Survey*. Frederick J. Newmeyer (ed.), 140–61. Cambridge: Cambridge University Press.
Silverstein, Michael (2003) Indexical Order and the Dialectics of Sociolinguistic Life. *Language and Communication* 23: 193–229.
Smith, Mark K. (2001) What is Community? *Encyclopedia of Informal Education*. Online available at: www.infed.org/community/community.htm (accessed 22 March 2014).
Spolsky, Bernard (forthcoming) *Chinese Language Management* (manuscript).
State Language Commission (2006–11) *The Green Cover Book: Language Situation in China*. Beijing: Commercial Press.
Tagliamonte, Sali (2012) *Variationist Sociolinguistics: Change, Observation, Interpretation*. New York: John Wiley & Sons.
The Five Graces Group (2009) Language Is a Complex Adaptive System. Position Paper. *Language Learning* 59(Suppl.1): 1–26.
Tönnies, Ferdinand (1955) *Community and Association*, London: Routledge & Kegan Paul.
Trudgill, Peter (2003) *A Glossary of Sociolinguistics*. Edinburgh: Edinburgh University Press.
van den Berg, Marinus (forthcoming) Special issue on Urban Language Survey, *Journal of Asian Pacific Communication*.
van den Berg, Marinus and Daming Xu 2010. *Industrialization and the Re-structuring of Speech Communities in China and Europe*. Newcastle: Cambridge Scholars.
Wagner, Leonie (2004/2005) Community – A Theoretical Approach to a Big Issue. *I.U.C. Journal of Social Work Theory and Practice* 10. Online available at: www.bemidjistate.edu/

academics/publications/social_work_journal/issue10/articles/2_Community.htm (accessed 22 March 2014).
Weinreich, Uriel, William Labov and Marvin I. Herzog (1968) Empirical Foundations for a Theory of Language Change. In: *Directions for Historical Linguistics: A Symposium*, Winfred P. Lehmann and Yakov Malkiel (eds), 97–188. Austin: University of Texas Press.
Xu, Daming (1992) A Sociolinguistic Study of Mandarin Nasal Variation. Dissertation, University of Ottawa.
——(1993) Unexceptional Irregularities: Lexical Conditioning of Mandarin Nasal Deletion. *Diachronica* 10(2): 215–36.
——(2004) *Yanyu shequ lilun* [Speech Community Theory]. *Journal of Chinese Sociolinguistics* 1: 18–28.
——(2006a) Urban Language Survey. *Journal of Chinese Sociolinguistics* 2: 1–15.
——(2006b) Nanjing Language Survey and the Theory of Speech Community. *Journal of Asian Pacific Communication* 16(2): 175–96.
——(2010) The Formation of a Speech Community: Mandarin Nasal Finals in Baotou. In: *Industrialization and the Re-structuring of Speech Communities in China and Europe*. Marinus van den Berg and Daming Xu (eds), 120–40. Newcastle: Cambridge Scholars.
——(2012) Speech Communities in Transformation: The Effects of Linguistic Urbanization in China. Plenary Speech at Sociolinguistics Symposium 19, Berlin, 21–24 August.
Xu, Daming and Yihong Gao (eds) (2005) *Urban Language Survey* (= *Journal of Chinese Sociolinguistics* 5).
Xu, Daming and Cuiqin Wu (2006) The Formation of the Kundulun Speech Community. Sociolinguistics Symposium 16: June, Limerick, Ireland.
Xu, Daming and Tiekun Wang (2012) *China Language Strategies*. Shanghai: Yiwen Press.
Xu, Daming and Xiaomei Wang (2009) *Quanqiu huayu shequ shuolue* [Global Chinese Community]. *Jilin University Journal* (Social Science Edition) 49(2): 132–37.
Yang, Jinyi (2002) Zhongguo xinxing gongyequ yuyan zhuangtai yanjiu [Study of the Language Situation of Newly Emerged Industrial Area in China], *Yuwen yanjiu* [Language Study] 1(2): 28–33.
Zhang, Jingwei and Daming Xu (2008) Renkou liudong yu Putonghua puji [Population Movement and the Popularization of Putonghua]. *Applied Linguistics* 3: 43–52.
Zhang, Qing (2005) A Chinese Yuppie in Beijing. Phonological Variation and the Construction of a New Professional Identity. *Language in Society* 34(3): 431–66.
Zhou, Minglang (2010) Sociolinguistic Research in China. In: *The Routledge Handbook of Sociolinguistics Around the World*. Martin Ball (ed.), 67–80. London and New York: Routledge.

8

LANGUAGE VARIATION AND CHANGE

The Indian experience

Shobha Satyanath

8.1 Introduction

One of the key questions in sociolinguistic studies of speech communities has been, "what makes people alter their speech behavior when presented with linguistic choices?" (Meyerhoff 2006: 4–5). This question is central to the study of intra-speaker variation and hence to "style shift". While structural constraints may be important to an extent in addressing the question, it is the social and attitudinal factors that have a clear edge over the structural in the study of style shift. Unlike structural factors, the social and stylistic factors are closely linked to social structure, including those cultural norms and expectations of the speech community from which they derive their meaning and interpretation. It is, therefore, likely that the internal workings of these factors may vary across societies.

Drawing on available studies on Indian speech communities in Cherukunnam (Kerala), Silchar (Assam), Calcutta (West Bengal), Delhi (Delhi) and Kohima[1] (Nagaland), this chapter seeks to explore what can be learnt with respect to this aspect of the relationship (involving intra- and inter-speaker variation) between language and society in India, which is home to a large number of diverse linguistic communities.

Considering that the sociolinguistic tradition of language variation and change is relatively young in India, the findings reported here are based on a small collection of available sociolinguistic studies of speech communities, which have largely been produced over the past decade or so.[2] The research cited here includes unpublished doctoral and pre-doctoral dissertations and research in progress. Partially transcribed and analysed speech corpuses are amongst the data that have been studied.

8.2 The Indian sociolinguistic setting

What makes India a worthwhile site for sociolinguistic exploration is the presence of multiple linguistic communities with both shared and diverse internal organizations and social practices. This diversity prompted the new Indian nation-state to recognize multiple official languages during the 1950s – one (or more) for each of its constituent states and union territories. This was a deviation from the widely followed European model of linking one language to one nation-state (Anderson 1983; Foley 1997). India has more than 1,500 mother tongues grouped under 122 languages from four major linguistic families spread over some 34 states and union territories; of these, some 22 languages serve as the principal official state languages (Census of India 2001). Therefore, no state within India is linguistically or culturally homogeneous. The increased mobility of, and contact among, the population has increased the diversity within each state. What is remarkable about this diversity is the way it is organized and the way it functions. Furthermore, this diversity is not held together by a single national language.

One implication of the current linguistic organization is a new bilingualism. This, together with the traditional bilingualism, has resulted in multiple layers of languages at various levels. At the centre are the home and intra-community languages spoken by different linguistic communities. At the next outer layer are the local lingua francas, which may be the same as (as it is in the union territory of Delhi) or different from (as may be seen in Nagaland state) the state languages. Then, there are the state languages themselves. The outermost layer is represented by Hindi and English at the national level, which mainly serve as inter-state communication tools. In those places where the home languages are different from the state languages, people are more likely to be bilingual when using home and state languages. Considering the fact that many mother tongues are grouped under a single language, it is not difficult to find bilingualism in both a home language and the state language. This is particularly the case in the so-called Hindi states, as there are more than 49 constituent varieties listed under Hindi (ORGCC 2001).

Based on what has been written about linguistic models, one may be inclined to interpret the Indian linguistic model as a hierarchical one, but in reality it is not, as will be demonstrated later in this chapter. One finds multi-layered multilingual speech communities in India where the linguistic diversity is held together by participation in the local linguistic and social practices on the one hand, and by continuing diverse practices on the other. In addition, there are languages with a long history of literary, grammatical and religious traditions, whereas a vast majority of the modern vernaculars have only recently developed a written tradition, and some of these still continue to be essentially oral. A variety of languages cutting across societal layers serve as the medium of instruction at schools. As one goes higher up in the educational system the choices get narrowed down to the state languages and English. English is the state language in three Indian states, is an important language for education, administration and also a language of socialization in urban areas. Though English has not replaced the local languages, it has replaced literacy in regional languages in major urban areas to a considerable extent due to rising English education, as was reported in Satyanath and Sharma (2012). So, the overall model that India presents is pluralistic, where multiple linguistic and cultural practices coexist without necessarily competing, even though the local political discourse seems to view plurality in terms of conflict. Capturing this in a sociolinguistic model that captures the situation described above is a challenge. It is against this background that I will discuss style shift.

8.3 Issue 1: style shift

As indicated above, the issue of linguistic choice in face-to-face interactions, whether in a monolingual or a multilingual setting, is always influenced by social structures. Looking at style shifts in different sociolinguistic settings will reveal language choices which are unique to India and countries like it. The five settings discussed next are: (1) a diglossic situation with a strong and long history of a literary language; (2) language variation in a dominant language in a multilingual urban setting; (3) a multilingual and multidialectal situation where the idea of a standard language is still very young, with less than 150 years of history of writing; (4) interactions in a monolingual setting (within a dialect) and interactions across dialects; and (5) language choice and use in a multidialectal urban setting.

So much has been written on style, all of which has been drawing from a variety of social settings, that it has become almost a contentious issue (see Eckert and Rickford 2001; Kiesling 2009). The two influential models that have emerged are Labov's model of style shift (1966, 1972, 2001a) and Bell's model of audience design (1984, 2001).

The Labovian model is based on the degree of attention paid to one's speech as a function of familiarity and comfort with the interlocutor as well as with the kind of speech activities one is involved in. The stylistic continuum from "careful" to "casual" intersects with the standard–non-standard continuum. This model is known to work in contexts of stratified societies, where the standard and the non-standard speech varieties form a continuum, and where there is salient social meaning attached to a variable in terms of its affiliation to the standard or non-standard.[3] Such evaluation cannot simply be termed as an attitude towards a particular vernacular or standard language as these are not constant, and shifts occur more as a function of appropriateness of a variant to a certain speech activity or task. While the audience is important, the intra-speaker shift occurs even when the audience is constant. All these factors allow monitoring the use of a variable according to the degree of attention paid to one's own speech by a speaker. The model has been replicated in many societies around the world (as indicated in numerous studies cited in Meyerhoff 2006), in Japan and Poland as pointed out in Smakman (2012) and in Russia and Indonesia as pointed out by my students.[4] The other influential model is Bell's audience design, where there is a noticeable shift in the use of a variable depending on who one is talking to. This model is much wider in its scope as it considers intra-speaker variation as derived from inter-speaker variation. The model applies to "all codes and levels of a language repertoire, monolingual and multilingual" (Bell 2001: 144). While possibly accounting for a very wide range of situations, the two models do not necessarily cover language use in all situations and speech communities, and they do not satisfactorily capture the Indian situation. Below, a number of diverse situations from India will reveal how style does or does not work in the Indian context.

8.3.1 Style shift in a diglossic situation

The first case study (Sunny 2013) deals with a diglossic Dravidian situation where the relevant language Malayalam has a long history of literary and grammatical traditions. The literary variety has to be learnt through schooling and differs from spontaneous speech both lexically and in the application of (morpho-)phonological processes. Certain agglutinating processes are more apparent in spontaneous speech than in the literary, standard variety. Sunny reports on the voiceless plosives in Malayalam in Cherukunnam, Kerala, which all variably undergo a number of phonological processes (voicing, weakening, deletion and nasal assimilation) resulting in multiple surface variants (see Sunny 2013 for detail). Following Labov (1972), the spontaneous speech data were categorized in terms of "careful speech", "casual speech" and "narratives" to test for style shift in spontaneous speech. Speech addressed to family members, neighbours and friends, as well as telephone conversations during the interview (described as "group" according to Labov's decision tree), were merged with "narratives" for the purposes of the analysis. In addition, speakers were also given reading tasks involving a word list, sentences and a passage. The results revealed no significant shift in favour of the unchanged plosives within the spontaneous speech across styles, nor was there evidence of a shift across reading tasks; instead, there was a significant opposition between spontaneous speech and read speech as a whole. Variation is, thus, a function of speech activity (Sunny 2013).

The findings of Sunny (2013) show that with the exception of voicing, the other processes apply significantly less in reading tasks than in spontaneous speech. Deletion and nasal assimilation show the steepest differences between the two speech activities, whereas there doesn't seem to be a difference in voicing (because of its high frequency) between the two styles. Is this style shift? In the strict Labovian sense it cannot be termed style, as style is not binary but exists in a continuum. What about audience? Sunny herself conducted both the interviews as well as the reading tasks, and the audience remained the same. The differences between the spontaneous speech and reading tasks are therefore not the result of whether more or less attention was paid to speech or to the audience, but due to the amount of attention paid to the written word. The differences between the literary style and spontaneous speech style appear to be relative, but they do not form a continuum. The literary variety represents standard Malayalam and has value, but there is no negative meaning attached to the non-standard either. There is no particular social meaning attached to the variants other than labels such as literary or read speech versus spoken speech. The various caste groups that Sunny (2013) drew her data from show a similar pattern in the two genera.

8.3.2 Style shift in Angami

The second example discussed here comes from Angami Naga, a Tibeto-Burman language from Kohima village, Nagaland (Suokhrie 2013, 2015). Unlike Malayalam, Angami Naga has existed primarily in orality and its written variant only came into existence about 125 years ago. Though Kohima forms a single village, the residences of Angamis within the village are organized in terms of clans and sub-clans referred to as *khels*. Angamis thus have a multi-layered cultural identity based on village and clan membership. There are about 92 villages in the Kohima district, each village having its own dialect. Angamis identify themselves according to their village (as *kewhi-mia*, "people of Kohima village"), then *khel* within the village and then in terms of the major clan they belong to within the *khel*. Each *khel* has its own *khel*-lect. The *khel*-lects are mutually intelligible but differ from each other to varying degrees. In contrast, not all village dialects are necessarily mutually intelligible.

8.3.2.1 Style shift in Angami as attention to speech

Two of the variables that Suokhrie (2013) studied include: (1) variation between a voiceless aspirated alveolar affricate and an aspirated palatal affricate; and (2) variation between a voiced alveolar fricative [z] and a voiced palatal fricative [Z]. The palatal variants are considered to be standard. Suokhrie did not find any evidence of style shift in spontaneous speech in her collected data. However, some shift was observed between spontaneous and read speech. The standard dialect of Angami, known as *Tenyidie*, is a subject taught in local schools. However, its status as standard does not prompt people to shift towards it. Instead, the standard serves more as a lingua franca across Angami village dialects. Nagamese (a contact language based on Assamese) is also used across villages if the dialects are not mutually intelligible. In Kohima town, where different village dialects co-exist, Tenyidie can be heard in Angami churches in the pastor's sermons.[5]

For the variable (1) one speaker showed complete shift and another speaker also showed a slight shift towards the standard in reading tasks. In the case of variable (2) there appears to be a general shift towards the standard with two speakers showing the strongest shift.

Suokhrie feels that the variable shifts in favour of the standard palatal variants were influenced by Tenyidie spellings. Even if it can be argued that the speakers were attempting to read the standard or Tenyidie properly (by following the spelling, thereby style-shifting in their reading task), it is doubtful that they were attempting to sound more educated or formal in their speech, as studying or speaking Tenyidie does not carry much positive connotation.

8.3.2.2 Audience design and style shift in Angami

The issue of style shift can be further elaborated by comparing the use of the two fricative variants, [z] and [Z], in the speech of those belonging to a single *khel* (a clan-based unit in Kohima village, as discussed above) and those from two different ones. In one research setting, the interlocutors are all from L. *khel* of Kohima village, while in another setting there is a speaker from D. *khel* interacting with an L. *khel* speaker. The results show that three speakers from L. *khel* are all using the alveolar variant (which is characteristic of an L. *khel*-lect), whereas in the mixed interlocutor setting the L. and the D. *khel* speakers continue to speak their own *khel*-lects, in this case [z] and [Z] respectively, without trying to accommodate each other. As was mentioned earlier, there are multiple identities to be found in the Kohima village. Given the absence of accommodation or neutralization of *khel*-lectal differences, it is possible to infer that the speakers perhaps mark or celebrate their own identities by not accommodating one another. This interpretation, however, is not very convincing. Though Angamis can identify a speaker's *khel*, they are not always successful in identifying all the *khels*. It is, for instance, hard to distinguish between L. and T. *khel*-lects and D. and P. *khel*-lects as they are relatively close to each other, and it is even more difficult for younger speakers to do so. Therefore, absence of mutual accommodation or shift in favour of the standard variant is an open acknowledgement of the linguistic differences that exist between speakers of the different *khels*.

A similar picture emerges from the use of Nagamese by different Naga linguistic groups. Nagamese is a vibrant language that is extensively used across various Naga linguistic communities. The use of Nagamese in Kohima town easily reveals a speaker's principal linguistic and cultural identity and can easily be recognized by listeners. I discovered this accidentally in 2009 when I was playing some of my Nagamese recordings to a Naga student. As he listened, he started identifying the speakers with ease. So, in addition to holding a collective identity as "Naga", the individual constituent identities are equally important in Nagaland.

8.3.3 Style shift in an urban setting, Delhi

The next example demonstrating Indian style shift comes from Sharma (2010, 2015), who reported on variation in vowels in English in Delhi. English is extensively used in Delhi across all domains and is actively code-mixed with Hindi and other local languages. English has emerged as the preferred language of education in Delhi (see Satyanath and Sharma 2012) and is probably valued over other languages in some respects. Amongst several variables that Sharma studied are included variation in (Kit) and (Face) vowels, which show a tendency for lowering and laxing. The variability is conditioned by linguistic factors (see Sharma 2010 for details). The lower variants seem to be on the rise: Sharma's study showed that there is a systematic shift across three speech styles (spontaneous speech and two reading styles) to a greater use of the lower/innovative variants in more careful speech.

Another variable that Sharma studied was vowel reduction in words such as *ago*, *galaxy* etc., where the unstressed vowel gets reduced in many ENL Englishes (English as a native language). Delhi English favours full vowels over reduced vowels. In addition to linguistic conditioning of vowel reduction, the full vowels are used more in careful speech styles. The greater use of the conservative variants may seem to suggest that speakers are using more ENL variants in careful speech.

However, the greater use of the innovative variants for (Kit) and (Face) vowels and conservative variants in the case of vowel reduction in careful speech are uninterpretable in the absence of any supporting evidence from social evaluation of the variants. Sharma conducted five different perception tests to explore the social meanings attached to the variants, but both the variants in the above mentioned variables were judged alike.

8.3.4 Style shift within and across dialects of Bengali

The fourth style shift demonstration comes from the Eastern Bengali dialect from Silchar, Assam (Dey 2010). The standard dialect represents a non-local variety (the western dialect), which is used in education, administration and state media, and is learnt through formal education. The two dialects differ from each other in the use of spirants [s, ʃ] in place of plosives [c, ɟ] and the greater use of alveolar over palatal sibilants. In one research setting, Dey (2010), herself a speaker of the eastern variety, conducted several interviews among the local speakers and found no evidence of style shift in the direction of the standard despite the fact that the standard is highly valued. This was rather unexpected as the Silchar Bengali community is functionally and essentially a monolingual (excluding Hindi–English) community and Bengali education is widely prevalent. Absence of a style shift, however, is understandable, considering that talking in the local dialect without shifting is identifying oneself with the local speech community (i.e. as in-group).

In another research setting, an eastern Bengali speaker was interviewed by telephone by a Bengali speaker who had a non-eastern dialect. A near-total shift was observed in the speech of the eastern Bengali speaker towards western Bengali, resulting in a much higher use of plosives instead of the corresponding spirants (i.e. those used in eastern Bengali), as well as an equally high use of palatal rather than alveolar sibilants. However, to interpret the shift as an attempt to identify with a higher prestige dialect would be misconstruing the facts. In an eastern–western Bengali mixed dialect group interaction it is not uncommon for an eastern Bengali speaker to switch back and forth between two dialects depending on the dialect affiliation of the addressees, and regardless of the presence of any auditors from other dialects. The shift towards the western dialect is therefore intended to facilitate comprehension by neutralizing marked differences between the dialects. This could possibly be argued as evidence of audience design, but with a critical difference, as was explained above. This may also suggest that speakers can simultaneously display multiple identities in a multidialectal setting. A similar case is demonstrated in section 8.3.5.

8.3.5 Mobility, linguistic pluralism and language use in an urban town.

Bhattacharya's (2013) study shows that Calcutta, which emerged as the base of operations of the East India Company in the seventeenth century, has its roots in multiple dialects from other dialect regions, particularly in erstwhile eastern Bengal. The town of Calcutta grew as a result of industrialization and urbanization. Its population grew from a mere 12,000 in 1706 to 51 million by 1931. The locally born children of the migrants learnt the local Calcutta dialect but also continued their parental dialects. This is in sharp contrast with what is reported in studies such as Kerswill (2010), which reported development of new urban town koines as a result of accommodation and neutralization of the marked regional variants. Either the diversity has been underestimated by Kerswill or the Indian migration to urban areas is significantly different from the one reported in the west. I would take the latter view. The Indian urban–rural relationship is defined not by a unilinear pattern of migration towards urban areas. It is a to and fro migration where the migrants continue to maintain strong family ties even after their migration (McGee 1977). The ties are sustained and strengthened by periodic visits to their homelands for festivals and other occasions, such as bringing brides and grooms from their villages, and receiving agricultural produce from the ancestral farmlands. Data from Bhattacharya (2013, 2015) suggest that the migration to Calcutta has resulted in multi-dialectalism among families, with several generations living together.

The language choice and use data among family members across generations when talking to the interviewer clearly demonstrate the multidialectal competence across generations. The family members used the western dialect with the interviewer (regarding her as an outsider) but switched back to the eastern dialect when addressing each other. This may be seen as audience-based design but there is a difference. The interviewer's presence does not cause a difference in the interviewee's own speech behaviour. Patterns of language choice are the same in this case as in the case of Silchar Bengali, involving interaction within and across dialect boundaries.

A similar pattern was observed in Guyana while interacting with members of an Indo-Guyanese family (Satyanath 1991). The family members spoke to me in English but switched to Creole when talking among themselves, despite my presence. Here the differential practice of language use suggests that the choice of a particular dialect marks an individual as a member of either the in- or out-group. So, speaking English with me in Guyana marked the fact that I am not a Guyanese. My Indianness, though, qualifies me for the friendship and trust of the Indo-Guyanese community but not for full membership as a local. In Guyana, the use of Creole with friends and family marks one as possessing in-group membership – in this case as Guyanese. The same is exemplified in the Calcutta example (Bhattacharya 2013).

8.3.6 Discussion

The five different cases discussed above raise the question of why there is no style shift. Why don't the standard and the non-standard form a continuum? Or, why is there no hierarchical evaluation of the standard and the vernacular? It is not enough to demonstrate the absence of a style shift. A search for an explanation is equally important. In the following paragraphs, I have discussed possible explanations for the absence of a style shift in an Indian context.

At the outset, it can be said that the history of standardization is not uniform across languages in India given their unequal history of writing. Furthermore, a steady increase in English education has interrupted the process of standardization of Indian languages. The increased use of a code mixed with English in the public sphere, in both print and in electronic media, has caused vernacularization of some of the standard spaces, which were once the exclusive domain of modern Indian languages. Equally important is the absence of a national language in India, which is in contrast to many other countries. The linguistic nationalist agenda flopped as Hindi could not be introduced as the national language. Finally, standard languages are increasingly seen as languages of writing and as lingua francas in India, rather than as symbols of social prestige in comparison with vernaculars. Though the discussion in this chapter only covers a minuscule fragment of the Indian experience, it is this commonality that binds languages like Malayalam and Angami, which are both situated at the two extreme ends on the timeline of writing. All these factors considered would suggest that perhaps the idea of a standard is, after all, different in the Indian context.

A second possibility is that perhaps style shift is an outcome of hierarchical societies where (standard) language is as much a source of social stratification as other measures, like having private possessions and access to resources. In the Indian scenario one finds that the relationship among languages is rather horizontal in both multidialectal and multilingual settings.

A history of pre-colonial India also suggests that pluralistic and inclusive practices were the order of the day with multiple literary and cultural representations coexisting side by side. In medieval India, language was not a symbol of identity. Further, the trans-spatiality of languages, scripts and texts suggest that these were meant for sharing, appropriating and adopting, and not meant for identifying, labelling or monopolizing. These resulted in multi-tier and inclusive systems rather than exclusive singular systems (see T. Satyanath 2011; and various chapters in Pollock 2003).

Ardhakathanak, a seventeenth-century text by a Jain Monk by the name of Banarasidas (1981 [1641]), provides a window into the various linguistic practices that existed at the time in India. The text, which is both historical and biographical, suggests that Sanskrit and Prakrit forms continued alongside regional forms like Braj, Awadhi and Hindvi/Hindustani (as it was called then) without erasing them until as late as the seventeenth century onwards (for more details see Satyanath 2008a, 2008b). The text is in a regional language (a mix of Braj Bhasha and Eastern Hindi) and contains Sanskrit *tatsamas*[6] (with conjunct consonants) co-occurring with Prakrit and regional variants, which avoid such conjuncts. Likewise, literary traditions of languages such as Hindi and Urdu, and of many others, were also complex and included participation of many other related languages, communities and religions. The models were not based on one religion, one language and one script or even one region.

This is not to suggest that "scripts" and "languages" have not become contentious issues in present-day India and that things have not changed. Changes have occurred, but somehow many elements of the earlier plurality have continued; India, with all of its plurality and some 22 official languages, continues to be more of a horizontal society than a vertical one, in terms of relationships among the different languages. This is despite the presence of many inequalities at various levels. Even caste, which has often been read as vertical (see, for instance, Chambers 1995: 52–53), is actually horizontal (see Deshpande 2003). Hence, it is not surprising that there are no strong social meanings attached to variants in terms of standard and vernacular. Instead of a standard–non-standard continuum one finds a binary opposition between a literary variety and one or more spoken varieties or vernaculars without a strong value judgement attached to either of them.

Even New Zealand, from where Bell (1984, 2001) drew his examples initially to support his audience-based design model, is a hierarchical society where ethnic identity is not completely independent of social class (see Holmes and Bell 1990). Some of the features that index ethnicity in New Zealand (Bell 2001) perhaps also index social class. A hierarchical relationship between standard and non-standard is also evident in Bell's study of language use on two radio networks (Bell 2001: 40) and elsewhere (see Meyerhoff 2006: 162, 164). Just as social class appears central to Labov's model of style as attention paid to speech, both social class and identity seem central to Bell's model of audience design.

The answers to the questions at hand must then lie in the nature of the speech community and the relationship among languages. It is possible to propose that the style shifts based on the standard–non-standard continuum are more likely to be the outcome of societies that are socially and linguistically vertical in nature. This applies to both models of style, where the nature of relationship among languages is vertical. The audience-based style shifts are more likely to be a product of pluralistic and simultaneously vertical societies. Only in the absence of social hierarchy can the audience-based designs be considered a product of horizontal societies.

As was already discussed above, the Indian context endorses a notion of standard language that is associated with a written form on the one hand, and with a lingua franca on the other. The results of the survey conducted to find out the meaning of a standard language following Smakman (2012) confirm the above proposal.

8.4 Issue 2: Local social factors other than class: caste, clan and gender

In this section I report on the role of three social factors in Indian society. One case study refers to the role of caste, religion and gender in Cherukunnam, Kerala (see Sunny 2013). The second one refers to the salience of *khel* (clans) in understanding social differentiation in a speech community.

8.4.1 Caste, religion and gender

The population of Cherukunnam comprises Christians (mainly Catholics and Jacobites) and Hindus (amongst others, Nairs, Parayas and Ezhavas). There are no Brahmins in the village. However, Nairs are considered a dominant caste group. Much has been written about the Nair women and the status they traditionally enjoyed (e.g. by Gough 1962a, 1962b). To test the salience of caste, religion and gender, Sunny (2013) selected two speakers each – one male and one female from two Christian and two Hindu groups. It must be mentioned that caste in India does not simply divide in terms of Brahmins and non-Brahmins, but that there are multiple castes and there are multiple sub-castes in each caste group, including Brahmins. For more discussion on caste and language readers may consult McCormack (1960), Bright and Ramanujan (1972), Shapiro and Schiffman (1981: 198–207) and Chambers (1995) on caste in India, and Gough (1962a, 1962b), Schneider (1962), Subramoniam (1974) and Nair (2008) on caste in Kerala. The findings of Sunny (2013) suggest that caste and gender interact; this is in line with the general, mainstream finding that gender and social class interact. The two factors, caste and gender, were, when tested independently, not selected as significant. However, a cross-tabulation of the two provides interesting patterns.

First of all it seems as though the four social groups show no hierarchy, and would hence work differently from social class. Caste (including Christian groups) does not reveal any salient patterns if taken by itself. Second, it would seem that in general women show more "no change" (meaning less shifts) compared with men, which implies that woman favour the use of more standard varieties in stable situations (Labov 1990, 2001b). The most striking finding is that the study of Nair women revealed a pattern which is consistently at variance with the rest of the women. Their unique behaviour is in line with what has been written on them, their matrilineal practices and the status they enjoyed vis-à-vis men and other caste women historically (see Gough 1962a, 1962b; Logan 2008). Unique behaviour of Nair women also tags Nair men's behaviour as marked compared with that of men from other castes/groups.

One of the suggested reasons why caste and gender as independent factors are not selected as significant in Sunny (2013) is that gender differences are not uniform across all women. Furthermore, gender interacts with caste and the two are uninterpretable without reference to each other.

8.4.2 Clan in Angamis

The best-known studies on clan so far are those of the Sui community of Southwest China reported in Stanford (2008a, 2008b). Like social class, membership of a clan again appears to be an important social factor in many communities, though it has not been widely reported. As mentioned earlier, Angamis are organized in terms of *khels* (the clan-based subunits of Kohima village). Kohima village, which is an Angami village, is divided into four *khels* comprising some 3374 houses (Suokhrie 2013). Women traditionally married outside their *khels*, but now marriages within the *khel* are also taking place. However, people with the same family name in a clan still do not marry. "Family name" here refers to shared surname and not to "family" itself. As in the Sui community, women in cross-*khel* marriages continue to speak their own *khel*-lects. As a result, one finds husband and wife speaking different lects. Their children learn either only father's *khel*-lect or show influence of both parents' *khel*-lects. These factors then act as salient factors in explaining variation within and across families.

In order to test the salience of clan Suokhrie interviewed several families from each of the four *khels* in Kohima village balancing between "same-*khel*" and "mixed-*khel*" marriages and by drawing data from different generations. Some of the variables that Suokhrie (2013) studied include: (1) variation between aspirated alveolar and palatal affricates; (2) variation between unaspirated alveolar and palatal affricates; and (3) variation between voiced alveolar and palatal fricatives. Two of the *khels*, L and T, favour alveolar variants whereas two other *khels*, P and D, favour palatal variants. The physical distances among the *khels* are not significant, it is the intensity of socialization in terms of daily interactions which explains why P and D are closer and L and T are closer to each other. The degree of daily contact is influenced by the location of the houses.

Suokhrie's (2013) findings suggest that in intra-*khel* marriages and marriages where all the family members are from the same *khel*, both parents and children show a similar pattern with respect to the variables mentioned above. In contrast, in mixed-*khel* marriages one finds variation in patterns displayed by husband and wife. Additionally, their children often show a pattern which is deviant in some ways from both their parents. In some cases one finds a split pattern with different variables following different parent's *khel*-lectal patterns. This suggests that inter-speaker variation, or lack of it, in Kohima village can be understood only in terms of clan membership, marriage practices and their impact on language acquisition by children.

The findings are suggestive of the role of clans and family as salient sociolinguistic variables in Angami community. Unlike Stanford's experience with the Sui community, the Angami community also shows the impact of contact on language acquisition. Kohima is more of an urbanized village with a fully-fledged infrastructure, including schools, churches and shopping places. As a result, there is a large amount of mobility within the community.

8.5 Conclusions

The various case studies discussed in the last few sections have shown that the model of style as attention paid to speech has little evidential basis in the Indian context. Lack of style shift is attributed to the non-vertical nature of the relationship between the standard and vernacular variants as well as among different social groups. It is further shown that despite the presence of inter-speaker variation, there is no evidence of either accommodation or of any attempt to identify oneself with the other. Instead, the relationship is more one of coexistence and cooperation among plurality. Therefore, audience-based design also does not work in the Indian context in the specific situations examined in the chapter. It is proposed here that style shift is an outcome of societies that are vertical in nature, both socially and linguistically; this in turn attaches social meanings to available choices, creating both a social and a linguistic continuum. The relationship between the so-called standard and vernacular in the Indian context is one of written versus spoken language, on the one hand, and that of a lingua franca on the other. Amid greater diversity, and when faced with the difficulty of comprehension across dialects, the standard language functions as the "common" one or the lingua franca. The two models of style nevertheless remain useful tools for both designing sociolinguistic interviews as well as analysing the data obtained through such interviews. I have avoided using dichotomies like "West" versus "East" as these underplay their internal diversity by imagining a homogeneous West as opposed to a homogeneous East. While it is easy to consider the West as representing class societies based on power and hegemony, I have preferred to use a broader and more neutral term such as "vertical". The cases studied here constitute only a minuscule part of the diverse sociolinguistic settings. The findings presented here, though they form a radical departure, are therefore by no means exhaustive and need to be further researched.

It has also been shown that in Kerala, where a number of caste groups and religious groups coexist, caste does not work in the same way as social class. This is contrary to the popular misconception of caste as being hierarchical. The findings are in line with the new analysis of class by Indian scholars (Deshpande 2003) who have demonstrated that caste in India is horizontal. The chapter has further shown that unlike the patrilineal societies, from where gender findings thus far have been reported, gender-related findings in other, less patrilineal, societies are very different. In Kerala, which is a mix of patrilineal and matrilineal communities, the behaviour of Nair women is different from the rest of the women from other groups, as well as that of Nair men. The Nagaland case study has shown that in Kohima village, the clan is salient and not social class. The variability in speech in a clan-based society is to be understood as an outcome of clan and exogamy, which brings women and men from different clans together and impacts language acquisition among children that grow up in these settings. These findings are also different from Stanford (2008a, 2008b), as local practices differ between the Angami of Kohima village and the Sui of Southwest China, despite both being clan-based societies.

Given the social underpinnings of sociolinguistic theory, these findings, though striking, are not surprising. The findings underscore the fact that not all societies are necessarily class based, and that social class is not always a powerful indicator of linguistic behaviour in every society. Similarly, not all societies are solely patrilineal in structure. There may be parameters other than class and patriarchy which structure societies and which may impact language differently. The findings reveal the issues with universalizing human linguistic behaviour amid diverse speech communities.

Notes

1 Unless otherwise mentioned, "Kohima" refers to "Kohima village".
2 However, see Gumperz (1971), Pandit (1972), Southworth and Apte (1974) and Shapiro and Schiffman (1981) for some of the early sociolinguistic studies on India.
3 Positive attitudes towards the standard language have been well demonstrated in numerous studies such as Labov (1972) and Kroch and Small (1978). The high status attached to one national language is shown in many countries (Foley 1997; Smakman 2012).

The seven countries surveyed in Smakman (2012) are from several parts of the globe, but they are mutually dissimilar to India in the sense that their standard/non-standard situation is predictable and straightforward. These data emphasize the difference between countries with an obvious, undebated national/standard language and those for which this is not so.

4 I am grateful to my graduate students Arif Rahman from Indonesia and Yevgenia Litvinova from Russia for pointing this out. Following Smakman (2012) I conducted a similar survey in my class with students from different parts of India and from countries such as Syria, Indonesia and China. The results demonstrated that within India a "standard" was viewed more as a written variety rather than a formal and a prestigious speech variety. In places such as Manipur and Nagaland a standard was equated with a lingua franca. In countries like Russia, Syria, Indonesia and China a standard variety is more clearly distinguished and it seems to function as a formal speech variety.

5 Use of Tenyidie in Angami churches is limited to reading excerpts from the Bible. I am thankful to Viya, a resident of Kohima town Terhiija, for pointing this out.

6 *Tatsama*, literally meaning "as it was", refers to words of Sanskrit origin found in other Indian languages in their original and unmodified form. An opposite of *tatsama* is *tadbhava*, referring to words borrowed from Sanskrit and modified.

Further reading

Cardona, George and Dhanesh Jain (eds) (2003) *The Indo Aryan Languages.* London: Routledge. (The volume provides linguistic descriptions of 20 Indo-Aryan languages, both big and small. Chapters 1–6 in particular provide a good coverage of issues covering diachrony of Indo-Aryan and sociolinguistically relevant information.)

Emeneau, Murray B. (1980) *Language and Linguistic Area: Essays.* Stanford: Stanford University Press. (This is a collection of essays by Emeneau on linguistic and sociocultural descriptions of India. The essays are based on his extensive collection of materials on India and oral texts covering Indo-Aryan, Dravidian and touching Tibeto-Burman language areas. The anthology provides a meaningful introduction to India including issues relating to contact and convergence.)

Ferguson, Charles A. and Gumperz, John J. (eds) (1960) *Linguistic Diversity in South Asia: Studies in Regional, Social and Functional Variation* (= *International Journal of American Linguistics* 26). (The volume explores linguistic diversity in South Asia, covering India and Pakistan with reference to social and cultural contexts. The articles focus on social dialects, literary and colloquial varieties of several languages, both Dravidian and Indo-Aryan.)

References

Anderson, Benedict (1983) *Imagined Communities: Reflections on the Origin and Spread of Nationalism.* London: Verso.

Banarasidas (1981 [1641]) *Ardhakathanak* (translated, annotated and introduced by Mukund Lath). *Half a Tale: A Study in the Interrelationship between Autobiography and History.* Jaipur: Rajasthan Prakrit Bharati Sansthan.

Bell, Allan (1984) Language Style as Audience Design. *Language in Society* 13(2): 145–204.

——(2001) Back in Style. Reworking Audience Design. In: *Style and Sociolinguistic Variation.* Penelope Eckert and John Rickford (eds), 139–69. Cambridge: Cambridge University Press.

Bhattacharya, Pratibha (2013) *Urbanity and Ethnography of Communication: Social Lives of Language: A Cardiff-Delhi University Symposium.* University of Delhi (16 August 2013).

——(2015) *Variation and Change: A Case Study of Calcutta Bengali.* Doctoral dissertation, University of Delhi (in progress).

Bright, William and A. K. Ramanujan (1972) Sociolinguistic Variation and Language Change. In: *Sociolinguistics. Selected Readings.* J. B. Pride and Janet Holmes (eds), 157–66. Harmondsworth: Penguin.
Chambers, Jack K. (1995) *Sociolinguistic Theory: Linguistic Variation and Its Social Significance.* Oxford: Blackwell.
Deshpande, Satish (2003) *Contemporary India: A Sociological View.* New Delhi: Penguin India.
Dey, Kakoli (2010) *Silchar Bengali: A Sociolinguistic Study.* Doctoral dissertation, University of Delhi.
Eckert, Penelope and John Rickford (eds) (2001)*Style and Sociolinguistic Variation.* Cambridge: Cambridge University Press.
Foley, William A. (1997) *Anthropological Linguistics: An Introduction.* Malden: Blackwell.
Gough, Kathleen (1962a) Nayar. Central Kerala. In: *Matrilineal Kinship.* David Murray Schneider and Kathleen Gough (eds), 298–384. Berkeley: University of California Press.
——(1962b) Nayar. North Kerala. In: *Matrilineal Kinship.* David Murray Schneider and Kathleen Gough (eds), 385–404. Berkeley: University of California Press.
Gumperz, John J. (1971) *Language in Social Groups* (compiled and edited by Anwar S. Dill). Stanford: Stanford University Press.
Holmes, Janet and Allan Bell (1990) Attitudes, Varieties, Discourse: An Introduction to the Sociolinguistics of New Zealand English. In: *New Zealand Ways of Speaking English.* Allan Bell and Janet Holmes (eds), 1–20. Clevendon: Multilingual Matters.
Kerswill, Paul (2010) Contact and New Varieties. In: *The Handbook of Language Contact.* Raymond Hickey (ed.), 230–51. West Sussex: Wiley-Blackwell.
Kiesling, Scott (2009) Style as Stance: Stance as the Explanation for Patterns of Sociolinguistic Variation. In: *Stance. Sociolinguistic Perspectives.* Alexandra Jaffe (ed.), 171–94. Oxford: Oxford University Press.
Kroch, Anthony and Cathy Small (1978) Grammatical Ideology and Its Effect on Speech. In: *Linguistic Variation: Models and Methods.* David Sankoff (ed.), 45–55. New York: Academic Press.
Labov, William (1966) *The Social Stratification of English in New York City.* Washington, DC: Centre for Applied Linguistics.
——(1972) *Sociolinguistic Patterns.* Philadelphia: University of Pennsylvania Press.
——(1990) The Intersection of Sex and Social Class in the Course of Linguistic Change. *Language Variation and Change* 2: 205–54.
——(2001a) The Anatomy of Style Shifting. In: *Style and Sociolinguistic Variation.* Penelope Eckert and John Rickford (eds), 85–108. Cambridge: Cambridge University Press.
——(2001b) *Principles of Linguistic Change. Social Factors.* Oxford: Blackwell.
Logan, William (2008[1887]) *Malabarile Janangal* (Malabar Manual Series II, translated by T.V. Krishnan). Kozhikode: Mathrubhumi Books.
McCormack, William (1960) Social Dialects in Dharwar Kannada. *International Journal of Dravidian Linguistics* 26: 79–91.
McGee, Terry G. (1977) Rural Urban Mobility in South and South East Asia: Different Formulations – Different Answers. In: *Third World Urbanization.* Janet Abu-Lughod and Richard Hay (eds), 196–212. New York: Maaroufa Press.
Meyerhoff, Miriam (2006) *Introducing Sociolinguistics.* London: Routledge.
Nair, Gopinathan B. (2008) Dialect Survey of Malayalam in Retrospect. *International Journal of Dravidian Linguistics* XXXVII(1): 169–189.
Office of the Registrar General and Census Commissioner (2001) *Census of India.* Online available at: www.censusindia.gov.in/Census_Data_2001/Census_Data_Online (accessed on 15 November 2011).
Pandit, Prabodh B. (1972) *India as a Sociolinguistic Area: Gune Memorial Lectures, 1968.* Ganeshkhind: Pune University Press.
Pollock, Sheldon I. (ed.) (2003) *Literary Cultures in History: Reconstructions from South Asia.* Berkeley: University of California Press.

Satyanath, Shobha (1991) Variation and Change. (DAZ) in Guyanese. Doctoral dissertation, University of Pennsylvania.

———(2008a) Reflections on Language in Society in Early Modern India: National Seminar on Understanding Language, Grammar and Literature. CIIL, Mysore, 6–8 February.

———(2008b) Rethinking Language and Identity. XXXII Indian Social Science Congress. Jamia Millia Islamia, New Delhi, 17–22 December.

Satyanath, Shobha, and Richa Sharma (2012) The Indian Experience with English from Classroom to the Community, from ESL/EFL to ENL. Tenth Asia TEFL International Conference. Delhi, 4–6 October.

Satyanath, T. (2011) Sectarian Texts and Syncretic Conventions: Hindus and Muslims in the Narratives of Medieval Karnataka. In: *Poetics and Politics of Sufism and Bhakti in South Asia*. Kavita Panjabi (ed.), 107–24. New Delhi: Orient Blackswan.

Schneider, David Murray (1962) The Distinctive Features of Matrilineal Descent Group. In: *Matrilineal Kinship*. David Murray Schneider and Kathleen Gough (eds), 1–29. Berkeley: University of California Press.

Shapiro, Michael C. and Harold F. Schiffman (1981) *Language and Society in South Asia*. Delhi: Motilal Banarsidass.

Sharma, Richa (2010) *Phonetic Realizations of Vowels in Indian English*. MPhil dissertation, University of Delhi.

———(2015) *A Sociophonetic Study of Variation in Vowels among Hindi/Punjabi-English Bilinguals in Delhi*. Doctoral dissertation. University of Delhi (in progress).

Smakman, Dick (2012) The Definition of the Standard Language: A Survey in Seven Countries. *International Journal of the Sociology of Language* 218: 25–58.

Southworth, Franklin C. and Mahadev L. Apte (eds) (1974) *Contact and Convergence in South Asia*. Trivandrum: Department of Linguistics, University of Kerala.

Stanford, James N. (2008a) Child Dialect Acquisition: New Perspectives on Parent/Peer Influence. *Journal of Sociolinguistics* 12(5):567–96.

———(2008b) A Sociotonetic Analysis of Sui Dialect Contact. *Language Variation and Change* 20(3): 409–50.

Subramoniam, V.I. (1974) *Dialect Survey of Malayalam Ezhava-Tiiya*. Trivandrum: University of Kerala.

Sunny, Neethu (2013) A Sociolinguistic Study of Malayalam in Cherukunnam. MPhil dissertation, University of Delhi.

Suokhrie, Kelhouvinuo (2013) Clan Identity and Language Variation in Kohima Village. Social Lives of Language: A Cardiff–Delhi University Symposium. University of Delhi, 16 August.

———(2015) Internal Variation in Angami: A Case Study of Kohima Village. MPhil dissertation, University of Delhi (in progress).

9

GENDER IN A NORTH AFRICAN SETTING

A sociolinguistic overview

Reem Bassiouney

9.1 The linguistic and historical context of Northern Africa

This chapter provides a snapshot of research on sociolinguistics in Northern Africa. The chapter concentrates on three sociolinguistic variables: gender, urbanisation and the symbolic function of language in this region. It focuses mainly on gender and will reveal how the Northern African gender situation cannot easily be captured by paradigms as found in mainstream sociolinguistics.

The North African countries comprise Egypt, Libya, Tunisia, Morocco and Algeria. All these countries have Standard Arabic as their official language and exhibit diglossia. That is, in addition to the prestigious colloquial variety there also exists a standard variety that is functionally distinct. Standard Arabic is not a spoken language anywhere in North Africa. According to Ferguson (1959), Standard Arabic is the language of heritage and culture, and is used in political speeches, mosque sermons, news broadcasts, literature and poetry as well as in written documents; this is still true today. The colloquial variety of each country is used in conversations amongst friends and family, in soap operas, in cartoons and in folk literature. This clear distinction between the colloquials and Standard Arabic has been challenged by linguists who found cases of switching between standard and colloquial in the same stretch of discourse with no change in context or topic (cf. Bassiouney 2006, for examples from Egypt). The most essential point that differentiates the linguistic situation in North Africa from that of other countries is that the standard variety is different from the prestige variety. For example, Standard Arabic is not necessarily the prestigious variety in Egypt; instead, the prestigious variety is a specific variety of Cairene Arabic.

In terms of urbanisation, colonisation and social composition, North African countries have developed differently from one another. For example, in Libya and Algeria the urban population accounts for well over 70 per cent of the total, compared to just over half in Morocco. Whereas in Libya and Tunisia, speakers of Berber languages represent only a small fraction of the population (estimated at 3 per cent and 1 per cent, respectively), some 25 per cent of the population in Algeria, and some 45 per cent in Morocco, are speakers of these languages (UN 2014).

By the beginning of the twentieth century the majority of Arab countries were either under British or French mandate. Egypt was the only country occupied by the British. In 1916, most of the Arab world, excluding Saudi Arabia and North Yemen, were divided between France and Britain. France controlled the Mediterranean coast of North Africa and what is now Syria and Lebanon, while Britain controlled Iraq, Transjordan, Egypt and the Sudan (Mansfield 2003). Most of the institutions of these countries were established during the colonial period, and were shaped to correlate with British and French models.

Following independence (in the 1950s and 1960s), North African countries followed a policy of Arabisation. Standard Arabic was a symbol of an identity that had long been suppressed. Immediately after achieving independence, Standard Arabic was seen as a language of independence, tradition, a glorious past, and even the language in which a sound moral system could be explained and maintained (cf. Saʿdī 1993). However, the use of foreign languages, French and English specifically, is still prevalent in North Africa, even more than at the time of colonisation, for reasons of economy and tourism.

9.2 Sociolinguistic research in the region

Descriptions of dialects and colloquial varieties in Northern Africa started to flourish during the period of colonisation (see Bassiouney 2009). However, studies correlating variables to linguistic variants explaining and contextualising language variation and change only emerged in the 1980s. The methodologies used by both Labov and Milroy in collecting data served as a template for studies in Northern Africa.

Like in other countries, studies in North Africa suffer from the methodological problem of the well-known "observer's paradox" (Labov 1972a; Milroy 1987). This problem is quite pertinent when studying gender. Milroy's method of collecting data was used in Haeri's study of sociolinguistic variation in Cairo (Haeri 1997). Haeri worked alone, and, as an Iranian woman she shared the religion of her informants (i.e. Islam). Therefore, it was easy for her to be both an insider and an outsider. She was able to study phonological variation in the speech of men and women in Cairo in relation to social class. She used the sociolinguistic interview in addition to radio and TV programmes for children and adults as well as a wordlist reading. She analysed the speech of 87 speakers and limited her study to traditional urban and modern or industrial urban groups. To overcome the observer's paradox, she used the social network approach, but also tried to speak about personal subjects with her informants, such as childhood games, school days, family, falling in love and local customs.[1]

9.2.1 Gender as a social variable

Gender has been defined by Coates (1993: 4) as "the term used to describe socially constructed categories based on sex". "Gender practices are not only about establishing identities but also about managing social relations" (Eckert and McConnell-Ginet 2003: 305). Thus gender is the product of social interaction. This chapter argues that quantitative sociolinguistic research in North Africa tends to treat gender as a given, and then proceeds to examine variation between males and females; categories such as social class, ethnicity and gender are treated as clear and simple categories that can be used directly to account for variation within a community. This is, however, an oversimplification.

Some scholars in the Western world claim that women use more prestigious language forms than men. Women, especially in the lower middle class, take the initiative in introducing new prestigious forms of many of the phonological variables studied in the US, UK and other industrialised societies such as Sweden (cf. Romaine 2003). Men, on the other hand, are seen to initiate language change from below (Labov 1990). This pattern may be related to economic and social factors (James and Drakich 1993). In studies examining language change in bilingual communities, women seem to be initiating a change towards the more prestigious variety (Gal 1978). Women in the Western world are assumed to be more status-conscious and less secure in their social position (cf. Romaine 2003). According to Trudgill (1972), language is used as a symbolic means of securing social status. He claims that women have a less secure position in society and therefore use more prestigious forms. This has been criticised as an overgeneralisation in a number of studies (cf. Holmes and Meyerhoff 2003).

The most important interpretation of Western studies, and the one that concerns us directly here, is that lower-middle-class women tend to use more prestige forms to compensate for their socially insecure position (cf. Trudgill 1972; Labov 1982; Paulston and Tucker 2003). However, Labov (1982: 201) claims that this is not the case in the Near East and South Asia and that women in these areas are not necessarily linguistically more conservative. But Labov may not have taken the difference between a prestige and a standard variety into account. Many linguistic studies in Northern Africa have shown that, at least in urban areas, a prestigious vernacular is used, the nature of which depends on a number of geographical, political and social factors. In Egypt, for example, this prestigious vernacular is Cairene Arabic. It is usually the dialect used in the larger cities. There is also a standard variety, Standard Arabic. Effects of urbanisation have led to a distinction between prestige and standard dialect. Miller (2004: 177) posits that "urbanization has been one of the greatest social changes of the last century in Arab countries". After that, a rapid growth occurred, for instance in Nouakchott, the capital of Mauritania (cf. Taine-Cheikh 2007), Casa Blanca, the capital of Morocco (cf. Hachimi 2007), and Tripoli in Libya (Pereira 2007). Growth in the urban populations has a number of linguistic ramifications, amongst others a mixing of dialects in the cities through contact. In a big city such as Tripoli, Standard Arabic is not the most prestigious dialect. According to Pereira (2007: 92) everyone in Libya is proud of their own dialect.

I argue that it is important to de-essentialise concepts of language and society in order to apply it to North Africa, especially in studies that correlate linguistic variation with independent factors.

Sadiqi (2003: 212–13) alludes to the fact that it is not helpful to look at the category of Moroccan women as one entity since diversity within Moroccan society is pervasive. According to Sadiqi, understanding this is essential for a clear understanding of women's position in society. If it is an oversimplification to speak about "Moroccan women", then it is also too simple to speak about "North African women" without acknowledging the diversity in their situations and positions. In the next section I will list studies that correlated linguistic variation to gender.

Trabelsi (1988) studied the use of diphthongs and monophthongs in relation to gender in Tunisia. Walters (1991) made a quantitative sociolinguistic study of Arabic as spoken in Korba, a small Tunisian town, and compared and contrasted his findings with Western studies. To collect his data, he used a male Tunisian teacher of French and a female student of language in order to examine whether the gender of the interviewer mattered. Walters was interested in phonological variables, especially the *ima:la* phenomenon, vowel raising (palatalisation, produced by a rising movement of the tongue towards the prepalatal region). He found that *ima:la* is used by older people, less educated people and women. It is considered a feature of the Korba dialect, which is now looked down upon, especially when used outside Korba.

In a different vein, Haeri (1996) was interested in Cairene Arabic variation between men and women, especially in the processes of fronting and backing. She noted that data from ten different communities in Cairo suggest that women take the lead in fronting processes. Haeri concentrates specifically on two variables: the degree of pharyngalisation and apical palatalisation. Pharyngalisation is a secondary articulation which involves the backing of the tongue towards the pharynx (cf. Jakobson 1978), while palatalisation is a fronting process that involves tongue fronting as well as raising (cf. Bhat 1978; Haeri 1996: 106). Haeri contends that social class plays an important role in this variation between men and women. She concluded that men use heavier pharyngalisation than women in order to sound tough and manly (Haeri 1996: 107), while weak or no pharyngalisation is characteristic of women in general and, in particular, of upper-middle-class men and women (cf. Royal 1985). Although strong pharyngalisation is a process found in classical Arabic, it tends to be avoided by women. For women, weak pharyngalisation is associated with upper class, civilisation and so on, while strong pharyngalisation or backing is associated with men generally and in particular with men from the lower class. Haeri (1996) found middle-class women initiated this change in Cairo. Variables associated with upper-middle-class women tend to become prestigious norms associated with refinement, and thus become models for lower-class women with social ambitions. Haeri argues that both class and gender interact as independent variables in Egypt and influence linguistic variation. However, a Modern Standard

Arabic variable such as the voiceless uvular plosive /q/ is used more frequently by men than women, almost across all classes.

Other studies also found that young, educated, middle-class women use more foreign lexical items than men do (cf. Lawson-Sako and Sachdev 2000, for a study on Tunisia). The above studies indicate, first, that women sometimes do not have access to education and professional life to the same extent as men and thus use Standard Arabic less often. On the other hand, when women do have a choice between the prestigious urban variety, a rural variety and Standard Arabic, they are more prone to choose the urban variety as a symbolic means of asserting their identity. Haeri (1996: 307) claims that "studies of gender differentiation have shown that women who have equal levels of education to men use features of classical Arabic significantly less than men" (see also Haeri 2006: 529). Note however that Mejdell (2006) found that this generalisation did not apply to some of her female informants.

9.2.2 Gender, politeness and universals

Some theories perceive gender as a binary opposition (Freed 2003: 702). Holmes (1998: 468, 472) suggests some language universals related to gender: First, women are more sensitive to emotions rather than the content of what is said, while men focus more on the information; second, women provide more encouragement, supportive feedback or minimal responses like "mm", "uh-huh" etc. in conversations between couples (Fishman 1980, 1983), in management discussion groups (Schick-Case 1988), in political debates (Edelsky and Adams 1990), and in interactions between women and men in laboratory or studio conditions (Leet-Pellegrini 1980; Preisler 1986). Women are more concerned for their partner's positive face needs. They value solidarity. Women tend to use linguistic devices that stress solidarity more often than men (for Mayan Indians see Brown 1980; for Javanese see Smith-Hefner 1988). Third, they also tend to often use hedges, tag questions and terms like "sort of" and "as you know", which are often interpreted as signals of uncertainty (Lakoff 2003). Fourth, interruptions come from men, not women, and men tend to speak more. Men want to maintain and increase their power, women tend to maintain and increase solidarity (Holmes 1998: 472). Note that Holmes acknowledges that there are some societies in which this is not true, for example in Madagascar.

I argue against the assumption that women are more polite than men and more concerned with solidarity while men are concerned with power (cf. Kiesling 2003: 514). I also argue that power is context-dependent. Power is indeed related to social status. Therefore, one question is whether there is a direct relation between politeness and the social status of women. Many studies argue that this is the case and that it is rooted in a lack of power of women: the less power one has in any given interactional context, the more likely one is to be concerned with expressing or displaying politeness, especially negative politeness. Deuchar (1989) applied Brown and Levinson's (1987) theory of politeness and face to the use of prestigious forms, and posited that powerless people usually monitor face more carefully than powerful ones. They do so by using more forms that encode status. One usually speaks respectfully to superiors no matter how well one knows them (Holmes 1995).

It is suggested that men in most cultures have more access to power and status than women. They can use more power-related techniques because their face is already protected. Women, on the other hand, cannot use more assertive techniques when speaking since this may be considered face threatening. This hypothesis is confirmed by studies that found women frequently using back-channel responses, simultaneous talk to show interest and support, and facilitative tag questions (Holmes 1995).

However, there are some studies that did not find any differences in the degree of politeness (Salami 1991). In a ground-breaking study examining the way Moroccan men and women bargain, Kharraki (2001) discusses the concept of politeness and face in relation to both sexes. The study analyses more than 60 bargaining exchanges. It concludes that it is men rather than women who use more linguistic solidarity devices; that is, it is men who use more positive politeness techniques than women in bargaining. In fact, women's use of insisting strategies is perceived as "a daring act of assertiveness" (Kharraki 2001: 623). Men, on the other hand, feel that such strategies could be face-threatening and reduce their social power. Men in this specific community derive their social status not by maintaining hierarchies, but by emphasising similarities. Women, on the other hand, emphasise their status by appealing to the hierarchical rank. Sellam (1990: 90) posits that, in general, the way Moroccans make requests is different from the way speakers of English do, for example. The women in the examples in this study are not particularly rude. In fact, the exchanges do not result in any damage to the face of either interlocutor. Insisting is another strategy of bargaining with vendors used by women. Other strategies also include repetitions, oaths or threatening to buy from another seller (Kharraki 2001).

At first sight, this difference between the way men and women bargain in this specific Moroccan community may seem bewildering. From the examples given by Kharraki (2001), women are more assertive than men and much more persistent. This may be, as Kharraki puts it, a way to demonstrate their skills as housewives. It may also have larger implications for the power spheres of both sexes in this community. The interaction between the women and the street vendors in Morocco is not just a manifestation of politeness and power relations. It is a manifestation of the intricate relation between politeness as a communicative resource and independent variables such as social class, tribal affiliations, ethnicity, age and so on (see Bassiouney 2009). Social class and status are at work. For example, upper-middle-class women in Egypt, when bargaining or arguing with male servants (porters, caretakers, street vendors, etc.), can seem very rude to an outsider, using insults, a higher pitch or omitting greetings. Men from the same class deal with the situation differently, being calmer, using greeting terms and rarely using verbal insults.

In a study of identity projections in the speech of educated women and men in Egypt, Bassiouney (2010) examines Modern Standard Arabic and Egyptian Colloquial Arabic use in talk shows. She examines two talk shows in which the participants are exclusively either male or female (the other three talk shows have both male and female participants). All the participants are in the same age group, 45–55.

She sheds light on code choice and code-switching by women specifically in relation to identity. The study also examines assertiveness techniques, such as interruption and floor-controlling by women. In doing so, Bassiouney challenges variationist studies on the Arab world that indicated that women have less access to education and professional life in comparison to men and thus use less Standard Arabic. Also, when women have a choice between the prestigious urban variety, a rural variety and Standard Arabic, they are more prone to choose the urban variety as a means of asserting their identity.

In spite of the fact that talk shows may not be representative as stratified samples of variationist research, talk shows can help demonstrate that certain general conclusions about the use of Standard Arabic by educated women should not be drawn. Educated women with access to Standard Arabic do in fact use it in certain contexts. It also shows that in specific contexts, Egyptian women are as assertive as men, if not more.

When discussing the use of code choice by women, linguists tend to concentrate on the disadvantages of women in the public sphere, while ignoring how code choice can be used as a means of attaining power by women and asserting their identity. Cameron (2005: 496) discusses how women are marginalised globally in public spheres and how women are silenced in public contexts or denied access to the "language literacies and speech styles" necessary to enter the public domain. Sadiqi (2007: 647), in discussing language and gender in the Arab world, postulates that women had to struggle to be able to enter the public arena; while this may be true, her other statements are too general. She claims that although literate women have a "less detached attitude" towards Standard Arabic, they, like illiterate women, are not encouraged to be in the public sphere, and use Standard Arabic less often than men. She also postulates that Standard Arabic is the "male domain", since it is the language of the public sphere and institutions. However, data suggest that this may not be the case in all contexts, and not for all Arab women. When women are in the public sphere, which occurs frequently in Egypt, especially on the media, they use the opportunity to establish their status and identity, and Modern Standard Arabic is one of the tools they use to do so. The diglossic situation in Egypt can be used by women to show their authority and expertise, and to appear emphatic and assertive.

There are numerous ways in which women in North Africa can invoke power. One of them is age; Eckert (2003) stresses the fact that gender has to be studied in relation to age. Arab women in general have increased status when they are older. Abu-Lughod (1987) mentioned, for example, that Bedouin women in the Western desert in Egypt tend to show their faces more and veil less when they have higher status or when they are older. A mother's status is much higher than a young woman's. The formidable power of mothers in the Arab world is reflected in language to a great extent. Mothers, by praying for or cursing their children, are thought to be able to give happiness or inflict misery. A mother can pray for her son and her prayers are believed to have the utmost effect, and the opposite is likewise perceived to be true. All in all, in many contexts women may have more power than men.

9.2.3 The symbolic function of language

Most acts of language choice by both men and women are a symbolic act of some sort. If, for example, women are seen as a symbol of tradition and the transmitters of history in a culture, then they may want to preserve this role by using a specific variety and this may not necessarily be the most prestigious one. Miller (2004) posits that in Arab cities where the old urban vernacular has been replaced by a new one, it is older women who retain linguistic features of the old dialect. Still, in other situations of language contact and change, young women tend to acquire features faster. Eckert states that one cannot make the generalisation that women are more or less conservative than men; one may only say that women use "symbolic resources" more than men to "establish membership and status" (1998: 73). It could also be that women evaluate and use the symbolic resources differently.

A study by Hoffman (2006) on women's use of Berber reveals that women have the role of maintaining and transmitting it. According to Hoffman, at a time when political and economic factors shape women's linguistic practices, it is still rural Berber women who are responsible for speaking the language and remaining monolinguals. If the language is to maintain its vitality, it falls to women to pass it on. In some cases it is the only language they have mastered. The Tashelhit language community of southwestern Morocco was specifically examined. Tashelhit Berber speakers reside in the Anti-Atlas mountains and Sous valley. Note that in public urban Berber, men who are usually bilingual in Arabic (standard and colloquial) and Berber languages are the prominent figures in the "Berber Rights Movement" (Amazigh Rights Movement) for valorising and preserving the language (Demnati 2001, cited in Hoffman 2006: 146). The reason why the women are practically monolingual and do not speak any Arabic, although this in fact affects their access to resources, is because of the closer relation they have to the land, which may be because of their exclusion from city life and other domains. In the Anti-Atlas mountains, women are the agriculturalists and men are considered unfit to farm, but more suited for clean city work (Hoffman 2006: 156). Hoffman argues that although men are not attached to the land they are still attached to the language, since it serves as a symbol of belonging to a tribe and a community.

In a similar vein, a study by Walters (1996) reveals how language can be used as one of the symbolic resources for women. He studied a diglossic community and a bilingual one simultaneously. He studied foreign wives coming from England, Canada or the USA, who were married to Tunisian men and living in Tunisia. These wives have integrated themselves into a new community. To some extent their status in this community is predetermined by specific factors, such as them being native speakers of English and their husbands' position in this community as well as their in-laws' positions. However, there is room for these women to shape and modify their status. The language used for communication can serve as one of the symbolic means of modifying a status. These women have four options: they can learn Standard Arabic, Tunisian Arabic, French or communicate in their native English.

While these women are expected to learn Tunisian Arabic to interact with family and friends, some still prefer French as a symbolic means of keeping their distance and not getting involved in family conflicts. French also serves as a symbol of their power and prestige. One of the goals of the study was to highlight the differences in outcome despite the similarities in the social positions of these women.

To summarise, the linguistic choices available to women are also not absolute, but are limited by a number of factors, such as their access to a language or variety, the context and domain in which they can use this language or variety and the ability of learning a different language or variety (as is the case with the Anglophone wives of Tunisian men discussed above). Finally, language can be used as a symbolic resource for both men and women.

9.3 Methodological challenges and theoretical implications

In terms of methodologies, there are two challenges: collecting thorough and representative data and contextualising findings in terms of social and individual identity construction in different communities and correlating these findings with language use.

Variationist research that relies on gender as a variable starts with categorising participants as male or female and places them into fixed social classes which may yield circular arguments. Language in this case will just be a reflection of already existing social identities rather than a construction of identities and communities (Romaine 2003). Two key factors in the variation of speech between men and women, according to Romaine (2003: 109), are "access" and "role". The amount of access that women have to the prestige language and the role that they play in their community is significant in their language use. Both factors have to be considered before any conclusions about variation and gender can be reached. The study by Hoffman mentioned above could also be studied within this framework.

Variationists claim that in the Middle East and North Africa women move away from the prestige forms (cf. Romaine 2003). This is not necessarily true and may be the result of the confusion between standard and prestige.

Analysts who want to study the relation between language and gender should begin with the assumption that gender will rarely stand alone but will interact in complex ways with other social variables – fixed and flexible ones, like class, education and ethnicity. Likewise, they should assume that the range of behaviours engaged in by women and men are not independent – that it is not a case of one being from Mars and the other from Venus – but that they overlap and are highly contextualised.

In comparing and contrasting sources and methods used to study gender by linguists, it has been concluded that the sources used by linguists in North Africa are varied to some degree (from obituaries to women in the market) but much research remains to be done. For example, we need more studies examining job interviews such as Bogaers (1998), or how women are linguistically represented in the media.

When it comes to the methods, one finds that linguists studying the Arab world use the same techniques as their Western counterparts: they concentrate on quantitative studies, they use social correlates and statistics, and they also try to overcome the observer's paradox (cf. Coates 1993, for an overview of some Western studies on gender). However, the observer's paradox has never been completely overcome. As Haeri (1996: 106) posits, "Investigating interactions between iconic values based on sex differences and social structure is an inherently difficult task, and the data that would be required to examine [the issue completely] are not available".

In addition, linguists studying language and gender need to expand their horizons and include more studies that examine gender in relation to code-switching; like the study done by Walters (1996) in Tunisia, for example, and indeed the diglossic situation in the Arab world should be considered more in studies. Further, pragmatic studies that examine the language of men and women in relation to politeness are needed. For example, Keating (1998) studied women's roles in constructing status hierarchies, by examining honorific language in Pohnpei, Micronesia. Similar studies need to be conducted for the Arab world, although Arabic does not have true honorifics, it has other means of showing status and hierarchies. As Meyerhoff (2011: 245) contends about gender studies:

> [O]ne of the clear changes that has taken place over the last few decades is an emphasis on not only analysing how different variants are used by women and men as groups but also on understanding how a social category like gender emerges in more particular, individualised interactions. This may entail more detailed analysis using methods from conversations or discourse analysis, and de-emphasises the role of generalisations across individuals or across interactions.

It was also argued in this work that there are two main approaches to studying gender from a linguistic perspective. The "binary approach" to gender assumes that men and women, because of the way they are brought up and treated in their community, are two different groups and therefore differ in their linguistic performances. The "construction approach" assumes that men and women together form and are formed by a community, which in turn is constructed and modified by independent variables. Individuals, whether they are men or women, within this community, project an identity on themselves which is usually reflected in their linguistic performance.

Evidence from data from talk shows, as well as evidence from different studies that concentrate on the performance of women in the Arab world, reveals the intricate nature of concepts such as politeness and variation in language use.

The social status of women continues to change, especially in the Arab world, as the result of the exposure of women to the outside world, education, and work situations (cf. Haeri 1996; Kapchan 1996; Daher 1999; Sadiqi 2003).

The diglossic situation in the Arab world and North Africa adds a new dimension to our understanding of language variation and change in the region. A salient phonological feature such as the /q/ is in fact a Standard Arabic variable. Its realisation by different speakers in different communities may be related to education and literacy as well as exposure to Standard Arabic.

The question of the ideological connotations of linguistic variation in North Africa as part of the Arab world is long overdue. As Suleiman (2011) argues, while correlating linguistic variables with sociolinguistic ones, such as gender, class and ethnicity, linguists analysing the Arab world neglect issues related to the symbolic function of Arabic and the relation between Arabic, the self and the formation of identity in the socio-political world. These issues, according to Suleiman, are essential for a thorough understanding of language change and variation in the Arab world. Cameron (1997: 59–60) criticises variationist research for a different reason. He argues that this research usually falls into the trap of "correlational fallacy", by which one independent variable is tied, sometimes arbitrarily, to a linguistic one in a causal link. As Benwell and Stokoe (2006: 27) explain, one can never be sure of the "implicit assumptions" of such variables: "A person may speak with a pronounced Scottish accent, but we cannot be confident that this is an expression of 'Scottish identity'."

In public discourse, the ideological component is prevalent. Occasionally, we have a case of someone admitting to speaking an Alexandrian dialect, in order to emphasise an Alexandrian identity that is also an Egyptian one. What distinguishes public discourse data from variationist research data are the ideological and indexical elements. The causal link between language and identity is, in fact, sometimes underpinned. At times, linguists yoke linguistic variation together with social variables with no consideration given to indexes or associations of different codes. Studies that incorporate the ideological and political component of codes and linguistic variation are indeed needed, especially in a region as extensive as North Africa, one that is undergoing socio-political changes.

Notes

1 Haeri used networks to recruit subjects, a fact that sometimes makes results less representative.

Further reading

Bassiouney, Reem (2009) *Arabic Sociolinguistics: Topics in Diglossia, Gender, Identity, and Politics.* Washington, DC: Georgetown University Press. (This book contains a general introduction to the language situation in North Africa, with a focus on language policy and language in education.)

Miller, Catherine, Enam Al-Wer, Dominque Caubet and Janet C. E. Watson (eds) (2007) *Arabic in the City: Issues in Dialect Contact and Language Variation.* London: Routledge. (This study of urban vernaculars deals with an important aspect of a feature of North African societies – urbanization – and its impact on language.)

Sadiqi, Fatima (2003) *Women, Gender and Language in Morocco.* Leiden: Brill. (This study on Morocco has a narrower geographic and thematic focus, but is one of the few thorough book-length studies on language and gender in the Arab world, and is thus valuable.)

Suleiman, Yasir (2011) *Arabic, Self and Identity: A Study in Conflict and Displacement.* Oxford: Oxford University Press. (This book discusses issues of language and identity in general, but refers to Egypt and the Maghreb in the part of the author's memoirs.)

References

Abu-Lughod, Lila (1987) *Veiled Sentiments: Honor and Poetry in a Bedouin Society.* Cairo: American University in Cairo Press.

Bassiouney, Reem (2006) *Functions of Code Switching in Egypt: Evidence from Monologues*. Leiden: Brill.
——(2009) *Arabic Sociolinguistics: Topics in Diglossia, Gender, Identity, and Politics*. Washington, DC: Georgetown University Press.
——(2010) Identity and Code-choice in the Speech of Educated Women and Men in Egypt: Evidence from Talk Shows. In: *Arabic and the Media. Linguistic Analyses and Applications*. Reem Bassiouney (ed.), 97–121. Leiden: Brill.
Benwell, Bethan and Elizabeth Stokoe (2006) *Discourse and Identity*. Edinburgh: Edinburgh University Press.
Bhat, Darbhe N. S. (1978) A General Study of Palatization. In: *Universals of Human Language* (Volume 2). Joseph H. Greenberg, Charles Ferguson and Edith Moravcsik (eds), 47–91. Stanford: Stanford University Press.
Bogaers, Iris (1998) Gender in Job Interviews: Some Implications of Verbal Interactions of Women and Men. *International Journal of the Sociology of Language* 129: 35–58.
Brown, Penelope (1980) How and Why are Women More Polite: Some Evidence from a Mayan Community. In: *Women and Language in Literature and Society*. Sally McConnell-Ginet, Ruth Borker and Nelly Furman (eds), 111–36. New York: Praeger.
Brown, Penelope and Stephen C. Levinson (1987) *Politeness: Some Universals in Language Usage*. Cambridge: Cambridge University Press.
Cameron, Deborah (1997) Performing Gender Identity: Young Men's Talk and the Construction of Heterosexual Masculinity. In: *Language and Masculinity*. Sally Johnson and Ulrike Hanna Meinhof (eds), 47–64. Oxford: Blackwell.
——(2005) Language, Gender and Sexuality: Current Issues and New Directions. *Applied Linguistics* 26(4): 482–502.
Coates, Jennifer (1993) *Women, Men, and Language*. London: Longman.
Daher, Jamil (1999) (θ) and (ð) as Ternary and Binary Variables in Damascene Arabic. *Perspectives on Arabic Linguistics* 12: 163–202.
Deuchar, Margaret (1989) A Pragmatic Account of Women's Use of Standard Speech. In: *Women in their Speech Communities: New Perspectives on Language and Sex*. Jennifer Coates and Deborah Cameron (eds), 27–32. London: Longman.
Eckert, Penelope (1998) Gender and Sociolinguistic Variation. In: *Language and Gender. A Reader*. J. Coates (ed.), 62–75. Oxford: Blackwell.
——(2003) Language and Gender in Adolescence. In: *The Handbook of Language and Gender*. Janet Holmes and Miriam Meyerhoff (eds), 381–400. Oxford: Blackwell.
Eckert, Penelope and Sally McConnell-Ginet (2003) *Language and Gender*. Cambridge: Cambridge University Press.
Edelsky, Carole and Karen Adams (1990) Creating Inequality: Breaking the Rules in Debates. *Journal of Language and Social Psychology* 9(3): 171–90.
Ferguson, Charles (1959) Diglossia. *Word* 15: 325–40. Reprinted in: *Language and Social Context*. Pier Paolo Giglioli (ed.) (1972), 232–51. Harmondsworth: Penguin.
Fishman, Pamela (1980) Conversational Insecurity. In: *Language: Social Psychological Perspectives*. Howard Giles, Peter W. Robinson and Philip M. Smith (eds), 127–132. Oxford: Pergamon.
——(1983) Interaction. The Work that Women Do. In: *Language, Gender and Society*. Barrie Thorne, Cheris Kramarae and Nancy Henley (eds), 89–101. Rowley: Newbury House.
Fontaine, Jacques (2004) La population libyenne, un demi-siècle de mutations. In: *La nouvelle Libye : Sociétés, espace et géopolitique au lendemain de l'embargo*. Olivier Pliez (ed.), 159–78. Paris: Karthala-IREMAM .
Freed, Alice. F. (2003) Epilogue: Reflections on Language and Gender Research. In: *The Handbook of Language and Gender*. Janet Holmes and Miriam Meyerhoff (eds), 699–721. Oxford: Blackwell.
Gal, Susan (1978) Peasant Men Can't Get Wives: Language Change and Sex Roles in a Bilingual Community. *Language in Society* 7: 1–16.

Hachimi, Atiqa (2007) Becoming Casablancan: Fessis in Casablanca as a Case Study. In: *Arabic in the City: Issues in Dialect Contact and Language Variation.* Catherine Miller, Enam Al-Wer, Dominique Caubet and Janet C. E. Watson (eds), 97–122. London: Routledge.
Haeri, Niloofar (1996) "Why do Women do this?" Sex and Gender Differences in Speech. In: *Towards a Social Science of Language: Papers in Honor of William Labov.* Volume 1. Gregory R. Guy, Crawford Feagin, Deborah Schiffrin and John Baugh (eds), 101–114. Amsterdam: John Benjamins.
——(1996) *The Sociolinguistic Market of Cairo: Gender, Class, and Education.* London: Kegan Paul International.
——(1997) The Reproduction of Symbolic Capital: Language, State, and Class in Egypt. *World Journal of Human Sciences* 38(5): 795–816.
——(2006) Culture and Language. In: *Encyclopedia of Arabic Language and Linguistics.* Kees Versteegh, Mushira Eid, Alaa Elgibali, Manfred Woidich and Andrzej Zaborski (eds), 527–36. Leiden: Brill.
Hoffman, Katherine (2006) Berber Language Ideologies, Maintenance, and Contraction: Gendered Variation in the Indigenous Margins of Morocco. *Language and Communication* 26: 144–67.
Holmes, Janet (1995) *Women, Men and Politeness.* London: Longman.
——(1998) Women's Talk: The Question of Sociolinguistic Universals. In: *Language and Gender. A Reader.* Jennifer Coates (ed.), 461–83. Oxford: Blackwell.
Holmes, Janet and Miriam Meyerhoff (eds) (2003) *The Handbook of Language and Gender.* Oxford: Blackwell.
Holt, Mike (1994) Algeria: Language, Nation, and State. In: *Arabic Sociolinguistics. Issues and Perspectives.* Yasir Suleiman (ed.), 25–41. Richmond: Curzon Press.
Jakobson, Roman (1978[1957]) Mufaxxama: The "Emphatic" Phonemes of Arabic. In: *Readings in Arabic Linguistics.* Salman Al-Ani (ed.), 269–81. Indiana: Indiana University Linguistics Club.
James, Deborah and Janice Drakich (1993) Understanding Gender Differences in Amount of Talk: A Critical Review of Research. In: *Gender and Conversational Interaction.* Deborah Tannen (ed.), 281–312. Oxford: Oxford University Press.
Kapchan, Deborah (1996) *Gender on the Market: Moroccan Women and the Revoicing of Tradition.* Philadelphia: University of Pennsylvania Press.
Keating, Elizabeth (1998) Honor and Stratification in Pohnpei, Micronesia. *American Ethnologist* 25(3): 399–411.
Keenan, Elinor (1974) Norm-Makers, Norm-Breakers: Uses of Speech by Men and Women in a Malagasy Community. In: *Explorations in the Ethnography of Speaking.* Richard Baumann and Joel Sherzer (eds), 125–43. Cambridge: Cambridge University Press.
Kharraki, Abdennour (2001) Moroccan Sex-based Linguistic Difference in Bargaining. *Discourse and Society* 12: 615–32.
Kiesling, Scott F. (2003) Prestige, Cultural Models, and Other Ways of Talking About Underlying Norms and Gender. In: *The Handbook of Language and Gender.* Janet Holmes and Miriam Meyerhoff (eds), 509–27. Oxford: Blackwell.
Labov, William (1972a) *Sociolinguistic Patterns.* Philadelphia: University of Pennsylvania Press.
——(1972b) *Language in the Inner City: Studies in the Black English Vernacular.* Philadelphia: University of Pennsylvania Press.
——(1982) Building on Empirical Foundations. In: *Perspectives on Historical Linguistics.* Winnfried P. Lehmann and Yakov Malkiel (eds), 17–82. Amsterdam: Benjamins.
——(1990) The Intersection of Sex and Social Class in the Course of Linguistic Change. *Language Variation and Change* 2(2): 205–54.
Lakoff, Robin (2003) Language, Gender, and Politics: Putting "Women" and "Power" in the Same Sentence. In: *The Handbook of Language and Gender.* Janet Holmes and Miriam Meyerhoff (eds), 159–78. Oxford: Blackwell.
Lawson-Sako, Sarah and Itesh Sachdev (2000) Codeswitching in Tunisia: Attitudinal and Behavioural Dimensions. *Journal of Pragmatics* 32(9): 1343–61.

Leet-Pellegrini, Helena (1980) Conversational Dominance as a Function of Gender and Expertise. In: *Language. Social Psychological Perspectives*. Howard Giles, Peter Robinson and Philip M. Smith (eds), 97–104. Oxford: Pergamon.
Mansfield, Peter (2003) *A History of the Middle East* (second edition). New York: Penguin.
Mejdell, Guvnor (2006) *Mixed Styles in Spoken Arabic in Egypt*. Leiden: Brill.
Meyerhoff, Miriam (2011) *Introducing Sociolinguistics*. London: Routledge.
Miller, Catherine (2004) Variation and Change in Arabic Urban Vernaculars. In: *Approaches to Arabic Dialects: A Collection of Articles Presented to Manfred Woidich on the Occasion of his Sixtieth Birthday*. Martine Haak, Rudolf de Jong and Kees Versteegh (eds), 177–206. Leiden: Brill.
Milroy, Leslie (1987) *Language and Social Networks*. Oxford: Blackwell.
Paulston, Christina and Richard G. Tucker (eds) (2003) *Sociolinguistics.: The Essential Readings*. Oxford: Blackwell.
Pereira, Cristophe (2007) Urbanization and Dialect Change: The Arabic Dialect of Tripoli (Libya). In: *Arabic in the City: Issues in Dialect Contact and Language Variation*. Catherine Miller, Enam Al-Wer, Dominique Caubet and Janet C. E. Watson (eds), 77–96. London and New York: Routledge.
Preisler, Bent (1986) *Linguistic Sex Roles in Conversation*. Berlin: Mouton de Gruyter.
Romaine, Suzanne (2003) Variation in Language and Gender. In: *The Handbook of Language and Gender*. Janet Holmes and Miriam Meyerhoff (eds), 98–118. Oxford: Blackwell.
Royal, Ann Marie (1985) Male/Female Pharyngalization Patterns in Cairo Arabic: A Sociolinguistic Study of two Neighbourhoods. PhD dissertation, University of Texas.
Sadiqi, Fatima (2003) *Women, Gender and Language in Morocco*. Leiden: Brill.
——(2007) Language and Gender. In: *Encyclopedia of Arabic Language and Linguistics*. Kees Versteegh, Mushira Eid, Alaa Elgibali, Manfred Woidich and Andrzej Zaborski (eds), 642–50. Leiden: Brill.
Saʿdī, ʿU. (1993) *al-Taʿrīb fī al-Jazāʾir: Kifāḥ al-shaʿb ḍidda al-haymanah al-Frankūfūnīyah* [Arabization in Algeria: The People's Struggle against the Francophone Dominance]. Algiers: Dār al-Ummah.
Salami, L. Oladipo (1991) Diffusing and Focussing: Phonological Variation and Social Networks in Ife-Ife, Nigeria. *Language in Society* 20(2): 217–45.
Schick-Case, Sesan (1988) Cultural Differences, not Deficiencies: An Analysis of Managerial Women's Language. In: *Women's Careers. Pathways and Pitfalls*. Suzanna Rose and Laurie Larwood (eds), 41–63. New York: Praeger.
Sellam, A (1990) Aspects of the Communicative Approach to Language Teaching. *Revue de la Faculté des Lettres* 1(1): 81–93.
Smith-Hefner, Nancy J. (1988) Women and Politeness: The Javanese Example. *Language in Society* 17(4): 535–54.
Spolsky, Bernard (2004) *Language Policy*. Cambridge: Cambridge University Press.
Suleiman, Yasir (2011) *Arabic, Self and Identity: A Study in Conflict and Displacement*. Oxford: Oxford University Press.
Taine-Cheikh, Catherine (2007) The (R)urbanization of Mauritania: Historical Context and Contemporary Developments. In: *Arabic in the City: Issues in Dialect Contact and Language Variation*. Catherine Miller, Enam Al-Wer, Dominique Caubet and Janet C. E. Watson (eds), 35–54. London: Routledge.
Trabelsi, Chadia (1988) Les usages linguistiques des femmes de Tunis. PhD dissertation, Université Paris III.
Trudgill, Peter (1972) Sex, Covert Prestige, and Linguistic Change in the Urban British English of Norwich. *Language in Society* 1: 215–46.
UN (2014) Morocco. Online available at: http://data.un.org/CountryProfile.aspx?crName=Morocco (accessed on 9 April 2014).
Walters, Keith (1991) Women, Men, and Linguistic Variation in the Arab World. *Perspectives on Arabic Linguistics* 3: 199–229.
——(1996) Gender, Identity, and the Political Economy of Language: Anglophone Wives in Tunisia. *Language in Society* 25(4): 515–55.

10

THE CREOLE-SPEAKING CARIBBEAN

The architecture of language variation

Hubert Devonish

10.1 Introduction

This chapter covers the main sociolinguistic theories that have been applied to a common sub-type of language situation in the Creole-speaking Caribbean. These theories attempt to explain the relationship between interlocking and/or overlapping language varieties. Typically, these language varieties have been described as operating within an overall system of diglossia, a concept developed by Ferguson (1959) and reviewed and revised by Hudson (2002). This description emphasises the differences between the language varieties. Interestingly, the Caribbean exemplar, Haiti, included in the original formulation of diglossia, was excluded by Hudson's (2002) comprehensive review of the concept in a special issue of the *International Journal of the Sociology of Language* on diglossia. This chapter will present a more nuanced version of diglossia which would indeed account for Haiti and similar Caribbean situations.

Alternatively, the Caribbean language situations have been viewed as creole continua, a concept originally introduced by Reinecke (1969 [1935]) to describe the language situation involving Hawaiian Creole and English. Within this scenario, the language situation is viewed as consisting of a seamless progression of minimally distinct language varieties from the acrolect, the high status European language, to the basilect, the low status Creole vernacular language variety most divergent from the acrolect. How these seemingly contradictory approaches, emphasising respectively difference and similarity, can be reconciled is the focus of this chapter.

The Creole-speaking Caribbean begins, at its most south-easterly extreme, on the shoulder of South America in French Guiana (Guyane), extending westward to include Suriname (formerly Dutch Guiana) and the Republic of Guyana (formerly British Guiana). The region then takes in the geographic Caribbean, the islands in the Caribbean Sea, from Trinidad in the south-east to the Bahamas in the north-west, as well as the parts of mainland Central America on the Caribbean coast, particularly

Belize. Those Caribbean territories in which Spanish is the dominant language – i.e. Cuba, the Dominican Republic and Puerto Rico – do not have a numerically significant Creole-speaking population and are, therefore, on linguistic grounds, excluded from this discussion. The territories in question have a numerically significant, typically a majority Creole-speaking population.

In the majority of cases, the local Creole language has a vocabulary that originated in the European language with which it currently co-exists. Within such situations, the Creole language is normally the language of private and informal interaction, and the European language the official language and language of public formal interaction, literacy and education. This is a pattern typical of Guyana, Trinidad, Saint Vincent, Jamaica, Bahamas and Belize (Taylor 1977).

10.2 The specific areas under investigation

There are also the cases of Haiti, Martinique, Guadeloupe and Guyane, in which French-lexicon Creoles coexist with French as official language. It is these cases that constitute the focus of this chapter. Excluded are Caribbean Creole-language situations in which the mass-based vernacular Creole language is not lexically related to the main official European language. Examples include the Spanish-Portuguese lexicon Creole, Papiamentu (co-existing with Dutch as an official language in Aruba, Bonaire and Curacao) and French-lexicon Creole (co-existing with English as the official language in Saint Lucia and Dominica).

The following, although describing Haiti, presents a broadly correct picture of the traditional language situation in the type of Caribbean Creole-speaking situation of interest to us:

> in Haiti, full participation in the life of the community requires knowledge of the vernacular as well as knowledge of and literacy in the official language. On the other hand, the majority of Haitians are monolingual speakers of Haitian Creole and are totally excluded from participation in official matters, for these are carried out in French.
>
> *(Valdman 1971: 61)*

10.2.1 Previous research

In the past five decades, language attitudes, language status and the domains within which the language varieties are used have changed, under the influence of mass movements associated with anti-colonialism, nationalism and democratisation. The Creole vernacular is increasingly coexisting with the lexically related European language in domains that were previously the preserve of the latter. This has increased the lack of clarity about the roles, functions and ultimately even the features of the specific coexisting language varieties. This fuzzy relationship between Creole and lexically related European languages within the same societies was a trigger for much of the early sociolinguistic work of the 1950s and 1960s.

Two different trends have emerged within sociolinguistic studies of the region. One looks at the macro-sociolinguistic level and focuses on the linguistic differences between the language varieties in use and the way these correlate with language function. This lies at the heart of attempts to apply or reject the application of Charles Ferguson's (1959) notion of diglossia to Caribbean Creole language situations. The other takes a micro-view, examining the accumulation of small linguistic differences which produce the large differences between the least prestigious language variety, the basilect, and the most prestigious, the acrolect. This is the concept of the Creole continuum (Allsopp 1958; DeCamp 1971). Much of the motivation for this kind of research is education policy and practice. The Creole-speaking Caribbean has been characterised, in the past five decades, by a rapidly expanding and democratising education system operating exclusively, and so far inefficiently, in the dominant European language (Le Page 1968; Craig 1971, 1999; Carpenter and Devonish 2012).

10.3 Separate language varieties, separate language functions: the case for conquest diglossia

Diglossia is a modern sociolinguistic theory developed explicitly to explain language behaviour in a part of the Creole-speaking Caribbean. It operates at the macro-level and seeks to predict and explain the distribution of language varieties, and the social functions that they perform in those special language situations deemed to be diglossic. Charles Ferguson (1959: 435, capitals in original), the originator of the concept, presents diglossia in the following manner:

> DIGLOSSIA is a relatively stable language situation in which, in addition to the primary dialects of the language, [...] there is a very divergent, highly codified [...] superposed variety, the vehicle of a large and respected body of written literature, [...], which is learned largely by formal education and is used for most written and formal spoken purposes but is not used by any sector of the community for ordinary conversation.

As distinct from the much looser definition provided by Joshua Fishman (1967), the original Ferguson (1959) proposal requires that two language varieties in the diglossia, which he labels "the primary dialects", must be similar enough to each other that members of the speech community could consider them forms of the same language. This is facilitated by an overlap in the lexicon of the two language varieties since, as Ferguson (1959: 434) states, "Generally speaking, the bulk of the vocabulary of H and L is shared, of course with variations in form and with differences of use and meaning". Even with this tight definition, however, a set of historically quite distinct language situations are pushed together under the umbrella of "diglossia" as we shall see.

Ferguson (1959) uses four defining situations to illustrate diglossia. Two of these, Greek and Arabic, involve classical/literary varieties of a language which can be viewed as "internal", that is originating within the speech community. This classical/literary language variety in each of these situations functions as the High or H language, the one used in public and formal interaction, the education system, religion and in formal writing. In the other two defining situations, German-speaking Switzerland and Haiti, we have cases in which the H language variety is an "external" language, an import from another country. These are respectively French (imported from France in the case of Haiti) and Standard German (an import from Germany in the Swiss example). The Swiss German and Haitian cases, in turn, represent two quite distinct sub-types among those diglossic situations with an "external" H. In the former case, the Swiss German community took a historically pragmatic decision during the nineteenth century to use an external norm, that employed in Germany, as the language of writing and formal interaction (Haas 1981: 36–41; Trudgill 1998: 28). By contrast, the presence of French in Haiti is the result of colonial conquest and domination. This produced the language situation of modern-day Haiti, in which an external norm, French, is the main language of writing, education and public-formal discourse, with Haitian Creole, subject to later qualification in this chapter, largely the language of private and informal domains. English and Dutch, elsewhere in the Creole-speaking Caribbean, also owe their presence in the Caribbean to conquest and colonial imposition.

The sub-types of diglossia being proposed here do not appear in the original Ferguson (1959) article, in part, at least, explaining the already mentioned exclusion of Haiti from diglossia by the Hudson (2002) review. It is Devonish (2003) who first introduces the term "conquest diglossia" to distinguish Haitian-type diglossic situations from the consensus-type diglossias such as that of German-speaking Switzerland. One key characteristic of the Haitian diglossia, and by extension other cases of conquest diglossia, emerges naturally from colonial origins of the language situation. Only a relatively small proportion of the speech community participates in that diglossia. For Haiti, the oft-quoted figure is 10 per cent. This bilingual educated elite are the only ones who have the linguistic repertoire required to behave in a diglossic manner. The remaining 90 per cent are stated to be monolingual in Haitian Creole, a monoglossic majority in an overall diglossic situation (Prudent 1980: 101). This exclusion of the majority both breeds and is an expression of language conflict (Prudent 1980: 103). The focus of this conflict is access to the power of a state whose internal functions are conducted almost exclusively in French. The Creole monolingual majority are perpetually, on the ground of language, excluded from those aspects of public, formal and written domains involving the exercise of the decision-making powers of the state. Language is functioning as the medium for the exercise of state power by a bilingual elite class over the monolingual Creole-speaking mass of the population.

Significantly different outcomes flow from the difference in the history of a consensus diglossic situation like that of German-speaking Switzerland. No section of the population of the Swiss German community would use Standard German for private informal situations and as a home language (Haas 1981: 36–41). There is much less clarity in Haitian and similar situations. Pompilus (1961: 93) refers to the results of a census carried out in Haiti in 1949, just ten years prior to Ferguson's 1959 diglossia article. These figures showed that in Port-au-Prince, the capital, 11.1 per cent of the population declared that they spoke French as their main language at home. This is consistent with the general trend in Caribbean Creole conquest diglossic situations. The local ethos values and promotes the use of the imported H in all domains, including those that are normally the preserve of the L. Very often, the motive is educational, to ensure that children get early and consistent exposure to the elite prestige H language variety. Observations made of the Haitian language situation during the 1970s and 1980s suggest that this state of affairs has continued. Valdman (1984: 79) and Dejean (1993) observe that French is used as a home language by members of the bilingual Haitian elite. This class, although capable of and using Creole when the circumstances require it, uses French for all vernacular purposes as well. On the other side of the fence, the monolingual Creole-speaking majority employ Creole in every domain and communicative situation.

According to the Ferguson (1959) version of diglossia, the H and L varieties are regarded as varieties of the same language. Dejean (1993: 75) claims that French and Haitian Creole are widely regarded as two separate languages. However, the language behaviours he reports (Dejean 1993: 81–82) indicate both attitudes and speech forms which do not maintain the distinction he maintains. He goes on to report that the bilingual elite group has "scorn and disdain for Creole, a conviction of the inferior and inadequate character of popular speech" (Dejean 1993: 79). This suggests a perception that, for them, popular speech, that is Creole, does not exist as an autonomous language form. Typical of diglossic situations, the existence of the L is often denied by speakers (Ferguson 1959: 430). The clear implication is that Creole is an inferior and inadequate form of the H, French.

10.4 The structure of the Haitian diglossia: a theoretical framework

Given the overlapping language functions, of what value is the concept of diglossia and its applicability to Haiti? The diagram by Valdman (1984: 80) showing the distribution of languages provides some guidance. Even though Haitian Creole had a standard writing system developed for it in the late 1970s, French was and continues to be the primary medium of writing. At the societal level, French is the predominant language of writing, with Creole and French both functioning as spoken languages. More specifically, domains that involve the internal functioning of the state apparatuses – e.g. the formal education system, the legal system, the political system, and, for instance, government administration – operate predominantly or entirely in French. This is to be distinguished from those domains requiring that these apparatuses communicate with the monolingual Creole-speaking majority over whom it governs. Then, Creole would be used. Examples of use of Creole by the state apparatuses include the conduct of court cases in rural areas, interaction with the general public in government offices and political speeches (Dejean 1993). For the bilingual elite, in private informal domains, language choice involves code switching between Creole and French, triggered by considerations of topic, style and interlocutor (Dejean 1993). For the diglossic elite, French is used in all the domains, including the private and informal. Creole coexists with French in private and informal interactions. Given this fluid situation, diglossia is a notion that does not allow one to predict language choice at the micro-level for a bilingual speaker in a private informal situation.

According to Ferguson (1959: 433): "Diglossia typically persists at least several centuries, and evidence in some cases seems to show that it can last well over a thousand years." This statement, one would suggest, may apply to consensus diglossic situations such as that of German-speaking Switzerland. It is, however, not valid in relation to situations of conquest diglossia. To be fair to Ferguson, he does envisage the possibility of change. It is for this reason that he presents a prognosis of ongoing "relative stability" for Swiss German, even while predicting "[s]low development toward a unified standard based on the L of Port-au-Prince" (Ferguson 1959: 437). This prediction is borne out by the way the politics of language is played out right across the Caribbean. No Swiss German-type national consensus on the language exists which could be the basis for stability. By 1987, less than 30 years after Ferguson applied the label of diglossia to Haiti, the new post-dictatorship constitution of Haiti was to declare: "Tous les Haitiens sont unis par une langue commune: Le Créole. Le Créole et le Français sont les langues officielles de la République" – "All Haitians are united by a common language, Creole. Creole and French are the two official languages of the Republic" (Constitution de la République d'Haiti 1987, Article 6). This was the outcome of fierce struggles over the extent to which the mass of the Haitian population should control state power. One manifestation of this was the drive to make Creole, the language of the popular masses, Creole, the language of the nation and of the state. This conflict over the role and status of a Creole vernacular language and a coexisting lexically related standard European language is very typical of the Creole-speaking Caribbean. This ongoing language conflict is documented in works such as Devonish (2007), for the general Caribbean, Christie (2003) for Jamaica and Dejean (1993) for Haiti.

Perhaps because Haiti is used by Ferguson (1959) as one of the exemplars of diglossia, the use of diglossia as a label for language situations in work on situations involving French and French-lexicon Creoles in the Caribbean has been fairly standard (Prudent 1980: 100–103). This is in spite of extensive criticism about the applicability of diglossia to Haiti and other Caribbean situations. In work on those Caribbean countries where English coexists with an English-lexicon Creole, typically, the word "diglossia" is not used. However, the concept does play a role in the way that these language situations are viewed.

A very important example of diglossic analysis which does not speak its name is *The Dictionary of Caribbean English Usage (DCEU)* (Allsopp 1996). This is a reference work and language standardisation instrument, painstakingly compiled over three decades by a linguist, Richard Allsopp. Its target is the educated classes of the 15 British or former British possessions in the Caribbean. These include countries such as Jamaica, Guyana, Barbados, Saint Vincent and Belize.

In these countries, English functions as the official and public formal language and English-lexicon Creoles as languages of private and informal interaction. Allsopp models aspects of a diglossic language ideology very clearly in the introduction to the *DCEU*. This work codifies Standard Caribbean English (SCE), the H variety in the diglossia that exists in the ex-British Creole-speaking Caribbean. In it, Allsopp (1996: lvi) defines Standard Caribbean English/Caribbean Standard English (SCE) as "The literate English of educated nationals of Caribbean territories and their spoken English such as is considered natural in formal social contexts". The definition of SCE as a written language, that is "literate English", and as one spoken naturally "in formal social contexts", is significant. These observations clearly underscore the role of SCE as the H variety in a diglossic situation. In the other domains, varying only in relation to their degrees of formalness, Allsopp (1996) claims the existence of an unnamed language variety or language varieties, variously described as Creole "remainder features", Creole "borrowings" or Creole "survivals". Typical of diglossic ideology, the notion of the L, English-lexicon Creole as a complete and coherent linguistic system, is absent from this representation. As Ferguson (1959: 431) states, "H alone is regarded as real and L is reported 'not to exist'". It is this same Allsopp (1958) who is first to apply the concept of the Creole continuum to Caribbean language situations. Within the Caribbean, the Creole continuum is often seen as a competing concept to diglossia and is the subject of the following section.

10.5 Bridging the linguistic extremes: the Creole continuum

As far back as his original article on diglossia, Ferguson (1959) had laid out the framework for an understanding of the micro-level aspects of diglossia. According to Ferguson (1959: 432), "The communicative tensions which arise in the diglossia situation may be resolved by the use of relatively uncodified, unstable, intermediate forms of the language […] and repeated borrowing of vocabulary items from H to L". Partially successful efforts at democratising access to education have led to an increase in the size of the diglossic educated classes. This has produced a sizable portion of the population engaged in continual and widespread switching between language varieties across constantly changing language situations. Speakers need to switch codes with minimum effort, while maintaining a sufficient distinction between the H and the L to signal the social differences associated with these language varieties. As Ferguson (1959: 433) suggests for diglossic situations in general, in the Caribbean situations under study, intermediate varieties have emerged. These reflect a process of mixing of the standard European language or H characteristics, on the one hand, and those of Creole or L, on the other. The research on these intermediate varieties in the Caribbean suggests that, far from being unstable, these varieties are quite stable and rule-governed. What specifically, then, did scholars have to say about these intermediate varieties?

Richard Allsopp (1958), with reference to the Creole continuum Guyanese Creole and English in what was then British Guiana, lists nine different possible ways of saying "I told him". Derek Bickerton (1975: 13) suggests that this list could not have been the result of a random mixing of features from coexistent linguistic systems since this could not explain "why only the outputs listed by Allsopp occur with any degree of frequency, while the majority of the twenty-four [theoretically possible combinations] never occur at all".

David DeCamp (1971) adds to the discussion of mixed features on the Creole continuum by explicitly demonstrating the constraints that affect the ability of variants from the acrolect, the high-status language variety, and the basilect, the low-status language variety, to co-occur. DeCamp's focus is the Jamaican language situation, involving, as in Guyana, an English-lexicon Creole coexisting with English. He demonstrates that the output of individual speakers can be ranked on an implicational scale.

By way of providing social background to the implicational scale, DeCamp (1971: 358) states,

> We may note, for example, that informant 5 [our Speaker 7], at one end of the line, is a young and well educated proprietor of a successful radio and appliance shop in Montego Bay; that informant 4 [our Speaker 1], at the other end of the line, is an elderly and illiterate peasant farmer in an isolated mountain village; and that the social and economic facts on the informants are roughly (not exactly) proportional to these informants' position on the continuum.

DeCamp (1971: 356) remarks that the implicational scaling technique he adopts "is based on the co-occurrence of features within each idiolect". Implicational scaling produces the $n+1$ rule; that is, if there are n variables with two variants each, and their co-occurrences are scalable, there shall be $n+1$ possible sets of co-occurrences (Rickford 2002: 143). The number of implicationally scaled idiolects that DeCamp can identify by this technique would be constrained by the $n+1$ rule.

Along similar lines, Bickerton (1973: 665–66), in relation to Guyana, presents examples of the co-occurrence restrictions produced by the implicational scaling of the linguistic variants of variables within the speech of his informants. According to Bickerton (1975: 203): "At different times and in different circumstances, given the switching capacities […] the same individual may be located at widely differing points on a scale, and his range must therefore be regarded as potentially spanning all the isolects between its extremes." This is part of a debate, which also involves Rickford (1987b: 136), about what constitutes appropriate data on which to base a linguist's construct of a lect or language variety on the implicationally scaled Creole continuum. Should it be the speech of the individual, the speech of an individual on a single speech occasion or some other body of linguistic data? Devonish (1989: 129–40, 1991: 565–84, 1998: 1–12) makes the specific claim that the unit within which linguistic interaction between Creole and English takes place is the clause. He points out, by way of support, that Bickerton's own examples of co-occurrence rules all occur inside the clause. Beyond the clause, speakers are free to shift language variety as their linguistic repertoires allow and as social factors require.

Situations in which English coexists with an English-lexicon Creole have been the focus of proposals about the Creole continuum. However, there has been a secondary discourse about the possibility of Creole continua in those parts of the Caribbean in which a French-lexicon Creole coexists with French. Ferguson (1959: 435) recognises intermediate varieties as secondary characteristics of diglossia, suggesting that "the communicative tensions" that arise in diglossia are resolved in Haiti by a "créole de salon", a heavily Gallicised variety of Haitian Creole used by the privileged bilingual minority of that country. Valdman (1968), supported by the observations of Dejean (1993), identifies the existence of intermediate varieties, constituting a continuum of sorts, ranging between French, creolised French, Gallicised Creole (urban Creole) and rural Haitian Creole. Valdman argues that, at the phonological level, there is a seamless continuum across these varieties, though, at the syntactic level, a structural gap might separate the varieties of French from the varieties of Creole. With reference to rural monolingual Creole speakers, Valdman (1968) also suggests they shift to the urban variety in the kinds of public formal domains which would trigger the use of French for the bilingual elite. For rural monolinguals, the urban variety was their H variety, their "French".

Lefebvre (1974) makes a claim for Martinique similar to that made by Ferguson (1959) for Haiti, that the intermediate varieties in her data represent unsystematic attempts to approximate French. This leads naturally to the conclusion that a continuum between French and Creole does not exist in these situations. The prevalence of this perspective is noted in Prudent (1980: 107). One can speculate that this claim may merely manifest the relative purist linguistic ideology of scholars working in the French tradition and on Caribbean territories in which French is the official language.

The conclusions of this section are consistent with the findings of Winford (1985), who examined the extent to which diglossia and the Creole continuum were compatible. He concludes that Creole continua of the type found in the Caribbean are simply a special sub-type of diglossia. There is a challenge here, however. The very concept of diglossia relies on there being two distinct language varieties being employed for different social functions. Intermediate varieties are accommodated on the fringes of diglossia theory, as being responses to "communicative tensions". How, then, could the concept of the Creole continuum, epitomising as it does the absence of clear distinctions between varieties, be accommodated within the concept of diglossia, with two discrete language varieties, an H and an L? This is addressed in the following section.

10.5.1 Supporting the bridge: load-bearing variables

The work of Irvine (2005) in relation to Jamaica suggests that speakers in a situation of coexisting language varieties, whose use has high social value, typically economise on the effort to produce and identify English and Creole. This economy is expressed, according to her, by way of "load-bearing" variables. Irvine (2005: 297) defines as load-bearing those variables containing a variant which, if not produced in

	Variable 1	(E) ~ (C)	Variable 2	(E) ~ (C)
1)		E		E
2)		E		C
3)		C		C

FIGURE 10.1 Use and effects of load-bearing variants

"significant quantities, the speaker will not be interpreted in the Jamaican speech community as someone speaking English". She suggests, in fact, that "it is the use of these load-bearing variants, and not English variants *per se*, that defines someone as speaking SJE". Put simply, of the E(nglish) variants that make up the language variety "English" within the speech community, some are highly valued as marking the use of English. These are load-bearing. Others are less valued for signalling use of English and are deemed non-load-bearing. This relationship can be illustrated on an implicational scale as in Figure 10.1.

Irvine (2005) defines load-bearing strictly in relation to what is or is not English. For her, therefore, Variable 2 would be load-bearing, carrying as it does the variant with the bold E, the variant highly valued as signalling the use of English. An approach that, simultaneously, looks at what is or is not Creole will come up with a somewhat revised picture. Variable 1, with its bold C highly valued for signalling the use of Creole, would be the Creole load-bearing variable, contrasting with Variable 2 performing the same function for English. Within this framework, some variables serve to distinguish between Creole and non-Creole; others signal the distinction between English and non-English. Without a clearly defined Jamaican Creole (JC), it would be impossible to have a clearly defined Standard Jamaican English (SJE) and vice versa. That load-bearing variables behave in a complementary fashion is a natural product of the language situation. This claim is demonstrated in Figure 10.1. In Variable 1, the use of the E variant simply tells us that Creole is *not* being used, since there is an intermediate variety that also allows for the use of that E variant. By contrast, the use of the C variant here tells us that Creole is being used. In complementary fashion, the use of a C variant for Variable 2 signals merely that English is not being used. It is the use of the E variant here that signals that English is being used.

The research on load-bearing variables shows that, in these Creole continuum situations, there is both a need for intermediate varieties and for the polar varieties at each extreme. There is constrained mixing, allowing both speaker and hearer to focus on just a subset of the features which differentiate the H from the L, the acrolect from the basilect.

The application of this load-bearing principle can be seen also at the lexical level. According to Sand (1999: 103–5), in SJE radio and newspaper texts, where SJE and JC have a common vocabulary, there is a preference, in SJE usage, for employing lexical variants that do not exist in JC. These tend to be very learned vocabulary items rarely used in similar texts in standard varieties of English outside of the Caribbean. In relation to one vocabulary item, she compares the frequencies in the Great Britain English corpus of the International Corpus of English Project with a parallel Jamaican one. She found that SJE is approximately five times as likely to record the use of the more formal variant as is British English. A similar trend is seen when SJE usage is compared with that of a New Zealand English corpus.

These lexical variables are all load-bearing. Their less formal SJE variants, which are shared with JC, when used, send no specific signal as to whether SJE or JC is being used. The formal variant carries the load of signalling that English is being used, hence their higher frequency in Jamaica, given the need to signal, in formal written contexts, that SJE rather than JC is not being used.

Load-bearing variables and the implicational scaling with which they are linked complement each other. Together, they serve to maintain difference, as required by diglossia, in a context of similarity, as required by the notion of the creole continuum.

10.6 Conclusion: apart at extremes, yet part of a whole

We have two frameworks within which to understand the language variation in Caribbean societies that has been the subject of this chapter. One framework is that of diglossia. It operates at the macro-level, and treats the H variety and its L counterpart as distinct language varieties. This approach proposes that the two varieties have complementary social functions, one as the language of the public and formal, the other as the speech form appropriate to the private and informal.

The competing framework is that of the (post-)Creole continuum. This is used to explain language behaviour in these societies at the micro-level. Language varieties can be ranged on a continuum from the acrolect to the basilect, with intermediate mesolectal varieties acting as transitional varieties between the extremes. The distinction between the acrolect and the basilect involves an accumulation of small differences between neighbouring varieties in the middle of the continuum.

How do we reconcile these radically different views of these Caribbean language situations? As part of a mathematical modelling of the Creole continuum in Guyana, Thomas and Devonish (2008) stumble on results that may help reconcile these seemingly contradictory perspectives of diglossia and Creole continuum. They presume that there were two historically distinct linguistic systems, English and Creole. They further presume that these two varieties have mixed to produce the intermediate varieties on the continuum. Their goal is to identify which of two mathematical models, one linear, the other non-linear, more closely approximates reality.

In the linear model, the $n+1$ rule applies as with the implicationally scaled Creole continuum. For every clausal string with n binary linguistic variables, each consisting of an E(nglish) variant and a C(reole) one, there is a single allowable combination of Es and Cs (Thomas and Devonish 2008: 13). Thomas and Devonish (2008: 15–16) also examine the alternative, a non-linear model. Thomas and Devonish (2008) plot a graph that shows what happens when co-occurrence takes place with a probability of 1.0; that is, E and C variants across variables are allowed to co-occur within the same clause without constraint. This produces an exponential increase in the number of possible combinations, as the number of variables in the clause increases. This is consistent with an "everything goes" relationship between Es and Cs, where English and Creole mix freely and in all combinations. This we know not to be the reality. Some co-occurrences of Es and Cs across variables within the clause are allowable. Others are blocked. This means that the actual probability of co-occurrences is less than 1.0. The results show what happens when the probability of Es and Cs co-occurring across variables in the same clause drops below 1.0. The number of possible combinations initially rises in a manner consistent with the *n+1* rule associated with implicational scaling. However, this rise is brief and as the number of variables within the clause increases, the possible number of combinations eventually trends down to two (Thomas and Devonish 2008: 16).

The seemingly contradictory outcomes of the two models suggest an important insight. When one is looking at the small number of linguistic variables that can coexist within a clause, perhaps between five and ten, the results may present themselves in a form that may be linearly modelled, involving something resembling the *n+1* rule, and an implicationally scaled continuum. However, when projected as should be the case, across the exceptionally large number of linguistic variables that can theoretically manifest themselves within a particular clause, the results look quite different. These results show a trend towards the existence of two discrete language varieties. In short, Creole and English interact with each other, producing clauses with mixed features which nevertheless can be assigned to one of two distinct language varieties.

The linear model, when the probability is 1.0, models the output of an implicationally scaled continuum. The non-linear model, by contrast, models the operations of the diglossia mode. Communication within the Caribbean situations under study involves, at the macro-level, crude, diglossic-type language choices influenced by considerations of domain. Communication here also involves, at the individual level, fine-grained language choices. These choices are influenced by the range of one's linguistic repertoire and the nuances of topic and tone, and slight changes of situation. Each mathematical modelling suggests the validity of each of these theories and points to the need for theorising about them in ways that integrate them. A linguistic bridge requires simultaneously two ends that are apart, the H and the L, as highlighted by diglossia. A set of structured, intermediate elements along a continuum constitutes the bridge between the two extremes, the acrolect and the basilect. Thus, a clause at the acrolectal English end may consist of an EEEEE string which gradually transitions, via the sequences EEEEC, EEECC, EECCC, and ECCCC, to the Creole basilectal end of the form CCCCC. A speaker using a variety with 3E and 2C is producing an approximation of the 5E variety at the acrolectal extreme. In a similar manner, if 2E and 3C are produced, the clause has to be treated as an approximation of the basilect with 5E at the other extreme of the continuum. Wholly apart at the extremes, the polar varieties are part of a whole, linked by the middle.

Further reading

Dejean, Yves (1993) An Overview of the Language Situation in Haiti. *International Journal of the Sociology of Language* 102: 73–83. (Based on personal experience as a Haitian and a linguist with broad experience of life and language in Haiti, Dejean contests the applicability of diglossia to Haiti, one of the exemplars of the concept used by Ferguson. Dejean contests the notion the Haitian Creole and French are, or function as, dialects of the same language. He also argues, with specific reference to the rural areas of Haiti, that Haitian Creole functions in all domains, public and private, formal and informal.)

Winford, Donald (1985) The Syntax of Fi Complements in Caribbean English Creole. *Language* 61(3): 588–624. (This paper presents a detailed comparison of the linguistic and sociocultural characteristics of Ferguson's defining diglossic situations with those described as constituting Creole continua in the Caribbean. He concludes that Caribbean Creole continuum situations have much more in common with diglossic ones than with any other type of language situation.)

References

Allsopp, Richard (1958) Pronominal Forms in the Dialect of English used in Georgetown (British Guiana) and its Environs by Persons Engaged in Nonclerical Occupations. MA thesis, London University.

Allsopp, Richard (ed.) (1996) *The Dictionary of Caribbean English Usage*. Oxford: Oxford University Press.

Bickerton, Derek (1973) On the Nature of a Creole Continuum. *Language* 49: 640–69.

——(1975) *Dynamics of a Creole System*. Cambridge: Cambridge University Press.

Carpenter, Karen and Hubert Devonish (2012) Boys Will Be Boys: Gender and Bilingual Education in a Creole Language Situation. In: *Language, Culture and Caribbean Identity*. Jeannette Allsopp and John R. Rickford (eds), 161–76. Kingston: University of the West Indies Press.

Christie, Pauline (2003) *Language in Jamaica*. Kingston: Arawak.

Craig, Dennis (1971) Education and Creole English in the West Indies. In: *Pidginization and Creolization of Language*. Dell Hymes (ed.), 371–92. Cambridge: Cambridge University Press.

——(1999) *Teaching Language and Literacy: Policies and Procedures for Vernacular Language Situations*. Georgetown: Education and Development Services.

DeCamp, David (1971) Toward a Generative Analysis of a Post-creole Speech Continuum. In: *Pidginization and Creolization of Languages*. Dell Hymes (ed.), 349–70. Cambridge: Cambridge University Press.

Dejean, Yves (1993) An Overview of the Language Situation in Haiti. *International Journal of the Sociology of Language* 102: 73–83.

Devonish, Hubert (1989) Language Variation Theory in the Light of Co-occurrence Restriction Rules. *York Papers in Linguistics* 13: 129–40.

——(1991) Standardisation in a Creole Continuum Situation: The Guyana Case. In: *English Around the World: Sociolinguistic Perspectives*. Jenny Cheshire (ed.), 565–84. Cambridge: Cambridge University Press.

——(1998) On the Existence of Autonomous Varieties in Creole Continuum Situations. In: *Studies in Caribbean Language* (Volume 2). Pauline Christie, Barbara Lalla, Velma Pollard and Lawrence Carrington (eds), 1–12. St Augustine: Society for Caribbean Linguistics.

——(2003) Language Advocacy and Conquest Diglossia in the "Anglophone Caribbean". In: *The Politics of English as a World Language*. Christian Mair (ed.), 157–78. New York: Editions Rodopi.

——(2007 [1986]) *Language and Liberation: Creole Language Politics in the Caribbean*. Kingston: Arawak Publications.

Ferguson, Charles A. (1964 [1959]) Diglossia. In *Language in Culture and Society*. Dell Hymes (ed.), 429–439. New York: Harper and Row.

Fishman, Joshua A. (1967) Bilingualism with and without Diglossia: Diglossia with or without Bilingualism. *Journal of Social Issues* 23(2): 29–38.

Haas, Walter (1981) Entre dialecte et langue – l'example du Schwyzertütsch. In: *Le Schwyzertütsch: 5e Langue Nationale? Actes du Colloque de la Commision Interuniversitaries Suisse de Linguistique Appliquée*. Françoise Redard, René Jeanneret and Jean-Pierre Métral (eds), 23–41. Neuchatel: Organe de la Commission Interuniversitaire Suisse de Linguistique Appliqué.

Hudson, Alan (2002) Outline of a Theory of Diglossia. *International Journal of the Sociology of Language* 157: 1–48

Irvine, Grace A. (2004) A Good Command of the English Language: Phonological Variation in the Jamaican Acrolect. *Journal of Pidgin and Creole Languages* 19(1): 41–76.

——(2005) Defining Good English in Jamaica: Language Variation and Language Ideology in an Agency of the Jamaican State. PhD dissertation, University of the West Indies, Jamaica.

Lefebvre, Claire (1974) Discreteness and the Linguistic Continuum in Martinique. *Anthropological Linguistics* 16(2): 47–78.

Le Page, Robert (1968) Problems to be Faced in the Use of English as a Medium of Instruction in Four West Indian Territories. In: *Language Problems of Developing Nations*. Joshua A. Fishman, Charles Ferguson and Jyotirindra Das Gupta (eds), 431–41. London: Wiley.

Pompilus, Pradel (1961) *La Langue Française en Haïti*. Paris: Institut des Hautes Études de l'Amérique Latine.

Prudent, Lambert-Félix (1980) *Des baragouins à la langue antillaise: Analyse historique et sociolinguistique du discours sur le créole* [From Jargons to the Antillean Language: Historical and Sociolinguistic Analysis of the Discourses about Creole]. Paris: Editions Caribéennes.

Reinecke, John (1969 [1935]). *Language and Dialect in Hawaii* (revised edition). Honolulu: University of Hawai'i Press.

Rickford, John (1987a) *Dimensions of a Creole Continuum: History, Texts and Linguistic Analysis of Guyanese Creole*. Stanford: Stanford University Press.

——(1987b) Decreolization Paths for Guyanese Singular Pronouns. In: *Pidgin and Creole Languages: Essays in Honor of John E. Reinecke*. Glenn Gilbert (ed.), 130–38. Honolulu: University of Hawai'i Press.

——(2002) Implicational Scales. In: *The Handbook of Language Variation and Language Change*. Jack K. Chambers, Peter Trudgill and Natalie Schilling-Estes (eds), 142–67. Oxford: Blackwell.

Sand, Andrea (1999) *Linguistic Variation in Jamaica: A Corpus-based Study of Radio and Newspaper Usage*. Tübingen: Gunter Narr Verlag.

Taylor, Douglas (1977) *Languages of the West Indies*. Baltimore: Johns Hopkins University Press.

Thomas, Ewart A. C. and Hubert Devonish (2008) Mathematical and Empirical Studies of English/Creole Language Variation. *E-Journal of the Caribbean Academy of Sciences* 3(2).

Trudgill, Peter (1998) Dialect and Dialects in the New Europe. *Etudes de Lettres* (Faculté des Lettres, Université de Lausanne) 4: 19–32.

Valdman, Albert (1968) Language Standardization in a Diglossia Situation: Haiti. In: *Language Problems of Developing Nations*. Joshua A. Fishman, Charles A. Ferguson and Jyotirindra Das Gupta (eds), 313–26. New York: Wiley.

——(1971) The Language Situation in Haiti. In: *Pidginization and Creolization of Languages*. Dell Hymes (ed.), 61–82. Cambridge: Cambridge University Press.

——(1984) The Language Situation in Haiti. In: *Haiti – Today and Tomorrow: An Interdisciplinary Study*. Charles Foster and Albert Valdman (eds), 77–99. Ladham: University of America Press.

Winford, Donald (1985) The Syntax of Fi Complements in Caribbean English Creole. *Language* 61(3): 588–624.

PART III
Developed countries

Introduction to Part III

In this section, South America, the Slavic area, Japan and the Mediterranean are discussed. In doing so, this section includes formerly colonising (e.g. Russia, Spain, Japan) as well as colonised countries (those in South America). While African countries were often colonised as late as the nineteenth century, South America's colonisation and the independence that ensued took place relatively early, and by the mid-1800s most of Latin America had achieved independence. The colonisers' languages, Portuguese and Spanish, are still dominant in South America and have had much time to develop new functions. They are now dominant lingua francas and are developing considerable prestige within their new homelands, and this prestige often supersedes even that of their European counterparts. Coloniser languages like Russian, Italian or Japanese may also be spoken outside their respective states, but are in decline there. The different fates of former colonial lingua francas thus constitute a relevant sociolinguistic research object.

Equally relevant are the different ideologies on how language is linked to speakers, identities, territories and ultimately the politics of language. The dramatic events unfolding in the Crimean peninsula and East Ukraine at the time when this volume was edited are not surprising from the perspective of a *longue durée* view on the dominant language ideologies of the region. However, rather unfortunately, mainstream sociolinguistic theory has paid relatively little attention to the experiences of what was formerly known as the "Second World". Mainstream sociolinguistics does not need to be applied to an ever-growing number of regions, languages or communities. It needs to take the sociolinguistic differences between regions into consideration, as well as their shaping over the centuries, so as to fathom their current state.

It has long been understood in sociolinguistics that social class should not be seen as a given and that it is not found in all types of socioeconomic organisations of societies; hence the emergence and growth of social network studies in linguistic anthropology since the 1950s. Mainstream sociolinguistic concepts of social class cannot be easily applied to some countries even if they rank high or very high on the Human Development Index. In South America, sociologists have therefore developed their own concepts of "social class", from which local sociolinguists have drawn in their research. Local theories on sociology and sociolinguistics are needed for this, and these are highly enlightening for readers not familiar with the regions under discussion.

Japan, too, boasts an impressive tradition of indigenous approaches to the study of language in society, and this tradition has not been receiving the attention from mainstream scholars that it deserves from the perspective of theory development. Japan's relatively independent construction of a sociolinguistic system over many centuries, together with its steady rise up the HDI ladder since the Second World War, make for a particularly relevant country for general sociolinguistics to learn from.

11

CLASS IN THE SOCIAL LABYRINTH OF SOUTH AMERICA

Elisa Battisti and João Ignacio Pires Lucas

11.1 The sociolinguistic situation of South America

South America, a continent of almost 400 million inhabitants, 12 countries and two non-sovereign states, provides a sociolinguistic setting that is intimately related to European expansionist actions carried out from the sixteenth to the nineteenth century. Territorial disputes between the Spanish and Portuguese crowns, French and Dutch invasions and the endeavour of exploring natural resources in the new lands brought big population groups to the continent, promoting the contact between people of different languages – indigenous languages, spoken by the native Americans; African languages, spoken by the enslaved peoples; and European languages, spoken by the settlers and by other more recent (early twentieth-century) immigrant groups, such as the Asian ones (Chinese, Japanese). The majority languages today – Spanish, Portuguese, French – have traces of this contact, which continues due to the existence of minority languages, spoken by bilinguals descended from settlers and immigrants.

The history of South America is responsible not only for advancing language contact, from which varieties of the languages involved were born – or due to which languages eventually became extinct (mainly the indigenous South American ones) – but also for the creation of a socioeconomic context of social inequalities with linguistic reflections. In Brazil, for example, Portuguese has at least two social dialects, cultivated and popular (Preti 2000), spoken, respectively, by individuals of a high and low level of education, a difference in educational levels that results mainly from inequalities in income distribution.

11.2 Social class as a sociolinguistic category

In the context described above, one would expect sociolinguistic research to take social class into account because of its potential to capture patterns of linguistic variation in local dialects. However, only a few South American studies actually take social class into account as an analytical category. No one doubts that accounting for social class is relevant, but the design of the category is especially challenging in the area, either on empirical or theoretical grounds. South American reality, with its perennial macro-structural instability and its significant social mobility, does not enable individuals to perceive their own social practices as class experiences, nor does it provide researchers with clear criteria for grouping individuals into classes.

Brazil in particular has been studied sociolinguistically. Labovian sociolinguistic research on Brazilian Portuguese varieties has obtained insightful results since the 1970s. It was introduced to the country by Anthony Julius Naro, a professor at the Federal University of Rio de Janeiro, the institution which also hosted Gregory Riordan Guy as a visiting scholar at that time. There was a clear adherence to Labovian principles and methodology, among them the idea that "the crucial division in the society from the point of view of language change was not middle class vs. working class, but rather centrally located groups as against peripherally located groups" (Labov 2001: 32) with the consequent need to distinguish at least "three, or preferably four, divisions of the social hierarchy" (Labov 2001: 31). Nevertheless, sociolinguistic studies on language variation done in Brazil rarely take social class into account. Researchers end up grouping individuals based on limited socioeconomic information, such as consumption of goods and, more generally, level of education, which is only indirectly related to social class.

A consequence of not stratifying variables according to social class is the impossibility of testing Labov's generalisations in local contexts, the most important one being the location of language innovators in the middle classes of the social hierarchy. Important cross-tabulations, such as those between gender and class, are not possible either. Gender differences in relation to social class cannot be interpreted in the same way that they are in other parts of the globe. It is also difficult to control effects, such as crossover, which emerge at the intersection of style and class.

In this chapter, we will show that the complexity of dealing with social class in South America is a result not only of reality, but also of the need to design a model of social class based on current social theories, a model which properly expresses the social distinctions of the South American scenario.

Dealing with social class is a difficulty that not only South American sociolinguists have experienced. According to Labov (2001: 58), the functioning and relatively stable model of social class put forward by US American sociology raises criticism from sociolinguists because it "accepted the social inequities that are a part of that system and overlooked the conflicts within American society". Even so, Labov defends the relevance of class for the social stratification of the larger society. He makes use of a hierarchy of at least five classes (Labov 1972): low working class, upper working class, low middle class, mid-middle class, and upper middle class.

Such a social scale is not easily available to South American sociolinguists. Despite the success of social scientists in formulating consistent theses about the social structure of the continent, they have had difficulty in applying European and

North American theories about social class to the continent. According to Marini (2000), Latin American sociologists made an attempt in the second half of the twentieth century to develop their own model of social class, based on a theory they named Dependency Theory. This theory has been used in important analyses about the specificities of social classes in the continent; but in general, theories were more likely to be imported than created locally.

The solutions proposed by South American sociolinguists in the rare studies that have grouped individuals in classes are dependent on those theories and the discussions about them. For this reason, the studies that we will review here – Bortoni-Ricardo (1985), Amaral (2003), Carvalho (2004) – will be dealt with as we address the progress of the discussions about social class by South American social scientists.

11.3 The social labyrinth

The first analyses of social classes in South America were those within a Marxist framework, and pointed to the difficulty that the proletariat had in gaining political power and sufficient popular support to assume its revolutionary role in the continent. They came up against three main obstacles: the power of the indigenous and poor rural populations in those countries historically settled by the Spanish, the large contingent of marginalised people in rural and urban areas in Brazil and the social labyrinth of South America, that is its complex social make-up. Besides including descendants of Spanish, Portuguese, African and indigenous people, South America later (in the twentieth century) encompassed other European and Asian immigrant populations. All these were fundamental in the constitution of working classes, as well as classes of small urban proprietors.

According to Fernándes (1978), during the period between the 1960s and the 1980s, which was marked by the impact of the Cold War and the civil and military dictatorships, South American scholars verified three problematic aspects in affirming the existence of a real class society in the region. These were the economic dependency of South American countries on Europe and the USA, the function of the political power in maintaining a dependent form of capitalism, and the existence of an archaic patrimonialist culture in dealing with public goods, which prevented the creation of a democratic culture.[1]

Gohn (1997) observes that the processes of democratic transition in the 1980s and 1990s, and the crisis of socialism, redirected the discussion of social classes. The notion of social class was abandoned in favour of a more open view of the aggregation of interests in the paradigm of the social movements. New social and political subjects – collective identities submitted to decades of marginalisation – were born at the end of the totalitarian regimes and recognised in studies, especially in the context of the Latin American indigenous groups. This took place as a consequence of two perspectives developed in Europe: multiculturalism (Taylor 1994) and recognition (Honneth 2003) of civil rights by the public power. These new views were brought to South America[2] in the discussion of the ways in which social groups are able to access basic goods, services and technological advances.

The sociolinguistic study of Bortoni-Ricardo (1985) from this period used the social networks approach to investigate phonetic-phonological variables in Brazilian Portuguese in the speech of a group of rural migrants in Brazlândia, a satellite city of Brasília, capital of Brazil. The variables investigated were peculiar to the Caipira dialect, a popular rural dialect: the reduction of proparoxitones ([ˈpesego] versus [ˈpezgo], "peach"), denasalisation ([ˈvirʒẽɲ] versus [ˈvirʒi], "virgin"), deletion of final vibrants ([luˈgar] versus [luˈga], "place"), diphthongisation in the context of a sibilant ([raˈpas] versus [raˈpajs], "boy"), among other processes. The study focused on variables that are associated with social changes, in this case migration from a rural to an urban area. Network analysis was necessary mainly because the individuals under investigation were part of the same social class; they were referred to by the author as "urban lower class". Thus the variables were not stratified into different social classes.

The analysis of Bortoni-Ricardo (1985) shows that individuals who are more integrated into the new urban network move away from the norms of the Caipira dialect. This new network is less multiplex than the old rural one, and is associated with a wider range of social contexts. The author gives the name "rurban" to the dialect of Portuguese spoken by the group of rural migrants in the urban area; a bit closer to the cultivated dialect, but with traits of the rural substrate.

The innovative solution of Bortoni-Ricardo (1985) was to make use of two indexes to measure the migrants' change in linguistic patterns and social relations: an index of integration to the network and an index of urbanisation. The first was calculated considering the relative number of friends that each of the 32 adult informants had. The second was calculated with the average score of the members of the network in seven indicators of the rural–urban transition, namely: level of education, kind of work, spatial mobility, participation in urban events, exposure to the media, political information and the circumstances in which the friendship bonds were formed. These indexes were later correlated to the linguistic variables. The indicators of the rural–urban transition were conceived by the author based on what she observed in the ethnographic field research that she carried out before interviewing the informants.

The study of Bortoni-Ricardo (1985) does not group individuals into different social classes. Therefore, no contrast was made between social groups regarding the application of the variable rules. But her study provided a picture of language variation and change in a specific group, casting light on the role of individuals in maintaining and diffusing speech patterns. In order to do this, especially when designing the urbanisation index, the author incorporated elements of the rural–urban contrast which revealed the gradual integration of the migrants to city life. She accounted for the movement of a social group and its integration to urban life in accordance with the debates in the social sciences at the time.

In this same period, scholars of social class in Latin America were also influenced by Bourdieu's (1998) *Distinction*, a book first published almost 20 years before (Bourdieu 1979). One of its main ideas is that the social mapping of tastes, habits and preferences of individuals allows one to depict the tension of cultural capital versus economic capital, social positions versus dispositions[3] from which a pattern of social classes can be built. This perspective, according to Pochmann (2012), tends to complicate the debate about social classes in Latin America, because the situation of indigenous people still weighs on Western liberal citizenship, just as the *campesino* context[4] continues to bring an intermittent contingent to big urban areas. New communication and information technologies remake the forms of social interaction through the use of virtual networks. Waged workers are fighting for better working conditions.

As a result of the social policies of leftist governments, such as the ones of Venezuela, Ecuador, Paraguay, Brazil, Argentina, Uruguay and Peru, new middle classes have emerged in Latin America, but their relationship with the society as a whole is precarious and far from consolidated.

The complexity of the debates of social scientists about social class in South America reaffirms the difficulty they have in establishing a functioning and stable social hierarchy which could be used in Labovian sociolinguistic studies. The researchers confront this difficulty by composing socioeconomic indexes based on the characteristics of the speech communities investigated. These indexes are then aligned with Labov's stratification by using his terminology to label the social groups. This is what Carvalho (2004) and Amaral (2003) appear to be doing.

Carvalho (2004) studied the sociolinguistic consequences of the recent urbanisation of rural areas in Uruguay. In one of them, located at the border with Brazil, the language spoken is not Spanish, the official language of the country, but rather a variety of Portuguese with rural characteristics, similar to the ones investigated by Bortoni-Ricardo (1985). In Uruguayan schools, only Spanish is taught; in big Uruguayan cities, only Spanish is spoken; Spanish is the language of official reports and documents. Due to its unofficial character, and also due to the interferences of Spanish, the speakers of Uruguayan Portuguese describe their own speech negatively, considering it to be ugly, corrupted, mixed, mistaken.

Carvalho (2004) controlled for socioeconomic status, not exactly for social class, although the factors in this group are named by her in the same way social classes are traditionally named: working class, lower middle class and mid-middle class. The object of the analysis is the palatalisation of the dental plosives /t/ and /d/ triggered by the following high front vowel (['dia] vs ['dʒia], "day"; ['tia] vs ['tʃia], "aunt"). The process is innovative and its results, the palatalised forms, have high prestige among speakers of Uruguayan Portuguese. This is a characteristic of Brazilian Portuguese which reaches rural Uruguayan communities mainly through television, but also in the contact Uruguayans have with Brazilians in Rivera and Santana do Livramento, the cities on either side of the border between Uruguay and Brazil, and in other Brazilian cities. Shopping in urban areas is a new habit resulting from the recent urbanisation of Uruguayan rural areas.

Carvalho (2004) integrated the frameworks of speech accommodation and acts of identity in the Labovian paradigm to explain the social distribution of palatalisation among Uruguayan Portuguese speakers. Fifty-six informants were interviewed in 1998. They were grouped according to three social parameters: age, gender and socioeconomic status. Socioeconomic status was measured based on a composite index in which three factors were taken into consideration: average household income, occupational status and level of education. These three factors were decided upon after participant observation and interviews revealed they were implicated in the social stratification of the variable. Each factor was given a different weight in the index, the highest being the weight of income (0.5), with the weight of occupational status and educational level being 0.4 and 0.3, respectively. The analysis showed that palatalisation in Uruguayan Portuguese is a variable clearly related to age. Socioeconomic status is the second social factor of relevance. Cross-tabulation of age across socioeconomic status confirmed the hypothesis of the author: the variable palatalisation in Uruguayan Portuguese is a change in progress. The young generation in the highest socioeconomic group, which the author named mid-middle class, is the one that palatalises the most. The palatalisation decreases in lower social classes and older age groups. The socioeconomic stratification of palatalisation is evident only in the younger groups.

The conclusion of Carvalho (2004), also based on her own qualitative study, is that Uruguayan Portuguese is a case of sociolectal extension due to its constant exposure to Brazilian Portuguese. In the border context, Uruguayan Portuguese is a low variety in a diglossic community subject to a change from above. Young people in the highest socioeconomic group use palatalised forms with a specific symbolic value: they signify urban orientation.

The study of Carvalho (2004) deals with social class in the context of the new middle classes in South America, which are not yet consolidated. The results of the study reveal the sociolinguistic consequences of urbanisation on the variety of language spoken in a rural community. The author sought to demonstrate that consequences are also found in general social practices.

More recently, according to Braga (2013), Brazil, Venezuela and Ecuador have developed programmes of income transfer to poor populations. As a result, poverty and extreme poverty have been reduced in an accelerated manner. The consumer market has grown more[5] than in European countries or the USA. Nevertheless, the questions of automation of production processes and of transnational companies versus large local companies remain unanswered. Even with a process of social inclusion under way in those countries, the world of work no longer recruits large contingents of manual workers. Unemployment rates among young people, for example, are not as high as in Europe, but nonetheless the situation is precarious. Therefore, in a global perspective, the kind of occupation and especially the kind of unemployment are central elements in any analysis of social class today. In countries like Brazil, position in the consumer market, a basic aspect in Weberian studies,[6] is not as important nowadays as it was in the past, because of access to credit.

Property, a central element for Marxists such as Wright (1997), is presently less important than previously, because owners of companies have been replaced as symbolic figures by waged executives, who are also workers. According to Hardt and Negri (2005), the main kind of property is now more intellectual and immaterial. Power and status – especially the status related to taste and distinction, as described by Bourdieu (1998) – are still fundamental aspects of the debate on social class. At the same time, the growth of social participation in face-to-face or virtual networks, at work or in leisure and cultural settings, motivates people to engage in biopolitics, a less traditional and more democratic kind of politics that emerges in political parties, unions, professional associations, as well as at school, in neighbourhoods and at home.

11.4 The importance of neighbourhood

Of the three studies reviewed here, that of Amaral (2003) was done with the most recent data. It is a Labovian analysis, greatly influenced by the ideas of Bourdieu, from the stratification of individuals in social classes to the discussion of results. In the composite index that the author used to stratify individuals, neighbourhood was the most expressive element, which is in accordance with what Meyerhoff (2011: 168) claims:

> [N]eighbourhood is a better predictor of attitudes and behaviours than occupation all alone, because the effects of occupation interact with a number of other factors, such as more complex family structures, whether or not a household has two incomes, the marital status of the heads of the household, and whether there are any children in the household at all.

The object of the analysis of Amaral (2003) is the second-person singular verb agreement in Brazilian Portuguese spoken in Pelotas, a city in the very south of Brazil, in the state of Rio Grande do Sul. Two forms alternate, one with the second-person inflection, the other with that for the third person (*tu falas* ~ *tu fala* "you speak", *tu falaste* ~ *tu falou* "you spoke"). The first is identified as a characteristic of the cultivated dialect, the second is identified with the popular dialect. However, the popular variant is not seen negatively, and in fact it is more frequently used in every Brazilian Portuguese dialect, not only in the speech of Pelotas. But in this city, as in others in the same state, the forms with the second-person inflectional suffix are resisting disappearance. One of the hypotheses of the author for the maintenance of this inflectional suffix is its local identification with highly educated people. It is also a way to signify social class.

Amaral (2003) treats the social class category with care. He groups individuals according to three kinds of social aspects: economic (purchasing habits, average income, goods and neighbourhood), professional (manual, technical and intellectual occupation) and educational (8, 13 and 17 average years of education). The statistical measures in the quantitative analysis of the variable data showed that neighbourhood (city centre, inner suburbs and outer suburbs[7]) is the aspect that most significantly correlates to second-person singular verb agreement. Level of education and kind of occupation, in turn, are correlated to neighbourhood. The author then stratifies individuals in three social classes he names upper middle class, lower middle class and working class. The individuals in the upper middle class that live in the city centre are highly educated and have intellectual occupations. The individuals in the lower middle class that live in the inner suburbs have an average level of education, and their occupations are either manual or technical. The informants in the working class live in the outer suburbs, have a low level of education and their occupations are typically manual.

The total frequency of second-person singular verb agreement in the speech of Pelotas is low, as it is in other varieties of Brazilian Portuguese. Even so, it is socially stratified. The conclusion of the author is that the retention of the second-person singular verb agreement is favoured by individuals in the upper middle class. People in the lower middle class are neutral and the ones in the working class disfavour the agreement.

Amaral (2003), like Carvalho (2004), converts indexes of socioeconomic status into three social classes named according to the groups usually considered in Labov's studies. The higher frequency of verb agreement in the speech of individuals in the upper middle class may be a cross-over effect, that is a result of stylistic practices related to the educational and cultural level of the upper middle class.

A suggestion that comes from postmodern discussions in the social sciences today (Jameson 2011) is to take into consideration at least three elements in investigations of social class. These elements aggregate behaviours and produce social organisations of a formal or informal character. They are employment/unemployment, power in social networks, and status derived from consumption practices. Converted into analytical categories, these elements would help to verify whether the occupation is material or immaterial, pays high or low wages, and whether it requires flexible or inflexible work hours; whether the power is virtual or face-to-face, global or local; whether consumption is more or less sustainable, functional or superfluous, of public goods or paid goods. Taking them into consideration will depend, on the one hand, on the knowledge South American researchers have of the discussions and models put forward by the social scientists; on the other hand, it depends on the careful identification of elements related to the social stratification of the communities investigated, an entailment of the big social differences derived from the recent transformations of the local societies.

11.5 Other mismatches of South American sociolinguistic research related to social class

Labov (2010: 197) claims that "typically, the differentiation of stable linguistic variables by gender varies across social classes" and that "one or the other gender is usually in advance for all social classes". Sociolinguistic studies in South America do find gender differences in the use of linguistic variable forms (Rigatuso 2005; Zilles 2005, to cite just two of many others). However, because of the complexities of dealing with social class that we have just discussed, the examination of gender variation across social classes is generally inconclusive.

Another challenge posed by those complexities is making generalisations on language variation and style across large social groups such as social classes, age, gender. As a consequence, researchers either investigate style as attention to speech – intraspeaker variation (Hora and Wetzels 2011) – or analyse stylistic variation in small, idiosyncratic communities (Mendes 2012).

11.6 Conclusion

Dealing with social class in sociolinguistic research is demanding for any sociolinguist, South American or not. The types of classes to be considered in an investigation require an interdisciplinary dialogue between sociolinguists and social scientists which is not simple to carry out. In South America, particularly, the context of constant economic and social transformations, but also of permanence of certain historical challenges, such as the question of the *campesinos* and of indigenous communities, obscures individuals' perception of their own social class and makes the categorisation of classes a difficult task for researchers.

South American sociolinguists, especially Brazilians, monitor for level of education as one of the elements related to social class. In the few studies that include social class as an analytical category, level of education is taken into account in composing indexes because it is related to social dialects, the cultivated and the popular, which, in turn, are relative to the patterns of income, occupation and urbanisation of the communities investigated. These indexes are used as a basis for grouping individuals in social strata labelled according to the classes of the standard Labovian social hierarchy, in an apparent attempt to align the results produced by South American sociolinguistic research with the ones generally published by American and European investigators.

The few attempts at dealing with social class in South America, particularly in Brazil, have obtained revealing results. We thus reaffirm the validity of taking social class into consideration in sociolinguistic studies in South America despite the complexity surrounding its definition.

Notes

1 "Por lo tanto, no fueron ni pocas las influencias que la sociedad y la cultura – y especialmente formaciones políticas patrimonialistas o patrimoniales burocráticas – ejercieron y ejercen 'en la producción social de la propia existencia' por los hombres." 'Therefore, the influence exerted by the society and culture – and especially bureaucratic patrimonial or patrimonialist political formations – was and is great in men's "social production of their own existence"' (Fernándes 1978: 217).
2 A study on these concepts related to Latin America is Souza Filho (2003).
3 "Social class is not defined by a property [...], nor by a collection of properties [...], nor even by a chain of properties strung out from a fundamental property (position in the relations of production) in a relation of cause and effect, conditioner and conditioned; but by the structure of relations between all the pertinent properties which gives its specific value to each of them and to the effects they exert on practices" (Bourdieu 1998:106).
4 *Campesino* context refers to the social situation of unemployed farm workers, temporary migrants who, even in the city, keep their link with the field either by being eventual farm workers or by living with their parents in small farms close to urban areas.
5 Analyses made by different institutions show the rapid growth of consumer demands in emerging markets like Brazil when their consumption is compared with the consumption

in North America and Western Europe. For example, "IHS Global Insight's Global Scenario and Global Consumer Markets econometric models predict that by 2015, US and Western European consumer spending combined will account for only 26 percent of world GDP [gross domestic product], down considerably from a 38.5-percent share in 2002. Compare this to the BRIC countries [Brazil, Russia, India, and China] consumer spending: after averaging 4.4 percent from 1995–2005, it accounted for 8.1 percent of world GDP in 2010 and is projected to reach nearly 12 percent by 2015." Online available at: www.supplychainquarterly.com/columns/201104monetarymatters/ (accessed on 7 February 2014).

6 Studies based on the theories of Max Weber. Goldthorpe (2000) is one of the sociologists who have followed these theories.

7 "Arrabalde" in Portuguese. It is an outlying area of the city, not exclusively residential.

Further reading

Bortoni-Ricardo, Stella Maris (1985) *The Urbanization of Rural Dialect Speakers: A Sociolinguistic Study in Brazil*. Cambridge: Cambridge University Press. (A sociolinguistic investigation of how Brazilian rural migrants adjust to an urban environment.)

Leite, Yonne and Dinah Callou (2002) *Como falam os brasileiros* [How Brazilians speak]. Rio de Janeiro: Zahar. (An account of divergent and uniform features of five urban varieties of Brazilian Portuguese.)

Mello, Heliana, Cléo V. Altenhofen and Tommaso Raso (eds) (2011) *Os contatos linguísticos no Brasil* [Language Contact in Brazil]. Belo Horizonte: Editora UFMG. (An account of language contact in Brazil in its historical, social and linguistic aspects.)

References

Amaral, Luís Isaías Centeno do (2003) A concordância verbal de segunda pessoa do singular em Pelotas e suas implicações linguísticas e sociais [Second Person Singular Verb Agreement in Pelotas and its Linguistic and Social Implications] Tese (Doutorado em Letras/Estudos da Linguagem), Universidade Federal do Rio Grande do Sul. Instituto de Letras. Programa de Pós-Graduação em Letras, Porto Alegre.

Bortoni-Ricardo, Stella Maris (1985) *The Urbanization of Rural Dialect Speakers: A Sociolinguistic Study in Brazil*. Cambridge: Cambridge University Press.

Bourdieu, Pierre (1979) *La distinction: Critique sociale du jugement*. Paris: Les Éditions de Minuit.

——(1998) *Distinction: A Social Critique of the Judgement of Taste*. London: Routledge.

Braga, Ruy (2013) *A política do precariado: Do populismo à hegemonia lulista* [The Politics of the Precariat: From Populism to the Hegemony of Lula]. São Paulo: Boitempo.

Carvalho, Ana Maria (2004) I Speak Like the Guys on TV: Palatalization and the Urbanization of Uruguayan Portuguese. *Language Variation and Change* 16: 127–51.

Fernándes, Florestán (1978) Problemas de conceptualización de las clases sociales en América Latina [Problems of the Conceptualisation of Social Classes in Latin America]. In: *Las clases sociales en América Latina* [Social classes in Latin America] (11th edition). Florestán Fernándes and R. B. Benítez Zenteno (eds), 191–276. Ciudad de Mexico: Siglo Veintiuno Editores.

Gohn, Maria da Glória (1997) *Teoria dos movimentos sociais: Paradigmas clássicos e contemporâneos* [Theory of the Social Movements. Classical and Contemporary Paradigms]. São Paulo: Loyola.

Goldthorpe, John (2000) *On Sociology: Numbers, Narratives, and the Integration of Research and Theory*. New York: Oxford University Press.

Hardt, Michael and Antonio Negri (2005) *Império* [Empire] (eighth edition). Rio de Janeiro: Record.

Honneth, Axel (2003) *Luta por reconhecimento: A gramática moral dos conflitos sociais*. [Struggle for Recognition. The Moral Grammar of Social Conflicts]. São Paulo: Editora 34.
Hora, Dermeval da and Leo Wetzels (2011) A variação linguística e as restrições estilísticas [Language Variation and Stylistic Constraints]. *Revista da ABRALIN* 1: 147–88.
Jameson, Fredric (2011) *Representing Capital: A Commentary on Volume One*. London: Verso.
Labov, William (1972) *Sociolinguistic Patterns*. Philadelphia: University of Philadelphia Press.
——(2001) *Principles of Linguistic Change: Social Factors*. Malden: Blackwell.
——(2010) *Principles of Linguistic Change: Cognitive and Cultural Factors*. Oxford: Wiley-Blackwell.
Marini, Ruy Mauro (2000) *Dialética da dependência* [The Dialectics of Dependency]. Petrópolis: Vozes.
Mendes, Ronald Beline (2012) Diminutivos como marcadores de sexo/gênero [Diminutives as Markers of Sex/Gender]. *Revista Linguística* 8(1): 113–24.
Meyerhoff, Miriam (2011) *Introducing Sociolinguistics* (second edition). London/New York: Routledge.
Pochmann, Marcio (2012) *Nova classe média? O trabalho na base da pirâmide social brasileira* [A New Middle Class? Work at the Base of the Brazilian Social Pyramid]. São Paulo: Boitempo.
Preti, Dino (2000) *Sociolinguística – os níveis de fala: Um estudo sociolinguístico do diálogo na literatura brasileira* [Sociolinguistics – Speech Registers: A Sociolinguistic Study of Dialogues in Brazilian Literature] (ninth edition). São Paulo: Editora da Universidade de São Paulo.
Rigatuso, Elizabeth Mercedes (2005) Contribución de la sociolingüística al estúdio del problema de la variación lingüística en la Argentina [Contribution of Sociolinguistics to the Study of the Problem of Language Variation in Argentina]. In: *Estudos de variação linguística no Brasil e no Cone Sul* [Studies of Language Variation in Brazil and in the Southern Cone]. Ana Maria Stahl (ed.), 229–56. Porto Alegre: Editora da UFRGS.
Souza Filho, Carlos F. M. (2003) Multiculturalismo e direitos coletivos [Multiculturalism and Collective Rights]. In: *Reconhecer para libertar: Os caminhos do cosmopolitismo multicultural* [Recognise to Release: The Ways of Multicultural Cosmopolitanism]. Boaventura de Sousa Santos (ed.), 71–109. Rio de Janeiro: Civilização Brasileira.
Taylor, Charles (ed.) (1994) *Multiculturalismo: Examinando a política do reconhecimento* [Multiculturalism: Examining the Politics of Recognition]. Portugal: Instituto Piaget.
Wright, Erik O. (1997) *Class Counts: Comparative Studies in Class Analysis*. Cambridge: Cambridge University Press.
Zilles, Ana Maria Stahl (2005) The Development of a New Pronoun: The Linguistic and Social Embedding of "a gente" in Brazilian Portuguese. *Language Variation and Change* 17(1): 19–53.

12

THE SLAVIC AREA

Trajectories, borders, centres and peripheries in the Second World

Marc L. Greenberg

12.1 Introduction

This overview of the Slavic area examines two case studies in the spirit of the *longue durée*,[1] focusing on the rise and fall of Russian as the language of an empire and thus as an example of an "other" (non-West-European) colonial/post-colonial paradigm, and the rise and fall of the Yugoslav project, an example of group formation and nation-building – where language plays a significant role – emerging from the peripheries of the Austro-Hungarian and Ottoman empires. As such, this chapter focuses less on *tools* than on the *perspective* in sociolinguistics. In taking the long view and contrasting with Anglophone concerns in sociolinguistics, these case studies explore the dynamics of language in the context of changing ideologies, border creation, and the invention and replication of identity with regard to multilingualism in contrast to the primarily synchronic bias found in Anglophone sociolinguistics and, indeed, linguistics in general. Turned the other way, this perspective examines what non-Anglophone Europeans often refer to as "ethnogenesis", a notion conflating language and ethnicity in the formation of ethnicities and nations and often with an emphasis on essentialism. This perspective also allows us to see what we might otherwise miss: Anglocentric discourse divides the world into first and third, leaving a major gap. The "Second World" is our object of study. In examining the European Second World, the events leading up to and following 1989 afford us an unprecedented opportunity to examine the competing elements of sociolinguistic systems more or less in real time of a period characterized by sudden and extreme socio-political change and its relation to sociolinguistic systems.

12.2 The Slavic language situation

The Slavic languages, spoken in Central and Eastern Europe and the territory of the former USSR, stretching seven time zones to the Pacific, offer a view of extremes, both in terms of the degree of organic language variation as well as in terms of the historical shifts connected with their arrangement into codified and officially valorized forms. On the one hand, Russian, spoken by some 160 million speakers (of which 137 million are in the Russian Federation) (per Ethnologue, Lewis et al. 2014), is among the least dialectally variegated (its spread over its current territory dates from the sixteenth century and reflects eastward colonization, not unlike the spread of American English, which expanded westward). Slovene, with some two million speakers, boasts 48 dialects, some mutually unintelligible to speakers of the standard and the central dialects around Ljubljana, the capital of Slovenia. The "language-formerly-known-as-Serbo-Croatian", associated with the rise and fall of the Yugoslav project (ca. 1830–1990), has mutually intelligible standard forms mapped onto four state-aligned standard languages, Bosnian, Croatian, Montenegrin and Serbian, though its organic dialects bespeak historical ties to other languages as well: Slovene (to Croatian) and Macedonian (to Serbian).

12.2.1 The Slavic difference

This chapter will focus on some examples where Slavic-language studies help us gain perspective on sociolinguistic systems in at least two ways: by demonstrating that colonial language policies and their implementation are of different types, entailing different outcomes; and by examining diachronic processes rather than focusing on synchronic typologies.

Anglophone literature focusing on colonialism and globalization, sociolinguistic primers being no exception, tends to foreground British and West European models of dominance to the exclusion of others (see, e.g., Errington 2008; Meyerhoff 2011). The principle on which this exclusion can be framed is whether or not the dominating group was historically seafaring, which occludes the dynamics of systems in landlocked territories (which, unsurprisingly, focus more energy on border formation, justification, and maintenance). Consequently, students' foundational knowledge about sociolinguistic systems in colonial settings is skewed towards dominant languages that expanded via global trade networks, resource exploitation, slavery, and so on. A student may conclude that English as the dominant prestige language plus a non-English (low-prestige) indigenous language is the one-size-fits-all colonial model. To illustrate, consider English in post-apartheid South Africa, which, though along with Afrikaans yielded constitutional rights to indigenous languages, remains the de facto pre-eminent language of state. English is also widely acknowledged to perform a unifying socio-political function in states like India and Pakistan. And English is virtually synonymous with the dominant ideology of the current age (Block et al. 2012). A glance at another vast multilingual state, the Russian Empire, succeeded by the USSR, reveals a different outcome than the unqualified language-of-the-hegemon-rules. This line of reasoning underpins the general assessment of the role of language policy and language entrepreneurs in the formation, reification and reinforcement of nationalisms and modern nation states (Anderson 2006, especially Chapter 5; Judson 2006).[2] Thus, for example, one might expect that despite the dissolution of the USSR in the 1990s Russian would remain the dominant language. In fact, the fate of Russian in the "near abroad" (a loan-translation of Russian *bližnee zarubež'e*) – territories in post-Soviet states, contiguous to the Russian Federation, where Russian was spoken widely by both ethnic Russians and others – has had varied outcomes depending on multiple factors (Laitin, 1998).

An equally compelling reason to examine the former USSR, Eastern Bloc and Yugoslavia is that the post-communist era has allowed a fundamental reassessment of the sociolinguistic issues connected with the region. First, socialist societies were officially classless; consequently, ideology precluded overt sociolinguistic investigation. Second, post-Cold-War openness has allowed domestic and international scholars unprecedented access to archives and society at large – access that has permitted a fuller picture and critical reassessment of the region to emerge. Adding this body of knowledge to our understanding of sociolinguistic systems gives us more complete data on which to build models and construct theories.

12.2.2 Language and empire: a Russian perspective

Colonization in the Russian Empire and its successor state, the Soviet Union, centres around internal developments rather than appropriation and domination of overseas territories. Broadly speaking, the policies of both states would strike the casual observer as moving inexorably towards Russification, consolidating over time from a multilingual and multiethnic state into a culturally homogeneous one. However, over time we observe a heterogeneous range of strategies, some of which will strike today's Western observer as remarkably liberal and pluralistic. On the one hand, as an example of conservatism, imperial policy towards minority languages (a proxy for ethnicities) conforms to the standard assumption, whereby state-driven Russo-centrism attempted to remove Polish and Lithuanian from public use in the period after 1863 through the first years of the twentieth century, following the uprising against the Russian Empire by proponents of the former Polish–Lithuanian Commonwealth, by both legal means (ban on publication, education in these languages) and vigorous enforcement of the law (Geraci 2001: 76–77; Staliūnas 2007: 196ff.). On the other hand, during the same period a relatively liberal and markedly sophisticated language policy was pursued with regard to the minorities along the Volga river and in western Siberia, including Islamic (e.g. Tatars), Buddhist (e.g. Kalmyk) and pagan (Volga Finnic) populations, which encouraged the active development of literacy in non-Russian languages. Imperial authorities fostered the activity of the ethnolinguist Nikolaj Il'minskij (1822–91), who aimed to develop literacy in minority languages to spread adherence to Orthodox Christianity as a means by which to integrate non-Russian populations as loyal subjects of the state.[3]

At first blush these contrasting language policies – neither of which succeeded from the Russian perspective – seem dissonant, if not incoherent. After all, their targets are in some respects similar in type, given that the northwest territories of the Russian Empire were also populated not only by non-Russian speakers (Polish,

Lithuanian, Yiddish speakers), as well as by peoples of non-Orthodox confessions (Catholics, Jews), who might also have been ripe for conversion. At least two factors help to explain the difference in strategy. First, the languages in the north-west territories have had long traditions of literacy and statehood. The languages could thus challenge Russian for prestige. Not so for the languages of the Turkic, Mongolic and Finno-Ugric speakers in the Russian interior. Second, to reinforce the territorial integrity of the empire, the borderlands called for an approach that sharpened the differentiation between those inside and outside the state, whereas matters of cohesion in the interior could unfold over a longer timeframe. The second point can be seen as an example of a top-down version of a process that has played out in the Slavic-speaking world also from the bottom up, where local patriots consciously sought to sharpen ethnic boundaries by discouraging bilingualism among German and Czech speakers in the last decades of the Austro-Hungarian Empire (for details see Judson 2006).

The immediate post-revolutionary period in the Soviet Union continued a language policy that at least in principle was more in line with Il'minskij's approach than with unilateral imperial Russification (Geraci 2001: 77). Leninist policy (formulated by Stalin) in the 1920s of *korenizacija* "nativization" aimed at aligning non-Russian-speaking peoples not with Orthodoxy, but with the new socialist ideology – bringing languages, many hitherto unwritten, to a level of literacy that would permit them to develop on the principle "national in form, socialist in content". Nevertheless, this policy was put into effect with the goal of achieving state unity, meaning that alongside elevating literacy in the more than 130 languages of the USSR, all Soviets were required to function in Russian (Smith 1998: 54; Grenoble 2003: 44).

Despite the ideological shift, the internal colonization of the non-Russian-speakers was structurally similar under the Tsar and the Soviets. The processes of incorporation of peripheral peoples followed three patterns: most-favoured-lord (the example of Ukraine), integralist (the Baltic states) and colonialist (Kazakhstan as emblematic of Central Asian states) (pace Laitin 1998: 59ff.; note the borrowing of terminology from Western colonial theory with new meanings), where language serves as a reflection of the relationship between the Russian centre and the non-Russian periphery. In the Ukrainian example, the structural and genetic closeness of Ukrainian to Russian makes mutual acquisition of these languages easy. During the Soviet period Ukrainian was permitted to flourish under the principle of *korenizacija* (in contrast to the late imperial period, when Ukrainian had been suppressed). While this meant that Ukrainian individuals had a high degree of mobility and access to power, even to the Muscovite centre, it also meant that Ukrainian as a language of the periphery was subject to a dynamic lowering of prestige with respect to Russian and the net effect was that many Ukrainians, particularly in the east of Ukraine, had become monolingual Russian speakers by the time of the dissolution of the USSR. Lithuanian and Latvian are Indo-European languages relatively closely related to but mutually unintelligible with Slavic languages; Estonian is completely unrelated to Slavic.

The Baltic states, independent up to the first half of the twentieth century, enjoyed high degrees of literacy and prestige within their own communities with regard to Russian and, crucially, see their countries as having been unjustly annexed to the Soviet Union. Baltic speakers were thus more resistant than Ukrainians to assimilation to Russian both socio-politically and linguistically. Finally, the colonialist model (the five primarily Muslim Central Asian Soviet Socialist Republics, corresponding to the now independent states Kazakhstan, Kyrgyzstan, Tajikistan, Turkmenistan and Uzbekistan) shared linguistic distance from Russian with the Baltics, e.g., the Turkic languages of the Kazakhs, Turkmen, or Uzbeks being unrelated to Russian (or, in the case of Tajik, an Indo-European language so distantly related as to have no mutual intelligibility), but had much lower degrees of literacy and social prestige compared to Russian. As the USSR disintegrated, the Baltic states had retained high levels of proficiency in their own languages and did not suffer linguistic assimilation, whereas the Turkic languages had yielded significantly to Russian.

The dissolution of the USSR gives us the opportunity to observe in real time the processes of systemic change in the immediate post-Soviet (or post-colonial) period. Laitin's study (1998) offers the first multi-national research project examining the development of sociolinguistic systems in the 1990s. In 1989 a series of language laws, engendered by the framework of *perestroika*, in the titular republics established the titular languages as legally equal to or superior to Russian – statuses which devalued Russian (usually the only language of ethnic Russians), reversing the only power relationship and attendant language hierarchy Soviet Russians had known. Russians in peripheral republics then found themselves virtually overnight as subjects of Estonia and Kazakhstan, for example, and were no longer citizens of the vast Soviet Union, where they could traverse seven time zones with a single passport and a single language (Laitin 1998: 88–93). Russians had equated their own identity with Soviet identity, in contrast to members of the titular republics, who held overlapping identities (e.g. Estonian and Soviet) and would not miss the larger state identity when it ceased to exist; in many cases these Russians had been born and raised outside of the Russian territory proper. After the USSR the question then became whether or not Russians in the "near abroad" decide to assimilate culturally and linguistically – in Gellner's (1983: 243) terms, turning from Megalomanians into Ruritanians, stay put and demand linguistic rights, or emigrate to the Russian Federation. Individuals decide on their own trajectories based on multiple factors, but the group trajectories could be characterized by the mid-1990s thus:

Kazakhstan: Russians were (of the four cases) least likely to assimilate (Kazakh is low prestige even among ethnic Kazakhs, low economic returns for assimilation, linguistically distant from Russian);

Estonia: Russians were slightly more likely to assimilate than not (Estonian is high prestige, high economic returns for assimilation, Estonian difficult to learn for Russians);

Latvia: Russians were likely to assimilate (Latvian is high prestige, relatively high economic returns for assimilation, Latvian less difficult to learn than Estonian);

Ukraine: Russians were as likely to assimilate as not (no palpable gain in prestige, some economic gain possible, easy to learn) (for details see Laitin 1998: 252ff.).

Of these, the Kazakhstan situation since then has changed somewhat, with Kazakh gaining ground against Russian, evidently as a function of Kazakh success in building its base of wealth, technocracy, and international prestige, as well as the out-migration of Russians (Pavlenko 2008: 72; Lillis and Cox 2013). Nevertheless, Russian persists as a strong second language among those belonging to the titular ethnicities because of the advantages of knowing Russian as a language of regional commerce as well as its function and prestige as language of a high culture and world literature. Additionally, there is a persistently higher level of proficiency in Russian by titulars than of the titular language by Russians (Pavlenko 2008: 64, 67, 72).

The flipside to the Russophone near-abroad is the post-Soviet language situation inside the Russian Federation, itself a complex multilingual territory. As with the peripheral republics of the former USSR, the titular republics within the Federation also developed language-revival policies during the period of *perestroika* aimed at reversing Russification and elevating titular languages, in this case primarily Turkic languages (Chuvash, Bashkir, Tatar) and Finnic languages (Karelian, Komi, Mari, Mordvin, Udmurt). These languages had in the Soviet period been treated as something less than republican languages and as such in the sphere of education had native-language instruction offered until, but not including, university; after the Second World War, however, the language of instruction was increasingly left to parental choice, which through socio-economic pressure yielded to Russian. It should be kept in mind that, particularly in cities, the best employment opportunities went to ethnic Russians or at least Russian quasi-native speakers. As a result, titular languages tend to be spoken in everyday communication primarily in rural areas and Russian has prevailed in urban centres, though gradations of styles of communication with admixtures of the titular language and Russian co-exist(ed) in everyday communication (Wertheim 2003: 353–57). Soviet-language policy regarding minority languages also included special cases of linguistic engineering. An interesting example is the attempt in the 1930s to create a Karelian language (and corresponding Karelian ethnic identity) from the Karelian dialect of Finnish spoken in the USSR by manufacturing an *Abstand* relationship between Karelian and standard Finnish with the goal of fostering distinct ethnic identities, that is in order to obviate common identity between Soviet Karelians and "bourgeois" Finns. The intended standard language turned out to be so artificial and removed from spoken Karelian – including many additions from Soviet Russian newspeak – that it failed to be accepted as a standard language (Austin 1992). Coupled with urbanization, Karelian as a language has largely yielded to Russian (Grenoble 2003: 80).

Zamyatin (2012) demonstrates in his concise but insightful study of the two decades of post-Soviet language planning in the Russian Federation that the republican titular languages and minority languages (e.g. Karelian, Veps) made significant headway in the education systems in the 1990s, during a period of economic growth, but the situation has largely reversed in the following decade, during an economic downturn, resulting in greater and lesser failures. The relative success versus failure largely depends on the starting points, with Turkic republics faring somewhat better than Finnic-language republics (Zamyatin 2012: 88). The major factors are demographics (the relative share of native titulars versus Russians), regional prestige of the titular language, coherence among local titular elites, as well as ideological considerations. Wertheim (2003: 368–69), for example, elucidates the relatively strong Islamist drive in the revival of Tatar, which reinforces the break with the recent Soviet past.

12.2.3 The-language-formerly-known-as-Serbo-Croatian

As an extension of the topic of Anglo-Western hegemony in sociolinguistic systems one finds a preoccupation in the sociolinguistic literature with synchronic typology of systems, rather than how such systems come into being, persist, and transform over time. (In the sociological and anthropological literature ontological and diachronic perspectives on group identity are coming [back] into fashion; see, e.g., Brubaker 2004; Wimmer 2013.) The case study of the Yugoslav project is illustrative, which began as a self-conscious early nineteenth-century experiment in language planning on a grand scale (the Illyrian project, see M. L. Greenberg 2011) that through vicissitudes resulted in the formation of "fraternal twin" standards, Croatian and Serbian. These standards lasted for nearly a century and a half (1850–1990) and are mapped to different confessional and ethnic groups, which are sometimes blithely compared in type to Hindi and Urdu (and vice-versa, e.g. van Olphen 1988: 743; Everaert 2010: 264–65). Further below, we shall explore the relationship between religion and language using the Yugoslav project as a model. In doing so we note that the study of the relationship between religion and language has remained relatively poorly understood (Darquennes and Vandenbussche 2011: 2). The erstwhile Serbian and Croatian languages have later (since 1990) fragmented into four separate state languages. But these comparisons hold true only if one is concerned with rough equivalences and only if one focuses on a short time segment and a particular historical perspective that allows one to match up their "moving parts". Furthermore, the comparison of Hindi–Urdu to Serbo-Croatian might be seen as a covert reflection of the Western colonial paradigm: Serbo-Croatian appears in the imagination of the West largely in the context of Tito's Yugoslavia in the same historical period (the Cold War) as India and Pakistan emerge from British colonial rule and could be viewed in this light as being cut from the same cloth of post-colonial self-determination.

Sociolinguistic literature on Serbo-Croatian[4] is preoccupied with the mid-nineteenth-century national revival (a preoccupation justifiable because of the period's dynamism), during which Serbian and Croatian emerge as standard languages (R. D. Greenberg 2004; Anderson 2006: 76). Studying this Slavic area allows us to focus on the rise and formation of national languages. But there is more to it than is usually treated in the handbooks. If one were to follow the trajectory of sociolinguistic systems in the Yugoslav territory over a longer time-frame – a millennium, for example – one would discover not only a much more textured narrative, but a dynamic sequence of configurations of which some may turn out to be singularities among sociolinguistic systems. In at least one respect, the comparison of Serbo-Croatian to Hindi–Urdu overlooks an essential mismatch. The Serbo-Croatian dichotomy reflects the cultural-confessional disjuncture between Eastern Orthodoxy

(Serbian) and Roman Catholicism (Croatian). However, the dichotomy excludes, and thus occludes, the Muslim speakers of this pair of languages (or language with two variants) – no corresponding glottonym nor a standard language was to be elaborated for this group, primarily situated in Bosnia (alongside Bosnian Catholic and Orthodox populations), though a distinct tradition of spoken and written practice among the Bosnian Muslims has long been noted (Mønnesland 2004), until after the dissolution of Yugoslavia in the 1990s. As Gellner (1983: 71–72) notes, the linguistic bifurcation reinforces the political pre-eminence of the historical Christian ethnic categories "because these identifications carried the implications of *having been* Orthodox or Catholic", reflecting the indigenous narrative about religious betrayal from the Christian-European viewpoint, whereby Slavophone Muslims are seen (even across centuries) as collaborators with the Ottoman Turks (beginning in the late fourteenth century) and therefore traitors to their Christian brethren (Wachtel 1998: 103–4). The indigenous interpretation of ethnic eschatology is sometimes accepted wholesale by outsiders, which can translate into real-life consequences in inter-ethnic conflict (see, e.g., Nilsen 1995).

Much scholarship on Serbo-Croatian focuses on the politics of standardization and the linguistic entrepreneurs who advanced the project. The story is indeed remarkable, as it developed from a grand vision to unite the South Slavic speakers (corresponding to today's Slovene, Croatian, Bosnian, Serbian, Montenegrin, Macedonian and Bulgarian) into a compromise language, a sort of South Slavic Esperanto, called "Illyrian" after the name of the pre-Roman inhabitants of the western Balkans.[5] This programme was driven largely by Croatian ethnolinguistic entrepreneurs, Ljudevit Gaj (1809–72) being the most prominent. A competing, contemporaneous movement on the Serbian side, centring around Vuk Karadžić (1787–1864), militated for a standard based on the Štokavian vernacular language, rendered in Cyrillic on the German orthoepic principle "Write as you would speak". The Illyrian project as such was abandoned in favour of a compromise, formalized in 1850 by an agreement signed in Vienna, on two varieties of standard vernacular Štokavian codes, labelled Croatian and Serbian, corresponding to Catholic (Latin-alphabet) and Serbian (Cyrillic-alphabet) written stylizations, respectively.

12.2.4 Borders and languages: religious and political factors

Border-making, both past and present, is a preoccupation in the former Yugoslav territories to which sociolinguistic systems have been put to service, which systems, in turn, reify older cleavages based on religion. In the 1913 report of the Balkan Commission of the Carnegie Endowment for International Peace, competing claims over "Macedonia" drew on different criteria: Turkish claims were based on confession per se, Bulgarian on national self-identification, and Greek on the influence of and traces of classical Greek civilization; but Serbian, which prevailed, focused on dialect and local customs. Aleksandar Belić's map including Slavic dialects of today's Macedonia into "Southern Serbia" and Jovan Cvijić's maps of anthropological features of the Balkans were decisive for the drawing of the political borders of the Kingdom of the Serbs, Croats and Slovenes (Kennan 1993 [1914]: 27–30). In accord with the focus in the sociolinguistic literature on nineteenth-century nation-building, and the European tradition of building nation states along ethnolinguistic boundaries, there is an attendant, usually unexpressed, belief that such ethnolinguistic divisions can be considerably older. In the nineteenth century this belief was mythologized, for example in the Illyrian ideologeme. We find a recent echo of this concern in handbooks on Croatian dialectology where, for example, the ancient division between proto-Croatian and proto-Serbian is emphasized (Lisac 2003: 16, map 6). The notion is not far-fetched, as it turns out, though the evidence usually presented is thin (i.e. not what is presented by Lisac and his predecessors). What was later to be "packaged" as Croatian and Serbian is reflected in sociolinguistic systems corresponding to the Orthodox–Catholic dichotomy, which can be observed as early as the turn of the first millennium AD. The terminus post quem of what will turn out later to be the Serbo-Croatian sociolinguistic system is reflected in the isogloss for the innovation of intervocalic /ž/ becoming /r/, e.g. *može* became *more*, "s/he can". This change occurred throughout the South Slavic area (today's Slovene, Bosnian/Croatian/Serbian, Macedonian, Bulgarian) in the last century of the first millennium AD, but by the fourteenth the innovation had receded to the point where all but a few traces are found in Orthodox areas, whereas in Catholic areas the change remained productive and proliferated in subsequent centuries, especially where it occurred in grammatical markers (r(e) vs. ž(e), originally being a focus marker and later a marker of subordination, for example *kada-r*, "whenever"). Notably, this sociolinguistic marker cuts across the Štokavian dialect, that is the dialect selected for the *Ausbau* basis of Serbo-Croatian, dividing it into western and eastern subzones (/r/ in the West, /ž/ in the East), where Slovene (another South Slavic language), Kajkavian and Čakavian share the innovation. In other words, carriers of the change were identifying themselves sociolinguistically as speakers of Catholic-style speech versus Orthodox-style speakers, signalled by the avoidance versus replacement of the innovative forms. Bosnian Muslim speakers of the language have both markers (for details see M. L. Greenberg 1999; Snoj and Greenberg 2012: 280–81, 304). Notably, the nineteenth-century standardization project proceeded without awareness of the earlier development, which speaks to the systemic, if not cyclical, nature of abstand formation and perhaps ethnic boundary formation in general.

Serbo-Croatian developed from the language of the subaltern in the context of empires to the language of the Yugoslav hegemon. The "first" Yugoslavia, formed in 1918, gave titular priority to Serbs, Croats and Slovenes – in this order: The name of the newly independent state was the Kingdom of the Serbs, Croats and Slovenes, the pecking order of the languages. Macedonian was codified as a standard and elevated as a titular republican language in 1944 at the conclusion of the Second World War (simultaneously with the establishment of the "second" Yugoslavia as a socialist federation under Marshal Tito). Although they had equal status at both the republican and federal levels, restated in the 1974 constitution, Slovene and Macedonian served almost exclusively at the republican level, while federal functions of the state – military, border security, external representation, political discourse and so on – were conducted *de facto* in Serbo-Croatian. However, the legal status of the republican peoples, partially mapped to their corresponding standard languages, was encoded through the distinction *narodi*, "nations" versus *narodnosti*, "nationalities", *nations* denoting the primary South Slavic republican groups Serbs, Croats, Slovenes, Macedonians, Montenegrins and Muslims; *nationalities* denoting even substantial groups whose majorities lay outside Yugoslavia, for example Albanians, Hungarians, Roma, Turks, Bulgarians. As the wars of succession played out in the 1990s, the close mapping of standard language with emergent nation states proceeded predictably, with the titular groups prevailing in the respective states. New standards emerged for the state of Bosnia and Herzegovina (corresponding to the ethno-religious category "Muslim", alongside Croatian and Serbian, used by the respective ethnicities) and Montenegro.

An intriguing aspect of the post-Serbo-Croatian period is the variety of strategies by which language planners have reinforced the differences among the standard languages. In addition to different alphabets – Croatian (Latin) and Serbian (Cyrillic) – Croatian has revived a trend, employed in earlier periods (mid-nineteenth century, the brief interregnum of the fascist Independent State of Croatia during the Second World War) of reinforcing purism, that is inventing new words through native word-formation to replace internationalisms, in contrast to the Serbian practice of remaining open to borrowings (for details see Langston 1999). Bosnian, written in the Latin alphabet, reinforces regional vocabulary of eastern origin, especially Turkish. Montenegrin (usually written in Cyrillic), the newest of the standards, foregrounds regional differences in phonology, lexicon, word-formation and syntax (MINA 2007). These developments have not unfolded without internal opposition, however. Some linguists have argued against the excessive strictness of official Croatian purism (see especially Kapović 2011; Kordić 2010).

A number of lessons can be derived from the rise and fall of the Yugoslav project, but perhaps the most important one challenging biases in Western views of sociolinguistic systems is the following: hegemons and their language can be of any size – they need only be bigger than *the other*; standard languages can be engineered to reflect and reify other differences (ethnic, religious, political) and are remarkably plastic. They are plastic especially when non-seafaring hegemons are forced to colonize internally, creating the conditions wherein group conflict reinforces boundary-making and language systems are ready-made material for establishing them.

12.3 Conclusion

The brief overview of the two case studies from the Slavic-language area, the case of the Russian/Soviet Empire and the post-Soviet space, and the rise and fall of the Yugoslav project, gives us the opportunity to examine the dynamics of linguistic systems in the wide interstice between the Western "First World" and the traditional view of the Western-colonized "Third World". The sociolinguistic systems that developed in the context of Slavic speech areas in the Russian, Austro-Hungarian and Ottoman Empires and their successor states allow us to examine closely the interplay between political, religious and ideological change, on the one hand, and language, on the other. In the Russian/Soviet case we observe a struggle between shifting patterns of regional power in which the dominant can quickly become the dominated and we have a rare opportunity to observe in real time how individual actors and groups can move, mirrored in their linguistic behaviour, from one group to another, in some cases even moving from Megalomanian to Ruritanian. In the case of the rise and fall of the Yugoslav project, we can observe the trajectory of Ruritanians to Megalomanians and back again to Ruritanians. In each case, sociolinguistic systems come into play both as a reflection of group formation and as a motivating factor for them.

12.4 Postscript (March 2014)

After the chapter was written, events in Russia and Ukraine brought to the fore language and cultural issues that from a Western perspective would seem to have been matters that belonged to the past. As I write these lines, Crimea has just been formally annexed to the Russian Federation and Russian troops are poised along the border with Ukraine, which NATO leadership is reading as a threat to annex further Ukrainian territory. Western newspaper editorials express their surprise at the turn of events, as though upsetting the projects of self-determination of nation states in Europe were unthinkable. However, students of language and culture in the former Soviet space can hardly have been surprised.[6] As was pointed out in this chapter, Russia's "top-down", long-term project of uniting its empire around the rationalization of language ("making Russians", as Staliūnas titled his 2007 book), through heterogeneous means, has been ongoing for centuries. The problem can also be viewed from the bottom up. As Laitin (1998: ix) characterizes them, Russians in the titular republics that broke away from the USSR constitute a "beached diaspora":

> Daily they face a set of questions about who they are and what they may become. Are they a people in diaspora, even if it was not they but their country that moved? Would they "return" to a homeland many of them had never seen? Would they join forces to fight politically for Russian rights in these republics, or even militarily for the right to reunite with the Russian Federation? If they remained as loyal citizens, would ethnic conflict between them and the titulars become a permanent feature of social life? Would a new identity form, not quite Russian, but not quite titular either? Would these Russians move along a path that leads, for their children if not for them, to assimilation with the titular nationality?

What was not foreseen was the other logical possibility, which is that Russia itself could reunite Russian speakers from outside the borders of the titular republics. To understand why this other possibility, not readily entertained in the West, is playing out, it helps to consider that, in addition to the realities faced by everyday people, there is an ideological underpinning to Putin's military intervention.

A strain of Russian thought to which President Putin evidently subscribes holds that Russia is destined to be the dominant political and cultural force in Eurasia, a great ethnic and socio-political complex ideologically and philosophically opposed to Western Europe (see Laruelle 2008). This powerful mythologem, whose roots are in the eighteenth century, was clearly articulated in the 1920s, where the great linguist Nikolai Trubetzkoy (1890–1938) was one of its early proponents; it continues in the work of Alexander Dugin (b. 1962), one of its most recent proponents. Eurasianist thought, never far from conservative nationalist programmes, has shaped the world-view of the Kremlin and the Russian intellectual circles (Shlapentokh 2007: 221): "Dugin's views have been absorbed more and more by segments of the Russian elite, even those who not only have never read Dugin but have never even heard of him." From a Western European or North American perspective, the Euromaidan protests seemed hardly more than a quotidian yearning to join other liberal democracies and market-based economies; from a Russian Eurasianist perspective, the protests were a harbinger of identity loss, a step beyond which there would be no return, since it has as a consequence the betrayal of one great civilization in favour of another.

Notes

1 *Longue durée* perspective has been advanced programmatically in sociolinguistics by Blommaert (1999), though the approach has gained little traction.
2 Geraci (2001: 76) notes that Benedict Anderson, in his *Imagined Communities*, cites imperial Russification as a parade example of "cultural homogenization".
3 This strategy echoes the beginnings of Slavic literacy in the 850s, when pagan Slavs were incorporated into the Hellenic culture by creating a Byzantine-style Slavic liturgical language.
4 To avoid confusion, we use the anachronistic but widely recognized term "Serbo-Croatian", which properly belongs to the erstwhile Yugoslav state (1918–91). Today four standards correspond to four post-Yugoslav nation-states, Bosnian, Croatian, Serbian and Montenegrin, sometimes referred to collectively in English as "Bosnian–Croatian–Serbian (BCS)".
5 The identification of Illyrian with the pre-Roman inhabitants, most likely the precursors to today's Albanians, was known at the time, but as an ideologeme in nineteenth-century popular imagination Illyrian referred to the early South Slavs, before their fragmentation into local identities (for details see Blažević 2008).
6 To wit, asked by a local reporter, shortly after I had returned from Kyiv in February 2014, whether I was surprised by the escalation in the conflict, I replied that I was not. The development fit Putin's "Eurasian model" of his world. Ben Unglesbee, "Ukrainian Natives and Experts at KU Forced to Watch Crisis from Afar", *Lawrence Journal-World*, 4 March 2014, [electronic edition] www2.ljworld.com/news/2014/mar/04/ukrainian-natives-and-experts-ku-forced-watch-cris/ (accessed 24 March 2014).

Further reading

Gerasimov, Il'ja, et al. (eds) (2011) *The Diversity of Otherness: Studies of the Second World and New Historical Paradigms* (*Ab Imperio* 1). Kazan: Ab Imperio.
Hroch, Miroslav (1999) The Slavic World. In: *Handbook of Language and Ethnic Identity*. Joshua A. Fishman (ed.), 319–33. Oxford: Oxford University Press.
Kamusella, Tomasz (2012) *The Politics of Language and Nationalism in Modern Central Europe*. Basingstoke: Palgrave Macmillan.

References

Anderson, Benedict R. (2006) *Imagined Communities: Reflections on the Origin and Spread of Nationalism* (revised edition). London: Verso.
Austin, P. M. (1992) Soviet Karelian. The Language that Failed. *Slavic Review* 51(1): 16–35.
Blažević, Z. (2008) *Ilirizam prije ilirizma* [Illyrism before Illyrism]. Zagreb: Golden Marketing/Tehnička knjiga.
Block, D., J. Gray and M. Holborow (eds) (2012) *Neoliberalism and Applied Linguistics*. London: Routledge.
Blommaert, Jan (1999) The Debate is Open. In: *Language Ideological Debates*. Jan Blommaert (ed.), 1–38. Berlin: Mouton de Gruyter.
Brubaker, R. (2004) *Ethnicity without Groups*. Cambridge, MA: Harvard University Press.
Darquennes, J. and W. Vandenbussche (2011) Language and Religion as a Sociolinguistic Field of Study: Some Introductory Notes. *Sociolinguistica* 25: 1–11.
Errington, J. J. (2008) *Linguistics in a Colonial World: A Story of Language, Meaning, and Power*. Malden: Blackwell.
Everaert, C. (2010) *Tracing the Boundaries between Hindi and Urdu: Lost and Added in Translation between 20th Century Short Stories*. Leiden: Brill.
Gellner, Ernest (1983) *Nations and Nationalism*. Ithaca: Cornell University Press.
Geraci, R. P. (2001) *Window on the East: National and Imperial Identities in Late Tsarist Russia*. Ithaca: Cornell University Press.
Greenberg, M. L. (1999) Multiple Causation in the Spread and Reversal of a Sound Change: Rhotacism in South Slavic. *Slovenski jezik/Slovene Linguistic Studies* 2: 63–76.
——(2011) The Illyrian Movement: A Croatian Vision of South Slavic Unity. In: *Handbook of Language and Ethnic Identity: The Success–Failure Continuum in Language Identity Efforts* (Volume 2). Joshua A. Fishman and O. García (eds), 364–80. Oxford: Oxford University Press.
Greenberg, R. D. (2004) *Language and Identity in the Balkans: Serbo-Croatian and its Disintegration*. Oxford: Oxford University Press.
Grenoble, L. A. (2003) *Language Policy in the Soviet Union*. Dordrecht: Kluwer Academic Publishers.
Judson, P. M. (2006) *Guardians of the Nation: Activists on the Language Frontiers of Imperial Austria*. Cambridge: Harvard University Press.
Kapović, M. (2011) *Čiji je jezik?* [Whose Language is it?]. Zagreb: Algoritam.
Kennan, G. F. (1993[1914]) *The Other Balkan Wars: A 1913 Carnegie Endowment Inquiry in Retrospect with a New Introduction and Reflection on the Present Conflict*. Washington, DC: The Carnegie Endowment.
Kordić, S. (2010) *Jezik i nacionalizam* [Language and Nationalism]. Zagreb: Durieux.
Laitin, D. D. (1998) *Identity in Formation: The Russian-Speaking Populations in the Near Abroad*. Ithaca: Cornell University Press.
Langston, K. (1999) Linguistic Cleansing: Language Purism in Croatia after the Break-up of Yugoslavia. *International Politics* 36: 179–201.
Laruelle, Marlène (2008) *Russian Eurasianism: An Ideology of Empire*. Washington, DC/Baltimore: Woodrow Wilson Center Press and Johns Hopkins University Press.
Lewis, M. Paul, Gary F. Simons and Charles D. Fennig (eds) (2014) *Ethnologue: Languages of the World* (seventeenth edition). Dallas: SIL International. Online available at: www.ethnologue.com (accessed 9 June 2013).
Lillis, J. and D. C. K. Cox (2013) Interview 180: Juggling the Roles of Kazakh and Russian Languages. *Eurasianet.org*. Online available at: www.eurasianet.org/node/66712 (accessed 19 August 2014).
Lisac, J. (2003) *Hrvatska dijalektologija 1: Hrvatski dijalekti i govori štokavskog narječja i hrvatski govori torlačkog narječja* [Croatian Dialectology 1: Croatian Dialects and Subdialects of the Štokavian Dialect Complex and the Croatian Varieties of the Torlak Dialect]. Zagreb: Golden Marketing/Tehnička knjiga.
Meyerhoff, Miriam (2011) *Introducing Sociolinguistics* (second edition). Abingdon/New York: Routledge.

MINA (2007) U slavistici odavno postoji naziv crnogorski [In Slavic Studies the Term Montenegrin has Long Existed], *Pobjeda (Internet izdanje dnevnog lista "Pobjeda")*. Online available at: www.pobjeda.cg.yu/naslovna.phtml?akcija=vijest&id=124322 (accessed on 19 August 2014).
Mønnesland, S. (2004) Is there a Bosnian Language? In: *Language in the Former Yugoslav Lands*. R. Bugarski and C. Hawkesworth (eds), 127–61. Bloomington: Slavica.
Nilsen, K. A. (1995) Bosnian Experts Accuse Stoltenberg. *Bosnia Report*. Online available at: www.bosnia.org.uk/bosrep/junaug95/expaccuse.cfm (accessed on 19 August 2014).
Pavlenko, A. (2008) Russian in Post-Soviet Countries. *Russian Linguistics* 32: 59–80.
Shlapentokh, Vladimir (2007) *Contemporary Russia as a Feudal Society: A New Perspective on the Post-Soviet Era*. New York: Palgrave Macmillan.
Smith, M. G. (1998) *Language and Power in the Creation of the USSR, 1917–1953*. Berlin: Mouton de Gruyter.
Snoj, M. and Greenberg, M. L. (2012) O jeziku slovanskih prebivalcev med Donavo in Jadranom v srednjem veku (pogled jezikoslovcev) [On the Language of the Medieval Slavic Population in the Area between the Danube and the Adriatic (from a Linguistic Perspective)]. *Zgodovinski časopis* [Historical Review] 66(3)–4[146]: 276–305.
Staliūnas, D. (2007) *Making Russians: Meaning and Practice of Russification in Lithuania and Belarus after 1863*. Amsterdam: Rodopi.
van Olphen, H. (1988) Religious Differentiation and National Languages. In: *Languages and Cultures: Studies in Honor of Edgar C. Polomé*. M. A. Jazayery, E. C. Polomé and W. Winter (eds), 741–47. Berlin: Mouton de Gruyter.
Wachtel, A. (1998) *Making a Nation, Breaking a Nation: Literature and Cultural Politics in Yugoslavia*. Stanford: Stanford University Press.
Wertheim, S. (2003) Language Ideologies and the "Purification" of Post-Soviet Tatar. *Ab Imperio* 1: 347–69.
Wimmer, A. (2013) *Ethnic Boundary Making: Institutions, Power, Networks*. New York: Oxford University Press.
Zamyatin, K. (2012) From Language Revival to Language Removal? The Teaching of Titular Languages in the National Republics of Post-Soviet Russia. *Journal on Ethnopolitics and Minority Issues in Europe* 11(2): 75–102.

13

THE STUDY OF POLITENESS AND WOMEN'S LANGUAGE IN JAPAN

Patrick Heinrich

13.1 Introduction

Japan is a group of islands dotting the Pacific Rim. It is a multilingual polity extending for almost 3,000 kilometres from Ainu Mosir (Hokkaido) in the north to the Ryukyu Islands in the south. Standard Japanese is the dominant language.[1] With more than 130 million first- and second-language speakers, Japanese is amongst the largest languages in the world. As an effect of urbanization and the influence of mass media, extensive dialect levelling has occurred in Japanese. The shift to Standard Japanese is also endangering Japan's indigenous languages – such as Ainu, Hachijo and the Ryukyuan languages – as well as Japanese Sign Language. Japanese, Hachijo and the Ryukyuan languages form the Japonic language family. Ainu is a language isolate.

This chapter first discusses the development of sociolinguistic studies in Japan. In order to meaningfully do so it is imperative to understand the reception and application of Western sociolinguistics in Japan, as we will see in the course of this chapter. Afterwards the study of politeness and women's language in Japan will be discussed. In doing so, it will become clear that Japan may apply models developed in Western sociolinguistics to Japanese but that it will maintain the perspective on Japanese language and society as set forth in its own sociolinguistic tradition. As an effect, modernist Japanese language ideology finds entry into this kind of research, and this stalls the development for more thorough investigations. This is also a problem because this kind of Japanese research then feeds back into mainstream sociolinguistic theory. It furthers the "exotification" of Japan and the Japanese language (e.g. Holmes 1992; Talbot 1998).

13.2 Indigenous and Western approaches to sociolinguistics

Japan can draw on a notable pre-modern tradition of linguistic research. Buddhist studies, the heritage of classical Chinese culture through Confucian studies, the philological work of the so-called school of *kokugogakusha* ("national philologists" or "Edo nativists") and translations at Court were the main sources of pre-modern linguistic studies. In particular, the work of the Edo nativists found entry into Japanese modern linguistics (Eschbach-Szabó 2000). The introduction of Western linguistics to Japan was never simply a transfer of information. It was a selection, interpretation and adaptation of Western linguistics according to the necessities, research gaps and the dominant ideologies existing in Japan. Indigenous and Western approaches coexist on all levels of description and all linguistic sub-disciplines (pragmatics, sociolinguistics, grammar, etc.). At times, although rather rarely, attempts have been made to unify indigenous and Western approaches (Heinrich 2002a). As a result, sociolinguistics in Japan is not a unified, monolithic discipline. Different traditions coexist and come up with different approaches and results.

13.2.1 Gengo seikatsu

Japan's own tradition of sociolinguistic study is called *gengo seikatsu* ("language life"). It has its roots in the effort to modernize the Japanese language. The legendary Ainu linguist Kindaichi (1933: 35, translation by the author) was the first to call for a structured approach to the study of language and society: "Our lives are one harmonious and synthetic unity. Hence, just as one can imagine to comprehensively study economic life, religious life, social life, intellectual life, aesthetic life, sexual life, and so on, there also exists the possibility to comprehend language life (*gengo seikatsu*) as such an abstract phenomenon."

Already before 1945, a number of important language life studies were conducted (see, e.g., Kikuzawa 1933; Tanabe 1936; Kindaichi 1941). More detailed research was launched after 1945 when the National Institute for Japanese Language and Linguistics (Kokuritsu Kokugo Kenkyūjo) was responsible for a veritable boom in language life studies.

Two distinct schools of studying language life developed. One was theoretically based on Tokieda's (1941) process theory of language. Based on his basic claim that language was first and foremost an "activity" (*kōi*), just like dancing or singing, Tokieda called for a study of language that paid regard to "context" (*bamen*). Besides physical aspects of context, Tokieda (1956) argued for a study of certain psychological factors – "attitudes" (*taido*), "frame of mind" (*kibun*) and "emotion" (*kanjō*) – in relation to language structures. Studies in this tradition include Tsukahara (1954) or Mio (1948). The second approach to language life was based on large-scale field surveys and the introduction of statistical analysis to Japanese linguistics. The National Institute for Japanese Language and Linguistics conducted large-scale surveys on literacy (YKNCI 1951), the standardization process in rural areas (KKK 1950), politeness (KKK 1957) and even made 24-hour-long language documentations (KKK 1951). This research did not include theoretical considerations (Heinrich 2002b). It was motivated by the objective of the institute, which called for research in order to "rationalize" (*gōrika*) the Japanese language. This objective reflected a language ideology, which perceived the Japanese language to be undemocratic per se and thus in urgent need of reform after the Second World War (Lewin 1979).

After the introduction of Western sociolinguistics from the early 1970s onwards, interest in *gengo seikatsu* declined. Today, the legacy of language life survives in studies on "new dialects" (*shin-hōgen*) or "neo-dialects" (*neo-dairekuto*) (Inoue 1985), in the study of "role language" (*yakuwarigo*) (Kinsui 2003) and in its geolinguistic variant called "dialect cosplay" (*hōgen kosupure*) (Tanaka 2011).

13.2.2 Imported sociolinguistics

Western sociolinguistics spread quickly in Japan. This manifested itself in a large number of translations of Western works into Japanese; for example, Fishman (1972) translated into Japanese in 1974, Trudgill (1974) translated into Japanese in 1975, or Hymes (1974) translated into Japanese in 1978. Concrete application of Western sociolinguistics started in the 1980s. The shift from language life to sociolinguistics was due to the fact that "problems of national language and script" (*kokugo kokuji mondai*) were no longer seen to be pressing. Hence, *gengo seikatsu* received less attention. The internationalization of Japanese universities and the employment of and exchange with Western sociolinguists such as Patricia Clancy, Senko Maynard, Florian Coulmas, Harald Haarmann, John Hinds, Leo Loveday, John Maher, Jiri Neustupny, Fred Peng, and many others, also played a crucial role. These scholars came to be known as the "imported fraction" (*gairaiha*) of sociolinguistic research in Japan. In 1987, a symposium was organized with the aim of unifying Western and Japanese approaches (see Ide 1988). Ambitions did not go beyond declarations of good intentions, though. In aiming at universal application and theory building, Western sociolinguistics is rather incommensurable with language life's insistence on emic approaches and data collections as its ultimate objective. Emic approaches indicate that no attempts were made to gain insights beyond the Japanese language and Japanese society.

From the very start of modern linguistics in Japan, more or less the same ideology emphasizing and promoting linguistic homogeneity has been upheld. Not conforming to such a stance has been rare (see Heinrich 2013 for discussion of an exception). Sociolinguistics continued this trend and reproduced the view of a classless, monolingual and homogeneous Japanese society. In particular, Japanese dialectologists who "converted" to sociolinguistics subscribed to this view and consequently neglected a wide range of sociolinguistic topics (Masiko 2014). Among other things, they ignored the study of social dialects and linguistic minorities in Japan, despite the reception of Western sociolinguistics introducing research on social stratification in urban centres, segregated minority settlements in cities, or code switching by migrants. Such issues started to be addressed only from the 1990s onwards when scholars from neighbouring disciplines started to take an interest in Japanese sociolinguistics.

13.2.3 Interdisciplinary sociolinguistics

Sociologists of education initiated long overdue research into how social class was reflected in language and culture. Researchers familiar with research trends outside

Japan, that is Katsuhiko Tanaka, Kiyoshi Hara, Hidenori Masiko, Goro Chrisoph Kimura, and many others, started pointing at an unequal distribution of power between the majority and minorities in Japan, and at the various forms of discrimination resulting from this. Linguistic diversity also became increasingly difficult to ignore. Ainu, Ryukyuans and the Deaf started calling for their recognition as cultural and linguistic minorities. A new generation of critical sociolinguistics began addressing these issues. They are aware that the image of an exclusively middle class and monolingual Japanese-speaking society is the legacy of the pre-war "one lord, the whole nation" (*ikkun banmin*) ideology. Interdisciplinary critical sociolinguistics is first and foremost seeking to shift the epistemology of Japan's sociolinguistic make-up (see, e.g., TGKK 2013). It departs from a view that Japan is a "multilingual society" (*tagengo shakai*) and a "disparate society" (*kakusa shakai*), contradicting the dominant and popular view of a linguistically homogenous Japanese society.

Interdisciplinary critical sociolinguistics can be characterized as being radical and anti-establishment. It is not simply applying Western models on Japan. It develops new approaches as well. These incorporate methods and perspectives from disciplines such as anthropology, sociology, pedagogy or legal studies. Noteworthy books in this tradition include Kadoya and Abe (2010), Masiko (2012), Noro and Yamashita (2009) or Yasuda (1997).

As we will see in the subsequent discussions on the study of women's language and politeness in Japan, the object of research is studied according to Western theories and methods but the object of research is constituted in the way that the indigenous traditions of Japanese linguistics have framed it. Hence, knowledge of different approaches to the study of Japanese sociolinguistics is indispensable for comprehensibly grasping the application of Western sociolinguistics.

13.3 Women's language

Just as many other sociolinguistic topics in Japan, women's language was already studied in the tradition of language life studies. Kikuzawa (1929) provides an early discussion along the lines of his theory of language "strata" (*isō*), which provides a view of Japanese as being constituted by various role languages. It was, however, only in the 1980s that the study of "women's language" (*joseigo* or *onna kotoba*) became a central topic in Japanese sociolinguistics.

The reception of Lakoff's (1975, translated into Japanese in 1985) *Language and Woman's Place* by scholars such as Ide or Reynolds proved important for a new wave of research on women's language in Japan. Lakoff (1975) maintained that women use tag-questions, hedges, intensifiers, hypercorrect forms, and so on, as a reaction to male domination, and do so more frequently than men. In so doing, women create a language that is perceived to be softer, more insecure and uncertain. According to such a correlational model, the variable gender was seen to prompt women's language unrelated to other aspects of female identity. Initially, this view also became widely accepted in Japanese research. However, Lakoff's (1975: 69) assertion that women's language was perceived to be deficient in comparison to male speech was instantly refuted (except for a few such as Reynolds 1985, 1990). In particular, Ide (2004: 185) claimed that women's language indexed elegance, prestige and power, and, what is more, that it had done so throughout history. Thus, while claiming that women's language was a well-defined and autonomous subset of Japanese language, it was argued that the dichotomy between male and female language did not translate into inequality in the case of Japan. The reason for this was perceived to lie in a different concept of society. An interpretation of women's language as being deficient would emerge only on the grounds of egalitarian idealism in individual societies. In Japanese group-orientated society, however, gendered speech was truly complementary and coexisted with male language (Ide and McGloin 1990).[2]

It is important to note that the idea of a well-defined women's language in Japan is rooted in the fact that men and women's language choices are "more clearly located in morphology than in languages like English" (Matsumoto 2004: 245). Important indexes of gender are the use of sentence-final particles and personal pronouns (Ide 1982; Shibamoto 1985; Okamoto 1995). As a result of such apparent linguistic differences, awareness of gendered language is without doubt higher in Japanese than in many other languages. Consider the gendered distribution of some sentence final particles (Ide and Yoshida 1999: 464). We find particles used predominantly by men such as *-ze* (100%), *-zo* (94%), *-na* (94%), *-saa* (86%) or *-ka* (84%), while others are predominantly used by women such as *-wane* (100%), *-noyo* (89%), *-wa* (85%), *-nano* (78%) or *-monne* (78%).

The view on language and gender structured by clear boundaries, creating a gendered binary, was severely undermined from the 1990s onwards. Two approaches can be identified, one historical and the second anthropological. On the one hand, the origin of the dominant ideology about women's language was traced back in history. It was thereby revealed that *joseigo* was a modernist construct, rather than a natural category (Endō 1997). On the other hand, a number of scholars started to examine women's language by taking a view from the social margin, that is a view removed from the middle class in Tokyo. This new wave on the study of women's language demonstrated that earlier research on this topic had confused a language ideology of gendered language with empirical facts (see, e.g., Shibamoto 1985; Okamoto 1995; Inoue 2006).

The most important work in the deconstruction of dominant views on women's language in Japan has been conducted by Inoue (2006). In taking her own linguistic socialization in rural Japan as a point of reference, Inoue (2006: 3) exposes ideas on women's language, and that these do not conform to sociolinguistic facts:

> But here is a little public secret: the very simple, yet obstinately disregarded, fact is that most women in Japan do not have access to – did not systematically learn and cannot skillfully produce – the speech forms identified as women's language in their habitual speech repertoire; particularly people in the cultural, class, and regional peripheries would tell us that statements such as "men and women speak differently" do not apply to their everyday linguistic experience.

In writing this, Inoue breaks an invisible veil in that those not proficient in what is seen as a legitimate language remain silent about their lack of proficiency, because lack of proficiency tends to be perceived as ignorance. Bourdieu (1991: 62) has aptly observed in this context that the recognition of a legitimate language is more widely accepted than it is possessed and that those not in possession of legitimate speech are usually compliant to the dominant view and silent about their difference (Bourdieu 1991: 90–104). Legitimate language as defined by Bourdieu is language invested with a symbolic power accepted by all members of a speech community. It is the language likely to be listened to. Lack of proficiency in legitimate language, on the other hand, condemns speakers to silence in most situations, or results otherwise in hyper-correctness.

In having Inoue refrain from keeping silent on her language repertoire which deviates from legitimate speech, a new perspective on women's language emerges. Consider Inoue's (2006: 6) recollection of her own linguistic socialization: "Growing up in a regional area in Japan, where no one speaks women's language, I never experienced as a child a face-to-face context of talking with or hearing someone who used the speech forms identified as women's language." Furthermore (Inoue 2006: 8):

> The place associated with women who speak women's language is Tokyo, an unmarked place, in the world of television, where everybody is middle class, every man wears a tie and commutes on trains and subways, and every woman wears a frilled apron or high heels. For me, women's language was the language spoken on the other side of the TV screen [...] cartoon characters, stuffed animals, [...] women in cooking shows, actresses in dramas, and popular singers. I heard the most authentic women's language from such inauthentic – electronically mediated – bodies, not the bodies of real people in face-to-face interaction with me.

In departing from Inoue's iconoclastic view on women's language, two new sets of questions become central in the study of women's language. How did the idea of women's language become popular and when, and whose language is Japanese women's language? Endō (1997) has convincingly argued that women's language is not the result of an evolutionary process descending directly from the Heian Period (794–1185) but that it has actively been manufactured in the Meiji Period (1868–1912). Inoue (2006) depicts how language planners, first and foremost through writers of the Japanese naturalism school of literature, created women's language in their books by applying a new literary language which sought to "unify the spoken and the written language" (*genbun itchi*) (see Twine 1978; Heinrich 2005).

The *genbun-itchi* literature invented a new spoken language for writing, but this language was received as spoken language by its readers. Women's language was thus initially not heard but spread through written language in novels or magazines. The case of women's language in Japan serves as a forceful reminder of the importance of written language with regard to ideologically constructed language norms.

Consider the changes that occurred in the gendered use of sentence-final particles in the period when Japanese was modernized. In order to illustrate these changes, Inoue (2006: 94) compares sentence-final particles in two works of literature. *Ukiyoburo* ("Bathhouse in the Floating World") by Shikitei was published in 1813. It consists in large parts of conversations between visitors of a public bath. *Sanshirō*, titled after the first name of the male protagonist, is a novel by Natsume. It was published in 1909 and is considered today to be a masterpiece of the Japanese *genbun itchi* literature. In contrasting particles used in *Ukiyoburo* and *Sanshirō*, the allocation of gender indexing in the course of Japanese language modernization becomes plainly obvious. (Note in this context that *da* is the informal form of the copula.) The copula and particles *da-na*, *da-ne*, *da-yo*, *da-ze* and *da-zo* were used both by men and women in *Ukiyoburo* but only by men in *Sanshirō*; *da-wa* used by men and women became restricted to use by women; *da-koto* was never used in the work of Shikitei but became employed in female speech in Natsume's novel.

Needless to say, such an invention of women's language was not undertaken for the sake of inventing women's language. Something larger was at stake and that was the social modernization of Japan. Natsume's use of gendered language, as found in *Sanshirō*, drew on the speech of young female students in Tokyo. Female students were of course a novelty in Japanese society then. Their language (and these young women themselves) was at the time subject of much negative judgement. Japanese women's language as it emerged in the modern novel was, however, not the same language as that which was used by these students. It is once more worth quoting Inoue (2006: 105) at length in this context:

> The emergence of women's language was and has been intensely modern and national. Indexing gender in the early-twentieth-century Japan involved imagining the voice of (the yet to be imagined) modern Japanese woman. It was in the "vulgar" speech of schoolgirls that the Meiji writers discovered the linguistic forms to represent the voice of modern women. This type of speech became elevated to the rank of "Japanese women's language" only after it was displaced, grafted, quoted, recycled, and circulated in the network of newly available representational genres and media. In this sense, there is no original or authentic speaking body that uttered women's language. It is *no one's language*; indeed, it is disembodied language.

The reason for crafting a language for women in the Meiji Period was caused by the necessity to imagine the role of Japanese women in modernity, and such a role needed to be indexed linguistically. The modern Japanese woman was thereby to follow the ideal of being a "good wife and wise mother" (*ryōsai kenbo*). The term *ryōsai kenbo* itself was coined by the Japanese educator and Confucian scholar Masanao Nakamura in 1875. According to this ideal, women were to excel in housekeeping and saving money as well as in raising intelligent children for the sake of the Japanese nation (Koyama 1991). The women's language, which emerged in the Meiji years, was the voice of the imagined modern woman corresponding to this ideal of womanhood (Inoue 2006: 149–59). It is this particular ideal of the role of women in Japan that underlies the reception of studies on women's language and that informs popular and academic discourse on women's language in Japan (Tanaka and Tanaka 1996) and also abroad (Shibatani 1990). Although shifting usage of the so-called "gendered particles" and "gendered pronouns" are sometimes depicted as recent phenomena (e.g. Okamoto and Shibamoto Smith 2004), these changes have been noted for over a 100 years (e.g. Reynolds 1985, 1990; Endō 1997; Nakamura 2011).

What sets Japan's *joseigo* apart from other examples of women's language is not the existence of a women's language shared by all since ancient time, but the extent and pervasiveness with which modernist ideology is reproduced in the study of women's language. An ideology has been created and remains in place for some reason. It is for this reason that Ohara (1999: 431) calls for a study of language and gender that attempts "to reach a deeper level, the level of common sense assumption that underlie the production and interpretations of the activities that constitute Japanese society". To be sure, sociolinguistics must be more sensible to the ways and the extent to which national ideology enters the study of language and society. Tracing ideology back into the past and studying women's language from a perspective of the margin have been the main approaches to deconstructing modernist views on Japanese language and society. Most of this research was, however, not undertaken by sociolinguists but by students of conversation analysis, history or linguistic anthropology.

13.4 Politeness

A survey of the classified content of the *Kokugo nenkan* ("Yearbook of National Language") between 1954 and 1991 shows that politeness was the most intensively researched topic in Japan of that period (Heinrich 2002a: 199). Politeness became a prominent topic in Japanese linguistics when the National Institute for Japanese Language and Linguistics (KKK 1952) published a booklet titled *Kore kara no keigo* ("Honorific Language Henceforth"). Therein, a new use of honorific language was promoted. The use of honorific language was to henceforth reflect the egalitarianism of a democratic society. According to the booklet, *keigo* (honorific language, literally "respect language") should be used in order to express mutual respect and should no longer be employed to reproduce social hierarchies in an authoritarian state (see Wetzel 2004: 56–65, 117–22). Just as women's language, honorific speech in Japanese is clearly marked by morphosyntactic and lexical means. Hence, awareness about politeness registers in Japanese is ever-present, and different registers of honorific language (self-humbling, respectful, linguistic beautification, etc.) are expressed very differently and follow different rules of grammar.

A perceived "confusion in national language" (*kokugo no midare*), seen as the result of social changes and language reforms in the post-war years (Heinrich 2002a: 92–95), led to surveys on honorific language by the National Institute for Japanese Language and Linguistics (KKK 1957). It revealed, amongst other things, that female informants tended to use polite forms more often, and that longer utterances and also Sino-Japanese vocabulary were perceived to be polite.[3] As is usual in the language life tradition, no attempts at theory building were made, but we do find in these works descriptions of socio-cultural contexts triggering the choice of *keigo* (see Wetzel 2004: 19–42 for a summary of this research). As Japan recovered from the Second World War, public interest in Japanese language reform declined and Japanese linguistics shifted focus to the study of regional varieties and historical linguistics (Masiko 2014).

Politeness re-emerged as a popular topic in the 1980s. While the earlier research on *keigo* had postulated rules how to speak politely to persons of respect, the new sociolinguistic approaches studied what kind of people were actually deserving of respect. Ide (1982: 366–71) identified four decisive factors prompting the use of honorific language: social position, power, age and situational formality. Based on these insights, she formulated three rules defining polite language use in Japanese: (1) be polite to persons with a high social status; (2) be polite to people with power; (3) be polite towards older people. Ide's initial interest in politeness had its origin in her studies on the language of women. Given the strong awareness of honorific language in Japanese and the interest of the polite speech of women, the work of Brown and Levinson (1987) was seen as a welcome contribution to the study of Japanese (see, e.g., Hori 1986; Schilling 1999). The work of Brown and Levinson proved crucial for a shift from descriptions of contexts to interactional strategies prompting politeness. Ide was among the first to consider this new approach to politeness, and she also proved influential for its spread.

Applying Brown and Levinson proved difficult, as the indigenous tradition to the study of *keigo* had shown that the use of polite registers hinged on context. The necessity to be polite was seen not to be an interactional strategy. In other words, it was claimed that communal obligations overrule individual choices in the case of Japan. As a consequence, the model of Brown and Levinson was criticized as being Eurocentric. Calls were made to look more closely into the culture-specific character of politeness, an important contribution to the subsequent development of politeness studies. Ide (1989a, 1989b) and Matsumoto (1989) claimed that the honorific language system in Japanese left little room for a choice of politeness strategies as described by Brown and Levinson. Hence, face-threatening acts were not responsible for prompting polite speech. Ide's (1989b: 227) argument is today a classic in research on politeness.

(1) * Sensei-wa kore-o   yonda.
    prof.-TOP this-ACC read-PAST
    The professor read this.

(2) Sensei-wa kore-o   oyomi ni-natta.
    prof.-TOP this-ACC read-REF.HON.PAST
    The professor read this.

Ide argued that a Japanese speaker had no other choice but utterance (2). Furthermore, the idea that speakers may decide how polite they want to make an utterance was seen to be based in individualistic societies. Ide did, however, not entirely refute the approach of Brown and Levinson, but argued that there existed a discernment–volition continuum in language, where Japanese was placed at the discernment end while English was placed at the volition end. In other words, politeness in Japanese was the effect of socio-cultural constraints while it was an instance of choice in the case of English. Note, however, that the fact that Japanese honorifics are obligatory in most situations does not mean that honorifics are not linked to face threatening acts at all. Not using honorifics where required very certainly constitutes a face threatening act (Fukuda and Asato 2004: 1997). In other words, most use of honorifics is linguistically unmarked or "politic" behaviour (Watts 2003), making its absence an instance of impoliteness.

According to Ide (1989b), the difficulty of applying the Brown and Levinson framework to the Japanese honorific system stems from the fact that they collapse "linguistic form" (= honorific) and "verbal strategies" (= politeness) into one category (politeness), and in doing so cannot account for honorific language use adequately. In order to fill this gap, she proposes to treat honorific linguistic forms as discernment. Another major difference between the two, that is politeness and discernment, is that politeness is used towards a hearer, whereas linguistic forms can be used towards a referent who is not the hearer. In other words, linguistic forms can be used for something else but to alleviate face-threatening acts, that is discernment. Fukuda and Asato (2004: 1996), however, rightly pointed out that Japanese honorifics do not work as described by Ide and that polite forms are required in what she calls discernment because the hearer stands in relation with the referent and it is this which triggers the necessity to use honorifics.

Matsumoto (1988), on the other hand, argued that the idea of face needed to be reconsidered for non-Western cultures. In Japan, she claimed, the preservation of face depended on the communicative context and one's place in society (Matsumoto 1988: 415). Just like Ide, Matsumoto (1988: 419) argued that politeness was not a free choice and that applying Brown and Levinson without any modification to Japanese would result in seeing all utterances using *keigo* as constituting face-threatening acts. Without modification, Ide and Matsumoto argued Brown and Levinson's approach could not be applied to types of societies where individuals gained their significance mostly from the social group to which they belonged.

In a comparative study between English and Japanese, Hill et al. (1986) proposed an entirely new approach to the study of cross-cultural politeness. It was maintained that politeness was instigated by two factors, volition and *wakimae* ("discernment"). *Wakimae* is a Japanese term used as a central theoretical concept in an otherwise English publication. The study concluded that *wakimae* played a more important role in the case of politeness in Japanese, and volition a bigger role in the case of politeness in the US. It is important to note here that while criticizing Brown and Levinson for not being of universal applicability, the Japanese emic concept of *wakimae* was chosen as a means for a comparative study of politeness.[4]

In a more recent book on politeness in Japanese, Usami (2002: 23) criticized that Ide and Matsumoto had confused politeness theory with the "politeness level of linguistic forms", in other words politeness with the Japanese honorific system. This confusion, Usami argued, is due to the fact that prior research had been limited to utterances and had neglected discourse. In studying linguistic politeness on the basis of 72 Japanese conversations, Usami maintained that politeness was not simply to be equated with the analysis of *keigo*, but included other aspects such as turn-taking or topic initiation. When paying attention to such issues, politeness does constitute a matter of choice in Japanese as well. In order to grasp such choices, researchers needed to shift their focus to the level of discourse. This, then, allowed for grasping the "functions of language manipulation that work to maintain smooth human relationships" (Usami 2002: 2).

With the benefit of hindsight, we understand today that much work "on politeness in Japanese to date has […] inherited a predisposition to explicating politeness primarily in relation to honorifics" (Haugh and Obana 2011: 147). Furthermore, just like women's language, *keigo* as we know it today took shape and was popularized only in the Meiji Period (1868–1912). As in the case with women's language, *keigo* ideology accompanied its creation and this ideology also found its way into sociolinguistic research (Wetzel 2004).

Sociolinguistic research on Japanese politeness has been essentialist, mapping fixed meaning onto specific expressions. However, Ide (1982: 378–81) herself had noted in one of her early publications on politeness that *keigo* was not polite per se and that it was also often employed for linguistic beautification by women, for speaking motherese, or for "hypocritical courtesy" (*ingin burei*). Sociolinguistic research has also been normative if not prescriptive, and deviations to such prescription can easily be found on the social margins of Japanese society (see, e.g., Dickel Dunn 1999). Usami (2002) is an important departure from such essentialist and prescriptive directions of research on politeness in Japan. It may, however, not be radical enough. Most important for the future development of sociolinguistic research on politeness may be to abandon the view that Japanese politeness is contingent on context and not subject to choice. Politeness is all about choice, and if *keigo* is not subject to choice then it is not related to politeness. *Keigo* is unmarked in most cases (see above), but politeness is about marked language. *Keigo* is applied to index inside–outside affiliation, social role, gender, formality and this may all be context driven, but it is not linguistic politeness.

Since Usami published her book, research in linguistic politeness has undergone what is called the "discursive turn" or "postmodern turn". The new approaches refute the idea about the existence of linguistic norms recognized as appropriate by all at all times, and they also reject the idea that interactants have set and fixed roles they have to follow by all means (Watts 2003; Kádár and Mills 2011). The contributions on Japanese politeness have played an important role in evoking this shift. Present-day research on politeness, Haugh and Obana (2011: 147) state, is a "debate between culture-specific and universal perspectives in politeness". Doing so requires a distinction between the way interactants and researchers interpret politeness (first and second orders of politeness). But while Japanese sociolinguists of the past have greatly contributed to the necessity of making such a distinction, they are found not to participate in exploring and shaping these new approaches at present (Kádár and Mills 2011: 2–3). Given the insights we have gained in this chapter this might be less surprising than appears at first sight. With the shift from languages and societies as units of analysis to context and individuals in politeness research (Eelen 2001), an essentialist view on Japanese language and cultures becomes impossible. Such essentialism is, however, the hallmark of dominant language ideology in Japan and it is intricately linked to ideas about *keigo* and politeness. Such an ideology waits to be purposefully challenged by Japanese sociolinguists.

13.5 Discussion

Four patterns can be identified that are relevant in discussing the theme of this volume:

(1) Japanese sociolinguistics is not simply an application of Western sociolinguistics. The reception of Western sociolinguistics is not a theoretical or methodological adjustment to Japanese data. The Japanese tradition of sociolinguistic study predates that of the West, and hence the object of research (here women's language and politeness) is seen through the lenses of the indigenous tradition. In other words, the theory and the methods may be Western but the epistemology remains Japanese. Therefore Japanese scholars develop their own approaches to studying the interrelations between language and society. In so doing, they stick to Japanese cultural frameworks.

(2) The application of Western sociolinguistics has had a strong tendency to reproduce dominant ideas about Japanese society. This ideology regards Japan as being an egalitarian, classless and monolingual society where women and men speak differently. Japanese Studies outside Japan, which often informs sociolinguistic studies, also frequently reproduces the dominant language ideology, in particular in Japanese foreign-language classes.

(3) Neighbouring disciplines such as sociology, history or legal studies have long challenged the ideological view of a homogeneous Japan and scholars with a background in these traditions have discussed and undermined the ideological bias in indigenous and dominant Western approaches to sociolinguistics. The same can be said of Japanese studies in linguistic anthropology conducted in the West.

(4) Specialists of women's language and of politeness who do not speak Japanese rely on Western sociolinguistics accounts and in so doing unconsciously reproduce the dominant modernist ideology about Japanese society and language. Critical interdisciplinary sociolinguistics in Japan is mainly concerned with challenging such ideology in Japan and does not publish in English. Too few scholars are conversant with Japanese and Western approaches of sociolinguistics in Japan to change the current trend.

As it stands, we can predict that various approaches to sociolinguistics will continue to coexist in Japan. Which one will become dominant and prevail in the long run ultimately depends on the place that Japan is seeking to fill in a globalizing world, and what image of society Japan wants to project in the future. Sociolinguists drawing on Japanese accounts for developing their arguments will involuntarily and unconsciously reflect this choice and will use such accounts for building sociolinguistic theory. As it stands, the way that the majority of sociolinguistic studies are conducted in Japan does not only stagnate the development of theories, it also furthers exotification of Japanese and downplays existing heterogeneity in Japanese society.

Acknowledgement

I am indebted to Yumiko Ohara, Hidenori Masiko and Dick Smakman for discussions on the subject of this chapter. All remaining shortcomings or mistakes are mine.

Notes

1 Transcriptions of Japanese follow the conventions of the modified Hepburn system.
2 It is noteworthy in this context that until today no popular movement has existed aiming at the elimination of gender differences or the creation of gender-neutral language use in Japan. This is, however, not based in an absence of sexist language use in Japan, but rather in a popular lack of awareness about sexist language (Gottlieb 2005: 109–10).
3 Note in this context that the Japanese lexicon consists by two-thirds of loanwords, mostly of Chinese origin.
4 Note also that cross-cultural comparison between the social roles in this study (professionals, teachers, family members, etc.) is not possible, because these roles are emic, too.

Further reading

Heinrich, Patrick and Christian Galan (eds) (2011) *Language Life in Japan: Transformations and Prospects*. London: Routledge.
Inoue, Miyako (2006) *Vicarious Language: Gender and Linguistic Modernity in Japan*. Berkeley: University of California Press.
Kádár, Dániel Z. and Sara Mills (eds) (2011) *Politeness in East Asia*. Cambridge: Cambridge University Press.

References

Bourdieu, Pierre (1991) *Language and Symbolic Power*. Cambridge: Polity Press.
Brown, Penelope and Stephen Levinson (1987) *Politeness: Some Universals in Language Use*. Cambridge: Cambridge University Press.
Dickel Dunn, Cynthia (1999) Coming of Age in Japan: Language Ideology and the Acquisition of Formal Speech Registers. In: *Language and Ideology: Selected Papers from the 6th International Pragmatics Conference*. Jef Verschueren (ed.), 89–97. Antwerp: International Pragmatics Association.
Eelen, Gino (2001) *A Critique of Politeness Theory*. Manchester: St Jerome Publishing.
Endō, Orie (1997) *Onna no kotoba no bunkashi* [A Cultural History of Women's Language]. Tokyo: Gakuyō Shobō. Translated by Orie Endō (2006) *A Cultural History of Japanese Women's Language*. Ann Arbor: Center for Japanese Studies.
Eschbach-Szabó, Viktoria (2000) Die Frühzeit der neueren japanischen Sprachforschung. In: *History of the Language Sciences* (Volume 1). Sylvian Auroux, E. F. K. Koerner, Hans-Josef Niederehe and Kees Versteegh (eds), 92–102. Berlin: Walter de Gruyter.

Fishman, Joshua A. (1972) *The Sociology of Language*. Rowley: Newbury House Publishers. (Translated by Yasutoshi Yukawa (1974) *Gengo shakaigaku nyūmon*, Tokyo: Taishūkan.)
Fukuda, Atsushi and Noriko Asato (2004) Universal Politeness Theory: Application to the Use of Japanese Honorifics. *Journal of Pragmatics* 36: 1991–2001.
Gottlieb, Nanette (2005) *Language and Society in Japan*. Cambridge: Cambridge University Press.
Haugh, Michael and Yasuko Obana (2011) Politeness in Japan. In: *Politeness in East Asia*. Dániel Z. Kádár and Sara Mills (eds), 147–75. Cambridge: Cambridge University Press.
Heinrich, Patrick (2002a) *Die Rezeption der westlichen Linguistik im modernen Japan*. Munich: Iudicium.
——(2002b) Gengo seikatsu: The Study of Language Life in Japan, 1945–95. *Historiographia Linguistica* 29(1/2): 95–119.
——(2005) Things You Have to Leave Behind: The Demise of "Elegant Writing" and the Rise of Genbun Itchi Style in the Meiji Period. *Journal of Historical Pragmatics* 6(1): 113–32.
——(2013) Hōgen ronsō: The Great Ryukyuan Languages Debate of 1940. *Contemporary Japan* 25(2): 167–87.
Hill, Beverly, Sachiko Ide, Shoko Ikuta, Akiko Kawasaki and Tsunao Ogino (1986) Universals of Linguistic Politeness: Quantitative Evidence from Japanese and American English. *Journal of Pragmatics* 10: 347–71.
Holmes, Janet (1992) *An Introduction to Sociolinguistics*. New York: Pearson Education.
Hori, Motoko (1986) A Sociolinguistic Analysis of Japanese Honorifics. *Journal of Pragmatics* 10: 373–86.
Hymes, Dell (1974) *Foundations in Sociolinguistics*. Philadelphia: University of Pennsylvania Press. (Translated by Norimitsu Tōsu (1979) *Kotoba no minzokushi: Shakai gengogaku no kiso*. Tokyo: Kinokuniya.)
Ide, Sachiko (1982) Japanese Sociolinguistics: Politeness and Women's Language. *Lingua* 57: 357–85.
——(1988) Shakai gengogaku no riron to hōhō: Nihon to ōbei no apurōchi ni tsuite [Sociolinguistic theory and methods: On Japanese and Western approaches]. *Gengo kenkyū* [Journal of the Linguistic Society of Japan] 93: 97–103.
——(1989a) How and Why Do Women Speak More Politely in Japanese? *Nihon joshi daigaku eibei bungaku kenkyū* [Japan Women's University Studies in English Philology] 24: 1–19.
——(1989b) Formal Forms and Discernment: Two Neglected Forms of Linguistic Politeness. *Multilinga* 8: 223–48.
——(2004) Exploring Women's Language in Japanese. In: *Language and Woman's Place. Text and Commentaries*. Mary Bucholtz (ed.), 170–86. Oxford: Oxford University Press.
Ide, Sachiko and Naomi McGloin, (eds) (1990) *Aspects of Japanese Women's Language*. Tokyo: Kurosio.
Ide, Sachiko and Megumi Yoshida (1999) Sociolinguistics: Honorifics and Gender Differences. In: *The Handbook of Japanese Linguistics*. Natsuko Tsujimura (ed.), 444–80. Oxford: Blackwell.
Inoue, Fumio (1985) *Atarashii nihongo* [New Japanese]. Tokyo: Meiji Shoin.
Inoue, Miyako (2006) *Vicarious Language: Gender and Linguistic Modernity in Japan*. Berkeley: University of California Press.
Kádár, Dániel Z. and Sara Mills (2011) Introduction. In: *Politeness in East Asia*. Dániel Z. Kádár and Sara Mills (eds), 1–17. Cambridge: Cambridge University Press.
Kadoya, Hidenori and Yasushi Abe (eds) (2010) *Shikiji no shakai gengogaku* [The Sociolinguistics of Literacy]. Tokyo: Seikatsu Shoin.
Kikuzawa, Sueo (1929) Fujin no kotoba no tokuchō ni tsuite [On the Characteristics of Women's Speech]. *Kokugo kyōiku* [National Language Education] 3: 66–75.
——(1933) *Kokugo isō-ron* [National Language Strata]. Tokyo: Meiji Shoin.
Kindaichi, Haruhiko (1967 [1941]) Ga-gyō bion-ron [Study of Velar Nasals]. Reprinted in: *Nihongo on'in-ron no kenkyū* [Studies in Japanese Phonology]. Haruhiko Kindaichi, 168–97. Tokyo: Tokyodō.
Kindaichi, Kyōsuku (1933) *Gengo kenkyū* [The Study of Language]. Tokyo: Kawade shobō.

Kinsui, Satoshi (2003) *Vācharu nihongo: Yakuwarigo no nazo* [Virtual Japanese: The Mystery of Role Language]. Tokyo: Iwanami.
Kokuritsu Kokugo Kenkyūjo (1950) *Hajijōjima no gengo chōsa* [Language Survey on Hachijō Island]. Tokyo: Shūei Shuppan.
——(1951) *Gengo seikatsu no jittai* [The Actual State of Language Life]. Tokyo: Kokuritsu Kokugo Kenkyūjo.
——(1952) Kore kara no keigo [Honorific Speech Henceforth]. Tokyo: Kokuritsu Kokugo Kenkyūjo.
——(1957) *Keigo to keigo ishiki* [Honorific Speech and Honorific Speech Awareness]. Tokyo: Kokuritsu Kokugo Kenkyūjo.
Koyama, Shizuko (1991) *Ryōsai kenbo to iu kihan* [The Norms of "Good Wife, Wise Mother"]. Tokyo: Keisō shobō.
Lakoff, Robin (1975) *Language and Woman's Place*. New York: Harper & Row. [Translated by Katsue Akiba Reynolds (1985) *Gengo to sei: Eigo ni okeru onna no ichi*. Tokyo: Yūshindō Kōbunsha.)
Lewin, Bruno (1979) Demokratisierungsprozesse in der modernen Sprachentwicklung. In: *Japan nach 1945*. Klaus Kracht (ed.), 87–101. Wiesbaden: Harrassowitz.
Masiko, Hidenori (ed.) (2012) *Kotoba, kenryoku, sabetsu: Gengo-ken kara mita jōhō jakusha no kaihō* [Language, Authority, Discrimination: Empowerment from Linguistic Perspectives of People with Inadequate Access to Information]. Tokyo: Sangensha.
Masiko, Hidenori (2014) Nihon no shakai gengogaku saikō [A Review of Japanese Sociolinguistics]. *Shakai gengogaku* [Sociolinguistics] 14: 1–26.
Matsumoto, Yoshiko (1988) Reexamination of the Universality of Face: Politeness Phenomena in Japanese. *Journal of Pragmatics* 12: 403–26.
——(1989) Politeness and Conversational Universals. *Multilingua* 8: 207–21.
——(2004) The New (and Improved?) Language and Place of Women in Japan. In: *Language and Woman's Place: Text and Commentaries*. Mary Bucholtz (ed.), 244–51. Oxford: Oxford University Press.
Mio, Isago (1948) *Kokugo-hō bunshō-ron* [Discourse Studies of National Language]. Tokyo: Sanseidō.
Nakamura, Momoko (2011) Historical Discourse Approach to Language and Gender: Framework and Theoretical Implications. *Shizen, ningen, shakai* [Nature, Human Beings, Society] 52: 21–47.
Noro, Kayoko and Hitoshi Yamashita (eds) (2009) *"Tadashisa" e no toi: Hihanteki shakai gengogaku no kokoromi* [Towards a Questioning of "Correctness": An Initiative in Critical Sociolinguistics] (second edition). Tokyo: Sangensha.
Ohara, Yumiko (1999) Ideology of Language and Gender: A Critical Discourse Analysis of Japanese Prescriptive Texts. In: *Language and Ideology* (Volume 1). Jef Verschueren (ed.), 422–32. Antwerp: IPrA.
Okamoto, Shigeko (1995) "Tasteless" Japanese: Less "Feminine" Speech among Young Japanese Women. In: *Gender Articulated: Language and the Socially Constructed Self*. Kira Hall and Mary Bucholtz (eds), 297–325. New York: Routledge.
Okamoto, Shigeko and Janet S. Shibamoto Smith (eds) (2004) *Japanese Language, Gender, and Ideology: Cultural Models and Real People*. Oxford: Oxford University Press.
Reynolds, Katsue (1985) Female Speakers of Japanese. *Feminist Issues* 5(2): 13–46.
——(1990) Female Speakers of Japanese in Transition. In: *Aspects of Japanese Women's Language*. Sachiko Ide and Naomi Hanaoka McGloin (eds), 127–46. Tokyo: Kuroshio.
Schilling, Ulrike (1999) *Kommunikative Basisstrategien des Aufforderns*. Tübingen: Niemeyer.
Shibamoto, Janet S. (1985) *Japanese Women's Language*. Orlando: Academic Press.
Shibatani, Masayoshi (1990) *The Language of Japan*. Cambridge: Cambridge University Press.
Sibata, Takesi (1975) On some Problems in Japanese Sociolinguistics. In: *Language in Japanese Society*. Fred C. C. Peng (ed.), 159–73. Tokyo: University of Tokyo Press.
Tagengo-ka genshō kenkyūkai (2013) *Tagengo shakai nihon: Sono genjō to kadai* [Japan as a Multilingual Society. Present State and Tasks]. Tokyo: Sangensha.

Talbot, Mary (1998) *Language and Gender: An Introduction*. Cambridge: Polity Press.
Tanabe, Juri (1936) *Gengo shakaigaku* [Sociology of Language]. Tokyo: Jichōsha.
Tanaka, Harumi and Yukiko Tanaka (1996) *Shakai gengogaku e no shōtai* [An Invitation to Sociolinguistics]. Tokyo: Minerva.
Tanaka, Yukari (2011) *"Hōgen kosupure" no jidai – nise kansai-ben kara gunma-ben made* [The Age of "Dialect Cosplay": From Fake Kansai to Fake Gunma Dialect]. Tokyo: Iwanami.
Tokieda, Motoki (1941) *Kokugogaku genron* [Principles of National Language]. Tokyo: Iwanami.
——(1956) Gendai no Kokugogaku [National Linguistics Today]. Tokyo: Yūseidō.
Trudgill, Peter (1974) *Sociolinguistics: An Introduction to Language and Society*. Harmondsworth: Penguin. (Translated into Japanese by Shigeru Tsuchida (1975) *Gengo to shakai*. Tokyo: Iwanami.)
Tsukahara, Tetsuo (1954) Bamen to kotoba [Context and Speech]. In: *Kōza gendaigo* [A Course in Contemporary Language] (Volume 1). Kenji Morioka (ed.), 228–50. Tokyo: Meiji Shoin.
Twine, Nanette (1978) The genbunitchi Movement: Its Origin, Development, and Conclusion. *Monumenta Nipponica* 33(3): 333–56.
Usami, Mayumi (2002) *Discourse Politeness in Japanese Conversation*. Tokyo: Hituzi Syobo.
Watts, Richard J. (2003) *Politeness*. Cambridge: Cambridge University Press.
Wetzel, Patricia J. (2004) *Keigo in Modern Japan: Polite Language from Meiji to Present*. Honolulu: University of Hawai'i Press.
Yasuda, Toshiaki (1997) *Shokuminchi no naka no "kokugogaku"* ["National Linguistics" in the Colonies]. Tokyo: Sangensha.
Yomikaki Nōryoku Chōsa I'inkai (ed.) (1951) *Nihonjin no yomikaki nōryoku* [Reading and Writing Proficiency of the Japanese]. Tokyo: Tōkyō Daigaku Shuppan.

14

POSITIVE POLITENESS IN THE EUROPEAN MEDITERRANEAN

Sociolinguistic notions

Irene Cenni

14.1 Introduction

The goal of this chapter is to discuss some distinctive sociolinguistic characteristics of the European Mediterranean. The Mediterranean countries are those that are surrounded by the Mediterranean Sea; consequently the Mediterranean region represents the crossroads between the three continents of Europe, Asia and Africa. This chapter will restrict the discussion to a specific part of this larger area – the European Mediterranean – and will focus more specifically on Spain, Italy and Greece. These European countries are positioned at the heart of the Mediterranean area and, as will become clear in the course of this chapter, have much in common: culturally, politically, linguistically and sociolinguistically.

This area differs from the main Anglo-Western model in various respects. More precisely, I will focus on the issues of politeness and gender, since these stand out due to their deviancy. For a better understanding of the following discussion, a short outline of the sociolinguistic background of Spain, Italy and Greece is presented.

14.1.1 Spain

Spain is situated on the Iberian Peninsula, in southwest Europe. Its population is approximately 47 million. A key sociolinguistic characteristic of Spain is the presence of recognised autochthonous minority languages, namely Basque, Catalan and Galician (Mar-Molinero 1997).

Key historical facts relevant for the linguistic history and development of Spain are the conquest and subsequent seven-century-long occupation (711 until 1492) of large parts of the peninsula by the Arabic-speaking Moors (Mar-Molinero 1997), the founding of the Real Academia Española in 1713 and the dictatorship of Franco during the twentieth century (Mar-Molinero 1997).

Considering the official recognition of bilingual regions where the autochthonous minority languages are co-official to Castilian, language planning and policy have been the central focus of sociolinguistic research. This topic has attracted considerable academic debate, especially in the post-Franco period, in which the co-official status of these regions has been recognised. From the second half of the twentieth century Spanish sociolinguistics saw a growth in dialectal studies, focusing for instance on vernacular peculiarities of rural and urban Spain (collected in Alvar 1996) and studies within variationist linguistics (summarised in Blas-Arroyo 2005). In recent years new topics of interest have arisen, for example research into language education and the study of linguistic behaviour of "new" immigrants from, principally, Latin America, Eastern Europe and North Africa. Finally, great attention has been paid to the fields of discourse analysis and pragmatics.

14.1.2 Italy

Italy is a peninsula in the heart of the Mediterranean Sea. With 60.8 million inhabitants, it is among the most populous countries in Europe.

Sociolinguistic research focusing on Italian issues is wide-ranging. The first major concern is the description of the ensemble of the Italian varieties, which constitutes a rich and multifaceted continuum. An influential model for the study of different varieties and registers of the Italian language is found in the work of Berruto (1987, 2012). Italian dialectology has been an important topic since the beginning of the twentieth century and continues to remain vital. Investigating the relation between Italian and dialects, issues such as language shift, bilingualism/diglossia and code-switching have also been extensively studied (D'Agostino 2007). Representative investigations on these issues are Alfonzetti (1998), Berruto (2005), Cerruti (2011) and Dal Negro and Vietti (2011). Another important topic of research is represented by the language planning and policy towards the 12 autochthonous languages of Italy, for example German (in South Tyrol) (see Toso 2008; Iannàccaro and Dell'Aquila 2011).

A field in which sociolinguistic research in Italy is quickly expanding is the investigation of so-called computer mediated communication, which consists of the study of the language use, amongst others of Italian varieties, in "new" channels of communication such as e-mails, blogs and social networks (Gheno 2011). The linguistic behaviour of young people has also been studied by various scholars; key works on this topic being the studies of Cortelazzo (1994) and Marcato (2006).

14.1.3 Greece

Greece has 11 million inhabitants. Modern Greek is the sole official language of Greece and one of the two official languages of Cyprus.

The Greek linguistic repertoire has for centuries been influenced by diglossia, since the spoken language diverged perceptibly from older norms that were adhered to by writers (Mackridge 2012). In the twentieth century the Greek language significantly moved towards standardisation (Mackridge 2012). This was realised by means of two major political acts, namely those of 1911 and 1976–77. In 1911 *katharevousa* was defined in the new Constitution as the official language. This language variety can be described as a hybrid written language based on a blend of ancient and modern linguistic features. But after the fall of the military dictatorship in 1976–77, "the language question" (*glossikozitima*) became close to being resolved through the abandonment of what had hitherto been the official language, *katharevousa*, and the adoption of another variety, *demotiki*. The latter is a codified and written version based more closely on the model of the spoken language, which was specified as the language of education and state administration, and labelled as "Modern Greek" (Mackridge 2012).

Even though it is claimed that Greece is one of the most homogeneous countries in Europe in terms of language, national consciousness and religion, languages such as Turkish, Italian, Albanian, Slavonic dialects and Ladin are also spoken on the Greek territory by minority communities (Mackridge 2012).

Thus, standardisation and bilingualism (Greek/minority language) in Greece are among the most studied sociolinguistic matters (see Kakava 2009; Georgakopoulou and Silk 2009; Mackridge 2012). Additionally, the issue of politeness, which will be discussed in the following section, has also assumed an important role within Greek sociolinguistic research (Bayraktaroglu and Sifianou 2001).

14.2 Politeness in the European Mediterranean

The past three decades have seen a rapid development in the study of linguistic politeness in different languages and cultures, reflecting the centrality that the topic has been accorded in the field of pragmatics.[1] This is also true for the languages spoken in the Mediterranean.

Brown and Levinson's theory (1978, 1987) represents one of the best-known theoretical frameworks in the study of politeness and has contributed to the fast growth of the investigation of linguistic politeness in many languages and societies. Nonetheless, some problematic concepts of this theory are represented by its universal applicability and the notion of face, specifically the notion of face threatening acts (Bravo 2008a, 2008b). These aspects have been criticised as a contemporary Western European construct based mainly on Anglophone socio-cultural contexts (Spencer-Oatey 2000; Kerbrat-Orecchioni 2004; Bravo 2008b). Similarly, Watts (2003) and Bravo (2008a) recommend caution when using the term "universal" and they underline that utterances should be seen as social acts and politeness as part of discursive social practices of a specific language and culture.

For all these reasons I would like to cast some light on the difficulties of applying this theory unreservedly to the group of Mediterranean languages under examination. I will discuss refinements and alternative formulations of this theory, thereby providing new theoretical insights and evidence based on data and previous studies of how politeness may be studied more fruitfully in the Mediterranean socio-cultural linguistic context. By doing so I will demonstrate how a theory with universal claims, such as the politeness theory by Brown and Levinson, does not easily fit in a more Southern European linguistic context. This notwithstanding, a number of insights can be gained from its application.

The reader will notice that the degree of attention to this specific issue is far from uniform across the different countries taken into account in this discussion. For instance, while the need to refine the theory of politeness has been extensively studied in Spain and Greece, there are fewer studies available on the same subject in Italian.[2]

14.2.1 A preference for positive politeness

According to various authors investigating the languages of the Mediterranean area, a tendency towards so-called positive politeness practices has been observed (Haverkate 2004; Held 2005; Hernandez-Flores 2004; Sifianou and Antonopoulou 2005; Nuzzo 2009). This may be somewhat unexpected given that, as claimed by Brown and Levinson (1987: 129–30): "When we think of politeness in Western cultures, it is negative politeness behaviour that springs to mind." That seems not to be the case when analysing polite speech in three of the most widely spoken languages of the European Mediterranean: Italian, Greek and Spanish.

Starting our discussion with Italy, we can affirm that one of the most significant priorities characterising Italian discourse is embodied by the act of conveying "social tact" in any interpersonal communication (Held 2005). Consequently, positive politeness seems to be preferred by speakers of Italian. More specifically focusing on actual linguistic practices, Nuzzo (2009: 1), for instance, notices that when making requests in Italian, "native speakers use plenty of linguistic devices that make them appear cautious in assigning obligations to their addressees". A variety of mitigating devices are adopted by Italian native speakers and, among the morphosyntactic ones, the most frequently used are: the past "imperfect" *imperfetto*, the impersonal construction, negative cleft clauses and the use of the conditional mood (Bazzanella 2008). Caution in making requests in Italian is also marked by a significant use of lexical modifiers, as courtesy markers *per favore* ("please"), downtoners *forse; un po'* ("maybe; a bit") and/or preparatory mitigating sentences, also known as "external modifiers" (Vedder 2007), such as *se non tidispiace* ... ("if you don't mind"), *se puoi essere così gentile da* ... ("if you could be so kind as to ... ") (Bazzanella 2008: 183). Other specific speech acts such as giving compliments, self-humbling forms and modesty formulas are typical features of Italian discourse (Held 2005). In everyday conversations, in a friendly, or familiar situation, distinctive expression of praise and appreciation can be found quite easily in Italian. They are frequently found in opening sentences, such as: *Come sei x oggi!* ("How x you are today!"), with any positive adjective in the x slot. The same compliments practice is present in Spanish, in the construction *¡Qué x estás!* ("How x you are today!") (Hickey 2005: 320).

A similar preference towards positive politeness has been attested in Greece. Key values identified for Greek society are not only freedom and personal autonomy but also sociability and solidarity, which all affect Greek politeness conduct (Hischon 2001). Prime linguistic examples of Greek positive politeness orientation are constituted by the extensive use of compliments, diminutives and approbation practices (Sifianou and Antonopoulou 2005: 263–68). Approbation expressions such as *bravo* and *congratulations* are used so extensively that some authors even speak about "abuse" of these linguistic expressives (Makri-Tsilipakou 2001). Their everyday use seems to be connected to the affiliate role that they play within Greek discourse, and a tendency to maximise praise within the same discourse (Makri-Tsilipakou 2001). Besides, diminutives are generally employed to convey the concept of smallness; however, in Greek diminutives often indicate "affection, endearment and informality" (Sifianou and Antonopoulou 2005: 266). Furthermore, diminutives are used more frequently than Greek speakers may realise (Sifianou 1992). As a matter of fact, it is quite common to hear a Greek person using diminutives when, say, ordering some *lemonaki* ("lemon.dim"); *krasaki* ("wine.dim"); *patatoules* ("potatoes.dim"); *kafedaki* ("coffee.dim") in a restaurant (Sifianou and Antonopoulou 2005: 266). It appears that their linguistic function is that of expressing informal, positive politeness, especially when making requests (Sifianou and Antonopoulou 2005). Finally, compliments are produced quite frequently in Greek as well. They have been primarily defined as "acts of courtesy" and are "generally viewed as expressions of praise, consolidating or increasing solidarity" (Sifianou 2001: 396).

A preference towards a positive and cooperative attitude has also been noted in turn-taking analysis. In Spanish, for instance, it was found that "negative politeness practices [such] as leaving in peace the interlocutor finds little favour among the speakers" (Hickey 2005: 317). The situation in Italian and Greek is similar. As noticed by Zorzi Calò (1990) frequent procedures of interruptions can be found in Italian conversations, but it is argued that these practices are in fact understood as collaborative rather than conflictual, contradicting some classical positions in ethnomethodology and discourse analysis (see Sacks et al. 1974). Very similar linguistic behaviour has been observed in Spanish, as stated by Hickey (2005: 318): "Spaniards talk over each other […] without any intention of impeding the beginning, middle or end of a message, but rather most often simply to express an opinion forcefully, showing enthusiasm, passion and positive involvement in the conversation, factors rated more highly than silently awaiting one's turn." Such co-construction of conversation has also been identified as a sign of positive politeness in Greek. For instance, Tzanne (2001) analysed the activity of panel discussions and observed that presenters do not hesitate to intervene in the middle of a guest's talk, thus apparently performing a face-threatening act, but they do so in order to express their agreement with and the approval of the point being made by the guest (Tzanne 2001). Thus, in these cultures, this linguistic behaviour is not perceived as aggressive, impolite or competitive. Instead, it seems to be used to create an atmosphere of closeness and solidarity, transmitting the idea of collaboration between speakers (Tzanne 2001; Hickey 2005).

14.2.2 Politeness in the European Mediterranean: need for refinement

This orientation towards positive politeness reveals some additional linguistic implications. First of all, this "Mediterranean" conduct is scarcely comparable with other European patterns (Hickey 2005); therefore, a need to refine the existing Anglo-centric theories has emerged. This is particularly true when focusing on Spanish and Greek studies, where alternative theories and modifications of Brown and Levinson's model have been proposed by various authors. Focusing on Spanish, Bravo (2008a, 2008b) underlines how every communicative situation is a "social practice" and that making a socio-pragmatic analysis increases the amount of shared knowledge between analyst and language users (Bravo 2008a: 564). Consequently, the phenomenon of politeness has been identified as both a pragmatic and a socio-cultural one. As a direct consequence, politeness practices and categories cannot be considered the same for all cultures (Bravo 2008a). For instance, in Spanish communities a new category that describes a typical linguistic behaviour has been introduced: the search for *confianza* (Hernandez-Flores 2004). This term defines the kind of relationship that aims at achieving close ties connected to familiarity and to the right to speak openly with one another, showing the individual as having integrated in the group (Bravo 2008b).

The key concept of face threatening acts in Brown and Levinson, though useful, appears not to be the most appropriate classification when it comes to linguistic behaviour in languages like Italian, Spanish and Greek. Within the Anglo-centric view speech acts such as compliments and expressions of admiration have been categorised as acts that primarily threaten the addressees' negative face, in that speakers enter the personal sphere of the interlocutor (Sifianou and Antonopoulou 2005). However, we have seen that in Southern European languages "viewing such acts as primarily face-threatening obscures their equally primary positive politeness function of enhancing one's interlocutor's face" (Sifianou and Antonopoulou 2005: 265). For these reasons an alternative categorisation of these acts has been proposed by various authors: the category of face-enhancing (e.g. Hernandez-Flores 2004) and face-flattering (e.g. Kerbrat-Orecchioni 2004) acts. These acts express concern and a friendly attitude towards the addressee; they focus on a positive relationship between the interlocutors (Hernandez-Flores 2004: 268), and are used by speakers when utilising flattering behaviour (Kerbrat-Orecchioni 2004). This practice obviously has the goal of showing politeness, but it also indexes familiarity and inclusion of the interlocutor in a specific in-group, bringing the speakers closer to each other and making their relationship stronger. This polite behaviour has been observed in empirical work in different cultural communities: as a way of engagement with social interaction in colloquial Spanish (Hernandez-Flores 2004), as boosting face in Greek simultaneous speech (Tzanne 2001) and as offering concern, understanding and collaboration in Greek compliments (Sifianou 2001).

Additional proof of this specific behaviour can be found when contrasting this conduct with the one present in Northern Europe. Enhancing and flattering the face of the interlocutor is common practice in familiar and informal conversation in Southern Europe, while it can be perceived as inappropriate and even disturbing in other socio-cultural contexts. For instance, in a Scandinavian communicative context, such as Swedish, face-flattering acts are not perceived as polite and are not adopted or appreciated in conversations. As a matter of fact "Swedish speakers orient their communicative behaviours towards a socio-cultural content of autonomy face based on the notion of self-sufficiency and of independence of the group" (Bravo 2008b: 566). Thus it appears that in Swedish, face-enhancing acts are not perceived as needed in producing polite acts; they do not even seem to be valued as pleasant and friendly, while this is the case within a Mediterranean socio-cultural context.

14.3 The interplay of language and gender

In European Mediterranean countries such as Spain and Italy, the discussion of the issue of language and gender came later than in other Western European countries. As a concrete example, the first study on language and gender in the Italian language is represented by *Il sessismo nella lingua italiana* ("Sexism in the Italian Language") by Alma Sabatini in 1987. It appeared almost 20 years later than similar initiatives for English and French (Cirillo 2002: 141). Moreover it differed from similar works produced in other countries in one significant way: it was stimulated from above rather than emerging as a critique from below. Since then, the debate on the issue of language and gender has continued. In fact, in Spain, the media has recently paid a large amount of attention to this topic. More specifically, *El Pais*, one of the most important national newspapers, published a special issue dedicated to this topic under the title of: *Sexismo lingüístico y visibilidad de la mujer* ("Linguistic Sexism and the Visibility of Women"). Despite having had a belated start in comparison to English-speaking countries, the study of the connection between language and gender has started to receive some attention in Mediterranean countries over the past decades. Nonetheless, this issue proves to still be controversial in literature and is in need of further investigation.

Sociolinguistics research on language and gender in these Mediterranean countries has pointed out some specific linguistic practices, such as the asymmetrical lexical and semantic references (this has especially been attested in dictionaries) and linguistic asymmetry in professional titles.

Concerning the linguistic practices in Italian and Spanish mentioned above, consider how distinct values are assigned in some cases to the feminine form of a lexeme. In Spanish, for example, in the case of words designating the two members of a married couple: in common use *mujer* (f.) ("woman") also signifies "wife", while *hombre* ("man") does not signify husband, a specific term, *marido*, being used for this. Other languages, for instance Dutch, show more symmetry: *vrouw* and *man* both have the double meaning of "woman" and "wife" and "man" and "husband". In addition, linguistic gender asymmetry in Italian and Spanish can be noted when pejorative value is added to feminine versions of words: while *un hombre público* refers to "a man concerned with public affairs", its feminine counterpart *una mujer pública* traditionally signifies "prostitute". The same happens in Italian; for instance, the noun *pescivendolo* (m.) ("fish seller") in its feminine counterpart, *pescivendola* (f.), signifies not only female "fish seller" but also "chatterbox".

Moreover, previous studies showed that in Italian and Spanish, linguistic gender bias is present in the institutional references of language codification, such as dictionaries. Cirillo (2002: 143), for instance, states that, in Italian, sexist principles rule all aspects of dictionary making. This is evident in the selection of entries, number of synonyms, in the ordering of definitions and in the selection of examples. Similar tendencies have been noted in Spanish, for instance by Guil (2006) investigating the dictionary function Thesaurus of Word.

An additional paradigmatic point of discussion on the issue of language and gender in these countries concerns the professional titles of women. Although the Italian and Spanish language systems theoretically allow for the grammatical gender-based splitting of most nouns concerned, this is not always the case in practice. Many work-related nouns have traditionally been used only in the masculine, and the new feminine forms, although properly derived, seem lacking in euphony and have not been entirely endorsed by the speakers (Robustelli 2011). Traditionally, the feminine version of the noun denoting an occupation was referring more often to "wife of ... " rather than directly referring to the woman who held the corresponding position. In Spanish *la médica* (the female "doctor") referred more often to the "doctor's wife" rather than to a female doctor (something that was considered exceptional in Spain until fairly recently) (Guil 2006). Nowadays, entries such as *avvocatessa*, *ministra* and *magistrata*, feminine nouns denoting "female lawyer", "female minister" or "female magistrate", exist prescriptively in the Italian language; however, when using professional nouns to address women in newspapers and other media, oscillation between female and masculine versions of the same professional title is the norm. More specifically, the masculine version of profession nouns remains dominant, especially those denoting positions of power.[3] Additionally, in some cases of work-related nouns, the feminine and masculine form of the same lexeme have acquired different values, the feminine corresponding to a less prestigious profession than the masculine, a paradigmatic case being: *secretaria* (f.)/*secretario* (m.) ("secretary") in Spanish and *segretaria* (f.)/*segretario* (m.) ("secretary") in Italian, the feminine version denoting a subordinate administrative employee, while the masculine one refers to a position of a certain importance within a company or organisation (Guil 2006). Indeed, in Italian, the masculine noun *segretario* is mainly used in connection to positions of power, such as *segretario di stato* ("secretary of state"), *segretario generale* ("secretary-general"), *segretario esecutivo* ("executive secretary"). Consequently, we are still far from an interchangeable use of professional titles in these societies.

Of course we have to keep in mind that language is the symptom of gender inequality, and in most cases not the cause. Hence, making language more symmetrical will not directly result in removing these inequalities. As underlined by Lepschy (1989), it is imperative to first abolish the biased distinction between women and men in all its implications, namely in the social, economic, political and juridical spheres, and then let language follow these changes. Since language represents the dominant public opinion, language will reflect a more equal society only when it will come into existence (Lepschy 1989).

The ambivalence in Italian and Spanish concerning professional titles and unbalanced references to women in everyday spoken language and in dictionaries seems to be in line with what has been noted by many commentators, most prominently Lakoff (2005: 161), who underlines how "the combination of women and power still has the capacity to confuse us all". Indeed, as we could see in the examples discussed above, the relation between women and power and their representation in society remains a very complex one. The motivation behind these practices, their frequency and the speakers' attitudes towards them in Spain and Italy represent aspects that need to be investigated in-depth in order to comprehensively identify and confirm possible differences from Anglo-centric sociolinguistics with respect to the issue of language and gender.[4] Indeed, although in the Anglo-Western model such sexism is incorporated as well, as it exists in English and European languages, it seems to be more pertinent and deeply engrained in the Mediterranean, and it is existent in a less gender-equal society. In particular, the study of these linguistic practices in connection with their specific socio-cultural context will be necessary (Eckert and McConnell-Ginet 2003) and could lead to remarkable results. More specifically, it would be interesting to understand the answer to certain questions: what are the power dynamics that influence these linguistic practices in these previously mentioned Mediterranean countries? How do these socio-cultural power struggles differ from the ones described in mainstream sociolinguistics studies? Which specific language ideology is connected to these language uses? How and why do speakers continue or change linguistic practices connected to the issue of gender? Is this process exactly the same when compared with tendencies examined in mainstream sociolinguistics? In other words, a more in-depth investigation of these specific linguistic practices intertwined with their specific socio-cultural contexts is needed. This could help us to detect and define distinctive linguistic patterns concerning the issue of language and gender in the European Mediterranean countries with more certainty.

14.4 Conclusions

This chapter's discussion of politeness in the European Mediterranean has presented a tendency towards positive politeness. At the phrasal level, this is attested by the frequent production of compliments and collaborative speech acts. Since this specific practice is scarcely reproduced in other parts of Europe, a re-examination of the Anglo-centric categories and most frequently used strategies is needed. These frequently used speech acts, such as compliments or encouraging sentences, have been re-defined by various authors as face-enhancing and face-flattering acts, which represent a pertinent label in the specific socio-cultural setting of the languages under discussion. These new categories are not mentioned in classical sociolinguistic textbooks, such as Meyerhoff (2011) and Mesthrie et al. (2009). Thus, the concepts of face-enhancing and face-flattering acts have to be understood as central concepts interacting with the politeness productions of Mediterranean speakers, since they seem to be more present in these cultures and, as such, they need to be actively involved in the study of politeness.

I have highlighted how the interplay of language and gender could represent an excellent field of study within the sociolinguistics of European Mediterranean countries. I believe that, in recent years, the awareness concerning matters connected to gender and language in countries such as Italy and Spain has grown and the socio-political and linguistic sensitivity regarding this issue has certainly increased (Cirillo 2002; Guil 2006). Nevertheless, further investigation in this field is surely needed. The specific socio-cultural context needs to be taken into account and a more detailed investigation of the whole issue could lead to interesting results, possibly confirming the mentioned set of potential divergent practices as distinctive when compared with mainstream sociolinguistics.

Acknowledgement

I would like to thank Claudia Crocco (Ghent University), Patrick Goethals (Ghent University) and Carmen Parafita Couto (Leiden University) for their valuable suggestions and remarks.

Notes

1 Even though we must keep in mind that mainstream attention of politeness study has moved to discourse analysis, to a combined approach of politeness and impoliteness and to individual perceptions of politeness (Watts 2003).
2 Presumably this is the case since in Italy, apart from a general and introductory work on politeness (Mariottini 2007), research in this field focused more on the issue of intercultural communication, thus discussing the relation of Italian with other languages; see Balboni (2007) *La comunicazione interculturale* or Pavan (2010) *Communicating in the Mediterranean Area: A Matter of Intercultural Awareness*. Furthermore, attention has been paid to the acquisition of pragmatic competence in Italian L2 (e.g. Vedder 2007) and to the issue of politeness in connection with translation issues (Bruti 2013).
3 For instance, referring to the female minister Rosi Bindi entries as *ministra Bindi* "minister Bindi" (f.) can be found in the corpus of *Repubblica*, one of the most popular newspapers in Italy. But, only eight entries have been found for the feminine version *ministra Bindi* versus 298 entries for *ministro Bindi* (m.).
4 Of course, in mainstream sociolinguistics, the discourse on language and gender has already moved beyond the present discussion, and new approaches have emerged. A new influential model, for instance, is represented by the work of Cameron and Kulick (2006), who focus on the complex relation of gender, sexuality and language. Indeed, they state that "there is growing interest among researchers, teachers and students in exploring the connections between language and sexuality" (Cameron and Kulick 2006: 1).

Further reading

Spain

Blas-Arroyo, José Luis (2005) *Sociolingüística del Español* [Sociolinguistics of Spanish]. Madrid: Càtedra.
Díaz-Campos, Manuel (2011) *The Handbook of Hispanic Sociolinguistics*. Oxford: Blackwell Publishing.
Mar-Molinero, Clare (1997) *The Spanish-speaking World: A Practical Introduction to Sociolinguistic Issues*. London: Routledge.

Italy

Berruto, Gaetano (1987, second edition 2012) *Sociolinguistica dell' italiano contemporaneo* [Sociolinguistics of Contemporary Italian]. Roma: Carocci editore.
D'Agostino, Mari (2007) *Sociolinguistica dell' Italia contemporanea* [Sociolinguistics of contemporary Italy]. Bologna: Il Mulino.

Greece

Georgakopoulou, Alexandra and Michael Silk (2009) *Standard Languages and Language Standards: Greek, Past and Present*. Burlington: Ashgate.
Kakava, Christina (2009) Sociolinguistics and Modern Greek: Past, Current, and Future Directions. *International Journal of the Sociology of Language* 126: 5–32.
Mackridge, Peter (2012) Multilingualism and Standardization in Greece. In: Matthias Hüning, Ulrike Vogl and Olivier Moliner (eds), 153–78. *Standard Languages and Multilingualism in European History*. Amsterdam: John Benjamins.

References

Alfonzetti, Giovanna (1998) The Conversational Dimension in Code-Switching between Italian and Dialect in Sicily. In: *Code-switching in Conversation: Language, Interaction, and Identity*. Peter Auer (eds), 180–214. London: Routledge.
Alvar, Manuel (ed.) (1996) *Manual de Dialectología Hispánica: El español de España* [Manual of Spanish Dialectology. The Spanish of Spain]. Barcelona: Ariel.
Balboni, Paolo E. (2007) *La comunicazione interculturale* [Intercultural Communication]. Venezia: Marsilio.
Bayraktaroglu, Arin and Maria Sifianou (eds) (2001) *Linguistic Politeness Across Boundaries: The Case of Greek and Turkish*. Amsterdam: John Benjamins.
Bazzanella, Carla (2008) *Linguistica e pragmatica del linguaggio: Un'introduzione* [Linguistics and Pragmatics of Language. An Introduction]. Roma–Bari: Laterza.
Berruto, Gaetano (2005) Dialect/Standard Convergence, Mixing and Models of Language Contact: The Case of Italy. In: *Dialect Change: Convergence and Divergence in European Languages*. Peter Auer, Peter Kerswill and Frans Hinskens (eds), 81–95. Cambridge: Cambridge University Press.
Bravo, Diana (2008a) (Im)politeness in Spanish-speaking Socio-cultural Contexts: Introduction. *Pragmatics* 18(4): 563–76.
——(2008b) The Implications of Studying Politeness in Spanish-speaking Contexts: A Discussion. *Pragmatics* 18(4): 577–603.
Brown, Penelope and Stephen Levinson (1978) Universals in Language Usage: Politeness Phenomena. In: *Questions and Politeness: Strategies in Social Interaction*. Esther N. Goody (ed.), 56–310. Cambridge: Cambridge University Press.
——(1987) *Politeness: Some Universals in Language Usage*. Cambridge: Cambridge University Press.
Bruti, Silvia (2013) *La cortesia. Aspetti culturali e problemi traduttivi* [Politeness. Cultural aspects and translation's problems]. Pisa: Pisa University Press.
Cameron, Deborah and Don Kulick (2006) *The Language and Sexuality Reader*. London/New York: Routledge.
Cerruti, Massimo (2011) Regional Varieties of Italian in the Linguistic Repertoire. *International Journal of the Sociology of Language* 210: 9–28.
Cirillo, Chiara (2002) Sexism and Gender Issues in the Italian Language. In: *Multilingualism in Italy: Past and Present*. Anna Laura Lepschy and Arturo Tosi (eds), 141–49. Oxford: Legenda.

Cortelazzo, Mauro (1994) Il parlato giovanile [Spoken Language of Young People]. In: *Storia della lingua italiana* [History of the Italian Language] (Volume 2). Trifone Pietro and Luca Serianni (eds), 291–317. Torino: Einaudi.
Dal Negro, Silvia and Alessandro Vietti (2011) Italian and Italo-Romance Dialects. *International Journal of Sociology of Language* 210: 71–92.
Eckert, Penelope and Sally McConnell-Ginet (2003) *Language and Gender*. Cambridge: Cambridge University Press.
Gheno, Vera (2011) I linguaggi della Rete [Languages of the Web]. In: *I linguaggi giovanili* [Youth Language]. Stefania Stefanelli and Valeria Saura (eds), 159–220. Firenze: Accademia della Crusca.
Guil, Pura (2006) Word's Spanish Thesaurus: Some Limits of Automaticity. In: *Gender, Language and New Literacy: A Multilingual Analysis*. Eva-Maria Thüne, Simona Leonardi and Carla Bazzanella (eds), 153–68. London: Continuum.
Haverkate, Henk (2004) El análisis de la cortesía comunicativa: categorización pragmalingüística de la cultura Española [Communicative Politeness Analysis: Pragma-linguistic Categorisation of the Spanish Culture]. In: Diana Bravo and Antonio Briz (eds), 55–66. *Pragmática sociocultural: estudios sobre el discurso de cortesía en español*, Barcelona: Ariel.
Held, Gudrun (2005) Politeness in Italy: The Art of Self-representation in Requests. In: *Politeness in Europe*. Leo Hickey and Miranda Stewart (eds), 292–305. Clevedon: Multilingual Matters.
Hernandez-Flores, Nieves (2004) Politeness as Face Enhancement: An Analysis of Spanish Conversations between Friends and Family. In: *Current Trends in the Pragmatics of Spanish*. Rosina Marquez Reiter and Maria Elena Placencia (eds), 265–84. Amsterdam: John Benjamins.
Hickey, Leo (2005) Politeness in Spain: Thanks but No Thanks. In: *Politeness in Europe*. Leo Hickey and Miranda Stewart (eds), 317–30. Clevedon: Multilingual Matters.
Hischon, Renée (2001) Freedom, Solidarity and Obligations: The Socio-cultural Context of Greek Politeness. In: *Linguistic Politeness Across Boundaries: The Case of Greek and Turkish*. Arin Bayraktaroglu and Maria Sifianou (eds), 17–42. Amsterdam: John Benjamins.
Iannàccaro, Gabriele and Vittorio Dell'Aquila (2011) Historical Linguistic Minorities: Suggestions for Classifications and Typology. *International Journal of Sociology of Language* 210: 29–45.
Kerbrat-Orecchioni, Catherine (2004) ¿Es universal la cortesía? [Is Politeness Universal?]. In: Diana Bravo and Antonio Briz (eds), 39–54. *Pragmática sociocultural: Estudios sobre el discurso de cortesía en Español* [Socio-cultural Pragmatics. Studies on Discourses on Politeness in Spain]. Barcelona: Ariel.
Lakoff, Robin (2005) Language, Gender, and Politics: Putting "Women" and "Power" in the Same Sentence. In: *The Handbook of Language and Gender*. Janet Holmes and Miriam Meyerhof (eds), 161–78. Oxford: Blackwell Publishing.
Lepschy, Giulio (1989) Lingua e sessimo [Language and Sexisim]. In: *Nuovi saggi di linguistica italiana* [New Essays on Italian Language]. Giulio Lepschy (ed.), 61–84. Bologna: Il Mulino.
Makri-Tsilipakou, Marianthi (2001) Congratulations and bravo! In: *Linguistic Politeness Across Boundaries: The Case of Greek and Turkish*. Arin Bayraktaroglu and Maria Sifianou (eds), 137–76. Amsterdam: John Benjamins.
Marcato, Gianna (2006) *Giovani, lingua e dialetto* [Youngster, Language and Dialect]. Atti del convegno di Sappada/Plodn, Belluno giugno 2005 [Proceedings of the Symposium of Sappada/Plodn, Belluno, June 2005]. Padova: Unipress.
Mariottini, Laura (2007) *La cortesia* [Politeness]. Roma: Carocci.
Mesthrie, Rajend, Joan Swann, Andrea Deumert and William L. Leap (2009) *Introducing Sociolinguistics* (second edition). Edinburgh: Edinburgh University Press.
Meyerhoff, Miriam (2011) *Introducing Sociolinguistics* (second edition). New York: Routledge.
Nuzzo, Elena (2009) Richiedere in italiano L1 e L2. Strategie di attenuazione della forza illocutoria [Requests in Italian L1 and L2. Strategies in Weakening the Illocutionary Force]. In: *Atti del Congresso internazionale "La comunicazione parlata"* [Proceedings of the

International Symposium "Spoken Communication"]. Napoli: Università degli studi di Napoli L'Orientale.

Pavan, Elisabetta (2010) Communicating in the Mediterranean Area. A Matter of Intercultural Awareness. *International Journal of Euro-Mediterranean Studies* 2(1): 121–39.

Robustelli, Cecilia (2011) Lingua, genere e politica linguistica nell'Italia dopo l'Unità [Language, Gender and Language Policy in Italy after Unification]. In: *Storia della lingua e storia dell'Italia unita* [History of the Language and the Unification of Italy]. Annalisa Nesi, Nicoletta Maraschio and Silvia Morgana (eds), 587–605. Firenze: Franco Cesati.

Sabatini, Alma (1987). *Il sessismo nella lingua italiana* [Sexisim in the Italian Language]. Commissione nazionale per la parità e le pari opportunità tra uomo e donna: Presidenza del Consiglio dei Ministri. Online availabe at: www.funzionepubblica.gov.it (accessed 18 August 2014).

Sacks, Harvey, Emanuel A. Schegloff and Gail Jefferson (1974) A Simplest Systematics for the Organization of Turn-taking for Conversation. *Language* 50(4–1): 696–735.

Sifianou, Maria (1992) *Politeness Phenomena in England and in Greece*. Oxford: Clarendon.

——(2001) "Oh! How Appropriate!": Compliments and Politeness. In: *Linguistic Politeness Across Boundaries: The Case of Greek and Turkish*. Arin Bayraktaroglu and Maria Sifianou (eds), 391–430. Amsterdam: John Benjamins.

Sifianou, Maria and Eleni Antonopoulou (2005) Politeness in Greece: The Politeness of Involvement. In: *Politeness in Europe*. Leo Hickey and Miranda Stewart (eds), 263–76. Clevedon: Multilingual Matters.

Spencer-Oatey, Helen (ed.) (2000) *Culturally Speaking*. London: Continuum.

Toso, Fiorenzo (2008) *Le minoranze linguistiche in Italia* [Linguistic Minorities in Italy]. Bologna: Il Mulino.

Tzanne, Angeliki (2001) "What You're Saying Sounds Very Nice and I'm Delighted to Hear It" – Some Considerations on the Functions of Presenter-initiated Simultaneous Speech in Greek Panel Discussions. In: *Linguistic Politeness Across Boundaries: The Case of Greek and Turkish*. Arin Bayraktaroglu and Maria Sifianou (eds), 271–306. Amsterdam: John Benjamins.

Vedder, Ineke (2007) Competenze pragmatica e complessità sintattica in italiano L2 [Pragmatic Competence and Syntactic Complexity in Italian L2]. *Linguistica e Filologia* [Linguistics and Philology] 25: 99–123.

Watts, Richard J. (2003) *Politeness*. Cambridge: Cambridge University Press.

Zorzi Calò, Daniela (1990) *Parlare insieme* [Talking Together]. Bologna: Cooperativa Libraria Universitaria Editrice.

PART IV
Unstable multilingual communities

Introduction to Part IV

The final part of this volume describes five sets of multilingual and/or diglossic communities. The selected communities are geographically and culturally disparate, yet they share many sociolinguistic patterns.

To various degrees, the indigenous language in these communities is suffering from the pressure of an H-language and is subject to shift. Idiosyncratic forces are at play in the speech community that harbours an indigenous language. Such communities share several features that distinguish them from larger regions. These communities typically have speakers with a high level of language awareness and a raised consciousness of the meaning of language choices, especially when it comes to preserving language and its cultural-historical legacies. The strong social effect of choosing the indigenous language is part of this shared consciousness, as is the less predictable social stratification of language variation. The geographic spread of the speakers is typically diverse and shows the importance of this aspect, revealing how speakers not living in the same place can nevertheless form a true community on the basis of a set of shared features. This is true in particular for speakers of Gaelic. Written and spoken language development is different in these areas, as a linguistically dominant area for the indigenous language is not usually present, and instead maintenance of the language rather than social factors are important sources of standardisation, codification and revitalisation. Also, speakers have various levels of proficiency, and this variation in proficiency is an important factor in social interaction. Such information is often treated as background information but can be considered central in the cases presented here. Authors were asked to move some of the "background" to the "fore" in this sense.

All five communities are increasingly in contact with, and influenced by, a linguistically and culturally dominant community, and members of this community are usually bilingual. Attention needs to be placed on language repertoires rather than on languages. Doing so allows us to analyse changing language repertoires rather than changes in language attitudes or changes in languages. This is desirable because after many decades of sociolinguistic study in these communities a great number of changes have become evident. L-codes are used in H-domains as an effect of social emancipation efforts, for instance. Ideas of High and Low may be questioned altogether as they include an assessment of power and prestige that may no longer be valid. Why should school be High and family Low in the first place?

Language vitality, once a mighty tool in sociolinguistics, may have suffered as a beacon over the years, as an ever-increasing number of factors impacting on vitality can be identified. Hence, the field saw a shift from sociolinguistic to ethnographic approaches. But that may not necessarily be the only possible direction to channel research to. Updating and adapting the sociological toolbox in sociolinguistics might be a viable strategy, too. Replacing social class by social networks or social milieus comes to mind. Other questions generated by this section include whether sociolinguistic concepts like diglossia should be expanded or diversified. Such directions are always necessary, because existing frameworks draw heavily on specific cases and experiences and have neglected others. Paying due attention to folk ideologies of community, education and communication, as is done in these chapters, is yet another important step in developing sociolinguistic theory. An Anglo-Western perspective presumes a typically Christian emphasis on people's relationships with each other and God, and less so with nature or the supernatural forces that are believed to spring from it. Ideologies derived from a special relationship with the natural world around us and the shapes given to the inexplicable are thus easily misunderstood, underestimated and dismissed, whilst being the main determiners behind ideology and, consequently, the connotations of language variation in some more isolated communities. Larger communities, on the other hand, like the Gaelic community, have culturally merged with the dominant surrounding culture and are dealing with the lack of visibility of their own culture.

Much can be learned from these communities, as they provide a more detailed insight into the idiosyncrasies of sociolinguistic systems at a smaller societal level, in which linguistic dominance of other languages and cultures strongly affects the daily language situation. These chapters on communities in particular unveil sociolinguistics as the study of speakers' choices in contact situations.

15

NIVKH WRITING PRACTICES

Literacy and vitality in an endangered language

Hidetoshi Shiraishi and Bert Botma

15.1 Introduction

Nivkh is a linguistic isolate spoken in the lower reaches of the Amur River and on the northern part of the island of Sakhalin, in the Russian Far East. In Western literature, Nivkh is often referred to as "Gilyak". In Russia, this term is regarded as derogatory, being associated with the image of the Nivkh as uncivilized (illiterate, eating raw fish, etc.). The Nivkh themselves prefer the self-referent form Nivkh [ɲivx] ("human being"). In the latest census, held in 2010, 4,652 persons identified themselves as Nivkh. Of these, 2,149 live in the Khabarovsk region and 2,290 on Sakhalin (Federal'naia Sluzhba Gosudarstvennoi Statistiki 2013).

In our contribution to this volume, we examine Nivkh against the backdrop of the sociolinguistic variable of language vitality, with special focus on literacy. Literacy and associated aspects such as publication and education are closely related to political, economic and cultural power (see, e.g., Fishman 2003; Coulmas and Guerini 2012), and are therefore considered important indicators of language vitality (Grenoble and Whaley 1998). Nevertheless, a language with a high literacy rate may be faced with a declining number of speakers. As we will see, Nivkh is one such language.

In common with other indigenous languages of Russia, the introduction of literacy in the vernacular language began in the 1930s, when Nivkh still had many speakers. We believe that this early initiative, while in itself unsuccessful, lay the foundation for the recent upsurge in Nivkh writing practices. Interestingly, these writing practices were undertaken when there were only few Nivkh speakers remaining, and Nivkh had ceased to be the language of daily communication. Models of language vitality, for example that of Giles et al. (1977), would depict the current situation as scoring high on literacy variables (such as "institutional support"), but low on other variables (such as "demography" and "status"). Given that the variables subsumed under language vitality are normally correlated (e.g. Meyerhoff 2011: 115), Nivkh presents an interesting case, which suggests that "writing" is a more complex variable than is often assumed in sociolinguistic work.

15.2 The Nivkh language and people

Traditionally, the Nivkh lived as fishermen, hunters and gatherers. They traded and bartered with the Ainu, with Tungusic tribes and with China (the Qing Dynasty), fur and silk being the main objects of exchange. This trade system developed under the political control of China and declined when Chinese influence in the region waned. In the second half of the nineteenth century, the newly formed border between Russia and Japan hindered the transport and exchange of goods, effectively putting a stop to the trade system. The high number of Tungusic borrowings in the Nivkh lexicon suggests a close contact between the Nivkh and Tungusic tribes, both on the continent and on Sakhalin (Takahashi 1934; Kreinovich 1955). The linguistic influence of Ainu, which used to be spoken on southern Sakhalin, has been far less extensive.

The traditional Nivkh religion is animistic. In it, the world is viewed as consisting of spiritual beings that assume the shape of humans, animals, natural phenomena and geographical objects (e.g. rocks, mountains, the sea). Religious practices changed little after Christianity was introduced by the Russians in the nineteenth century. A bigger threat to the maintenance of traditional Nivkh religion came from the repression of the shamans in the 1930s and, following this, by the introduction of compulsory education at boarding schools (Vysokov 1999).

Nivkh has two dialect groups. The Amur dialects are spoken in villages located along the lower reaches of the Amur river and on the west coast of northern Sakhalin. Both dialect groups consist of several sub-dialects.

The national censuses carried out in the last decades show that the number of Nivkh speakers is declining. In 1959, 71.1 per cent of the Nivkh population reported that Nivkh was their mother tongue.[1] This had dropped to just 23.3 per cent in 1989 (Gruzdeva 2011). In the most recent census, held in 2010, 395 people reported Nivkh as their mother tongue and 4,232 people Russian. In the same census, 183 people claimed to have some command of Nivkh, 56 in the Khabarovsk region and 118 on Sakhalin (Federal'naia Sluzhba Gosudarstvennoi Statistiki 2013). This amounts to a language maintenance rate of 2.6 per cent in Khabarovsk and 5.2 per cent in Sakhalin. However, a problem with these statistics is that the censuses are based on a questionnaire that does not test speaker proficiency. As a result, people with sometimes widely differing proficiency levels may state that they have "some command of the language" – which clearly is not very insightful. Our own fieldwork experience suggests that the number of speakers sufficiently proficient to serve as language consultants is no higher than 50. None of them are monolingual, as a language shift to Russian is complete. The most proficient speakers were born before 1930. There are perhaps fewer than five of these speakers left; they speak imperfect Russian, with a strong Nivkh accent.

In the Amur region, Nivkh ceased to be the language of daily communication in the 1950s. The language held out for a little longer on Sakhalin (Eremin et al.

1988). At present, transmission of the language to younger generations has been disrupted for at least half a century. In 2000, UNESCO evaluated the language as "nearly extinct" (Janhunen and Salminen 2000). Fieldwork-based descriptions of the sociolinguistic situation which throw some light on the process of language shift include Novikova and Savel'eva (1953), Vysokov (1985, 1999), Eremin et al. (1988), Gruzdeva and Leonova (1990), De Graaf (1992) and De Graaf and Shiraishi (2013). Descriptions of specific aspects of language loss are discussed in Gruzdeva (2002, 2004), Shiraishi (2006) and Botma and Shiraishi (2014).

Most of the research on Nivkh that is sociolinguistically relevant is based on demographic data supplied by the national census, held every ten years. However, as we have seen, this data is coarse-grained and difficult to evaluate, so that even today an accurate estimate of the number of fluent speakers is hard to give. Gruzdeva and Leonova (1990) conducted a survey aimed at obtaining more detailed sociolinguistic data, in the village of Nogliki on eastern Sakhalin. Of the total of 315 responses, 75 people (23.8 per cent) claimed to know and use Nivkh. This number has decreased drastically since the time of this survey. Given the current sociolinguistic situation, a survey of a similar scale as that of Gruzdeva and Leonova would be unrealistic.

15.3 Literacy as an indicator of language vitality

Of the variables that pertain to language vitality, the status of literacy is somewhat unclear. Some models of language vitality do not in fact mention literacy explicitly. For example, the model of Giles et al. (1977), cited in Meyerhoff (2011), recognizes its role only indirectly through variables like "education" and "mass media", which fall under the rubric of "institutional support" (see Giles et al. 1977: 309). (A general problem of this model is that it is not clear how it can be applied to languages that lack a tradition of popular writing.) The model of Edwards (1992) contains more variables, and so captures finer-grained details of language vitality, but it, too, makes no direct mention of literacy. The relevance of literacy is recognized by Grenoble and Whaley (1998: 31), who acknowledge that it plays "a significant role in speech communities and in the relative vitality of threatened languages". This leads them to propose that literacy (and related variables such as "standardization", "educational program" and "publications") should form an integral part of models of language vitality.

Grenoble and Whaley's argument is justified to the extent that literacy practices are correlated with other variables of language vitality, such as the number of remaining speakers. These two variables do indeed correlate often: vital languages with a sufficient number of speakers tend to exhibit vigorous literacy practices, and vice versa. This is the reason why literacy programmes are being established in many parts of the world, often with the support of UNESCO (UNESCO Institute for Lifelong Learning 2013). Many linguists working on endangered languages also firmly believe in the empowerment of a language and their speakers through literacy, which is deemed to play a crucial role in language revitalization (see e.g. Hinton and Hale 2001; Grenoble and Whaley 2006).

The relation between literacy and language vitality is not always straightforward, however. Notably, there are cases where a language with a high literacy rate exhibits a declining number of speakers. This is the case for some languages in the Pacific, such as Rotuman. Vamarasi (2000) reports that children learn to write Rotuman in primary school, but are unable to practise their writing skills sufficiently, since there are few occasions to write Rotuman. A similar situation is found in Māori (see Parr 1961, 1963; Benton and Benton 2001). In the early nineteenth century, European missionaries successfully introduced writing to the Māori, which led to a rapid increase in literacy rate and a growing number of literacy practices in the vernacular language. At the same time, however, the number of Māori speakers steadily declined, until counter-measures were taken in the second half of the twentieth century (Benton 1981; Grenoble and Whaley 1998).[2]

These two cases show that literacy and language vitality are not directly related. Languages may score high on literacy variables but have a low number of speakers. This is the situation that we also encounter in Nivkh. While the last couple of decades have witnessed an increase in the number of publications, the number of speakers has declined, to such an extent that the future of the language is decidedly uncertain.

In what follows, we discuss the Nivkh case in some more detail. We begin by examining the historical context in which writing was established. We then describe the current situation, in which we find a proliferation of vernacular publications in the context of severe language endangerment.

15.4 The historical context of Nivkh writing practices

The first attempts to introduce a writing system for Nivkh were undertaken in the early stages of the post-revolutionary period (the 1920s), when writing systems were being developed for many indigenous languages of Russia. This formed part of a top-down initiative of the new Soviet government, whose political agenda included the improvement of the country's literacy rate, which in 1920 stood at a mere 44.1 per cent (Comrie 1981: 28). The new government wanted indigenous people to "climb up the evolutionary ladder" (Slezkine 1994: 156) to rid themselves of their "backwardness" and take part in the modernization of the state under the *korenizatsiia* ("nativization" or "rooting") policy (Grenoble and Whaley 2003; Hogan-Brun and Melnyk 2012; see also Greenberg, this volume). The socialist ideal behind this policy was to ensure the equality of all USSR citizens; this included the right to use one's own language in education and in other cultural contexts (Comrie 1981).[3] A practical reason for the dissemination of literacy in vernacular languages was to attract non-Russian nationalities to the Bolshevik side (Kreindler 1985). This was especially important in the Russian Far East, where the Civil War continued throughout the early 1920s. Nivkh was one of the nine minority languages of the "Peoples of the North" for which the *korenizatsiia* policy was first put into practice (Grenoble and Whaley 2003: 112).[4]

In 1926, Eruhim Kreinovich (1906–85), a young student of linguistics, was sent from Leningrad to the Nivkh homeland to implement the *korenizatsiia* policy. After intensive fieldwork with the local population, he created the first Nivkh orthography, which he submitted in 1931 to the Institute of the Peoples of the North in Leningrad. Kreinovich based his orthography on the Amur dialect, which he considered "the dialect of the Nivkh people who are superior in number and culture" (Kreinovich 1934: 187). In 1932, this orthography was officially recognized at the first All-Russian Conference on the Development of the Language and Literacy of the Peoples of the North. As was the norm at that time in the USSR, Kreinovich used the Latin (Roman) rather than the Cyrillic alphabet.[5] In 1932, Kreinovich also published the first Nivkh primer (*Cuz Dif,* "New Word") with the aid of Nivkh students who had come to Leningrad. This was followed by two readers, two arithmetic textbooks and a booklet on the October Revolution. The textbooks were used at schools and *likbez* (writing courses for adults) in *kul'tbaza* (social centres established by the Soviet government to implement its cultural policies).[6] Since there were no textbooks for the Sakhalin dialect, pupils who lived there used those for the Amur dialect (Tangiku 2009). The teachers were young local Nivkh, some of whom had acquired their formal education in Leningrad (Taksami 2005). Around the same time, the Nivkh language newspaper *Nivkhgu Mykyr Qlai-Dif* ("The true words of Nivkh") was launched in the city of Nikolaevsk-na-Amure. Its chief editor, K. Kando, was one of Kreinovich's former students (Roon 2001). A total of 11 editions of the newspaper were published, the last in 1935 (Gruzdeva 2011).

The time of language pluralism was short-lived. As early as in the mid-1930s, the tide began to turn under the highly centralized Stalinist regime. Kreinovich's orthography did not survive the strong pressure of Russification; in 1936, the Latin script policy came to an official end. A practical reason for its abandonment was the ever-growing contact with the Russian-speaking population, which made the acquisition of Russian and Cyrillic unavoidable (Comrie 1981; Grant 1995; Taksami 2005). Learning the Latin alphabet was no longer necessary, and was even thought to impede the acquisition of Cyrillic (Sergeev 1956, cited in Kaneko 2000). For Nivkh, several attempts were made to create a Cyrillic-based orthography, most notably by Valentina Savel'eva (in 1953) and Kreinovich (in 1961). Although both these orthographies were based on the Amur dialect, they assign different letters to sounds, suggesting that there was little cooperation between the two linguists.

During the time when these new orthographies were developed, USSR language policy had already undergone a drastic change towards total Russification. Russian had become the language the Nivkh were supposed to learn and use in all social contexts. Education in Nivkh was abolished, and children were removed from their parents and placed in *shkola-internat* ("boarding schools"), which were often located several hundred miles away from their homes. There they were forced to speak Russian, and were often punished by teachers and dormitory masters for not doing so (Shiraishi and Lok 2008; Paklina 2011). In addition, the diverse linguistic background of the children enrolled in these schools meant that Russian was the lingua franca in the playground (see Forsyth 1992; Grenoble and Whaley 2003). At school Nivkh children came into contact with children from Tungusic communities (such as Uilta, Evenki and Negidal) and with Russian-speaking teachers and children (Taksami 2005). As a result, most of them never mastered Nivkh orthography, a fate that Nivkh shares with many other indigenous languages of Russia.

Despite this dire background, new attempts to foster the use of a Cyrillic-based Nivkh orthography were undertaken as early as in the 1950s. The initiative for this came from two Nivkh intellectuals, the ethnologist and former director of the *Kunstkamera* (the current Peter the Great Museum of Anthropology and Ethnography) in Leningrad, Chuner Taksami (1931–2014), and the writer Vladimir Sangi (1935~). Taksami worked with Savel'eva. In 1956, the two published a Nivkh primer, which was followed by the first Russian–Nivkh dictionary (in 1965) and the first Nivkh–Russian dictionary (in 1970). The dictionaries had a tremendous effect on the propagation of their Nivkh orthography.

Sangi's work began locally. In 1960, he published a booklet of poems (some his own, some translations of Russian poems) in his hometown of Nogliki (*Znamia Truda* 1998). Sangi's mastery of Nivkh and his rich stock of traditional folklore knowledge (which he had acquired from elderly Nivkh) were put to full use in his later work, which made him one of the most successful writers in the country. Sangi also became a senior advisor to the Ministry of Culture. In this capacity he was actively involved in helping to re-introduce vernacular languages in elementary school education. Thanks in part to his efforts, this policy was implemented in 1977. Sangi also created an orthography for the Sakhalin dialect (his mother tongue), which was officially approved in 1979 (*Znamia Truda* 1998). Using this orthography, Sangi published a number of textbooks in collaboration with the Nivkh linguist Galina Otaina (1935–95). In 1981, a Nivkh language course was launched in two primary schools on Sakhalin. The teachers were Nivkh who had been trained at the Faculty of Peoples of the North at the Gertsen Pedagogical Institute (currently Herzen University) in Leningrad. While these courses have so far not led to a new generation of Nivkh speakers, they did stimulate literacy practices among the Nivkh (see Polet'eva 2003).

The historical overview sketched above suggests that we can distinguish between three critical periods in Nivkh writing practices. The first involved a top-down attempt to introduce literacy in the 1930s. Although this initiative was short-lived, and its social and practical impact negligible at the time, we believe that it did provide the basis for the current proliferation of Nivkh writing practices, which are based on a modified version of the orthography that was introduced in this period. The second attempt, by Nivkh intellectuals in the 1950s, also failed to provide an impetus to writing practices, occurring as it did during the days of total Russification, when the use of vernacular languages in public was strongly suppressed. It was only during the third period, in the 1980s, that writing practices among the Nivkh began to flourish. This happened as the result of a bottom-up development, in a period when the number of Nivkh speakers had already declined sharply.

During this third period, writing practices were initially restricted to professional activities of writers, journalists and teachers. Later on, others also took up writing, often after retirement. These writers used the Cyrillic script, but they did not make use of the established orthographies because, as we have seen, most Nivkh had never had the opportunity to learn these. The new writers came from a generation who had received their schooling exclusively in Russian. They could therefore transfer their knowledge of Russian orthography to Nivkh.

The topics on which people wrote were diverse: folk tales, traditional customs, lyrics, conversations, lists of words, proper names, toponyms, ways of counting, and so on. Some wrote with the aim of publishing their work and actively sought sponsors (such as local administrations and oil companies) for this. Others took up writing simply for the sake of it. During our own fieldwork we encountered a number of manuscripts produced in this way – some typed, others handwritten, sometimes on pieces of crumpled paper. Some writers reported that they had produced their work to keep the language and the memories of their ancestors alive. Practices of this kind are an instance of "folk writing", that is writing done by people who are informally trying to write their language (Hinton and Hale 2001: 246). The writing was not exclusively done in Nivkh, however. Some Nivkh wrote in Russian, no doubt because their Nivkh writing skills were insufficient.

A milestone in the practice of Nivkh literacy was the launch of the free monthly newspaper *Nivkh Dif* ("The Nivkh Language") in 1990. This newspaper is bilingual, with Nivkh and Russian printed in parallel columns. By December 2013, 249 editions had been published. The Sakhalin government recognizes *Nivkh Dif* as an official newspaper, which in the eyes of the local population lends an air of authority to Nivkh writing. The editorial staff, whose headquarters are located in the northern Sakhalin village of Nekrasovka, strive to show that writing in Nivkh can be maintained even in the face of a small number of native speakers. *Nivkh Dif* is viewed by many as the bulwark of Nivkh language maintenance and revitalization.

Technological advances have given a further boost to writing practices. Personal computers have made documents available to a wider public and have facilitated the printing of small publications. Since the 1990s, many posters, pamphlets and booklets have been produced in this way. In the late 2000s, electronic publications made their first appearance. Since then several pedagogical works have been published (e.g. Portal Khabarovsk 2009, 2010). These contain audio-visual material and are a valuable tool for educational purposes and language documentation. Many of these works contain recordings of the last speakers of Nivkh dialects.

Table 15.1 provides an overview of published titles in Nivkh written by Nivkh people. (School textbooks have been excluded, as has material which is written primarily in Russian.)

TABLE 15.1 Number of publications by Nivkh speakers in Nivkh

Period	Type of publication			
	Literature	Pedagogical	Academic	Political	Other
1982–1989	3				
1990–1999	1	2			1
2000–present	11	15	2	1	

Notice that the increase in titles over time is inversely proportional to the decline in the number of Nivkh speakers.

15.5 Nivkh writing practices against the background of Soviet language policies

Kreindler (1985: 2) likens the Soviet language policies in the twentieth century to a seesaw. In the early days of language pluralism the regime promoted vernacular languages. Then, in the 1930s, Stalin's policy of Russification slowed the seesaw into equilibrium. After this, the intensified Russification imposed by the Communist Party in the period following Stalin's rule promoted Russian at the cost of vernacular languages. The effects of this seesaw are still visible today. As we noted at the outset of this chapter, Nivkh, like most indigenous languages of Russia, faces a sharp decline in its number of speakers. The language appears to be moribund, and many Nivkh sub-dialects have already become extinct.

The effects of the Soviet language policies are no different from those that we see in other parts of the world, where dominant languages are also growing at the expense of vernacular ones. In Russia, the timely introduction of orthographies and literacy programmes appears to have contributed little to the maintenance of ethnic cultures, mainly because these programmes were not sufficiently propagated among the local population. Grenoble and Whaley (1998: 49) assert that "the loss of indigenous languages is clearly the direct result of policies implemented by Soviet language planners which created macro-level factors favoring acquisition of Russian at the expense of the native tongue". They examine the case of Evenki, a Tungusic language of Siberia, and criticize the way in which the Soviet regime implemented its language policy (see Grenoble and Whaley 1998, 2003, 2006). One of the main problems was that there were no contexts in which vernacular Evenki writing could be used, given that in Siberia, as elsewhere in the country, Russian fulfils all language functions related to writing. As a result, literary practices in Evenki remain modest until this day, and writing has not become part of everyday Evenki culture.

Other linguists pass milder judgment on the effects of Soviet language policy. Comrie (1981) and Kreindler (1985) both point to the success of the early policy of language pluralism, while noting the central role played by the introduction of vernacular orthography. For example, Comrie (1981: 24) observes that

> the development and implementation of these writing systems, even where flaws can be detected in the details of individual writing systems, must be seen as one of the most impressive achievements of Soviet language policy, given that this policy was not dictated by short-term economic or political gain. Only in very recent years have other countries with similar multilingual problems started attempting to implement similar policies.

As noted, we, too, are inclined to locate the roots of the recent proliferation of Nivkh writing in the days of the early Soviet language policy. When the Nivkh themselves look back on the history of their literacy practices, they point to 1931–32 as a memorable and decisive period, as it was then that the language got an authorized writing system and an orthography designed for public use (Eremin et al. 1988; Polet'eva 2003; Taksami 2005). The Nivkh have retained a modified version of this writing system even through the 1960s and 1970s, when the use of Nivkh in public was strongly discouraged by the authorities.

How did Nivkh writing practices survive this period of fervent language suppression? The first reason that comes to mind is that institutional support for Nivkh was never disrupted. The Gertsen Institute maintained its curriculum of language courses and continued to function as a home base for Nivkh students. There they had the opportunity to take courses taught by Valentina Savel'eva and Chuner Taksami, and meet with specialists like Eruhim Kreinovich, Vladimir Panfilov, Vladimir Rushchakov and Vladimir Nedialkov, and Nivkh intellectuals like Vladimir Sangi, Leonid Tyvus and Galina Otaina. The contribution of Kreinovich in particular cannot be overestimated. Former students fondly remember how he invited them into his Leningrad house and spoke to them in Nivkh. These encounters made a tremendous impact. Many students later reported that this was the first time they met a Russian who spoke Nivkh (Roon 2001).

Another boost for the survival of Nivkh literacy practices was the publication of Savel'eva and Taksami's Russian–Nivkh and Nivkh–Russian dictionaries. Although the number of copies was low (1,500 and 2,000, respectively), many Nivkh households had these books on their shelves. Both dictionaries were based on the Amur dialect, but the Nivkh–Russian dictionary also listed some lexical forms that were used in the Sakhalin dialect. Although this dictionary has often been criticized for containing many lexical items from Russian (e.g. *aviatransport* "air transport", *institut* "institute"), it is still the largest Nivkh dictionary, with a total of 13,000 entries.[7] The editors of the dictionary used a writing system that differed minimally from Russian Cyrillic orthography and that made minimal use of diacritics and new graphs. As a result, readers could use the dictionary without having any prior knowledge of Nivkh orthography, or even without knowing any Nivkh at all. Today, both dictionaries are widely used as an aid for writing, and they often provide a source of relief when people find words in them that they could not recall.

Finally, we should not overlook the role of Nivkh intellectuals. The ethnographer Taksami and the linguist Otaina were both leading figures in their field. And we have already mentioned Vladimir Sangi, a famous writer who used his political influence to help introduce education in vernacular languages. These Nivkh built their careers in Leningrad, Moscow and Vladivostok – big cities far away from their homeland – but kept in touch with local Nivkh through fieldwork trips, lectures and family visits. These contacts have helped to cultivate Nivkh literacy practices from the 1980s onwards.[8]

The above factors have ensured that Nivkh maintained some prestige, even during the darkest days of Russification. Without them, the development of Nivkh language maintenance activities in the 1980s would have been impossible.

15.6 The sociolinguistic relevance of the Nivkh situation

As for Evenki, the Soviet language planners failed to provide a suitable social context in which the Nivkh could employ their literacy skills. For Nivkh, too, orthographies were introduced top-down, and the linguists that were appointed to implement the language policy "arrived in communities uninvited and started working" (Grenoble and Whaley 2006: 73). A successful literacy programme needs bottom-up support: "Ideally, literacy will be the product of a grassroots kind of movement, coming from within the community itself and involving community participation in all phases of development" (Grenoble and Whaley 2006: 103). We have seen that for Nivkh this happened a good 50–60 years after the introduction of an orthography, and that participation of the community was possible only because some speakers had retained the practice of writing during the years of intense Russification.

The history of Nivkh writing practices illustrates that language policies may have long-term effects that are unexpected for the language planners who initiated them. This holds true in particular in Russia. On the one hand, Russian language policies have been subject to quite radical changes in a relatively short time. On the other, the country's immense size and complex bureaucratic system meant that new language policies were implemented at a slow pace and did not always undo the effects of previous policies, especially in a remote corner such as the Russian Far East.[9] For example, the Gertsen Pedagogical Institute has always continued to offer Nivkh language courses and train Nivkh teachers, even when there were no schools in which Nivkh could be taught. In our view, the complex of Russian language policies constitutes a unique socio-historical development which has resulted in language communities such as the Nivkh, and to which standard models of language vitality cannot be readily applied.

15.7 Conclusion

The Nivkh case surveyed in this chapter shows that a severely endangered language can still produce a high number of vernacular publications. We believe that this is an important observation for sociolinguistic research. It shows that literacy is not always a reliable indicator of language vitality.

Despite the recent upsurge in Nivkh publications, the future of Nivkh literacy practices is far from certain. Clearly, the greatest danger is the dramatic decline of the number of speakers. Another cause for concern is that the published genres are not evenly balanced, a problem that is also reported for other endangered languages (see, e.g., Benton and Benton 2001 on Māori). Nivkh publications on educational support and documentations of linguistic and cultural aspects heavily outweigh those in other genres. There are very few publications that adults can read for entertainment, for example.

Finally, an important question which we have not addressed here is what the Nivkh case tells us about language revitalization. It will be evident that writing practices can, and do, play a positive part in the revitalization of a language.

However, the Nivkh case also suggests that language revitalization is a more complex and multi-faceted issue than is sometimes suggested in the sociolinguistic literature.

Notes

1 By "mother tongue" we mean the language that is acquired first, not the language in which a speaker is most proficient (which for most Nivkh is Russian).
2 This scenario has led some linguists to claim that literacy in the vernacular language may also lead to language endangerment, in that the acquisition of literacy facilitates acquisition of the dominant language in the region. Mühlhäusler (1990) calls this "transitional literacy".
3 Kreindler (1985) notes that the early Soviet policy of language pluralism owes much to the personal prestige of Lenin, as language pluralism deviates from the orthodox Marxist belief in language unity – a common language for all people. For discussion of language policies in the USSR, see Comrie (1981); Grenoble (2003); Grenoble and Whaley (2003); Hogan-Brun and Melnyk (2012).
4 "Peoples of the North" is an administrative term that was used in the USSR to refer to the indigenous peoples in northern Russia, Siberia and the Russian Far East.
5 For discussion of this, see, e.g., Comrie (1981); Grant (1995); Kaneko (2000); Grenoble and Whaley (2003).
6 On the historical role of *likbez* and *kul'tbaza*, see Slezkine (1994) and Grant (1995). There were a total of 20 schools (13 in Amur, seven on Sakhalin) for Nivkh in this period (Forsyth 1992).
7 Chuner Taksami later reported that these Russian items could not be eliminated due to political pressure (Taksami 2005).
8 The initiatives of Maria Pukhta (in Nikolaevsk-na-Amure) and Nadezhda Bessonova and Zoia Liutova (in Nekrasovka) deserve special mention. In the late 1980s Pukhta and Bessonova launched a Nivkh radio programme. Around the same time, Pukhta and Liutova set up Nivkh "language circles" where local Nivkh could familiarize themselves with their language and orthography.
9 From a Western perspective, we could say that Russia finds itself in a "dissonant social system"; see Greenberg, this volume.

Further reading

Grant, Bruce (1995) *In the Soviet House of Culture: A Century of Perestroikas*. Princeton: Princeton University Press. (This book describes the drastic change of lifestyle that the Sakhalin Nivkh people underwent in the twentieth century.)

References

Benton, Richard (1981) *The Flight of the Amokura*. Wellington: New Zealand Council for Educational Research.
Benton, Richard and Nena Eslao Benton (2001) RLS in Aotearoa/New Zealand 1989–99. In: *Can Threatened Languages be Saved?* Joshua A. Fishman (ed.), 423–50. Clevendon: Multilingual Matters.
Botma, Bert and Hidetoshi Shiraishi (2014) Phonological and Phonetic Aspects of Nivkh Palatalization: Articulatory Causes and Perceptual Effects. *Phonology* 31(2): 181–207.
Comrie, Bernard (1981) *The Languages of the Soviet Union*. Cambridge: Cambridge University Press.
Coulmas, Florian and Federica Guerini (2012) Literacy and Writing Reform. In: *The Cambridge Handbook of Language Policy*. Bernard Spolsky (ed.), 437–60. Cambridge: Cambridge University Press.

De Graaf, Tjeerd (1992) Small Languages and Small Language Communities: News, Notes and Comments 9 – The Small Languages of Sakhalin. *International Journal of the Sociology of Language* 94: 185–200.

De Graaf, Tjeerd and Hidetoshi Shiraishi (2013) Documentation and Revitalisation of two Endangered Languages in Eastern Asia. Nivkh and Ainu. In: *Sustaining Indigenous Knowledge*. Erich Kasten and Tjeerd de Graaf (eds), 49–64. Norderstedt: SEC Publications.

Edwards, John (1992) Sociopolitical Aspects of Language Maintenance and Loss: Towards a Typology of Minority Language Situations. In: *Maintenance and Loss of Minority Languages*. Willem Fase, Koen Jaspaert and Sjaak Kroon (eds), 37–54. Amsterdam: John Benjamins.

Eremin, S., Chuner Taksami and V. Zolototrubov (1988) *Nivkhi Sakhalina* [The Nivkh of Sakhalin]. Novosibirsk: Nauka.

Federal'naia Sluzhba Gosudarstvennoi Statistiki (2013) Vserossiiskaia perepis' naseleniia 2010 [Russian census 2010]. Natsional'nyi sostav i vladenie iazykami, grazhdanstvo [Language Proficiency per Nationality]. Available online at: www.gks.ru/free_doc/new_site/perepis 2010/croc/perepis_itogi1612.html (accessed on 26 March 2014).

Fishman, Joshua A. (2003) Languages Late to Literacy: Finding a Place in the Sun on a Crowded Beach. In: *When Languages Collide*. Brian Joseph, Johanna Destefano, Neil Jacobs and Ilse Lehiste (eds), 97–108. Ohio: Ohio State University Press.

Forsyth, James (1992) *A History of the Peoples of Siberia*. Cambridge: Cambridge University Press.

Giles, Howard, Richard Bourhis and D.M. Taylor (1977) Towards a Theory of Language in Ethnic Group Relations. In: *Language, Ethnicity and Intergroup Relations*. Howard Giles (ed.), 307–48. London: Academic Press.

Grant, Bruce (1995) *In the Soviet House of Culture: A Century of Perestroikas*. Princeton: Princeton University Press.

Grenoble, Lenore (2003) *Language Policy in the Soviet Union*. Dordrecht: Kluwer.

Grenoble, Lenore and Lindsay Whaley (1998) Toward a Typology of Language Endangerment. In: *Endangered Languages: Current Issues and Future Prospects*. Lenore Grenoble and Lindsay Whaley (eds), 22–54. Cambridge: Cambridge University Press.

——(2003) Evaluating the Impact of Literacy: The Case of Evenki. In: *When Languages Collide*. Brian Joseph, Johanna Destefano, Neil Jacobs and Ilse Lehiste (eds), 109–21. Ohio: Ohio State University Press.

——(2006) *Saving Languages*. Cambridge: Cambridge University Press.

Gruzdeva, Ekaterina (2002) The Linguistic Consequences of Nivkh Language Attrition. *SKY Journal of Linguistics* 15: 85–103.

——(2004) Numeral Classifiers in Nivkh. *Sprachtypologie und Universalienforschung* 57: 300–329.

——(2011) Nivkhskii iazyk [The Nivkh Language]. In: *Nivkhi* [Nivkh]. Tat'iana Roon (ed.), 37–49. Yuzhno-Sakhalinsk: Energy Press.

Gruzdeva, Ekaterina and Julia Leonova (1990) K izucheniu nivkhsko-russkogo dvuiazychiia v sociolingvisticheskom aspekte [On the Study of Nivkh-Russian Bilingualism in a Sociolinguistic Aspect]. In: *Sistemnye otnosheniia v sinkhronii i diakhronii* [Systematic Relations in Synchrony and Diachrony]. N. Andreev (ed.), 48–55. Moscow: AN SSSR Institut Iazykoznaniia.

Hinton, Leanne and Ken Hale (2001) *The Green Book of Language Revitalization in Practice*. San Diego: Academic Press.

Hogan-Brun, Gabrielle and Svitlana Melnyk (2012) Language Policy Management in the Former Soviet Sphere. In: *The Cambridge Handbook of Language Policy*. Bernard Spolsky (ed.), 592–616. Cambridge: Cambridge University Press.

Janhunen, Juha and Tapani Salminen (2000) *UNESO Red Book on Endangered Languages: Northeast Asia*. Online available at: www.helsinki.fi/~tasalmin/nasia_report.html# (accessed 22 March 2014).

Kaneko, Toru (2000) Latin-shiki shokihou shimatsuki [The Latin Script Policy in the USSR]. *Journal of Chiba University Eurasian Society* 3: 1–20.

Kreindler, Isabelle (1985) The Non-Russian Languages and the Challenge of Russian. In: *Sociolinguistic Perspectives on Soviet National Languages*. Isabelle Kreindler (ed.), 345–67. Berlin: Mouton de Gruyter.
Kreinovich, Eruhim (1934) Nivkhskii (giliackii) iazyk [The Nivkh Language]. In: *Iazyki i pis'mennost' narodov severa* [Languages and Orthography of the Peoples of the North] 3. Ia. Al'kor (ed.), 181–222. Leningrad: Instituta Narodov Severa.
——(1955) Giliiatsko-tunguso-manchurskie iazykovye paralleli [Nivkh-Tungus-Manchu Language Parallels]. In: *Doklady i soobscheniia instituta iazykoznaniia* [Reports and Squibs from the Institute of Linguistics] (Volume 8). V. Vinogradov (ed.), 135–67. Moscow: AN SSSR.
Meyerhoff, Miriam (2011) *Introducing Sociolinguistics* (second edition). London: Routledge.
Mühlhäusler, Peter (1990) "Reducing" Pacific Languages to Writing. In: *Ideologies of Language*. John E. Joseph and Talbot J. Taylor (eds), 189–205. London: Routledge.
Novikova, K. and V. Savel'eva (1953) K voprosu o iazykakh korennykh narodnostei sakhalina [Linguistic Topics of the Indigenous Peoples of Sakhalin]. In: *Iazyka i istoriia narodnostei krainego severa SSSR* [The Languages and History of the Peoples of the North in USSR], 157 (2): 84–133. Leningrad: Lenigradskii Gosudarstvennyi Universitet. Reprint of the English translation by Takeshi Hattori appeared in (2000) in *Takeshi Hattori – Selected Writings*, 309–41. Sapporo: Hokkaido Shuppan Kikaku Center.
Paklina, Galina (2011) Vospominaniia detstva [Memories of Childhood]. In: *Nivkhi* [Nivkh]. Tat'iana Roon (ed.), 63–65. Yuzhno-Sakhalinsk: Energy Press.
Parr, C.J. (1961) A Missionary Library: Printed Attempts to Instruct the Maori, 1815–45. *The Journal of the Polynesian Society* 70(4): 429–50.
——(1963) Maori Literacy 1843–67. *The Journal of the Polynesian Society* 72(3): 211–34.
Polet'eva, Svetlana (2003) Prepodavanie nivkhskogo iazyka v shkole (iz opyta raboty) [Teaching Nivkh in Elementary Education (from My Work Experience)]. In: *Narody i kul'tury dal'nego vostoka: vzgliad iz XXI veka* [Peoples and Cultures in the Far East: Perspectives from the 21st Century]. Tatiana Roon and Mikhail Prokof'ev (eds), 209–15. Yuzhno-Sakhalinsk: Sakhalin Regional Museum.
Portal Khabarovsk (2009) *Nivkh dif* [The Nivkh Language]. Khabarovsk: Portal Khabarovsk.
——(2010) *Nivkhskii iazyk za 30 dnei* [The Nivkh Language in 30 Days]. Khabarovsk: Portal Khabarovsk.
Roon, Tatiana (2001) Zhizn' v nauke [Life in Academism]. In: *Nivkhgu* [The Nivkh People]. O. Kuznetsov (ed.), 3–41. Yuzhno-Sakhalinsk: Sakhalinskoe Knizhnoe Izdatel'stvo.
Savel'eva, Valentina and Chuner Taksami (1965) *Russko-nivkhskii slovar'* [Russian–Nivkh Dictionary]. Moscow: Sovetskaia Enciklopediia.
——(1970) *Nivkhsko-russkii slovar'* [Nivkh–Russian Dictionary]. Moscow: Sovetskaia Enciklopediia.
Sergeev, Mikhail (1956) *Nekapitalicheskii put' razvitiia malykh narodov Severa* [Non-capitalistic Path of Development for the Small Peoples of the North]. Moscow-Leningrad: Academy of Sciences USSR.
Shiraishi, Hidetoshi (2006) Topics in Nivkh Phonology. PhD dissertation, University of Groningen.
Shiraishi, Hidetoshi and Galina D. Lok (2008) *Sound Materials of the Nivkh Language* (Volume 5). Sapporo: Sapporo Gakuin University.
Slezkine, Yuri (1994) *Arctic Mirrors*. Ithaca: Cornell University Press.
Takahashi, Moritaka (1934) Giriyakzoku ni okeru gairaigo oyobi gairai bunka ni tsuite [Foreign Words and Culture of Nivkh Clans]. *Toyogaku sohen* [Philologia Orientalis] 1: 185–211.
Taksami, Chuner (2005) *NHK roshiago kaiwa* [Conversation in Russian]. Tokyo: NHK.
Tangiku, Itsuji (2009) *Ygh mif nivgun t'ylgur' p'urkkhun* [Interviews with the Sakhalin Nivkh]. Tokyo: Research Institute for Languages and Cultures of Asia and Africa.
UNESCO Institute for Lifelong Learning (2013) *Global Report on Adult Learning and Education. Rethinking Literacy*. Hamburg: UNESCO Institute for Lifelong Learning.

Vamarasi, Marit (2000) All Literate and Nothing to Read: The Problem of a Lack of Written Literature in Rotuman. In: *Proceedings of the Foundation for Endangered Languages Conference* (Charlotte, North Carolina, 21–24 September). Nicholas Ostler and Blair Rudes (eds), 119–22. Bath: Foundation for Endangered Languages.

Vysokov, Mikhail (1985) Sovremennaia iazykovaia situatsiia v raionakh prozhivaniia Sakhalinskikh nivkhov [The Current Linguistic Situation of the Sakhalin Nivkh]. *Ethnograficheskie issledovaniia Sakhalinskogo oblastnogo kraevedcheskogo muzeia* [Ethnographic Studies of the Sakhalin Regional Museum] 2: 71–76.

——(1999) Korennoe naselenie Sakhalina na poroge tret'ego tysiachletiia [Indigenous Peoples of Sakhalin towards the Third Millennium]. *Kraevedcheskii biulleten'* [Bulletin of Local History] 4: 18–47.

Znamia Truda (1998) Pervaia broshura na nivkshkom [The first Booklet in Nivkh]. *Znamia Truda* [Banner of Labour (a local newspaper)]. 29 January.

16

THE JAMAICAN LANGUAGE SITUATION

A process, not a type

Hubert Devonish and Kadian Walters

16.1 Typologizing the Jamaican language situation – diglossia

Jamaica is an island nation of approximately 2.9 million people in the Caribbean, some 120 miles to the west of Haiti, the country used by Ferguson (1959) as one of the exemplars of the concept of diglossia. Jamaica, like Haiti, has a predominantly creole-speaking population and is, second to Haiti, the largest single creole-speaking speech community in the world. Jamaican Creole (JC) is an English-lexicon creole language coexisting with English. JC, like nearly all the creole languages of the region, has been involved, from the 1960s onwards, in a process by which it is increasing in status and expanding in functions.

Of the approximately 15 English-lexicon creole languages spoken in the Caribbean, JC has as many speakers as the others combined. It is, therefore, a good choice for studying how diglossic-type behaviour is implemented in an English and English-lexicon Caribbean creole context. This matches the much better known case of Haiti, involving French and a French-lexicon creole. Hudson (2002), in his extensive and thorough review of the literature on diglossia, is inclined to exclude Haiti and, by extension, other Caribbean creole-type situations from the category of diglossia. Against this background, therefore, it becomes interesting to explore the relationship between the Jamaican language situation and the essential features of diglossia as identified by him. The essence of diglossia, Hudson (2002: 40) argues, is that the situations fitting this concept are unified by their having

> a quite specific set of relationships between functional compartmentalization of codes, the lack of opportunity for the acquisition of H as a native variety, the resulting absence of native speakers of H, and the stability in the use of L for vernacular purposes.

This arises in a context where

> there typically does not develop a prestige community of native speakers of H that might serve as a reference group for native speakers of L, thereby providing the social impulse for shift from L to H as a native variety. Exogenous language contact, on the other hand, is an entirely different matter. Here, two separate cultural-linguistic traditions come into contact and therefore into competition with each other for at least some of the same socioecological niches.
>
> *(Hudson 2002: 40)*

For Caribbean creole language situations to fit into diglossia depends on if, and to what extent, there is "opportunity for the acquisition of H as a native variety" and whether there is "the social impulse for shift from L to H as a native variety". The notion of the (post-)creole continuum, originally developed by Reinecke (1969 [1935]) for Hawai'i and adopted and expanded for application to Jamaica (DeCamp 1971), hangs on two beliefs. One is that there is indeed opportunity to acquire the H as a native language, and the other that there is a prestige community of native speakers of H who are in a position to trigger a language shift from L to H. Winford (1985) suggests that creole continuum situations, of which Jamaica is one, are special cases of diglossia. This is most intriguing and is worth exploring in the conclusion.

16.2 Typologizing the Jamaican language situation: the (post-)Creole continuum

The linguists who described Jamaican Creole (JC) in the 1960s, notably DeCamp (1971), tended to work within the life-cycle theory of pidgin-creole, as presented by Robert A. Hall (1962). According to this theory, in the beginning, a pidgin develops as a contact language, deriving most of its vocabulary from the most socially dominant language in the contact situation. The pidgin is used as a lingua franca to bridge the language gap. The pidgin becomes a creole when it is learnt as a native language by new generations of children born into a pidgin-speaking environment. The end of the life cycle is presented by DeCamp (1971: 349) as consisting of four options. The creole in question could continue "without substantial change", presumably as an L variety in a diglossic relationship to the socially dominant language from which it derives its vocabulary. Alternatively, the creole language may become extinct, displaced by the socially dominant language. As a third option, the creole language may evolve into a "normal" language, becoming standardized and performing the entire range of communicative functions of the speech community. Fourthly, the creole language "may gradually merge with the corresponding standard language, as is happening in Jamaica" (DeCamp 1971: 348). He goes on to state that the post-creole continuum model which he adopts for describing Jamaica is for communities "in which a creole is in the process of merging with a standard" (DeCamp 1971: 349).

Within the framework developed by Hudson (2002), DeCamp's post-creole continuum is really just a special case of language shift from a lower prestige language to one with higher prestige. The post-creole continuum implicational scale constructed by DeCamp is simply a linguistic ladder. It is used by individual speakers of the more divergent basilectal creole language varieties to climb to higher and higher levels of linguistic conformity with English, the high prestige acrolectal language variety. Simultaneously, the entire speech community, and social groups within it, are climbing upward on this ladder, from generation to generation, as part of this societal language shift.

We are now 45 years on from the late 1960s, the time of DeCamp's early field work in Jamaica. Jamaica gained its political independence from Britain in 1962. In the decades since independence, there has been massive spending on public education with English as the medium of instruction and of literacy. There has been a generalized spread of literacy, in English only, and a greatly increased access to tertiary education, available again only in English. However, as of 2014, the predicted language shift has not taken place. JC continues as a robust language, distinct from English and is recognized as such by its speakers. The vast majority of young Jamaicans, like their elders, have JC as their native language

In the second decade of the twenty-first century, the post-creole continuum model is relevant to the speech behaviour of a minority within the speech community, particularly older speakers. The more general trend seems to be towards diglossia. This involves the consolidation of Jamaican Creole (JC) as the language of private and informal interaction, and hence a reduction in the opportunities for learning English as a native language. Furthermore, there are the steps being taken to standardize the orthography, morpho-syntax and lexicon of JC for use in formal settings, and a campaign to have the language recognized as one of the official languages of Jamaica. This development suggests a move in the direction of the third of DeCamp's options, that is creole becoming a "normal" language.

Why was DeCamp wrong? Projecting backwards from the present language situation, it is clear that language attitudes and conditions did exist for the predicted language shift. Attitudes to JC were negative and many speakers were seeking to carry out a language shift from JC to English, if not for themselves, for their children. There still exists a minority within the speech community who do not recognize JC as a valid code and try, both at the level of advocacy and language use, to exclude JC from the Jamaican speech community. As seen in the Language Attitude Survey of Jamaica (JLU 2005), however, there is a decrease in negative attitudes to JC across the age groups. The oldest, those over 50, born in 1955 or before, are the most negative. The youngest, born after 1975, are the most positive. What, then, would have shifted the balance of public attitude in favour of JC, first as a legitimate L language partner in a diglossia, and more recently as an official language alongside English?

A huge transformation of Jamaica, and its attitude towards its popular culture and national identity, took place in the two decades immediately following independence, that is the 1960s and 1970s. A series of symbols, including popular music, African awareness and Rastafari, as well as the "language of the people", that is JC, become markers of identification with the nation. In this context, a language shift to English would not achieve the objective of marking the Jamaican nation off as distinct from all other nations. Ironically, the momentous event that triggers this transformation occurs in 1968, just a few months after the conference in Jamaica at which DeCamp presents the earlier version of his 1971 paper. The Rodney Riots of October 1968 in Jamaica are the catalyst for the development and spread of the Black Power movement in the country, a movement for the empowerment of the black oppressed masses of the country. An outpouring of cultural expression, in the form of the spread of the culture of Rastafari, and Jamaican reggae music, recognized internationally by way of the Jamaican icon Bob Marley, follows. JC, as the language of Jamaican national identity and cultural expression becomes reinforced, as part of these changes. Any tendency towards JC either disappearing or merging with English is stopped dead in its tracks. The use of JC in informal situations, across all social classes, including those that have traditionally used English as a home language, strengthened. This results in an ongoing reduction in the opportunities to acquire English as an L1.

The current language situation can be summed up in the following way. Standard Jamaican English (SJE) operates as the only official language, language of education and government administration in Jamaica. It is also the primary language within which literacy is exercised, and the main language of public communication in the print and electronic media. It is the speech form learnt through exposure to the formal education system. JC, by contrast, is the predominant language of private and informal interactions and of expressions of popular culture such as music lyrics. The preceding description, however, is but a crude approximation of the language behaviours which manifest themselves in the Jamaican speech community. The following sections add detail and texture to this crude description and provides the basis to return to the question, in the conclusion, of the application of (post-)creole continuum theory and diglossia to the Jamaican language situation.

16.2.1 Language use: the macro level

The 1,000 informant National Language Attitude Survey of Jamaica or LAS (JLU 2005) asked a series of questions about language use. Approximately 89 per cent of those interviewed claim that they speak English, and the same percentage claim to speak JC. Of the total number of informants, 78 per cent claim to speak both (JLU 2005: 8). Given the existing language ideology, which assigns high status to English and low status to JC, the 89 per cent claim for English is probably somewhat higher than the number who actually use the language. Similarly, the figure for users of JC is probably lower than the actual number of users.

According to the LAS (JLU 2005: 8), 57 per cent claim to speak English to strangers and co-workers, and 63 per cent claim to use JC with friends and family only. These represent the portion of the sample who declare stereotypically diglossic behaviour. Nine per cent claim to speak English to no one, presumably representative of the monolingual JC-speaking population. Five per cent claim to speak

JC to no one, representing a mix of those genuinely monolingual in English and those choosing to claim not to speak it for reasons of status. Furthermore, 26 per cent and 29 per cent claim, respectively, to speak English and JC to everyone. These figures would include the genuine monolinguals in each of the two languages, and bilinguals who claim to switch between languages freely, whether influenced by stylistic considerations or by the linguistic competence of the listener.

There is an interesting decline in the number of those declaring to speak English only, from the oldest 50+ group, at 15 per cent, to the youngest, 18–30, at 8 per cent (JLU 2005: 10), There is a parallel fall in the numbers of those claiming to speak JC only, from 13 per cent in the oldest group to 6 per cent in the youngest group. The claimed users of both languages move from 72 per cent in the oldest group to 86 per cent amongst the youngest informants. These claims are supported by the results of the National Language Competence Survey or LCS (JLU 2005: 19). Using the more relevant results, those for informants approached in English, we see demonstrated competence in English only, decreasing from 21 per cent amongst the oldest group to 16 per cent among the youngest. Similarly, demonstrated competence in JC alone falls from 41 per cent in the oldest to 36 per cent amongst the youngest informants. To match these, demonstrated bilingual competence increases from 40 per cent to 50 per cent from the oldest to the youngest.

Returning to the LAS (JLU 2005: 12), the numbers of those who claim to use English to strangers and co-workers moves from 48 per cent amongst the oldest group to 67 per cent amongst the youngest. At the same time, the number who claim to speak JC to family and friends moves from 54 per cent amongst the oldest group to 73 per cent amongst the youngest. The trend, as observed by the differences across the age groups, is for an increased number to declare use of both languages, that is bilingualism, amongst the younger groups, relative to older groups. This complements their higher tendency to declare diglossic behaviour, that is English with strangers and co-workers versus JC with family and friends. These results support the proposal already made in the preceding section. According to this, there is an older tendency in Jamaica, characteristic of the period up to the 1960s, for there to be higher levels of monolingualism in each of the two languages. This would have been a situation that favoured an eventual language shift from the lower-prestige JC to the higher-prestige English. According to the argument, this tendency has, since the 1960s, been replaced by another, one which is diglossic in character. The claim for this transformation is supported by the distinction in language behaviour claims being made by the older groups and the younger ones in the LAS.

16.2.2 Language use: the micro level – formal

A crude macro-level statement can be made that English is the language of government administration, the education system, the legislative and legal systems, formal writing and for formal communication in the mass media. A similar one can be made that JC is the language of the home, private and informal interaction, the street, the playground, folk traditions, popular music and culture. One immediately has to qualify these general statements, however, because the two languages are, on a daily basis, tightly intertwined in these domains.

An example of language use in parliament that came to public attention in Jamaica illustrates decades-old conventions of language use in that domain. English is used in this domain, but not infrequently, either for emphasis or other stylistic effect, speakers do switch to JC. In 2013, the Minister of Justice, Mark Golding, speaking in the Senate, proceeded to thank workers and other social partners for their cooperation with the government in its belt-tightening measures in preparation for an agreement with the International Monetary Fund. The following is a quote from a newspaper report on what transpired:

> "Respec' due to those patriotic Jamaicans," Golding said when Senate President Reverend Stanley Redwood broke his strides.
> "Sorry to break your flow but the language used in the Senate must be standard English," Redwood told Golding.
> The minister had no choice but to relent, and instead of saying respec' due, resorted to respect is due.
>
> *(Luton 2013)*

What is instructive, however, is the outpouring of ridicule on the head of the President of the Senate by newspaper columnists and the public generally that follows this incident. Thwaites (2013), in a satirical piece entitled "Rev. Senator Sir Stanley of Redwood: Dost Thou Jest?", comments on the event, making several observations that are of relevance to an understanding of the language situation. His column makes remarks that indicate that the Minister, Mark Golding, is of a privileged socio-ethnic background which one associates with having English as a home language. The affirmation is also made that Golding can carry on a conversation for half an hour in English. We learn from this two things. The first is that, for this class of individual, conversations in English do take place. Second, with relevance to the minister's choice of language in the Senate, the implication is that his use of JC is not a result of lack of competence in English. The other comment is that the Senate President, coming as he does from a rural area, St Elizabeth, widely stereotyped as having the most basilectal variety of JC in the country, is somewhat out of place to be correcting the speech of the minister. The article ends satirically, with an injunction in JC for the President of the Senate to stop the nonsense and "low de business fi gwaan wid likkle Patwa inna it", that is "allow business to continue with a little 'Patwa'/JC" in it" (Thwaites 2013). The writer is here affirming the norm for this kind of official speech since the 1970s, that of English with JC allowed for stylistic and emotional effect.

Another formal domain we can examine is that involved in speaking on the telephone to the customer service representative (CSR) of a public agency. It is formal since the call is to an agency of the state about the business of that agency, with the CSR speaking on behalf of and with the authority of the state. The caller and the CSR at the other end of the line are typically unknown to each other, requiring presumably the language choice one makes when speaking to strangers. As the informants of Beckford-Wassink (1999) indicate, they would typically answer the phone in English, with only 8 per cent declaring that they would use JC for this purpose. This is supported by the LAS where we have already seen that 57 per cent are claiming English as the automatic language of choice with strangers.

In research done by Walters (forthcoming), one is able to study the results of a matched guised test in which a CSR is called by telephone on two separate occasions, once using English and the other JC. In the majority of JC calls, the CSRs accommodate linguistically to the caller, providing in JC the information requested in a manner evaluated by the caller as courteous. However, in about 40 per cent of the JC calls, things do not go quite so smoothly. There are requests for the callers to identify themselves very early in the interaction, much earlier than in those calls made in English. In addition, the nature of the request for identification is different. The JC calls have as their identity-checking devices: "Who is this person?", "Who is this?", "Excuse me? Who am I speaking to?" and "Do I know you?" This contrasts with the calls made using the English guise, where identity checking by the CSR takes the form of polite queries such as, "May I ask who is calling?", "Whom may I say is calling?" and "To whom am I speaking?" The earlier introduction by the CSR of an identity check, and the use of a third-person reference in the first two of these, is linked very much to the assumption of familiarity which the use of JC to open an interaction implies. The "Do I know you?" question here occurs against the background that 63 per cent of informants claim that they use JC exclusively with family and friends (JLU 2005: 9). A classic example of the "friend" effect of initiating an interaction in JC occurs when, in response to the caller using JC to initiate the conversation, the CSR asks, in JC, "A uu soun laka wehn Baanz?" – "Who is this that sounds like Barnes?" The CSR next asserts that it is indeed Barnes. When the MC denies that he is Barnes, the CSR asks, in JC, "Uu dis?" – "Who is this?"

CSRs in JC encounters adopt other measures to bring the JC callers into line linguistically. They sometimes engage in the correction of the caller. They make a disaffiliative code-switch in the direction of the caller's JC speech, mimicking and mocking them. This supposedly should draw the attention of callers to their unconventional language choice, and trigger a switch to SJE. Another method of "other correction" employed by CSRs in JC encounters involves phrases like "pardon me" or "excuse me". These typically appear after the "trouble-source", usually the caller's use of the JC to make a request, and are uttered to force a switch to SJE by the caller.

One can contrast the beginnings of such CSR interactions with the way they conclude. As a friendly interaction comes to an end, even one initiated by the caller in English, CSRs switch in the direction of JC to bid the caller farewell. At that stage of the interaction, the interlocutors are no longer total strangers. The way is open for a relaxation of language-use rules as a recognition of this emerging familiarity.

16.2.3 Language use: the micro level – informal

In the case of informal interactions, the sociolinguistic backgrounds of the interlocutors play an important role. For the uneducated and more generally monolingual or near monolingual, all such interactions take place in JC. For bilinguals, however, several options present themselves. For what one might term first-generation bilinguals, informal interaction typically takes place in JC. Their exposure to English has been as a result of formal education and they have little exposure to the use of English in informal contexts. Language choices are different for non-first generation bilinguals. These would, to varying degrees, have been exposed to English language use in informal situations and even at home. They find themselves, therefore, free to select from the two languages in their repertoires as style, topic and tone require.

Stereotypically, if the conversation is one about an informal topic, such as an amusing incident, a quarrel, anything emotional, the likely language is JC. If, however, the topic is more formal, covering some issue associated with formal education, or derived from a source that is English, such as an academic topic, a technical argument concerning law or politics, the likely language of choice is English.

The statements made here represent a gross simplification of language choice, since language competence varies, as do language values and attitudes. The result is that it is often not possible to predict language choice. Rather, once it is made, one can interpret what the intended meaning of that choice is. A classic example of this is the frequent tendency to say something already uttered in one language in the other. One of the reasons for this is emphasis. Thus, it is possible to hear the following parental injunction to a child, "Come here! … Mi se fi kum ya." The second part, which means in JC "I said, come here!", is an attention-gathering device, along with the implication that the parent is serious. This is a result of JC being a language bilinguals choose to use when they are most concerned about communicating meaning forcefully.

Another example of the unpredictability of language choice is what we shall call "the one-sentence switch to English". This usually occurs in informal conversations taking place in JC. Usually, a short JC sentence, either a question such as "Im di de?" or a statement such as "Mi neva nuo", is immediately followed by its English equivalents, "Is he there?", "I didn't know". Sometimes the one-sentence switch occurs because the speaker feels the listener may not have properly heard the sentence when it is first produced. It sometimes, however, is done instantaneously, before the listener has had a chance to give any feedback. In such cases, one has to view it as an attention-gathering device, the switch alerting the listener to focus on the information contained in the sentence presented in the two languages.

16.3 Jamaica: (post-)Creole continuum, diglossic and bilingual

What we have explored is a Jamaican language situation that historically straddles three different types of language situation. We assume the accuracy of the (post-)creole continuum of DeCamp (1971) in capturing important characteristics of the Jamaican language situation up to the early 1960s. In this context, even though JC was widespread, it coexisted with English, a minority language spoken natively by a tiny privileged minority within the society. This was an orthodox low prestige versus high-prestige language situation which was predicted, with the spread of education and modernity, to lead to language shift in the direction of the high-prestige variety, English. Then, the 1960s happened. There was political independence and the awakening of Jamaican political and popular cultural expression. JC emerged as the medium of linguistic expression to discuss all things Jamaican. The popular and mass domains within which it predominated were now highly valued. The language was now cemented in these domains as the symbol of national identity. The scene was now set for the emergence of diglossia via a societal recognition that JC had a permanent role to play in Jamaican society as the language of a very highly valued mass cultural expression. With this came the acceptance of the legitimacy of JC as the main language of private and informal expression, even amongst the traditional elite English-speaking social groups. This brought with it a decline in the opportunities for exposure to English in such settings. A consequence of that is a reduction in the chances of speakers learning English as an L1, even amongst the groups who traditionally used English as a home language.

The fact that the appreciation of Jamaican music, culture and language has not simply been local but international has had a feedback effect. The pride coming from this international recognition has contributed to Jamaican language attitudes moving beyond a mere accommodation of JC in its L role as a private and informal language in a diglossic situation. This shows itself in the results of the LAS in relation to aspirational questions on language. Of the informants in the LAS (JLU 2005: 34), 71 per cent favoured schools that were fully bilingual in JC and English, with the percentages increasing from 63 per cent in the oldest age group to 75.1 per cent in the youngest. A similar trend was observed in relation to the question of whether JC should be declared an official language alongside English. There was a 69 per cent overall support for this proposition. The oldest group supported at 64.8 per cent but the youngest at 72.1 per cent (JLU 2005: 37).

In Jamaica, diglossic behaviour by large sections of the population represent but a way post on the road to the recognition of the national vernacular L variety as a co-official language alongside the pre-existing externally imposed H. This process is driven by the nationalist aspirations of individual speakers, even as they manifest diglossic behaviour. This instability is typical of language situations such as those of Haiti and Jamaica which can be designated as "conquest diglossia" (Devonish 2007: 158–61). In Jamaica, the people are speaking and they will have the last word on the matter.

Further reading

Beckford-Wassink, Alicia (1999) Historic Low Prestige and Seeds of Change: Attitudes towards Jamaican Creole. *Language in Society* 28(1): 57–92. (This is a study of language attitudes towards the traditionally low-status Jamaican Creole, looking at both covert and overt prestige. The findings suggest ambivalence towards the language, with its use being deemed more appropriate the smaller the social distance from and the greater the solidarity with the interlocutor.)

Christie, Pauline (2003) *Language in Jamaica*. Kingston: Arawak Publications. (This work, which is aimed at the educated non-linguist, attempts to bring into the public domain of the discussion of language in Jamaica the insights of linguists and sociolinguists. It gives a review of the changing roles and functions of English and Jamaican Creole, documenting the rise in status and functions of Jamaican Creole and the adjustments to the status and functions of English.)

Jamaican Language Unit (2005) *The Language Attitude Survey of Jamaica*. Kingston: University of the West Indies. (This was a 1,000 person survey of language attitudes in Jamaica. It came up with the unexpected finding that attitudes to Jamaican Creole had become quite positive and that approximately 70 per cent of informants would support it being granted co-official status and being used as a formal language of education. The results confirm and complement the findings of Beckford-Wassink.)

References

Beckford-Wassink, Alicia (1999) Historic Low Prestige and Seeds of Change: Attitudes to Jamaican Creole. *Language in Society* 28: 57–92.

DeCamp, David (1971) Toward a Generative Analysis of a Post-creole Speech Continuum. In: *Pidginization and Creolization of Languages*. Dell Hymes (ed.), 349–70. Cambridge: Cambridge University Press.

Devonish, Hubert (2007) *Language and Liberation: Creole Language Politics in the Caribbean*. Kingston: Arawak Publications.

Ferguson, Charles A. (1959) Diglossia. *Word* 15: 325–40.

Hall, Robert A. (1962) The Life Cycle of Pidgin Languages. *Lingua* 11: 151–56.

Hudson, Alan (2002) Outline of a Theory of Diglossia. *International Journal of the Sociology of Language* 157: 1–48.

Jamaican Language Unit (2005) *The Language Attitude Survey of Jamaica 2005*. Kingston: University of the West Indies. Online available at: www.mona.uwi.edu/dllp/jlu/projects/survey.htm (accessed on 25 March 2014).

Luton, Daraine (2013) English Only in the Senate, President tells Justice Minister. *The Gleaner*. 8 March. Online available at: http://jamaica-gleaner.com/latest/article.php?id=43329 (accessed on 25 March 2014).

Reinecke, John (1969 [1935]) *Language and Dialect in Hawaii* (revised edition). Honolulu: University of Hawai'i Press.

Thwaites, Daniel (2013) Rev Senator Sir Stanley of Redwood: Dost thou Jest? *The Gleaner*. 27 March. Online available at: http://jamaica-gleaner.com/gleaner/20130327/cleisure/cleisure4.html (accessed on 25 March 2014).

Walters, Kadian (forthcoming) Linguistic Discrimination by Customer Service Representatives in Jamaica, PhD dissertation, Kingston, University of the West Indies.

Winford, Donald (1985) The Concept of Diglossia in Caribbean Situations. *Language in Society* 14: 345–57.

17

NUTEMLLAQ YUGTUN QANERYARARPUT

Our very own way of speaking Yugtun in Alaska

Theresa Arevgaq John

17.1 Introduction

This chapter discusses the Yugtun language. It is the language spoken in my own community of Toksook Bay in South Central Alaska. Yugtun means a way of speaking a Yup'ik language; Yup'ik refers to one person. Central Yup'ik is the most prolific indigenous spoken language in Alaska. The fast-paced language shift that this community is suffering from – a shift from a Yup'ik-dominant to an English-dominant community in one generation – has led to language revitalization programmes. The Yugtun language and culture in Toksook Bay have been remarkably resilient. The traditional lifestyle is still very much alive and the heritage language is still the default language used among villagers today. The Yugtun community has been more successful in language maintenance than surrounding communities because it does not separate Yup'ik language from Yup'ik culture.

This chapter starts by describing the language situation in the area. Then, the three main themes are discussed. First, the way to incorporate sociolinguistic information in determining who "speaks" Yugtun is briefly discussed. Second, there is the village and its culture. Village autonomy is discussed, as well as the role of the individual in the community, the role of elders and leadership, life orientation, ceremony and rituals. These points are illustrated largely through the importance of dance – the role of dance in communication and in information continuation in this community is explained in detail. Finally, education as a sociolinguistic factor is discussed, particularly the conflicting educational ideologies between the community and the dominant, Western culture. Assumptions underlying how language in communities works or how it should work underlie such a conflict.

These three approaches will reveal how culture is part of the language and that without culture there is no fully-fledged language – a theme which is touched upon in mainstream sociolinguistic theory but not seen as an indispensable factor. It reveals a unique and intricate connection between language and the passing on of cultural information to subsequent generations. Sociolinguistic descriptions and general approaches usually focus on language utterances and the analysis thereof in correlation with well-known social factors, such as age, gender and class. Aspects of the local culture – and how they not only relate to, but are part of the language – are often mentioned in passing as being relevant but are not usually investigated in a systematic way. The current chapter shows some, perhaps unexpected, aspects of a complete sociolinguistic analysis of small speech communities.

17.2 The sociolinguistic situation in the community of Toksook Bay

In the vast state of Alaska, which is over five times the size of Arizona, the diverse landscape and majestic mountains provide resources (fish, moose, caribou, mink, beaver, marine mammals, seal oil, tundra berries and beach greens) that are necessary for the survival of Alaska's Indigenous peoples. There are multiple Indigenous societies that inhabit Alaska. There are over 200 federally recognized villages in Alaska. Traditionally, rural communities in Alaska spoke their heritage languages to pass down their own knowledge through language and culture (Napoleon 1996; John 2009). Nowadays, however, the heritage languages are no longer spoken in the majority of these communities.

17.2.1 Yup'ik

Yup'ik, like other languages, is gradually becoming one of the endangered languages. The Yup'ik Region consists of more than 60 villages and is home to approximately 23,000 Yup'ik Eskimos (Counceller et al. 2012). Villages are not connected by any roads, which means that possible modes of transportation are limited to airplanes, boats and snowmobiles. Currently, the local residents lead a traditional lifestyle that is solely based on annual hunting and gathering. The Bering Sea provides an abundance of multiple stable food sources. Traditional ecological knowledge is a critical aspect of cultural self-sustenance.

There are approximately 20,000 (Central Alaskan) Yup'iks, some 10,500 of which speak their ancestral language. Children still grow up speaking Yup'ik as their first language in about one-third of the Yup'ik villages, mainly those on the lower Kuskokwim River, on Nelson Island, and along the coast and in the tundra area between the Kuskokwim River and Nelson Island. In the other Yup'ik villages most children grow up speaking English as their first language and it is only the older generations who still speak Yup'ik there (Jacobson 1995). According to Krauss (1997) only about one-quarter of all Yup'ik villages have large numbers of children growing up with Yup'ik as their first language. Morrow (1990: 5) notes that there is a strong tradition of respect for village autonomy. This autonomy extends to the degree to which local villages choose to maintain Yup'ik customs, traditions and languages. While Morrow (1990: 8) reported 96 per cent of respondents felt

Yup'ik language and culture should be taught in school. Joshua (2011) in her study of parental preferences in Eek, Alaska reports that 76 per cent of the respondents felt that Yup'ik should be taught at school. The Lower Kuskokwim School District serves 22 villages, including 14 of the 17 villages identified as having significant numbers of child speakers.

17.2.2 The successful maintenance of Yugtun

Yugtun, one of the Yup'ik languages, was the only language spoken by the residents of our village of Nightmute, Alaska, in 1963 – when I was in second grade. Everyone communicated with our heritage language, and used it to govern and to educate children. This was the sociolinguistic situation for all of the children in our community at this time. However, along with two-thirds of the population of Nightmute, my family relocated to Toksook Bay in 1963, which was 15 miles westwards, to be closer to coastal resources. I am 59 years old now, and we are the first generation from our village that was exposed to the Western education system around 1960. Today, the younger Yup'ik generations are multicultural and multilingual.

An account by an anonymous village student quoted in Counceller et al. (2012) is worth quoting at length in this context:

> I had a fortunate opportunity to speak my language as a child. In fact back then it was not considered a fortune; it was a standard practice, and most often the only language of communication. Everyone in my community spoke Yugtun. Yugtun permeates every aspect of our living. Whether it was play, worship, or relaxation through evening stories told by parents and elders, we heard and spoke Yugtun. Although I grew up speaking both my father's and mother's dialects, and therefore chose when it was opportune to speak either, I felt safe to express myself in the language of my own choosing until I entered my public school years through the auspices of the Bureau of Indian Affairs (BIA). English did not make any sense to me and my schoolmates, whose parents exclusively spoke Yugtun at home and within the community. We learned rote English that we could not make any sense of, but since we were forced by our teachers to learn, we pretended to speak until we finally managed to utter English enough to satisfy our teachers.

A large percentage of the children still speak Yugtun in the community of Toksook Bay today. This may be surprising as current studies reveal a significant language shift in the majority of the surrounding villages. As will become clear in the course of this discussion, this is due to strong community leadership, geographic isolation and a strong cultural parental pedagogy. Christianity and federal education systems also arrived much later to the community of Toksook Bay. The heritage language is still the default language used among villagers today, and this may have spared them from assimilation and acculturation patterns that affected other communities in the area. In Toksook Bay, Yugtun is spoken at home, in church, at the post office, the grocery stores, in the community club house, at three governing agencies (traditional, municipal and corporate), and during subsistence activities today. Elders provide critical ancient oral narratives to the children, parents and adults. The church hymns and service books are also written and practised in Yugtun. Consequently, the local workers at the governing offices, school, church and recreation centres are fluent Yugtun speakers.

The Yugtun community has been more successful in language maintenance because it does not separate Yup'ik language from Yup'ik culture. The heritage language is an integral part of the culture. It is essentially intact, in daily communication and in social events. The elders, parents, leaders and Yugtun classroom educators are all fluent speakers, and so are educators of the children at home and at kindergarten to third grade school.

17.2.3 Social factors in defining "speaker"

How many speakers there are of Yugtun depends on whether one applies the local norms or the general definitions of what a speaker of this language is. McArthur's (1992) and Saville-Troike's (2007: 3) definitions of the degree to which one "speaks" a language focus on at what age one started to speak it. Lippi-Green's (2012: 45–46) definition also takes this well-known approach. Such definitions mainly focus on general fluency and on choice between variants. This approach, however, is not usually applied by Yugtun speakers. The local definition of a "speaker" in my community is a person who has the ability to carry on a conversation with an elder. The Yugtun term for a fluent speaker is called *puqilria*. In contrast, the person that is not a fluent speaker is called *puqialnguq*. The criterion of determining fluent speakers is a combination of actual fluency and the skill of communicating with a central member of the community. The former Director of the Alaska Native Language Center, Michael Krauss (2007), identified two critical problematic category types in language scholarship. The first is determining who counts as a speaker, and the second is determining who is a member of the indigenous community. Counceller et al. (2012) similarly addressed the same concern: "Generally, fluent speaker counts only identify those with advanced or higher language ability according to the American Council on the Teaching of Foreign Languages (ACTFL) standard […]. In threatened languages where no standard method of fluency assessment exists, scholars must sometimes use social rather than scientific tools."

17.3 Dance as a factor in communication

History, oral narratives and traditional cultural values and principles are taught to children at home and elementary school through the medium of Yugtun. The annual cultural rituals and ceremonial practices are taught and performed using the heritage language. Children and adults alike learn to sing the songs and their dances only using Yugtun year after year. The children have their own cultural dance group at the school, which has a repertoire that is different from that of the local native dance. The youth dance group composes their songs at school and performs them during community celebrations. The children can compose and choreograph their own dances with the help of professionals from the community, such as the elders, drummers and singers.

The language revitalization process is successful in the community because children and their collaborators speak Yugtun fluently and they still can communicate with elders and local experts efficiently. The fact that elders either did not attend federal school to learn English, or had very little schooling, motivated the parents as family leaders to perpetuate Yugtun, their only village communication tool. The unified collaborative efforts of the school administrators and respective local leaders for the younger generation to be proactive community members by speaking the language and keeping the culture alive inspires the young villagers to be proud of who they are as Yup'ik. This communal language, cultural practice and pedagogy are some of the ways to keep the language and culture alive and intact within the village. The Yup'ik educational framework of using Yugtun as a medium keeps the language maintenance strong in the community. Yup'ik dance is alive and vibrant in our village, which keeps Yugtun and cultural practices alive throughout the year. It is essential now to briefly explain how dance plays a critical role in the Yup'ik indigenous knowledge system in reference to language revitalization and cultural maintenance as described in my dissertation on dance (John 2010).

The transmission and construction of the Yup'ik indigenous knowledge system in dance involves both collaboration and communal creation. It requires socially mediated cooperative participation and learning. The elders and dance experts explain the lyrics. Song context and dance gestures are taught to children and adults alike in the community centres during ceremonies and ritual recitals. Since the dances portray historical and contemporary societal accounts, the hidden epistemic messages of music are explained to the participants.

Education in Yugtun epistemology requires multiple conceptual frameworks and methodologies (John 2009, 2010). They are crucial tools for passing down oral narratives and socio-cultural concepts from one generation to another. The complex Yup'ik "educational frameworks" (*qanruyuutet*) include words of wisdom that inscribe "proper ways of living" (*qaneryarat, ayuqucirtuutet, inerquutet, alerquutet, elucirtuutet, piciryarat* and *yagyarat*). Furthermore, the Yup'ik tools of "advice" (*qaneryara*), oral traditional stories of "ancestors' accounts" (*qulirat*) as well as "personal accounts" of events and activities (*qanemcit*) are part of the traditional knowledge transmission and construction system (for a detailed discussion, see John 2009).

The complex Yugtun terminologies used for dances are important for education. *Ellugcaraq* is an ancient form of "prayer dance", a way of cleaning a body from physical, mental and spiritual illness. *Arulayaraq* is defined as a way to enact a story through gestures, each of which is connected to a specific song text. *Kass'ikegcaraq* is defined as an exaggerated body movement in dance that includes the head, neck, arms, body and legs. It is an elaborate exhibition of unified body movements that awaken the characters and actions of the song text, such as a flying bird, swimming seal, cutting a fish or a caribou hunt dance. The accompanying music is called a *yuarun*. Dancers are called *yurartet* while the specific multiple forms of gesturing are referred to as *yagirayarat*. The composers are called *yuarucistet*, while dance choreographers are known as *yagiracistet*. *Yuraq* orchestrators are referred to as *agniurtet* or *apallirturtet*. They need to ensure that there is unison in lyrics, drumbeat, music, gesture and audience response.

Four key entities in Yugtun dance exist: "ancestors" (*ciuliat*), "shamans" (*angalkuut*), "drums" (*cauyaq*) and "song structures" (*yuaruciyaraq*). Ancestors, first of all, are regarded with respect and believed to be part of the living in our cosmology. The Emmonak documentary film entitled *Uksuum Cauyai: Drums of Winter* (Elders and Kamerling 1988) reveals a conceptual framework that pertains to the dead. An unidentified woman states: "[R]emembering their dead ones, people go the kashim [a communal centre] [...] and give gifts to everyone there." The Yupiit (plural for Yup'ik) socio-conceptual framework conveys a perception that life is immortal. The ancient belief system in the continuum of ancestors' lives brings us the notion of an intertwined holistic, spiritual and social web. The term *ciuliat* defines the functional role of ancestors as our leaders.

Shamans constitute the second key entity in dance. An Emmonak elder and leader Tucker describes (personal communication, 2008; my translation from Yup'ik) the role of shaman as the primary leader, petitioner and a trans-mediator between the human and non-human spiritual worlds in association with music, dance and masks. The shaman's professional responsibility is to enact ancient forms of prayer in order to request the survival of the people. The specified masks depict survival essentials requested in ceremonies. Tucker argues that in masked dancing, the consecutive verses in music function as tools in human/non-human spiritual mediation. The first verse specified ocean produce that includes mammals, fish, seashells and waterfowl. The second verse specifies the mainland natural resources such as moose, caribou, mink, wolf, berries, vegetables and driftwood. Tucker states: "This ancient form of prayer enacted by shamans was a central part of the Yup'ik cultural, social and spiritual way of living long before Christianity taught us about God."

Drums, the third component, are the only musical instrument used. It is played with a hand-carved wooden "drumstick" (*mumeq*). The drum is made with a round bentwood frame with a hand-crafted and specially designed handle. Traditionally, the "drum cloth" (*eciq*) was made out of fine mammalian stomach lining. The drum was to be treated with respect and used for ceremonial purposes only.

Finally, Yup'ik dance song structures used during ceremonies are composed and choreographed differently. The ceremonies are accompanied with music and must adhere to the same specific composition formalities practised by our ancestors. The songs vary in text, length, rhythm, drumbeat and melody. The people respect the old songs because, according to them, these songs have power. Some are afraid of some of the songs because of their meanings, but other songs are considered good. These songs give strength and well-being, and help us emotionally. Our songs assure success in hunting and some in fishing (Elders and Kamerling 1988).

Today, Toksook Bay youth dancing remains very popular in the different villages and helps to revitalize and maintain both the language and cultural knowledge.

The traditional pedagogical dance system explored and explained in this section was passed on to me by my parents, grandparents and extended relatives through the oral tradition, the knowledge system that enhances self-awareness and embraces a holistic, interconnected understanding of the human, the land and the sacred world. Yup'ik dance terminologies encapsulate important cultural patterns and knowledge still practised in the community. Most indigenous peoples' worldviews in the area aim towards harmony and integration with all life, including the spiritual, natural and human domains (Kawagley 1995) that were orally transmitted to the younger generation by prominent elders, shamans, educators and leaders of the communities (John 2010).

17.4 Language ideology in education

Several Yugtun teacher training and language development projects exist today. They were successfully acquired by the Alaska Native Language Center faculty from the Federal Education Agency in an effort to counter the language shift in the region. These projects started in early 2000. They include the Alaska Native Education planning grant, Second Language Acquisition Teacher Education, *Piciryaramta Elicallra* (ancestral knowledge) and Alaska Native Education Computer-Assisted Language Learning. Unfortunately, educational ideologies held by the indigenous community and state institutions are in conflict.

It has been well established in the literature that indigenous students face many challenges in educational settings. Native Alaskan students have high drop-out rates in high school, and only a small percentage of indigenous students pursue a form of higher education (Faircloth and Tippeconnic 2010; DeVoe and Darling-Churchill 2008). The recent Yugtun language programme implemented by the Lower Kuskokwim School District is discussed below. Counceller et al. (2012) articulate a conflict between practices commonly found in mainstream education in both Western school system and post-secondary school settings. A number of scholars have suggested that this situation may be attributed in part to a mismatch between these practices and Alaskan native cultural norms (Kawagley 1995; Barnhardt and Kawagley 2005). Yup'ik society, for instance, is undergirded by a cooperative rather than competitive orientation toward goal completion (Siekmann and Charles 2011). In addition, instead of celebrating individual knowledge, Yup'ik society highly values a communal source of knowledge (Fienup-Riordau 2005: 2–3).

The LKSD Advisory School Board are required to host public meetings every three to five years where the community members are asked to select a language programme for their local sites (Wyman et al. 2010a). These include the Yup'ik First Language and later the Yup'ik Language Development, English Language Development and a Dual Language Program. This third and final programme type is the so-called Gomez and Gomez Dual Language Program.

One major pressure that Yup'ik educators are facing in these language programmes is the complexity of the uneven processes of language shift. Each individual, family, village and school history varies, thereby creating a wide-ranging diversity of experiences and language repertoires between children (Smith 1999; Nicholas 2009). Research into differing language repertoires documented that three out of 11 sites have remained relatively stable multilingual environments in 2007. In each of these three sites, participants reported that very few to none of their youngest children "speak mostly English and hardly any Yup'ik". Two of these sites reported that well over 80 per cent of these children speak Yup'ik well for their age (Wyman et al. 2010b). This same data suggests that a language shift is well under way in two villages in the study, and the remaining six villages (3–8) appeared to be on the tipping point of language shift (Wyman et al. 2010b).

The Yugtun language programmes of South-Central Alaska were developed in an effort to resolve the conflicts between Yugtun and English educational institutions and ideologies in the region. The aim of the effort to develop effective language programmes is to resolve the conflict between the two by bridging Yugtun and Western knowledge systems. The Lower Kuskokwim School District has adopted and implemented the Gomez and Gomez Dual Language model. Key elements of this model include the requirements that at least 50 per cent of all instruction up to the age of ten must be in a Yup'ik medium. Adopters of this model are also encouraged to extend the age to 17 years. Instruction is divided according to subject. Math is in English, Science and Social Studies are in Yup'ik, and Language Arts is in Yup'ik from kindergarten to first grade. The teaching of language use for non-instructional purposes up to ten years is in both English and Yup'ik, and is alternated every three days – Monday, Wednesday, Friday is Yup'ik; Tuesday and Thursday is English (Marlow and Siekman 2013).

17.5 Conclusion

The sociolinguistics of Yugtun is not easy to capture, because it incorporates a large pallet of factors, some of which only the local population have a proper grasp of. There is the abundance of natural food resources and the living traditional ecological knowledge, both of which help to sustain a strong sense of heritage language and a vibrant culture within the community. The dance repertoire strengthens the social intergenerational connections among diverse community generations. These are aspects of a traditional subsistence lifestyle, and along with ceremonial and ritual practices provide critical sociolinguistic conceptual contexts that enhance and embrace strong language skills, cultural maintenance and revitalization. There are the elders, who, in collaboration with classroom teachers and parents, educate the children in the classroom and at home, teaching them hunting and gathering survival skills, traditional knowledge of the environment, narrative historical and contemporary accounts, and cyclic rituals and ceremonies. Such factors and concepts cannot be described by means of simple questionnaires but require interviews and other qualitative investigative means, and, most importantly, help from within the community. Such authentic descriptions can help put endangered languages on the sociolinguistic map in a more constructive way, and help advance theories on the intricate connections between language and culture.

Further reading

Fienup-Riordau, Ann (2005) *Wide Words of the Yup'ik People: We Talk to You Because We Love You* (translations from Yup'ik by Alice Rearden). Lincoln: University of Nebraska Press.
Kawagley, Oscar Angayuqaq (1995) *A Yupiaq Worldview: A Pathway to Ecology and Spirit.* Long Grove: Waveland Press.
Wyman, Leisy Thornton (2012) *Youth Culture and Linguistic Survivance.* Bristol: Multilingual Matters.

References

Barnhardt, Ray and Oscar Angayuqaq Kawagley (2005) Indigenous Knowledge Systems and Alaska Native Ways of Knowing. *Anthropology and Education Quarterly* 36: 8–23.
Counceller, April et al. (2012) A Decade of Language Revitalization: Kodiak Alutiiq on the Brink of Revolution. *Journal of American Indian Education* 51(3): 15–28.
DeVoe, Jill Fleury and Kirsten E. Darling-Churchill (2008) *Status and Trends in the Education of American Indians and Alaska Natives.* Online available at http://nces.ed.gov/pubs2008/2008084.pdf (accessed 17 March 2014).
Elders, Sarah and Leonard Kamerling (1988) *Uksuum Cauyai. Drums of Winter* [DVD]. Elders and Kamerling.
Faircloth, Susan C. and John W. Tippeconnic (2010) *The Dropout/Graduation Rate Crisis Among American Indian and Alaska Native Students: Failure to Respond Places the Future of Native Peoples at Risk.* Los Angeles: The Civil Rights Project. Online available at: www.civilrightsproject.ucla.edu (accessed 17 March 2014).
Fienup-Riordau, Ann (2005) *Wide Words of the Yup'ik People: We Talk to You Because We Love You* (translations from Yup'ik by Alice Rearden). Lincoln: University of Nebraska Press.
Jacobson, Steven A. (1995) *A Practical Grammar of the Central Alaskan Yup'ik Eskimo Language.* Fairbanks: University of Alaska Fairbanks Alaska Native Language Center.
John, Theresa (2009) Nutemllaput: Our Very Own – A Yup'ik Epistemology. *Canadian Journal of Native Education* 32(1): 54–72.
——(2010) *Yuryararput Kangiit-llu*: Our Ways of Dancing and their Meanings. PhD dissertation, University of Alaska Fairbanks.
Joshua, Mary J. (2011) Language Planning for Eek School. Master thesis, University of Alaska Fairbanks.
Kawagley, Oscar Angayuqaq (1995) *A Yupiaq Worldview: A Pathway to Ecology and Spirit.* Long Grove: Waveland Press.
Krauss, Michael E. (1997) The Indigenous Languages of the North: A Report on their Present State. *Senri Ethnological Studies* 44: 1–34.
——(2007) Native Languages of Alaska. In: *The Vanishing Voices of the Pacific Rim.* Osahito Miyaoka, Osamu Sakiyama and Michael E. Krauss (eds), 406–17. Oxford: Oxford University Press.
Lippi-Green, Rosina (2012) *English with an Accent: Language, Ideology, and Discrimination in the United States* (second edition). London: Routledge.
Marlow, Patrick and Sabine Siekman (eds) (2013) *Communities of Practice: An Alaskan Native Model for Language Teaching and Learning.* Tucson: University of Arizona Press.
McArthur, Tom (ed.) (1992) *The Oxford Companion to the English Language.* Oxford: Oxford University Press.
Morrow, Phyllis (1990) They Just Want Everything: Results of a Bilingual Education Needs Assessment in Southwestern Alaska. Paper presented at the 12th Annual Congress of Anthropology of Ethnological Sciences, University of Zagreb. Zagreb, Yugoslavia. Online available at: http://files.eric.ed.gov/fulltext/ED320725.pdf (accessed 17 March 2014).

Napoleon, Harold (1996) *Yuuyaraq: The Way of the Human Being* (edited by Eric Madison). Fairbanks: University of Alaska Press.
Nicholas, Sheilah E. (2009) "I Live Hopi, I Just Don't Speak It" – The Critical Intersection of Language, Culture and Identity in the Contemporary Lives of Hopi Youth. *Journal of Language, Identity, and Education* 8(5): 321–34.
Saville-Troike, Muriel (2007) *Introducing Second Language Acquisition*. Cambridge: Cambridge University Press.
Siekmann, Sabine and Walkie Charles (2011) Upingakuneng (When They are Ready). Dynamic Assessment in a Third Semester Yugtun Class. *Assessment in Education: Principles, Policy and Practice* 18(2): 151–68
Smith, Linda T. (1999) *Decolonizing Methodologies: Research and Indigenous Peoples*. London: Zed Books.
Wyman, Leisy Thornton, Patrick Marlow, Fannie Andrew, Gayle Miller, Rachel Nicholai and Nlita Rearden (2010a) Focusing on Long-term Language Goals in Challenging Times: Yup'ik examples. *Journal of American Indian Education* 49(1/2): 22–43.
——(2010b) High Stakes Testing, Bilingual Education and Language Endangerment: A Yup'ik Example. *International Journal of Bilingual Education and Bilingualism* 13(6): 701–21.

18

VARIATION IN NORTH SAAMI

Ante Aikio, Laura Arola and Niina Kunnas

18.1 Introduction

This chapter discusses some aspects of the sociolinguistic variation and change in North Saami, a Finno-Ugric (Uralic) minority language traditionally spoken in the northernmost parts of Norway, Sweden, Finland, and nowadays also in urban centres outside the traditional speaking area. We shall discuss issues that seem to make North Saami sociolinguistically different from the dominant majority languages surrounding it. The chapter is mostly based on field experience, as there is a near-total lack of research on North Saami sociolinguistics.[1] Hence, the sociolinguistic observations described below must be treated with some caution, and in-depth research would obviously reveal a much more elaborate picture of the phenomena discussed in this chapter.

  North Saami is one of ten distinct Saami languages traditionally spoken in Lapland, in an area reaching from Central Scandinavia in the southwest to the tip of the Kola Peninsula in the East. North Saami is the largest of the Saami languages with approximately 25,000 speakers. The figure is a rough estimate, as there are no good demographic data on speakers of Saami languages, and, moreover, the legislations of Sweden and Norway forbid gathering of demographic data related to ethnic identity. The traditional speaking area of the language is divided between three countries: Norway, Sweden and Finland. North Saami speakers form the majority of the population only in the municipalities of Kárášjohka (Karasjok) and Guovdageaidnu (Kautokeino) in Norway, and possibly also Ohcejohka (Utsjoki) in Finland; everywhere else the speakers are in the minority. The speech community is undergoing language shift, but the language is still transmitted to children in its core speaking area, and there are also active efforts to revitalize the language. North Saami is classified as "definitely endangered" in the UNESCO Atlas of the World's Languages in Danger (Moseley 2010).

Due to its geopolitical position, North Saami is spoken in a sociolinguistically unusual context. Because the language is spoken in three Nordic states, different parts of the speech community are strongly influenced by three different majority languages. Practically all speakers of North Saami are bilingual in North Saami and the majority language of their state of origin. In recent decades there has also been a massive emigration from the speaking area, and consequently many speakers now live in urban centres outside the traditional area.

The Saami are the only officially recognized indigenous group within the European Union. In spite of speaking several distinct but related languages, the Saami people form one ethnic group with a diverse array of shared ethnic markers (e.g. traditional livelihoods such as reindeer herding, traditional costumes, handicrafts, singing style, a Saami flag and a national anthem). As a minority, the Saami show an exceptionally high level of political organization; each of the three countries has a Saami parliament, an elected representative body of people of Saami ethnicity and ancestry.

The emergence and changes of state borders have had an impact on Saami languages and culture, as they have split traditional speech communities between different states. From the nineteenth century onwards the Saami people have experienced a history of assimilation followed by recognition in all three Nordic countries but the actual policies have varied from the harsh assimilation in Norway (known as the "Norwegianization" policy) to cultural segregation of reindeer herding Saami in Sweden (known as the *Lapp skall vara lapp* – "Lapp must remain Lapp" – policy). Today the Saami people have both legally and in practice the strongest position in Norway – which has, for instance, ratified the ILO Indigenous and Tribal Peoples Convention C169 – but in all three countries there is an official Saami administrative area that ensures basic linguistic rights. However, a large part of the Saami nowadays live outside of the Saami administrative areas, and thus have very limited linguistic rights.

In describing the sociolinguistic situation of North Saami, it has to be borne in mind that the language is currently spoken in a very heterogeneous speech community. Seven major factors must be taken into account:

(1) In each of the three countries North Saami is spoken in, the language is influenced by a different majority language (Norwegian, Swedish, Finnish). Practically all speakers older than six are bilingual in North Saami and the majority language of their state.
(2) The number of speakers varies greatly between countries: there are about 20,000 speakers in Norway, 5,000 in Sweden, and 2,000 in Finland.
(3) There are notable differences between the legal and educational systems of the three countries. One of the key issues is that in the Saami administrative areas of Norway and Finland there are primary schools where all of the education is provided through the medium of North Saami. There are special "Saami schools" in Sweden, too, but the use of Saami as a medium of teaching varies considerably.

(4) The vitality of the language shows major geographic variation. A high resistance to assimilation as well as strong revitalization efforts and engagement in the Saami ethnopolitical movement can be observed in the core areas, as opposed to language shift in many peripheral areas. In core area villages the language is transmitted to children, whereas many peripheral villages have undergone language shift since the 1960s and there may currently be few or no native speakers below the older or the middle-aged generations (e.g. Aikio 1988 is an in-depth study of the language shift in the Vuohččú area, the southern-most North Saami speaking area in Finland). Due to the ongoing language shift, there are also a large number of semi-speakers with varying degrees of proficiency in the language.

(5) Active efforts at language revitalization began in the 1980s, and some of these have been quite successful. As a result of revitalization efforts and generally increased interest in the language, the number of L2 speakers (which include both ethnic Saami and non-Saami) has also increased substantially. There are also L2 speakers transmitting the language to their children.

(6) There has been massive emigration from the traditional speaking area, and as a result many speakers especially in the younger generations now live as a small minority in cities, for instance in the capital regions of the three countries. According to the statistics of the Finnish Saami Parliament, 65 per cent of ethnic Saami (and 75 per cent of ethnic Saami under the age of ten) reside outside the Saami administrative area in Finland. The area of residence shows a remarkable correlation with language competence – a recent survey of the language situation among the urban Saami in Finland (Arola, forthcoming) reveals that only 6.8 per cent of the ethnic Saami residing outside the Saami administrative area have registered Saami as their mother tongue in the Population Information System of Finland, as opposed to 43 per cent within the area. In total, 79 per cent of the ethnic Saami who have registered Saami as their mother tongue reside within the Saami administrative area. Also, the rate of language transmission in urban environments is very low: the survey revealed only a couple of individual respondents who reported that their children speak Saami on a native level. Moreover, the questionnaire was distributed via Saami organizations, and can thus be assumed to have primarily reached people with an interest in Saami issues.

(7) The written standard of the language is relatively recent, stemming from 1979 (the first North Saami texts, grammars and dictionaries were, however, published in the eighteenth century). The overall literary proficiency in the language is relatively low, especially among middle-aged and older generations. Most North Saami speakers have not received education in their language and their main literary language is the majority language of their state, even in the core speaking area (see, e.g., Marjomaa forthcoming).

Thus, the "speech community" of North Saami could be conceived in many different ways; if understood to refer to "all people who speak North Saami relatively fluently", the diversity of the community is huge. It must be noted that the phenomena described in this chapter are largely based on observations of language use in the parts of the speech community that show a relatively high degree of language vitality, that is among speakers actively using the language in daily life. The realities of North Saami use in other contexts are likely to be quite different.

As regards the application of mainstream sociolinguistic theories to the description and study of North Saami, problems are encountered especially in the core subject matter of sociolinguistics, in the fields of variation and language change. Some quite common assumptions and predictions fail to hold in the speech community, as some basic variables such as speech situation do not correlate with variation in the manner predicted by mainstream theories. On the other hand, factors such as bilingualism and multilingualism, which are not of primary importance in largely monolingual majority language societies, turn out to be major factors causing variation and motivating language change. We have singled out two topics for discussion: the relationship between bilingualism and dialect variation, and the factors that contribute – or, contrary to expectations, fail to contribute – to variation on the speaker level.

18.2 Dialectal variation and bilingualism

In a traditional dialectological analysis the North Saami-speaking area is divided into four main dialect areas, the Eastern Inland, Western Inland,[2] Torne and Sea dialects (Table 18.1), each of which is in turn divided into a number of local sub-dialects (Sammallahti 1998: 9–20). The differences between the regional dialects arose much earlier than political boundaries in the region, and because of this the dialect borders do not coincide with state borders. The differences between the traditional regional dialects of North Saami are rather well understood. The phonological systems of the traditional dialects are described in great detail by Sammallahti (forthcoming). Lexical and morphological differences have been somewhat less systematically described (see, e.g., Nesheim 1967 and Rydving 2013 on lexical differences; the information on morphological differences is scattered in a wide range of publications). There is a near-complete lack of sociolinguistic studies regarding dialectal variation in North Saami.

As pointed out by Stanford and Preston (2009), "many indigenous languages exist in situations of extensive multidialectal or multilingual contact with ambiguous boundaries and no established single standard." This starkly contrasts with linguistically more homogeneous societies where most research on variation has been conducted. An interesting topic is how patterns of bilingualism and multilingualism are affecting the dialectal configuration of the language. Most parts of the North Saami-speaking area have been bilingual or multilingual for a substantial period of time, and North Saami has developed under contact with neighbouring Saami languages (Lule Saami to the west and Inari Saami and Skolt Saami to the east),

Scandinavian languages (Norwegian, Swedish) and North Finnic languages (Finnish, Karelian). Trilingualism has been common in local communities where North Saami speakers were simultaneously in contact with speakers of Scandinavian (Norwegian or Swedish) and Finnish (Helander-Renvall 1984; Andrezén 2007).[3]

Naturally, the different patterns of language contacts on the local level have influenced dialect diversification. It has been observed that as a result of the influence of different majority and state languages on different parts of the speaking area, the national borders have started rapidly developing into new dialect borders (Rydving 1986; Hansegård 1988: 74). This has not, however, resulted in the levelling of differences between the traditional regional dialects within each country. Instead, the result is a "new" pattern of dialectal differentiation that is largely complementary with the old divisions between the traditional regional dialects. On the one hand, the old differences between regional dialects mainly encompass phonology, the shape of certain morphological endings, and traditional lexicon; on the other hand, the "new" dialect differences that have arisen as the result of the uneven influence of different majority languages mainly involve features of phonetics and intonation, syntax and words for new concepts that have become known during modernization.

This implies that present-day dialects of North Saami must be classified on a two-dimensional matrix of dialect groupings. Each present-day dialect can be classified on the basis of both (1) which traditional regional features it represents and (2) from which state language it shows significant contact influence. Thus, we get the following matrix of modern North Saami dialects, in which eight major dialect groups can be distinguished:

TABLE 18.1 A two-dimensional classification of modern North Saami dialects

Regional basis:	Type of contact influence:		
	Finnish	Norwegian	Swedish
Eastern Inland	+	+	
Western Inland	+	+	
Torne	+	+	+
Sea		+	

It should be noted that the traditional regional model is practically exclusively used when the dialectal divisions of North Saami are described in both scholarly sources (e.g. Sammallahti 1998) and more popular texts such as schoolbooks (Palismaa and Eira 2001); the "new" dialectal differences resulting from different types of contact influence have received less attention in linguistic description. However, this does not mean that the latter kind of variation would be any less significant from a synchronic perspective. In fact, as far as mutual comprehension is concerned, the situation is rather the opposite: the old regional dialect differences pose few problems for communication, whereas the more recent majority language influences often do. We have both observed and heard many reports of cross-border communication problems between North Saami speakers. For example, students from the Norwegian side who have worked as teacher trainees in North Saami schools in Finland have reported having initially faced notable problems of mutual comprehension when working with pupils. These problems have been mainly caused by dialect differences originating in the influence of the different state majority languages – especially as regards the lexicon and idiomatic expressions, in the form of calques and loanwords. As a counterforce to such perceived problems of majority language induced lexical differences, vocabulary development programmes have been set up, and they have had some impact, especially on the language used in the media.

Thus, the dialectal divisions of modern North Saami illustrate that in a minority language community, the dialectal configuration of a language may become drastically altered if different patterns of bilingualism or multilingualism develop in different parts of the speech community. When dialectal variation is described, classical dialectological approaches often tend to ignore this kind of variation and stick to the traditional regional approach; if recent majority-language influence is treated at all, it is usually conceived of as a type of "interference" rather than "dialectal variation", even if the studied features and patterns have already become established in the language. However, it can be proposed that languages like North Saami should be described as showing more than one pattern of dialectal divisions, which are overlapping in geographic space, but complementary in regard to what parts of language they manifest in.

18.3 Speaker-level variation

According to previous research, linguistic variation in endangered languages is socially differently motivated from, for example, state languages (Wolfram 2002: 777–78). In a minority language community, linguistic variation is typically not an effect of the speakers' socioeconomic background, social class or education. As noted above, in the case of North Saami, the two most important correlates of linguistic variation are (1) the official language spoken in the area in question (Finnish, Norwegian or Swedish) and (2) the region (village or town) the speaker is coming from.

The linguistic variation in North Saami is thus very different from that of majority languages in Finland and Scandinavia. The most striking difference is that there is no single prestigious speech style of North Saami that would be pursued by a large segment of speakers of the language. For example in Finland and in Denmark, the regional dialects of Finnish and Danish are markedly influenced by the varieties spoken in capitals – in the Helsinki region and in Copenhagen, respectively (Mantila 2004; Kristiansen 2009). Moreover, variation of North Saami is fundamentally different from that of Finnish, for instance, because there are no clear signs of dialect levelling taking place in North Saami (see Meyerhoff 2011: 239). Whereas Finnish dialects are changing under the influence of (1) standard written language, (2) the speech style of the capital region and (3) the variety spoken in the nearest "big town", the dialects of North Saami seem to be relatively stable in the sense that native speakers generally do not opt for using phonological or morphological variants from varieties other than their own dialect.

The relationship of regional dialects to standard language differs from majority societies, too. The modern North Saami written standard is a rather new creation (the current orthography has been in use since 1979); a large part of North Saami speakers have not received education in their language and are unable to write the language fluently. Even in the written standard areal variation is prominent; for example, dialectal differences in basic vocabulary and in the shape of certain inflectional endings are often maintained in writing. Also, there is no spoken correlate to the written standard – that is no speech variety that could be characterized as "non-dialectal" or as a "spoken standard". As most research on variation in Nordic countries has been made on state languages that are strictly standardized, research on North Saami variation would undoubtedly yield some entirely different perspectives.

As Meyerhoff (2011: 239) points out, the process of dialect levelling is often the result of increased mobility of speakers, and social changes in the twentieth century have affected dialect diversity. After the Second World War, many speakers of North Saami emigrated from their home villages either to cities or to other parts of the North Saami region; nowadays there is even a saying that Oslo is "the biggest Saami village". It is common that in these new places of residence speakers of different dialects of North Saami encounter, and are in communication with, each other. Nevertheless, we have observed no clear signs of dialect levelling; it seems that at least the first generation of Saami emigrants quite strictly keep to their local dialects of North Saami even when they have become members of social networks that include people from different dialect areas.[4] What makes this phenomenon even more remarkable is that speakers generally do not exhibit the same behaviour in relation to their native dialects of the state majority language.

The general lack of dialect levelling could in part be attributed to the lack of a prestige variety and a spoken standard language, as in such a situation no variety will form a point of convergence toward which dialect levelling would take place. For the same reason, no diglossia within North Saami can be observed, at least as far as the structure of the language is concerned (obviously, however, there is diglossia between North Saami and majority languages). As regards actual phonological and grammatical forms, people tend to speak in the same way regardless of the situation. Also, there are dialectal differences in basic vocabulary items (e.g. "speak", "hope", "think", "man", "boy", "friend") that tend to be strictly kept. Thus, situational language variation among North Saami speakers is different from that in majority speech communities. The only feature regarding actual forms and structures that seems to show major situational variation is the extent of code switching and use of unassimilated loanwords from the state majority language. For example, in order to achieve mutual comprehension such features of language use need to be avoided when speaking to a North Saami person from another country.

An illuminating example of the lack of situational variation is provided by radio programmes in which speakers of different North Saami dialects are communicating with each other. The typical situation is that each participant speaks their own regional dialect and does not attempt to accommodate their speech towards the dialect(s) of the interlocutor(s). In this context, a prediction of speech accommodation theory fails: According to the theory, a speaker accommodates their speech on all levels of language towards the interlocutors' speech to achieve approval (e.g. Giles 1973; Giles and Smith 1979: 46–47, 49; Giles and Powesland 1997 [1975]: 233–34; Schilling-Estes 2002: 383–84, 388). When two or more speakers of different North Saami dialects meet, however, no notable attempts at speech accommodation can usually be observed either on the level of structure (phonology, morphology) or basic vocabulary.

This situation has a plausible explanation in the social norms regarding the use of North Saami. According to speech accommodation theory, the convergence of linguistic norms between interlocutors is motivated by desire of social approval. We suggest that in the North Saami speech community a person cannot gain social approval by speech accommodation, because this would be a breach of the norm of "keeping to one's own dialect". Dialect purism appears to be a sociolinguistic norm in the North Saami speech community, and crossing the boundary of one's own regional dialect of North Saami appears to be commonly regarded substandard or incorrect language use. We may note that this norm is in congruence with a generally high degree of linguistic purism. According to Länsman and Tervaniemi (2012) North Saami speakers require that the language should be spoken purely, and most of their respondents say that it sounds ugly if someone cannot speak North Saami properly. Also, ethnolinguistic purism has been reported: according to Lilja (2012: 141–42) many native speakers of North Saami do not accept the language spoken by "outsiders" (i.e. others than ethnic Saami) even if the speakers' language proficiency was very good.

As a result of the norm of keeping to one's own dialect, dialectally mixed idiolects of North Saami are rare and always seem to result from the language being acquired or learned under unusual circumstances. Also, such mixed varieties tend to be stigmatized: in the course of personal communication we have become aware of numerous cases of L2 speakers of North Saami (including ethnic Saami and non-Saami alike) who report having often received negative feedback for mixing features of different regional dialects in their speech. Thus, a norm of keeping to one's "own" dialect concerns not only native speakers but also the L2 speakers of North Saami. When studying North Saami as a second language, one tends to learn the dialect of the teacher; if a person wants to learn North Saami outside a classroom, he or she has to choose a certain dialect of North Saami and study that.

When it comes to stylistic variation, it seems that different regional variants of North Saami dialects do not have clear stylistic values. Thus, the division of linguistic variants into "indicators", "markers", and "stereotypes" (e.g. Labov 1971; Eckert 2008; Meyerhoff 2011: 22–23) does not fit very well in the context of North Saami. The idiolect of a speaker simply seems to serve as an indicator of which dialect area and which country he or she is coming from. An indicator is also called a "first-order index" (Silverstein 2003) and it simply indexes membership in a population – it designates people as Beijingers or Detroiters (Eckert 2008: 463) or, in the case of North Saami, as people from Ohcejohka (Finland) or Guovdageaidnu

(Norway), for example. However, the features of North Saami regional dialects do not seem to have the kind of social meaning that one could draw "an indexical field" for a certain variant. For example, a certain phonological variant of North Saami is not likely to reveal how old a speaker is, whether the speaker is a man or a woman, or whether they are rural-oriented or urban-oriented (see Eckert 2008: 466).

In North Saami, the lexicon is the only level of language where some kind of *social variation* is obviously manifest. In this context, especially, the degree to which unassimilated loanwords from majority languages are used displays great variation between idiolects. Apparently, academically educated people and elderly people who have a very high competence in North Saami do not use unadapted loanwords as frequently as other speakers of the language tend to do.

As numerous studies have shown, it is typical in many contemporary Western state-language contexts that women lead dialect change in the way that they use more prestigious variants as well as variants belonging to the standard language than men (e.g. Labov 1966; Romaine 2003: 109). Such a tendency is not obvious in North Saami, because there is neither a single prestige variety of the language nor any kind of standard pronunciation. Also, according to field observations, the standard written language does not seem to affect spoken varieties much, apparently because a large part of the North Saami speech community has little literary proficiency in the language. Also, gender does not appear to be a social variable with obvious correlates in the phonological or morphological variation within North Saami dialects, even though minor differences might be uncovered by in-depth analysis. One cannot characterize, for instance, phonological or morphological variants of North Saami dialects as feminine or masculine, as one can for example in the case of Finnish (see Mantila 2004: 329). However, there would seem to be pragmatic variation between the speech of male and female speakers of the same North Saami dialect, but the issue requires further study. The situation is similar to what Kendall has described concerning gender differences in the USA:

> Women and men do not generally choose linguistic options for the purpose of creating masculine or feminine identities; instead, they draw upon gendered linguistic strategies to perform pragmatic and interactional functions of language and, thus, constitute roles in a gendered way.
>
> *(2003: 604)*

Social class has long been considered a crucial factor in variation of majority languages (see Labov 1966, 1972, 2001). As in many other indigenous communities (Stanford and Preston 2009), the social classes in the North Saami community are not very distinct, and socioeconomic stratification does not seem to be a major factor in the variation of North Saami. The only effect might again be observed on the level of lexicon; for example, people working in traditional livelihoods may be more knowledgeable of vocabulary describing the natural environment, whereas educated people are generally more aware of newly constructed lexical items connected to societal life.

This is not to say that hierarchies within the North Saami community do not exist, however. A hidden prestige of particular geographical areas may be more important than overt prestige of particular social classes in the North Saami community. For example, hidden prestige may be attached to dialects spoken in core areas where the vitality of the language is the strongest (e.g. the Guovdageaidnu dialect in Norway). Also, hidden prestige may be attached to rural areas and to traditional livelihoods in general: people practising traditional livelihoods are respected as linguistic models and considered to be richer and purer in their use of language. There are also certain areas that seem to be considered linguistically "rich" in popular understanding – for example, the dialect of Badje-Deanu (upper Tana river) is often characterized as "rich" in its vocabulary and idiomatic expressions by people acquainted with the dialect. As the communities are small, there may also be certain ways of speaking typical to certain extended families.

18.4 Summary and discussion

In this brief chapter, we have shown that the nature and causes of variation in North Saami are partially different from those of the surrounding majority state languages. Currently, the main driving force of variation and change in present-day North Saami seems to be the complete bilingualism of the speech community, nearly every member of which is also a native-level speaker of at least one of three dominant majority and state languages: Norwegian, Swedish or Finnish. This situation has resulted in extensive contact influences that affect both different parts of the speech community and different levels of language in different ways. The result is a drastic alteration of the traditional dialectal configuration of the language that has resulted in a two-dimensional pattern of dialect variation: each modern dialect and idiolect of North Saami can potentially be classified on the basis of both its traditional regional features and the type of majority-language induced contact influence it displays.

On the other hand, the rapidly increased mobility of North Saami speakers since the Second World War seems to have had surprisingly little effect on variation, as practically no levelling of traditional dialectal distinctions can be observed as of yet, unlike what has occurred in languages with large numbers of speakers in the context of modernization. There is also a curious lack of situational variation of dialectal features, which seems to result from a lack of a prestige variety and especially from a sociolinguistic norm of "dialect purism" in the speech community, which disallows crossing dialect boundaries in language use. Thus, certain types of puristic language ideologies may work as an effective counterforce minimizing variation where it might otherwise be expected.

Hence, there are notable differences between the factors actually affecting variation and change in North Saami and the factors emphasized in mainstream sociolinguistic theories, which have been developed predominantly in the context of standardized majority languages spoken in largely monolingual speech communities. However, at least some of the motives for variation in North Saami appear to be typical of smaller languages spoken in multilingual communities, a situation that is (or at least has been) characteristic of the majority of the world's languages. As a certain "Eurocentric" viewpoint can be discerned in mainstream sociolinguistic theories, it seems apt that North Saami as a European language can challenge some of the common theoretical assumptions made in the study of linguistic variation. However, there is a regrettable lack of sociolinguistic research on the Saami languages; it will be a task for future research to examine the variation of North Saami from a fresh theoretical perspective, and seek solid empirical verification of the sociolinguistic patterns in which the language seems to differ from the surrounding majority languages.

Acknowledgement

We are obliged to Pekka Sammallahti for comments on an earlier draft of this chapter.

Notes

1 Issues in the sociology of language have, however, been studied from various perspectives (see, e.g., Helander-Renvall 1984; Aikio 1988; Huss 1999; Lindgren 2000; Jansson 2005; Rasmussen and Nolan 2011; Rasmussen 2013; Marjomaa forthcoming).
2 The Eastern and Western Inland dialects have been traditionally called "Eastern Finnmark" and "Western Finnmark" dialects (e.g. Sammallahti 1998). These terms are somewhat awkward, because both dialects are also spoken outside the Norwegian county of Finnmark, whereas dialects belonging to the Sea group are also spoken within Finnmark.
3 The Far-Northern dialects of Finnish traditionally spoken in Northern Sweden and Northern Norway have recently gained official statuses as independent minority languages, and are now commonly called Meänkieli (in Sweden) and Kven (in Norway).
4 The situation may, of course, change in the future. A partial exception to the general rule of keeping to one's own dialect may be found in the town of Inari, which has in recent years rapidly grown to become a sort of "capital" of the Saami administrative area in Finland, with many North Saami speakers moving in from other areas. Today one can observe a number of interdialectal influences in the speech of some young North Saami speakers in Inari, but it is as yet too early to tell whether the dialect contacts will lead to any widespread dialect leveling in the community. Another factor whose future effect is difficult to estimate is language revitalization programs, as children acquiring North Saami in language nests and language immersion are often exposed to input in more than one dialect spoken by teachers and language nest staff.

Further reading

Huss, Leena (1999) *Reversing Language Shift in the Far North: Linguistic Revitalization in Northern Scandinavia and Finland* (= Studia Uralica Upsaliensia 31). Uppsala: Uppsala Universitet.
Jansson, Annika (2005) *Sami Language at Home and at School: A Fieldwork Perspective* (= Studia Uralica Upsaliensia 36). Uppsala: Uppsala Universitet.
Rasmussen, Torkel and John Shaun Nolan (2011) Reclaiming Sámi Languages: Indigenous Language Emancipation from East to West. *International Journal of the Sociology of Language* 209: 25–55.
Sammallahti, Pekka (1998) *The Saami Languages: An Introduction*. Kárášjohka: Davvi Girji.

References

Aikio, Marjut (1988) *Saamelaiset kielenvaihdon kierteessä?: Kielisosiologinen tutkimus viiden saamelaiskylän kielenvaihdosta 1910–1980* [The Saami in a Cycle of Language Shift: A Study in Language Sociology on the Language Shift in Five Saami Villages in 1910–80]. Helsinki: Suomalaisen Kirjallisuuden Seura.

Andrezén, Sölve (2007) Finska språket: Torne Lappmarks lingua sacra [The Finnish Language. The lingua sacra of the Swedish Lapland]. In: *Ordens makt och maktens ord. Svenskt i Finland – Finskt i Sverige* [The Power of Words and the Words of Power: Swedish in Finland – Finnish in Sweden]. Olli Kangas and Helena Kangassharju (eds), 115–59. Skrifter utgivna av Svenska litteratursällskapet i Finland 682: 4. Helsingfors: Svenska litteratursällskapet i Finland.

Arola, Laura (forthcoming) *Saamen kielen tilanne saamelaisten kotiseutualueen ulkopuolella: Raportti* [The Situation of the Saami Language outside the Saami Administrative Area (of Finland): A Report].

Eckert, Penelope (2008) Variation and Indexical Field. *Journal of Sociolinguistics* 12(4): 453–76.

Giles, Howard (1973) Accent Mobility: A Model and Some Data. *Anthropological Linguistics* 15: 87–105.

Giles, Howard and Peter F. Powesland (1997 [1975]) Accommodation Theory. In: *Sociolinguistics: A Reader and Coursebook*. Nikolas Coupland and Adam Jaworski (eds), 232–39. London: Macmillan.

Giles, Howard and Philip M. Smith (1979) Accommodation Theory: Optimal Levels of Convergence. In: *Language and Social Psychology*. Howard Giles and Robert N. St Clair (eds), 45–65. Oxford: Blackwell.

Hansegård, Nils-Erik (1988) *Språken i det norrbottensfinska området* [Language in the Norrbotten Finnish Area] (= Arbetsrapport 3/1988, Lärarutbildingarna, Högskolan i Luleå). Luleå: Högskolan i Luleå.

Helander-Renvall, Elina (1984) *Om trespråkighet: En undersökning av språkvalet hos samerna i Övre Soppero* [On Trilingualism: A Study of Language Choice among the Saami in Övre Soppero] (= Umeå Studies in the Humanities 67). Umeå: Umeå Universitet.

Huss, Leena (1999) *Reversing Language Shift in the Far North: Linguistic Revitalization in Northern Scandinavia and Finland* (= Studia Uralica Upsaliensia 31). Uppsala: Uppsala Universitet.

Jansson, Annika (2005) *Sami Language at Home and at School: A Fieldwork Perspective* (= Studia Uralica Upsaliensia 36). Uppsala: Uppsala Universitet.

Kendall, Shari (2003) Creating Gendered Demeanors of Authority at Work and at Home. In: *The Handbook of Language and Gender*. Janet Holmes and Miriam Meyerhoff (eds), 600–23. Malden: Blackwell.

Kristiansen, Tore (2009) The Macro-Level Meanings of Late-modern Danish Accents. *Acta Linguistica Hafiensia* 41: 167–92.

Labov, William (1966) *The Social Stratification of English in New York City*. Washington: Center for Applied Linguistics.

——(1971) The Study of Language in its Social Context. In: *Advances in the Sociology of Language* (volume 1). Joshua A. Fishman (ed.), 152–216. The Hague: Mouton.

——(1972) *Sociolinguistic Patterns*. Philadelphia: University of Pennsylvania Press.

——(2001) *Principles of Linguistic Change* (volume 2). Oxford: Blackwell.

Länsman, Anne and Saara Tervaniemi (2012) *Saamen kielen käyttö Utsjoella* [The Usage of the Saami language in Utsjoki]. Saamelaiskäräjät: Utsjoki.

Lilja, Niina (2012) Kieli saamelaisuutta määrittämässä: Saamelaissyntyisten henkilöiden haastattelupuheessa rakentuvat saamelaisuuden kategoriat [Language as a Definer of Saami Identity: The Categories of Saaminess in Interviews of People of Saami Ancestry]. *Puhe ja kieli* [Speech and Language] 32(3): 127–50.

Lindgren, Anna-Riitta (2000) *Helsingin saamelaiset ja oma kieli* [The Saami of Helsinki and their Own Language]. Helsinki: Suomalaisen Kirjallisuuden Seura.

Mantila, Harri (2004) Murre ja identiteetti [Dialect and Identity]. *Virittäjä* [Tuner] 108: 322–45.

Marjomaa, Marko (2014) *North Sámi in Norway*. ELDIA: Case-Specific Report.

Meyerhoff, Miriam (2011) *Introducing Sociolinguistics* (second edition). London: Routledge.
Moseley, Christopher (ed.) (2010) *Atlas of the World's Languages in Danger* (third edition). Paris: UNESCO. Available online at: www.unesco.org/culture/en/endangeredlanguages/atlas (accessed on 3 May 2014).
Nesheim, Asbjørn (1967) Eastern and Western Elements in Lapp Culture. In: *Lapps and Norsemen in Olden Times*. Instituttet for Sammenlignende Kulturforskning (ed.), 104–68. Oslo: Universitetsforlaget.
Palismaa, Maaren and Inger Marie Gaup Eira (2001) *Gielas gillii, mielas millii 9: Davvisámegiela suopmanat* [From Language to Language, from Mind to Mind 9: The Dialects of North Saami]. Kárášjohka: Davvi Girji.
Rasmussen, Torkel (2013) *Go ealáska, de lea váttis dápmat: Davvisámegiela etnolingvisttalaš ceavzinnávccaid guorahallan guovtti gránnjágielddas Deanus ja Ohcejogas 2000-logu álggus*. [When It Comes Back to Life, It Is Hard to Tame: A Study of the Ethnolinguistic Vitality of North Saami in Two Neighboring Municipalities, Deatnu and Ohcejohka, in the Beginning of the 21st Century]. PhD dissertation, University of Tromsø. Available online at: http://hdl.handle.net/10037/5593 (accessed on 3 May 2014).
Rasmussen, Torkel and John Shaun Nolan (2011) Reclaiming Sámi Languages: Indigenous Language Emancipation from East to West. *International Journal of the Sociology of Language* 209: 25–55.
Romaine, Suzanne (2003) Variation in Language and Gender. In: *The Handbook of Language and Gender*. Janet Holmes and Miriam Meyerhoff (eds), 98–118. Malden: Blackwell.
Rydving, Håkan (1986) Neskol'ko zamechaniy o rezul'tatakh issledovaniya saamskoy dialektologii v predelakh ALE [A Few Remarks on the Study of Saami Dialectology in ALE]. *Sovetskoye Finno-Ugrovedeniye* [Finno-Ugric Soviet] 22: 198–202.
——(2013) *Words and Varieties: Lexical Variation in Saami* (= Mémoires de la Société Finno-Ougrienne 269). Helsinki: Société Finno-Ougrienne.
Sammallahti, Pekka (1998) *The Saami Languages: An Introduction*. Kárášjohka: Davvi Girji.
Sammallahti, Pekka (forthcoming) *Jietnadatoahpa vuoddolursa* [Basic Course in Phonology].
Schilling-Estes, Natalie (2002) Investigating Stylistic Variation. In: *The Handbook of Language Variation and Change*. Jack K. Chambers, Peter Trudgill and Natalie Schilling-Estes (eds), 375–401. Oxford: Blackwell.
Silverstein, Michael (2003) Indexical Order and the Dialectics of Sociolinguistic Life. *Language and Communication* 23: 193–229.
Stanford, James and Dennis Preston (2009) The Lure of a Distant Horizon: Variation in Indigenous Minority Languages. In: *Variation in Indigenous Minority Languages*. James Stanford and Dennis Preston (eds), 1–20. Amsterdam: John Benjamins.
Wolfram, Walt (2002) Language Death and Dying. In: *The Handbook of Language Variation and Change*. Jack K. Chambers, Peter Trudgill and Natalie Schilling-Estes (eds), 764–87. Oxford: Blackwell.

19

GAELIC SCOTLAND AND IRELAND

Issues of class and diglossia in an evolving social landscape

Cassie Smith-Christmas and Tadhg Ó hIfearnáin

19.1 Introduction

This chapter examines some aspects of social class and diglossia in Scottish and Irish Gaelic communities. The Gaelic languages, once dominant in Ireland, Scotland and the Isle of Man, form a distinct branch of the Celtic language group. They are more distantly related to the Brittonic languages spoken in Brittany, Cornwall and Wales, which form the other surviving branch of the Celtic languages. The Gaelic languages began their sociolinguistic decline as a consequence of English's rise to dominance in the polities within which they are spoken. Although Modern Irish and Scottish Gaelic are customarily referred to as distinct languages, they are not monolithic units but form the remains of a geographic dialect continuum, such as exists, for example, across the Scandinavian language area. Indeed, the languages themselves do not have distinct words to refer to each other. As an Irish academic who spent much of his career in Scottish Gaelic studies has said (Ó Baoill 2000: 132):

> While it is becoming fashionable among the educated in Ireland to equate *Gaeilge* with "Irish" and *Gàidhlig* with "Scottish Gaelic", and while some writing in Scottish Gaelic like to use *Gaeilge*, as if it existed as a separate word in their own Gaelic, to mean "Irish (Gaelic)", in the spoken language there is only one word, varying in dialect from *Gaolainn* in the south of the continuum to *Gàidhlig* in the north. This word denotes all the Gaelic dialects, and the terms *Gàidhlig na h-Eireann* ["The Gaelic of Ireland" as expressed in Scottish Gaelic] and *Gaeilge* (etc.) *na hAlban* ["The Gaelic/Irish of Scotland" as expressed in Irish] are needed to point up national differences.

The similar yet distinct sociolinguistic situations of Scottish and Irish Gaelic speakers present a fruitful locus for questioning the extent to which mainstream sociolinguistic paradigms may or may not be applied to these communities.

19.2 Sociohistorical background

The historical association of Scottish Gaelic with poverty and backwardness, coupled with a period of forced migration of many Gaelic speakers during the "Clearances" (1792–1886), has resulted in small, low-density populations of Gaelic speakers as well as the language's low prestige vis-à-vis English. According to the 2011 census (National Records of Scotland 2013), there were 87,056 people over three years old in Scotland who had some Gaelic language ability (1.7 per cent of the total population of Scotland), of whom 57,375 (1.1 per cent) claimed to be able to speak it. Over half the speakers live in what the census reports term "the main Gaelic areas", which correspond to the mountainous north and west area of Scotland, known as the Highlands, and the islands off the west coast, known as the Hebrides, to which Gaelic had become more or less confined by the nineteenth century following its initial retreat from the south and east of Scotland in late medieval times (Withers 1984). Within the "Gaelic areas" in 2011, numbers were concentrated in Na h-Eileanan Siar (the Western Isles), where the 14,066 speakers made up 52 per cent of the local population and 25 per cent of all Gaelic speakers in Scotland, with a further 15,490 speakers in the Highland and Argyll and Bute council areas. Referring to the 2001 Census (General Registrar for Scotland 2005), MacKinnon (2009: 589–90) points out, in contrast to the scenario a century ago, everyday Gaelic usage has now become a minority activity in its own "heartland" areas; by 2001, only 4,774 speakers (8.1 per cent of the total) lived in areas where 70 per cent or more spoke it, and this has now considerably reduced.

Today, all Gaelic speakers are bilingual, and thus when referring to "Gaelic-speaking communities", it is important to emphasise that in reality the current application of this term refers to communities in which, if speakers *do* speak Gaelic, they also speak English natively as well. Further, the linguistic competencies of speakers in "Gaelic-speaking communities" may vary considerably (cf. what Dorian (1981, 1986) famously refers to as "semi-speakers"). Even within three generations of an extended family living under one roof, Scottish Gaelic linguistic abilities can be highly variable (Smakman and Smith-Christmas 2008; Smith-Christmas 2012), and it is not uncommon for younger speakers (under 40 years old) who were brought up with Scottish Gaelic as their sole home language to have decreased proficiency in the language due to the adoption of English as their peer group language (see Smith-Christmas and Smakman 2009).

In Ireland, geographic areas where native Irish speakers are concentrated have been defined as Gaeltacht since the early twentieth century, shortly after the foundation of the state (Ó hIfearnáin 2009: 557–64), and the sociolinguistic dynamics of these communities parallel some of the Scottish Gaelic experience (Ó hIfearnáin 2013). Ó Riagáin (1997: vii) observes, however, that, unlike other minority language situations, in Ireland the state attempted to deal with its minority language problem by seeking to establish Irish as the national language. With respect to social class and diglossia, it is this long-standing institutionalisation of Irish that differentiates it most from Scottish Gaelic. According to the 2011 census of population (Central Statistics Office 2012), there are 1,774,437 speakers of Irish (40.6 per cent of the state population), and based on a national sample of 1,015 adults, Mac Gréil and

Rhatigan (2009) show that 84 per cent of the Irish-born population have some ability in Irish, largely because it is an obligatory subject throughout schooling. However, despite the high proportion of speakers who *can* use the language to some degree, the number of people *actively* using the language remains limited. The 2011 Census reported that only 77,186 (1.8 per cent of the total population) spoke Irish on a daily basis outside education. Although 69 per cent of the Gaeltacht population (96,628) speak Irish, only 23,175 do so daily. In Northern Ireland, the 2011 census revealed that 184,898 (10.65 per cent of the total population of Northern Ireland) has some ability in Irish, while 4,164 declared it as their "main language". One cannot be completely precise, but it thus appears that there is a core population of around 81,349 regular Irish speakers in the country, the majority dispersed but one quarter of whom are concentrated in the Gaeltacht regions and 5 per cent in Northern Ireland.

19.3 Social class as a sociolinguistic variable

Since Labov's (1966) landmark New York City study, the variable of "social class" has become an important construct used to demonstrate the link between language and society. Not only has this variable become paramount to categorisations of groups of speakers, that is labels denoting MC (middle class), WC (working class) and so on (see, for example, Williams and Kerswill 1999; Stuart-Smith et al. 2007), but it has been an important explanatory factor in conceptualising language variation and change. Trudgill (2000: 33) writes that the variable of social class can be measured "relatively easily (it is still far from simple) by the sociological method of assigning individuals a numerical index score on the basis of their occupational, income, educational and/or other characteristics" and introductory sociolinguistics textbooks describe the relationship between language and social class as an accepted rule rather than a testable hypothesis. Take, for example, Holmes (2001: 135): "Bank managers do not talk like office cleaners, lawyers do not speak in the same way as the burglars they defend." This section will primarily focus on the concept that social class lacks importance when discussing variation *within* Gaelic language use; historically speaking, Gaelic's status as a minority language owes much to the conception that its use connoted membership in the "lower" class and thus use of English, not Gaelic, often indexed a desire for social mobility, for example Dorian's report (2010: 241) of Gaelic speakers perceived as "too proud" to use Gaelic. Because this particular Gaelic–English dichotomy will be investigated in the section discussing "diglossia", this particular section will interrogate assumptions underlying the variable "social class" as well as discuss how social class does not necessarily correlate with certain linguistic practices.

19.3.1 Is social class always a useful analytical construct?

What about communities that evidence a high amount of linguistic variation but that are more or less socially homogeneous? MacKinnon (1977: 171), for example, describes the Scottish Gaelic heartland community of Harris as "classless", further writing that "it is certainly less divisive, socially, than is the class-structure of urban Britain generally". Even in instances in which differences in social class may be gauged by the traditional rubric as explicated by Trudgill (2000), these differences may not in fact be salient within the community. MacKinnon (1984: 491–92) writes:

> The persistence of Celtic ethnic cultures and speech communities in what is now a large-scale and highly centralised industrial state provides us with an interesting problem requiring some explanations [...] In the case of Gaelic Scotland, the sociological understanding of its problems is very much bound up with the consideration of the relationships of core and periphery in wider society. The traditional Highland society was not organised on class lines as such, and the ways in which it has been incorporated in wider society still render analysis in strictly class terms inadequate.

The nature of the small, relatively isolated communities that epitomise "traditional" Gaelic-speaking communities also presents a contrast to Holmes' (2001: 135) assertion that people of different occupations necessarily speak differently, or that the relationship will necessarily conform to preconceived Western industrialised hierarchies, such as the bank manager automatically being assigned a higher social status than the cleaner. In small, primarily endogenous communities, for example, the bank manager and the cleaner could easily be relatives, as well as belong to a number of the same organisations, such as the local football club or church – attributes that may take precedence over the social hierarchy assumed from someone's occupation (which consequently is presumed to account in part for language use). The nature of small communities means that members within a particular community may take up multiple social roles vis-à-vis each other. As Dorian (2010: 61) writes of the East Sutherland Gaelic community:

> The combination of uniform occupation, residential segregation, affiliation with one religious domination [...], and a long-standing socially enforced endogamy meant that the residents of any one fishing community typically stood in multiplex social roles to one another. It was more nearly the rule than the exception that any two men who were fellow crew members in a boat would also be kinsmen (brothers, cousins, father and son, uncle and nephew, say) and fellow congregants at a local church.

However, despite relatively high social homogeneity, substantial linguistic variation may exist within the community, as discussed extensively in Dorian (2010). Focusing on the East Sutherland Gaelic community that was also subject of her famous (1981) monograph, Dorian questions (2010: 3) how such "an extraordinary degree of linguistic variation can coexist with an extraordinarily homogenous speaker population". MacKinnon (1977: 178) writes of the Harris community (in comparison to the London Cockney-speaking community): "Speech variation does not signify a social divide between persons. It signifies the differentiation of social function within an individual's behavioural repertoire." Although recent directions in sociolinguistics, such as what Eckert (2005) terms "second and third wave" studies, have focused their attention on how social categories arise from *within* particular communities, as exemplified, for instance, in Eckert's (1989) famous "Jocks and Burnouts" study, the point to be made is that in mainstream sociolinguistics social class is often treated as sine qua non to exploring language use. This is not to say that social class does not have an important place in explaining language variation and change but, rather, that this relationship has been underpinned by Western industrial (and largely urban) conceptions of "class". For some communities, social class differentiations may be nearly non-existent, or may take entirely different forms from the way class is demarcated in urban, industrialised societies. What makes Scottish Gaelic potentially an interesting case in point is the liminal existence of many of its speakers as part of a Western industrial urbanised society, on the one hand, and, on the other, a relatively endogenous remote rural entity. As well, recent Scottish Gaelic revitalisation efforts have projected the language into new domains, which offer new possibilities for conceptualisations of "social class" in a Scottish Gaelic context. McEwan-Fujita (2008), for example, coins the term "white collar Gaelic worker", a term that clearly articulates social class in terms of urban, industrial ideologies. The implications of this and the emergent domain re-allocations will be further discussed when examining diglossia.

19.3.2 Difficulties in correlating linguistic practices to social categories

It is estimated, in the absence of census data during the years of conflict between 1911 and 1926, that a little under 20 per cent of the population spoke Irish at the time that it was made the official language of the new Irish state. Whereas we have seen that Irish language policy has ensured some acquired language ability in the majority of the population in the following century, most of those who could speak Irish in the 1920s were native Irish speakers from the impoverished rural peripheries of the country that were known as the "Congested Districts" under British rule. The absence of a literate, well-educated, Irish-speaking middle class was a major challenge to implementing the new role assigned to Irish as a language of administration, education and national development. Building such a professional group was a key strategy for early language planners who emphasised the teaching of Irish in all schools; the promotion of secondary education and teacher training in the Gaeltacht areas; ability in Irish as an obligation for employment in many publicly owned or controlled professions, such as the civil service, teaching and policing; as a compulsory exam subject in school and a matriculation requirement for the National University. Critics such as Borooah et al. (2009) have claimed that a century's institutionalisation has led to Irish speakers not only being advantaged over monolingual English speakers in state employment but in the labour market more generally, forming an Irish-speaking elite that is rooted in Irish-medium education. However, in a detailed report, Watson and Nic Ghiolla Phádraig (2011) show that such claims are without foundation as they conflate those who claim to speak Irish in the census with a notion of membership of a distinct linguistic community. In particular, they point out that there are not enough Irish-medium schools in the country to meet the needs of the dispersed regular Irish speakers, and that where such schools do exist, less than 15 per cent of their pupils use Irish at home. Watson and Nic Ghiolla Phádraig (2011) argue that the advantage, then, rather than belonging to any Irish-speaking group, is actually held by a so-called "middle-class" elite who claim an ability in Irish due to higher educational attainment at school but may not actually speak the language regularly or well. The institutionalisation of Irish and its role in national identity and policy has thus to an extent masked the existence of an Irish-speaker community which, like in Scotland, is multi-layered in its professional and social diversity, but not primarily divided by social categories in its linguistic practices.

The communities where the Gaelic languages are spoken have maintained the language in part because of their marginalisation and isolation from the social changes produced by urban industrialisation, on which mainstream sociolinguistics has developed many of its paradigms. In the sections above, we have teased apart certain assumptions underpinning mainstream sociolinguistic views of "social class". In the Scottish Gaelic context, it is argued that for the most part, social class is not a useful construct when looking at the sociolinguistics of Scottish Gaelic communities, as in many instances, communities where Gaelic is still spoken are not socially stratified like urban, industrialised areas. In Ireland, although the longevity of educational policy may seem to have associated Irish with social advancement, the connection is actually superficial, and perceived relationships between social class and linguistic practices are opaque. Elements of these themes will be carried forth into the next section, which discusses the concept of diglossia.

19.4 Diglossia

Since Ferguson's (1959) conception of "diglossia", whereby two varieties of a language exist in complementary social circumstances and Fishman's (1965, 1967) expansion of diglossia to include different *languages* in complementary distribution, diglossia has played an important role in describing and explaining the sociolinguistics of bilingual communities. Within the diglossic paradigm, the H (High) language indexes power and prestige, and is used in H domains, which normally encompass higher education, national media, religion, government and the workplace. In classic diglossia, H forms also encompass literary works and religious texts. In contrast, the L (Low) language indexes solidarity and its functions generally include the home and community sphere. Fishman (1967) argues that diglossia can be a stable situation but once the separate functions for each language begin to blur, there is the potential for one language to displace the other, resulting in language shift. Conversely, he proposes, stable diglossia can be a tool to maintain a lesser-used language. This section will take a diachronic perspective in exploring the theme of diglossia, demonstrating how Gaelic's historical resilience in a particular H domain complicates traditional notions of diglossia. Then the chapter will move on to examining recent revitalisation efforts and their implications for fitting Gaelic into a diglossic paradigm.

19.4.1 High without Low?

Historically speaking, the evolution of Gaelic literacy provides an insight to how Gaelic communities complicate the traditional diglossic model. Until the defeat of the Gaelic order in the seventeenth and first half of the eighteenth century, a unified written variety (Classical Irish) had been used as a form of prestige koine by the literate classes in both Ireland and Scotland, and the memory of this H language was very much alive in the surviving literate families. However, in a period when Anglicisation was becoming entrenched and Protestantism promoted vernacular literacy, Scottish Gaels nevertheless adopted religious texts that were based on conservative Classical Irish/Classical Gaelic (see MacCoinnich 2008). This development meant that an important H domain remained the remit of Scottish Gaelic rather than falling exclusively to English; therefore, although for the most part English was being established as the H language, Scottish Gaelic maintained a high literary form, especially in religious texts. The fact that the orthography adopted for these texts was based on a conservative Irish/Classical Gaelic far removed from the local vernaculars of its speakers meant that a separate religious register developed. Thus, it was possible even until contemporary times that certain speakers (i.e. clergymen) could speak the H variety but not the local L variety, a phenomenon that Dorian (2002) observes in the East Sutherland Gaelic community, where speakers who had access to and who propagated this H variety could not speak the L East Sutherland variety of Gaelic, as they came from other Gaelic-speaking communities. Dorian argues that this anomaly complicates traditional notions of diglossia and the separation of languages according to function, as Gaelic, and specifically a certain register of Gaelic, retains one of the most important H domains in Scottish Gaelic community life.

Dorian's illustration of speakers being proficient in the H variety but not necessarily the L variety resonates with present-day observations of the relationship between Gaelic use and domains. Recent revitalisation efforts have projected Gaelic into a variety of new H domains. For example, Gaelic is now present at the national (Scottish) level, as the 2005 Gaelic Language Act declared Scottish Gaelic an official language of Scotland with equal standing as English, however much this remains somewhat ambiguous at present (Dunbar 2006; Walsh and McLeod 2007); for the purposes of discussing diglossia, though, it is important to note that Gaelic is present in the Scottish Parliament, both as a language that can be used in parliamentary debates and as a language used on official documentation and signage (see MacCaluim 2011). The revitalisation efforts have been an important impetus in the creation of a Gaelic professional workforce, such as McEwan-Fujita (2008) describes in her ethnographic observations of the organisation Commun na Gàidhlig (CnaG). Maintenance efforts have further secured the status for national Scottish Gaelic media such as radio (see Lamb 1999) and TV (see Cormack 2010). However, entry to H domains does not necessarily mean that Scottish Gaelic is being maintained in L domains, as discussed in Munro et al.'s (2011) study of the Scottish Gaelic "heartland" community of Siabost, on the Isle of Lewis, which found that intergenerational transmission and community use of the language had all but ceased. It is even possible that in some instances a "reverse diglossia" is emerging in which, in their daily lives, a number of bilinguals (namely, the ones who are in professions in which the diglossia model could be applicable, i.e. H professions) will maintain exclusive use of Scottish Gaelic for H functions and use English or frequent code switching between English and Scottish Gaelic for L functions; for example, Dunmore (2013) discusses the phenomenon of a speaker (who acquired the language through Gaelic Medium Education) who speaks Gaelic in his professional workplace, but English at home with his wife (who is also a Gaelic speaker). This example is emblematic of the "reverse diglossia" and how it is brought about: a number of speakers working in Gaelic professional occupations have acquired Gaelic as an L2, or acquired both Gaelic and English as their L1, but due to the dominance of English in their sociocultural environments, prefer to speak English, as this is the language in which they feel more comfortable (cf. Oliver 2006 for a similar discussion of language choice in Gaelic Medium Education students). As Dunbar (2011: 115) observes:

> Undoubtedly, many L2s have attained quite high levels of fluency, both in written and spoken Gaelic, and also often have a strong command of the more technical vocabulary, where such exists, that would be appropriate for certain H domains. However, for virtually all of these L2s English (or, in some cases, some other L1, often together with English) would remain the dominant language, in terms of competence (if not always in terms of personal preference), in virtually all domains. Also, given the nature of adult language acquisition, many L2s have a limited knowledge of registers and even vocabulary appropriate to intimate or informal L domains – formal university level courses, night school classes and self-instructional material have tended not to focus on such forms.

Although much more in-depth research is needed to confirm the extent to which this "reverse diglossia" is emerging, the concept that Scottish Gaelic is used in a number of H functions but not in its traditional designated role of the home/community sphere points to the need to re-conceptualise diglossia concurrent with the still-evolving status of the language, both in terms of its status in H as well as L domains. This emergence of a type of "reverse diglossia" is perhaps even foreshadowed by Fishman's (1991: 380) well-known critique of Irish language policy for having mismatched priorities and Scottish Gaelic for relying on too many "higher order props" (i.e. the emergence of the language in H domains while at the same time losing ground in L domains, and especially in intergenerational transmission within the family).

As discussed above, a concern of language management in Ireland has been to re-establish Irish usage in H domains, from which it had been excluded since the fall of the Gaelic order and the establishment of English-speaking elites from the eighteenth century onwards. The institutionalisation of Irish has led to considerable investment in corpus planning. A century's experience in education and research, in broadcasting, and more recently in information technology means that Irish, in contrast to many minority languages, is linguistically relatively well equipped to repossess H domains. This does not mean, however, that the cultural division of labour that was present in the pre-independence era has been completely dispelled. Like Scottish Gaelic, Irish survived best in areas where there was a local subsistence economy that was strong enough to provide for the local community, but not strong enough to participate in the larger, English-speaking economy of the urban and more developed agricultural areas from which they were geographically isolated. Social stability was thus maintained within a fragile local labour market. If the local subsistence economy failed, the population had to seek employment in the English-dominant world. If it grew more prosperous, the local population would doubtless increase social and commercial contact with the wider English-speaking market. It is a paradox that either increasing wealth or increasing poverty thus both favoured the advance of English. In the Béarra peninsula, in west Cork, for example, this is well illustrated by the local mining industry, where all miners spoke Irish and lived in the local Irish-speaking community, while the engineers and managers were English speakers from outside. The community remained Irish-speaking until the mines closed, causing emigration on the one hand and local suppliers to seek markets beyond the miners on the other. As is the case in Gaelic Scotland, nowadays all Irish-speaking communities are bilingual, and the linguistic division of domains is now blurred. A key issue and challenge for the diglossic paradigm is to what extent the H domains of contemporary Irish are accessible for those who speak a local variety of Irish, and whether or not dialectal Irish should be considered an L variety at all in the context of the revival movement. Further, continued societal language shift towards English in the Gaeltacht demonstrates that providing the linguistic tools and the creation of professional and social H domains for Irish has not served as a buttress to maintain the language. In fact, one can hypothesise that the H and L domains in the bilingual Irish-speaking community are in fact shared. Irish-speaking employment does not therefore necessarily lead to language maintenance and intergenerational transmission.

19.4.2 Register and prestige

The expansion of Gaelic into H domains such as the media and Gaelic organisations has resulted in new registers, as described in detail in Lamb (2008). Lamb finds that a number of linguistic features distinguish the media register from the conversational spoken register (i.e. the register that would most likely be used in L functions), and both Lamb (2008) and McEwan-Fujita (2008) note that one of the most telling features of these emergent new registers is the avoidance of any English borrowings or code-switching. McEwan-Fujita (2008: 87), for example, describes how one native Scottish Gaelic speaker reports that although she would use the English word "answering machine" in casual Gaelic conversation, at work she feels compelled to use the Gaelic term *"inneal-freagairt"*, which she feels "silly" saying. The association of this Scottish Gaelic register with H functions such as the media and the workplace implies that this particular register may be considered the H register, and, in following the traditional model of diglossia, it would be expected that the H form would carry with it the connotations of power and prestige. However, it does not necessarily do so. Within the wider sociocultural entity of Scotland, Gaelic certainly does not afford power and prestige, and within what can be termed "Gaelic-speaking communities", the H register can connote a sense of artificiality, due in part to the lack of borrowing or code switching, which is a prevalent feature of natural Scottish Gaelic conversations (see MacAulay 1982; Cram 1986; Smith-Christmas 2012). Further, the prevalence of L2 speakers in H functions means that the H register also can connote non-nativeness and the perceived lack of fluency that entails, a conflict that is described in detail in MacCaluim's (2007) work on adult learners of Scottish Gaelic. Thus, even in the "reverse diglossia" model that has been tentatively suggested in this paper, the demarcation of the languages in terms of power/prestige vs. solidarity axis does not necessarily fit neatly, either.

The linguistic form of the contemporary H variety and its relationship with a learner variety, or varieties, is an under-researched area in the contemporary sociolinguistics of minority languages generally. Most Irish speakers who live outside the Gaeltacht regions tend to valorise one of the regional dialects, broadly defined, and seek to use it as a target speech variety, either because of direct association with one of the regions or because of experience through school of one such variety. These varieties form something of an intermediary speech located between the core features of west Ulster, southwest Connacht or Munster dialects and the national standard, promoted as a written variety but increasingly oralised by learners and Irish language professionals (Ó hIfearnáin and Ó Murchadha 2011). A similar situation prevails among speakers of other minority languages, where speakers negotiate a linguistic identity located somewhere between the traditional communities and their own socio-economic lives. However, as Mac Mathúna (2008: 87–89) points out, in Ireland this tendency is put under strain when revivalist groups, often associated with the Irish-medium schools, do not have constant access to such traditional language models, and adds that "most non-native speakers of Irish converse almost exclusively with other non-native speakers, interaction with the Gaeltacht community being peripheral to their social and economic needs and interests". This has led to the emergence of a variety of Irish which does not share all aspects of the common linguistic core of all traditional Gaeltacht Irish varieties as described, for example, by Ó Siadhail (1989). There is a perception among many Gaeltacht speakers that the standard and this learner speech are elements of the same variety. The emergence of proficient learner and levelled native language varieties, be they spoken forms of the written standard through education or by speakers' accommodation of different dialectal varieties through the broadcast media and general social mobility, is a reality. The Irish of young Gaeltacht speakers, however traditional their linguistic background, is now also moving very rapidly from the local variety to one that is influenced by contact with English and with the non-native revivalist varieties that are very much present in the broadcast and social media. This is heard at phonological, lexical, grammatical and syntactical levels in everyday speech. As neither the traditional local variety nor the standard target variety provided by schools appears to exercise linguistic authority in contemporary times, it is important to understand how the prestige attributed to different linguistic forms plays a role in the language practices and ambitions of the younger generations (Ó Murchadha 2013) and how this might affect our understanding of diglossia.

Critiquing the traditional model of diglossia is certainly not a new endeavour in sociolinguistics (see Hudson 2002; Romaine 2006), but this section has hopefully shown how what is often taken as a paradigm for describing bilingual communities – the complementary use of two languages depending on domain and where they fall in terms of the power/prestige vs. solidarity axis – constantly needs to be thought of in terms of the sociocultural realities as they evolve *in situ*. Diglossia was conceptualised without allowing for situations where second language speakers of minority languages such as Irish and Scottish Gaelic take on prevalent roles in the speech communities; additionally, the diglossic model was conceptualised before marginalised languages such as Scottish Gaelic gained access to certain domains. From the discussion in this chapter, it is evident to see that although diglossia was not necessarily conceived out of the Western industrialised vein of sociolinguistics, changes in the state of the language, such as the emergence of a sizeable proportion of L2 speakers in a community, calls for established paradigms to be thought of in new ways.

19.5 Conclusion

This chapter has illustrated how two sociolinguistic constructs – social class and diglossia – are difficult to apply directly to the case of the Gaelic languages. First, the chapter argued that the variable "social class", which is a hallmark of mainstream sociolinguistic theories of language variation and change, does not serve as a satisfactory explanatory construct when looking at Gaelic, neither linguistically nor with regard to the linguistic division of society. It postulated that this was because the variable was conceived out of Western industrialised urban ideas about "class", and argued that communities such as those where Gaelic is spoken do not necessarily fit within the bounds of industrial urban notions of social class. It then looked at the notion of diglossia, and discussed the difficulty of defining H and L varieties in bilingual communities and the possible reversal of roles in terms of traditional designations of the H and L variety in some circumstances. The examples presented were not intended to show that Gaelic studies radically depart from sociolinguistic theory but, rather, reiterate some of the emergent "take home" messages of this volume: first, that in many ways what are sometimes taken to be absolute "truths" within sociolinguistic theory have been influenced by studies on large, Western industrialised urban societies and therefore may only be "truths" for certain societies; and second, that as sociolinguistic circumstances change within certain communities, so too do ways of thinking about well-established sociolinguistic paradigms. In order to understand "sociolinguistics", therefore, it is important to investigate communities that challenge these well-established paradigms and not necessarily take communicative and social norms within Western urban industrial societies as the blueprint for how all peoples speak and interact with each other.

Further reading

Ball, Martin J. and Nicole Müller (eds) (2009) *The Celtic Languages* (second edition). London and New York: Routledge. (Survey essays in this collective volume cover the historical linguistics and sociolinguistics of all the Celtic languages.)

Durkacz, Victor E. (1983) *The Decline of the Celtic Languages: A Study of Linguistic and Cultural Conflict in Scotland, Wales and Ireland from the Reformation to the Twentieth Century*. Edinburgh: John Donald. (This book, written in English, provides a good overview of Gaelic language issues.)

Munro, Gillian and Ian Mac an Tàilleir (2010) *Coimhearsnachd na Gàidhlig an-Diugh/Gaelic Communities Today*. Edinburgh: Dunedin Academic Press. (This book, with some chapters written in Scottish Gaelic and some in English, provides a good overview of sociolinguistic issues in Gaelic communities, and situates the Gaelic languages within the larger realm of Celtic languages by including sections dealing with Welsh.)

Nic Pháidín, Caoilfhionn and Seán Ó Cearnaigh (eds) (2008) *A New View of the Irish Language*. Dublin: Cois Life. (The volume provides accessible discussions of many of the linguistic, sociolinguistic, political, educational and cultural issues surrounding contemporary Irish.)

References

Borooah, Vani K, Dónal A. Dineen and Nicola Lynch (2009) Language and Occupational Status: Linguistic Elitism in the Irish Labour Market. *The Economic and Social Review* 40: 435–60.

Central Statistics Office (2012) *This is Ireland: Highlights from Census 2011* (Part 1). Dublin: Stationery Office.

Cormack, Mike (2010) Gaelic in the New Digital Landscape. In: *Coimhearsnachd na Gaidhlig an-diugh/Gaelic Communities Today*. Gillan Munro and Iain Mac an Tailler (eds), 127–39. Edinburgh: Dunedin Academic Press.

Cram, David (1986) Patterns of English–Gaelic and Gaelic–English Code-Switching. *Scottish Language* 5: 126–30.

Dorian, Nancy C. (1981) *Language Death: The Life Cycle of a Scottish Gaelic Dialect*. Philadelphia: Pennsylvania University Press.

——(1986) Making Do with Less: Some Surprises along the Language Death Proficiency Continuum. *Applied Psycholinguistics* 7(3): 257–75.

——(2002) Diglossia and the Simplification of Linguistic Space. *International Journal of the Sociology of Language* 157: 63–69.

——(2010) *Investigating Variation: The Effects of Social Organization and Social Setting*. Oxford: Oxford University Press.

Dunbar, Robert (2006) Gaelic in Scotland: The Legal and Institutional Framework. In: *Revitalising Gaelic in Scotland*. Wilson McLeod (ed.), 1–23. Edinburgh: Dunedin Academic Press.

——(2011) Bilingualism: Conceptual Difficulties and Practical Challenges. In: *Strategies for Minority Languages: Northern Ireland, the Republic of Ireland, and Scotland*. John M. Kirk and Dónall P. Ó Baoill (eds), 150–63. Belfast: Cló Ollscoil na Banriona.

Dunmore, Stuart (2013) The Language Usage, Ideologies and Identities of Gaelic-educated Adults in Scotland: A (Past) Community of Practice? Paper presented at the 44th British Association of Applied Linguistics Conference. Edinburgh: Herriot Watt University.

Eckert, Penelope (1989) *Jocks and Burnout: Social Categories and Identity in the High School*. New York: Teachers College Press.
——(2005) Variation, Convention, and Social Meaning. Paper presented at the Annual Meeting of the Linguistic Society of America. Oakland, CA.
Ferguson, Charles (1959) Diglossia. *Word* 15: 325–40.
Fishman, Joshua A. (1965) Who Speaks What Language to Whom and When? *La Linguistique* 1(2): 67–88.
——(1967) Bilingualism With and Without Diglossia – Diglossia With and Without Bilingualism. *Journal of Social Issues* 23(2): 29–38.
——(1991) *Reversing Language Shift*. Clevedon: Multilingual Matters.
General Registrar for Scotland (2005) *Scotland's Census 2001: Gaelic Report*. Edinburgh: General Register Office for Scotland.
Holmes, Janet (2001) *An Introduction to Sociolinguistics*. Edinburgh: Pearson.
Hudson, Alan (2002) Outline of a Theory of Diglossia. *International Journal of the Sociology of Language* 157: 1–48.
Labov, William (1966) *The Social Stratification of English in New York City*. Washington DC: Center for Applied Linguistics.
Lamb, William (1999) A Diachronic Account of Gaelic News-Speak: The Development and Expansion of a Register. *Scottish Gaelic Studies* 19: 141–71.
——(2008) *Scottish Gaelic Speech and Writing: Register Variation in an Endangered Language*. Belfast: Cló Ollscoil na Banríona.
Mac Gréil, Micheál and Fergal Rhatigan (2009) *The Irish Language and the Irish People: Report on the Attitudes Towards, Competence in and Use of the Irish Language in the Republic of Ireland 2007–08*. Department of Sociology: National University of Ireland, Maynooth.
Mac Mathúna, Liam (2008) Linguistic Change and Standardization. In: *A New View of the Irish Language*. Caoilfhionn Nic Pháidín and Seán Ó Cearnaigh (eds), 76–92. Dublin: Cois Life.
MacAulay, Donald (1982) Register Range and Choice in Scottish Gaelic. *International Journal of the Sociology of Language* 35: 25–48.
MacCaluim, Alasdair (2007). *Reversing Language Shift: The Social Identity and Role of Adult Learners of Scottish Gaelic*. Belfast: Cló Ollscoil na Banriona.
——(2011) From Politics to Practice. Creating the Scottish Parliament's Gaelic Language Plan. In: *Strategies for Minority Languages: Northern Ireland, the Republic of Ireland, and Scotland*. John M. Kirk and Dónall P. Ó Baoill (eds), 192–95. Belfast: Cló Ollscoil na Banriona.
MacCoinnich, Aonghas (2008) Where and How Was Gaelic Written in Late Medieval and Early Modern Scotland? Orthographic Practices and Cultural Identities. *Scottish Gaelic Studies* 24: 309–56.
MacKinnon, Kenneth (1977) *Language, Education and Social Processes in a Gaelic Community*. London: Routledge.
——(1984) Power at the Periphery: The Language Dimension – and the Case of Gaelic Scotland. *Journal of Multilingual and Multicultural Development* 5(6): 491–510.
——(2009) Scottish Gaelic Today: Social History and Contemporary Status. In: *The Celtic Languages* (second edition). Martin J. Ball and Nicole Müller (eds), 587–649. London and New York: Routledge.
McEwan-Fujita, Emily (2008) Working at "9 to 5" Gaelic: Speakers, Context, and Ideologies of an Emerging Minority Language Register. In: *Sustaining Linguistic Diversity: Endangered and Minority Languages and Language Varieties*. Kendall King, Natalie Schilling-Estes, Lyn Fogle, Jia Jackie Lou and Barbara Soukoup (eds). 81–95. Washington, DC: Georgetown University Press.
Munro, Gillian, Iain Taylor and Timothy Armstrong (2011) *The State of Gaelic in Shawbost: Language Attitudes and Abilities in Shawbost*. Teangue, Isle of Skye: Bòrd na Gàidhlig.
National Records of Scotland (2013) *Scotland's Census 2011: Shaping our Future*. Release 2A (26 September 2013). Online available at: www.scotlandscensus.gov.uk/en/censusresults/ (accessed on 3 March 2014).

Ó Baoill, Colm (2000) The Gaelic Continuum. *Éigse* 32: 121–34.
Ó hIfearnáin, Tadhg (2009) Irish-speaking Society and the State. In: *The Celtic Languages* (second edition). Martin J. Ball and Nicole Müller (eds), 539–86. London and New York: Routledge.
——(2013) Family Language Policy, First Language Irish Speaker Attitudes and Community-based Response to Language Shift. *Journal of Multilingual and Multicultural Development* 34: 348–65.
Ó hIfearnáin, Tadhg and Noel P. Ó Murchadha (2011) The Perception of Standard Irish as a Prestige Target Variety. In: *Standard Languages and Language Standards in a Changing Europe*. Tore Kristiansen and Nikolas Coupland (eds), 97–104. Oslo: Novus.
Ó Murchadha, Noel P. (2013) Authenticity, Authority and Prestige: Teenagers' Perceptions of Variation in Spoken Irish. In: *Experimental Studies of Changing Language Standards in Contemporary Europe*. T. Kristiansen and S. Grondelaers (eds), 97–104. Oslo: Novus Press.
Ó Riagáin, Padraig (1997) *Language Policy and Social Reproduction. Ireland 1893–1993*. Oxford: Clarendon Press.
Ó Siadhail, Micheál (1989) *Modern Irish: Grammatical Structure and Dialectal Variation*. Cambridge: Cambridge University Press.
Oliver, James (2006) Where is Gaelic? Revitalisation, Language, Culture, and Identity. In: *Revitalising Gaelic in Scotland*. Wilson McLeod (ed.), 155–68. Edinburgh: Dunedin Academic Press.
Romaine, Suzanne (2006) Planning for the Survival of Linguistic Diversity. *Language Policy* 5: 441–73.
Smakman, Dick and Cassandra Smith-Christmas (2008) Gaelic Language Erosion and Revitalisation on the Isle of Skye, Scotland. In: *Endangered Languages and Language Learning. Proceedings of FEL XII*. Tjeerd de Graaf, Nicolas Ostler and Salverda Reinier (eds), 115–22. Leeuwarden: Fryske Akademy.
Smith-Christmas, Cassie (2012) I've lost it here dè a bh' agam: Language Shift, Maintenance, and Code-Switching within a Bilingual Family. PhD dissertation, University of Glasgow.
Smith-Christmas, Cassie and Dick Smakman (2009) Gaelic on the Isle of Skye: Older Speakers' Identity in a Language Shift Situation. *International Journal of the Sociology of Language* 200: 27–48.
Stuart-Smith, Jane, Claire Timmins and Fiona Tweedie (2007) Talkin' Jockney: Variation and Change in Glaswegian Accent. *Journal of Sociolinguistics* 11(2): 221–60.
Trudgill, Peter (2000) *Sociolinguistics: An Introduction to Language and Society*. London: Penguin.
Walsh, John and Wilson McLeod (2007) An Overcoat Wrapped around an Invisible Man? Language Legislation and Language Revitalisation in Ireland and Scotland. *Language Policy* 7(1): 21–46.
Watson, Iarfhlaith and Máire Nic Ghiolla Phádraig (2011) Linguistic Elitism: The Advantage of Speaking Irish Rather than the Irish-speaker Advantage. *The Economic and Social Review* 42: 437–54.
Williams, Anne and Paul Kerswill (1999) Dialect Levelling: Continuity versus Change in Milton Keynes, Reading, and Hull. In: *Urban Voices. Accent Studies in the British Isles*. Paul Foulkes and Gerard Docherty (eds), 141–62. London: Arnold.
Withers, Charles W.J. (1984) *Gaelic in Scotland 1698–1981: The Geographical History of a Language*. Edinburgh: John Donald.

CONCLUDING REMARKS

Dick Smakman and Patrick Heinrich

We started this volume by stating that the motivation of the editors for its creation was an awareness of a Western dominance in sociolinguistic theory making. All authors assembled in this book shared this view. They were aware that theoretical inconsistencies have to be bridged when applying mainstream sociolinguistics to the language communities in the regions of their expertise. As a result, the chapter authors call for more attention to be paid to distinct types of communities and societies. Several of the societies studied in this volume do not easily match the imagined societies popular in current sociolinguistic theory. Mainstream sociolinguistic theory is generally seen to be helpful, but it needs to be further refined in order to do justice both to the societies and languages studied in this volume, and to other societies. Different types of societies must give rise to different types of sociolinguistic study. What gives structure to a given society needs to be taken into account first before specific sociolinguistic theories are applied. Obversely, more emphasis and reflection may be paid to how society is seen to be structured in sociolinguistic theory before it is applied to new contexts and regions. The societies studied are in no way homogeneous and cannot always be studied by applying the well-known macro-categories of gender, social class or age. More diversified approaches therefore need to be applied towards this end.

On a general plane, the results presented in this volume point to a necessity to consider anew how the emic and the etic relate in sociolinguistic theory building and in the development of adequate research methods. The need to put considerations as to how etic and emic perspectives relate in the study of sociolinguistics has become a prominent topic in the study of politeness in the last decade. In place of the once impressively catch-all mainstream theories, we witness the emergence of what is in German referred to as *Theorien mittlerer Reichweite* ("mid-range theories"), as a result of enriching and adjusting mainstream theories for the study of distinct cultures of communication. This might well become a hallmark of a more consistently globalised study of sociolinguistics.

Does that mean dismissing mainstream or global sociolinguistics? Not necessarily. In fact, in the chapters of this book, mainstream sociolinguistics approaches were never entirely refuted. Quite the contrary, authors often drew on them heavily and willingly and few visions were expressed of their replacement with wildly novel sociolinguistic strategies. Current sociolinguistic theory will therefore probably remain to be part and parcel of sociolinguistic education and training in years to come; a point of departure. However, how it is taught might very well be changing with many of the old certainties about women and men, standard and dialect, working and middle class, politeness and so on changing. Nothing in this book hints at a return of these certainties on the basis of some improved sociolinguistic theories. Hence, these uncertainties will remain and will need to be addressed and discussed in sociolinguistic courses. Of course, uncertainty or a novel level of reflection on categories and the epistemology behind them alone will not suffice. Methods on how to apply sociolinguistic theory in an interconnected, diverse and layered world need to be added to the current toolbox. But this is a topic too large to discuss in these brief concluding remarks. It is probably no exaggeration to state that it constitutes a topic worthy of an entire volume in its own right.

INDEX

accent 84–5, 133, 210
accommodation 99, 112–18, 157, 229–31, 249–50
acrolect 137, 139, 144, 146, 148, 157, 225; *see also* Creole
age 99–100, 128–9, 157–8, 225–7, 234–5
American bias *see* Anglo-Western bias
Ammon, Ulrich 24–5
Anglo-Western bias 17, 31, 164, 173
anthropology 1, 3, 86–7, 170–3, 182, 185, 189, 214
assimilation 168, 174, 235, 244–5
audience design 109–18
Auer, Peter 44

basilect 137, 139, 144, 146–8, 225, 228; *see also* Creole
Bell, Allan 108–18
Bernstein, Basil 18, 32
Bourdieu, Pierre 11, 46–7, 86, 156–9, 183
Brown, Penelope and Stephen Levinson 17, 68–9, 186–7, 196–9

Cambridge University Press (publishing house) 22
caste 110, 116–7, 119
Central America 22, 26, 30, 137
clan 7, 111, 116–9
classical language 126–7, 139–40, 171, 178, 262
code-switching 42–8, 58–60, 86–9, 113–14, 141–4, 227–30, 249, 263–5
codification 47, 81, 142–3, 172, 195, 201–2, 214, 217

collaboration 3–4, 11–13, 33, 198–9
colloquial speech 123–4, 128, 130, 199
colonialism: attitudes 6, 12, 138, 140; effects 17–18, 66–7, 123–4; history 40, 54–6; paradigm 164–5, 166–8, 170; rule 80–5,
colonial language 56, 58–9, 80–4, 87, 140–3
community 47–9, 54–62, 83–5, 95–104, 113–18, 138–40, 233–40, 259–66; *see also* speech community
constraint pattern 98–100, 107, 144, 148, 187
continuum: Creole 139, 143–7, 224–5, 230; dialect 18–19, 111, 165, 195, 210, 246–52, 259, 265; standard – non-standard 49, 114, 116, 118; *see also* standard language
conversation analysis 132, 185
corpus linguistics 32, 107, 147
Coulmas, Florian 16, 20, 80–1, 209
Creole 55–6, 60–1, 137–48, 223–31; *see also* continuum

deficit hypothesis 19
De Gruyter (publishing house) 22
dependency theory 155
dialect: attitudes 15, 125–6, 159, 180, 250–2; contact 99–100; in daily communication 18, 83, 109, 111; definition 41, 46–7, 49; leveling 6, 83, 96, 178, 249; maintenance 7, 130; social 8, 81, 153, 161; transmission 5, 7, 114, 235

dialectology 2–3, 19–20, 172, 195
diglossia 58–9, 70–4, 110, 137–46, 147–58, 195, 223–31, 256–66; *see also* high variety, low variety
Discourse and Society (journal) 21
discrimination 84, 181
domain: analysis 4–5, 148, 260, 264; functional allocation 46, 58–9, 130, 140–2, 145, 228, 231, 261–3; proficiency 9, 89; *see also* diglossia

Eckert, Penelope 2, 9–11, 104, 125, 129–30, 259
editors 17, 21–2, 31, 174, 213, 215, 217
education first 23
elaborated code 18, 47–8, 81; *see also* Bernstein, Basil
endangered language *see* language endangerment
English Proficiency Index 23
enlightenment 18
epistemology 181, 189, 237, 271
ethnogenesis 164
ethnolinguistic vitality 42–3, 209–19, 233–40, 245; *see also* language endangerment
essentialism 11, 163, 189
European Union 18, 244

face: face-threatening acts 62, 69, 127–8, 186–7, 196, 198–9; negative 68, 199; positive 68–9, 127, 199–200, 202
Ferguson, Charles 5, 123, 137, 139–45, 223, 261
fieldwork 4, 12, 101, 210–11, 213, 215, 217
Finegan, Edward 46–7
Fishman, Joshua 20, 59, 139, 180, 261, 263

gender 116–19, 123–33, 154, 181–5, 188, 200–3, 251
gengo seikatsu 12, 179–81
genre 184, 218
geolinguistics 180
globalization 1–13, 83–5, 100, 160, 165, 190, 270–1
Grice, Paul 68
Gumperz, John J. 1, 44

Haugen, Einar 72–3, 81–2
high variety (H) 5, 59, 70–1, 139–41, 143–5, 224, 231, 261–266
honorific language 132, 185–8; *see also* politeness

Hudson, Alan 71, 137, 140, 223–5, 266
hypercorrection 181

Ide, Sachiko 180–2, 186–8
identity: ethnic 70, 88, 116, 164, 169, 243–4; gender 127–29, 181; individual 44, 101, 112, 128–9, 131, 265; national 124, 133, 168–9, 174–5, 225, 261
indexicality 95, 97, 104, 250–1
immigration *see* migration
impoliteness 187, 198, 203, *see also* politeness
indigenous language: ecological setting 40, 47, 49, 56–9, 67, 71–2, 81, 83; identity 56; study of 40–1, 46, 87, 165, 246; writing 209, 212, 214
inequality 94, 182, 201
Inner Circle 28–33, 84
Inoue, Miyako 182–4
institutional support 30, 42–3, 61, 209, 217, 257, 260–1, 263; *see also* language policy
International Journal of the Sociology of Language (journal) 21–2, 27–8, 137
internet 20, 22, 32

Jenkins, Jennifer 24
Journal of Linguistic Anthropology (journal) 21–2
Journal of Sociolinguistics (journal) 21–2, 29

Karchu, Braij 28, 84, 100

Labovian approach 84–7, 109–10, 154
Labov, William 4, 21, 87, 109–10, 154
Lakoff, Robin 127, 181, 202
language: border formation 81, 165, 171–2, 247–8; extinction 73, 209–19; official 40–3, 55–8, 70–1, 138, 225–6, 231, 260, 262; written 48, 143, 183, 248, 209–19
language attitudes 100, 178, 208, 231
language border 25, 81, 167, 171–2, 246–7
language concealment 72–5
language contact 42, 57–60, 71–2, 99–100, 224, 246–7, 252, 265
language documentation 2, 10, 40, 67, 73, 215, 218
language ecology 72–3
language endangerment 73, 209–19, 233–40, 243–53, 256–66
language ideology 143, 145, 164–75, 178–80, 185, 189, 226, 239–40
Language in Society (journal) 20–1, 27

language maintenance 73, 204, 215–17, 234–7, 240, 256–66
language policy 42, 56–7, 70, 143, 164–75, 218, 244, 260–3
language reform 179–80, 185–6
language revitalization 55, 73, 211, 215, 218, 233–40, 245
language shift 55, 58–60, 204, 210–11, 224–7, 233–35, 243–253, 256–66
Language Variation and Change (journal) 21–2, 29
language vitality *see* ethnolinguistic vitality
loanwords 72, 86–7, 143, 167, 210, 248–9, 264
lingua franca 40, 46–9, 81, 111, 115–16, 119, 213, 224
linguistic landscape 262
linguistic urbanisation 96, 101–2, 113, 125–7, 156–8, 178, 249
literacy 108, 138, 166–8, 209–18
load-bearing variants 145–7; *see also* Creole
low variety (L) 5, 59, 70–1, 139–41, 143–5, 224, 231, 262–6

mainstream *see* Anglo-Western bias
Markedness Model 60
Marxism 155, 158
Matrix Language Framework 60
maxims *see* politeness
mesolect 147; *see also* Creole
Mesthrie, Rajend 4, 82, 84–6
Meyerhoff, Miriam 6–7, 29, 107, 132, 159, 249
migration: language diffusion 73, 100, 114; policy 19, 66, 257; rural-urban 101, 114, 156, 244–5; societal diversification 17, 96
Milroy, Lesley 47, 124
missionaries 40, 61, 82, 212
multilingualism 56–9, 67, 70, 83, 87–9, 108
Myer-Scotton, Carol 43–5, 60, 87–8

nationalism 48, 138, 164–75
national language 41–3, 49, 70–2, 115, 170, 257; *see also* standard language
nation state 18, 54–6, 108, 172–4
native speaker (definition) 8–10, 236, 250
negative face 68; *see also* politeness
New Englishes 60–2, 70, 84–5, 112–13, 142–3, 146–7, 226

off-record strategies *see* politeness
official language *see* language
oral tradition 108, 110, 236–7, 239
Outer Circle 84

perestroika 169
pidgin 60–1, 224;
politeness 62, 67–70, 127–8, 185–9, 196–200; cooperative principle 68, 198; face 62, 68, 187, 196, 199–200; face-threatening act 62, 68–9, 128, 186–7, 198–9; face-enhancing act 199–200; negative face 69, 199; negative politeness 68, 199; maxims 68–9; off-record strategies 69; positive face 68, 127; positive politeness 194, 197–8;
positive face *see* politeness
pragmatics 96, 132, 179, 195–6, 199
prestige 81–9, 125–31, 167–70, 224–31, 251–2, 264–6
Preston, Dennis 29, 246–7, 251
professional titles 200–2

reform *see* language
restricted code *see* Bernstein, Basil

Sage and Wiley (publishing house) 22
Second World War 169, 172–3, 179, 186, 249, 252
second-wave sociolinguistics *see* sociolinguistics
sexist language 190, 200–2
social class 7, 110–11, 116–19, 251–2, 258–61
social networks 7, 124, 156–7, 195, 249
society: horizontal 115–16, 119; vertical 115–6, 118–19
sociolinguistics: African 20, 40–1, 55–6, 84, 124, 132; Arabic 20, 123–33; Chinese 2, 11, 20–1, 95–104, 117; Hispanic 20, 194–5, 199–201; introductions 20–2, 29, 61–2, European 18–19, 25, 194–96, 243; Japanese *see* gengo seikatsu; journals 12, 20–2, 29, 61–2, 96; British (United Kingdom) 18, 83–4; American (United States) 19, 83–4; South American 154–5, 160; waves 2–3, 10–13, 259
sociology 98–9, 103, 154–5, 180–1, 189, 259
speech acts 70, 109–10, 197, 199, 202
speech community 9–10, 97–102, 113, 116, 139–40, 224–6, 244–52
standard language 83, 115, 123–4, 129–31, 164–70, 178, 226, 251; definition 5–7, 19, 42, 46–9; standardisation 81–2, 178; construction 72, 170–1, 196, 245
Stewart, William 42–3
style shift 109–13; *see also* continuum

third-wave sociolinguistics *see* sociolinguistics
tone 7, 148
trilingualism 45, 46, 247
Trudgill, Peter 83–4, 99–100, 125, 258–9
Tagliamonte, Sali 98–9

urbanisation *see* linguistic urbanisation

vitality *see* ethnolinguistic vitality

Weberian model 158, 162
Weinreich, Uriel 1, 43–4, 102–3
WEIRD ('Western, Educated, Industrialised, Rich and Democratic') 3–4
western bias 3–4, 17, 31, 16–33, 164, 173–75, 179–81, 196
written language *see* language

Xu, Daming 97–100

youth language 40, 81, 83, 86, 89

eBooks
from Taylor & Francis
Helping you to choose the right eBooks for your Library

Add to your library's digital collection today with Taylor & Francis eBooks. We have over 50,000 eBooks in the Humanities, Social Sciences, Behavioural Sciences, Built Environment and Law, from leading imprints, including Routledge, Focal Press and Psychology Press.

Choose from a range of subject packages or create your own!

Benefits for you
- Free MARC records
- COUNTER-compliant usage statistics
- Flexible purchase and pricing options
- 70% approx of our eBooks are now DRM-free.

Benefits for your user
- Off-site, anytime access via Athens or referring URL
- Print or copy pages or chapters
- Full content search
- Bookmark, highlight and annotate text
- Access to thousands of pages of quality research at the click of a button.

Free Trials Available

We offer free trials to qualifying academic, corporate and government customers.

eCollections
Choose from 20 different subject eCollections, including:

- Asian Studies
- Economics
- Health Studies
- Law
- Middle East Studies

eFocus
We have 16 cutting-edge interdisciplinary collections, including:

- Development Studies
- The Environment
- Islam
- Korea
- Urban Studies

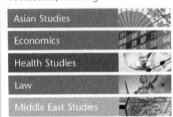

For more information, pricing enquiries or to order a free trial, please contact your local sales team:

UK/Rest of World: **online.sales@tandf.co.uk**
USA/Canada/Latin America: **e-reference@taylorandfrancis.com**
East/Southeast Asia: **martin.jack@tandf.com.sg**
India: **journalsales@tandfindia.com**

www.tandfebooks.com